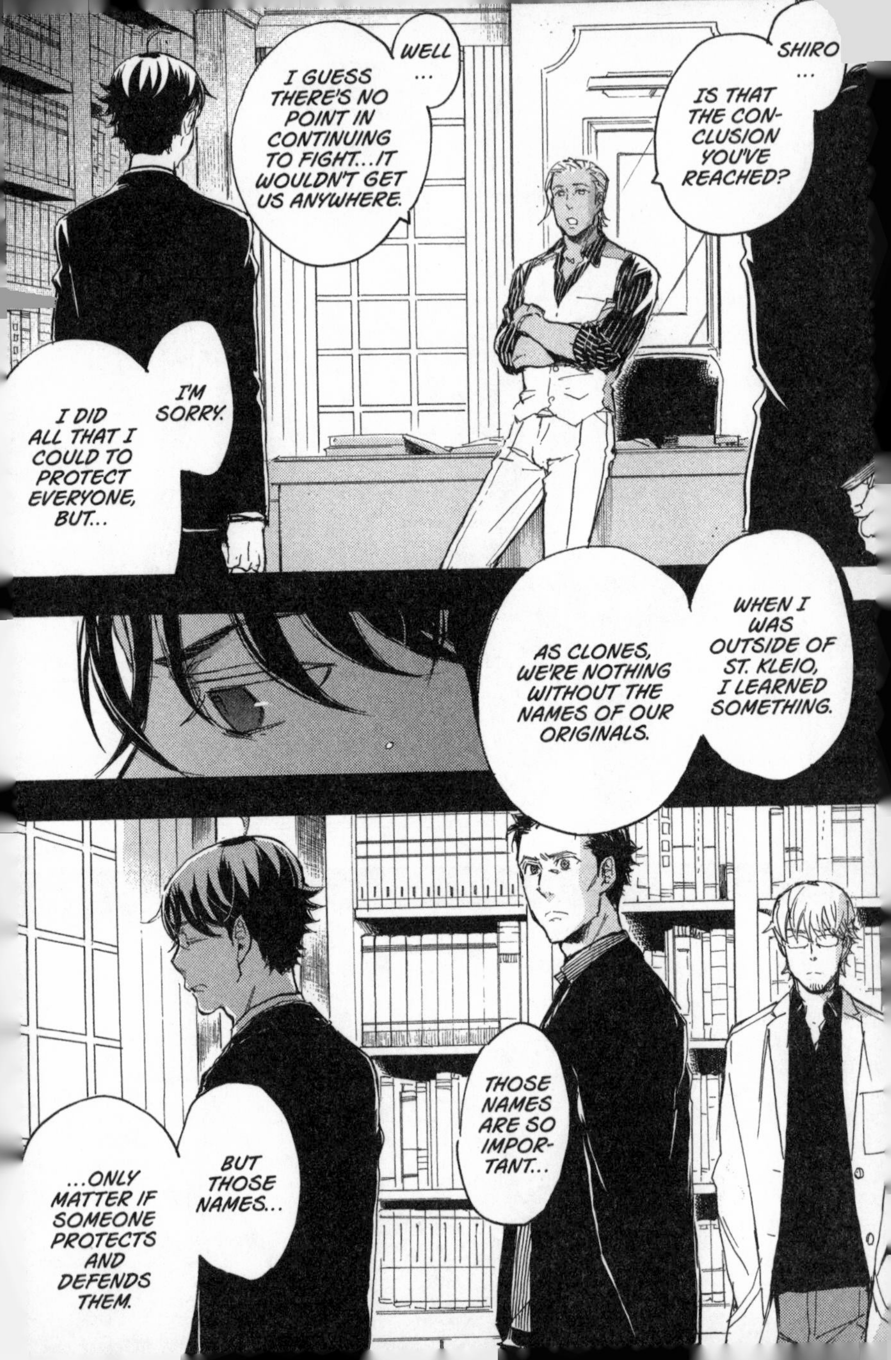
SHIRO... IS THAT THE CONCLUSION YOU'VE REACHED?
WELL... I GUESS THERE'S NO POINT IN CONTINUING TO FIGHT...IT WOULDN'T GET US ANYWHERE.
I'M SORRY.
I DID ALL THAT I COULD TO PROTECT EVERYONE, BUT...
WHEN I WAS OUTSIDE OF ST. KLEIO, I LEARNED SOMETHING.
AS CLONES, WE'RE NOTHING WITHOUT THE NAMES OF OUR ORIGINALS.
THOSE NAMES ARE SO IMPORTANT...
BUT THOSE NAMES...
...ONLY MATTER IF SOMEONE PROTECTS AND DEFENDS THEM.

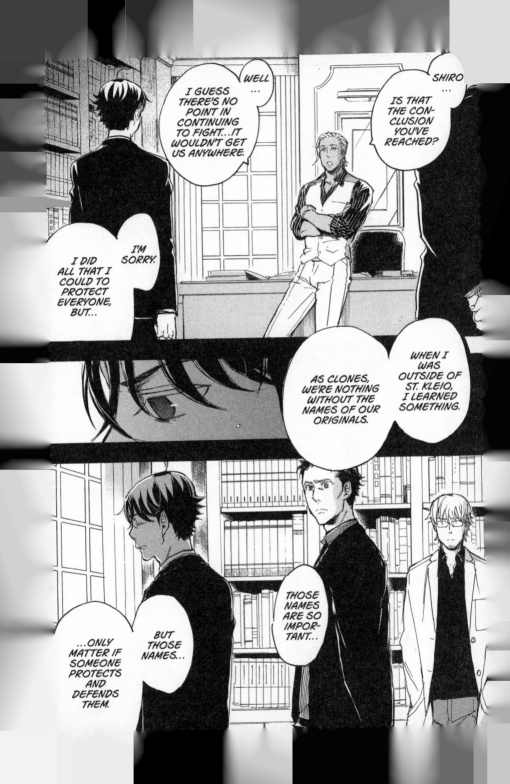

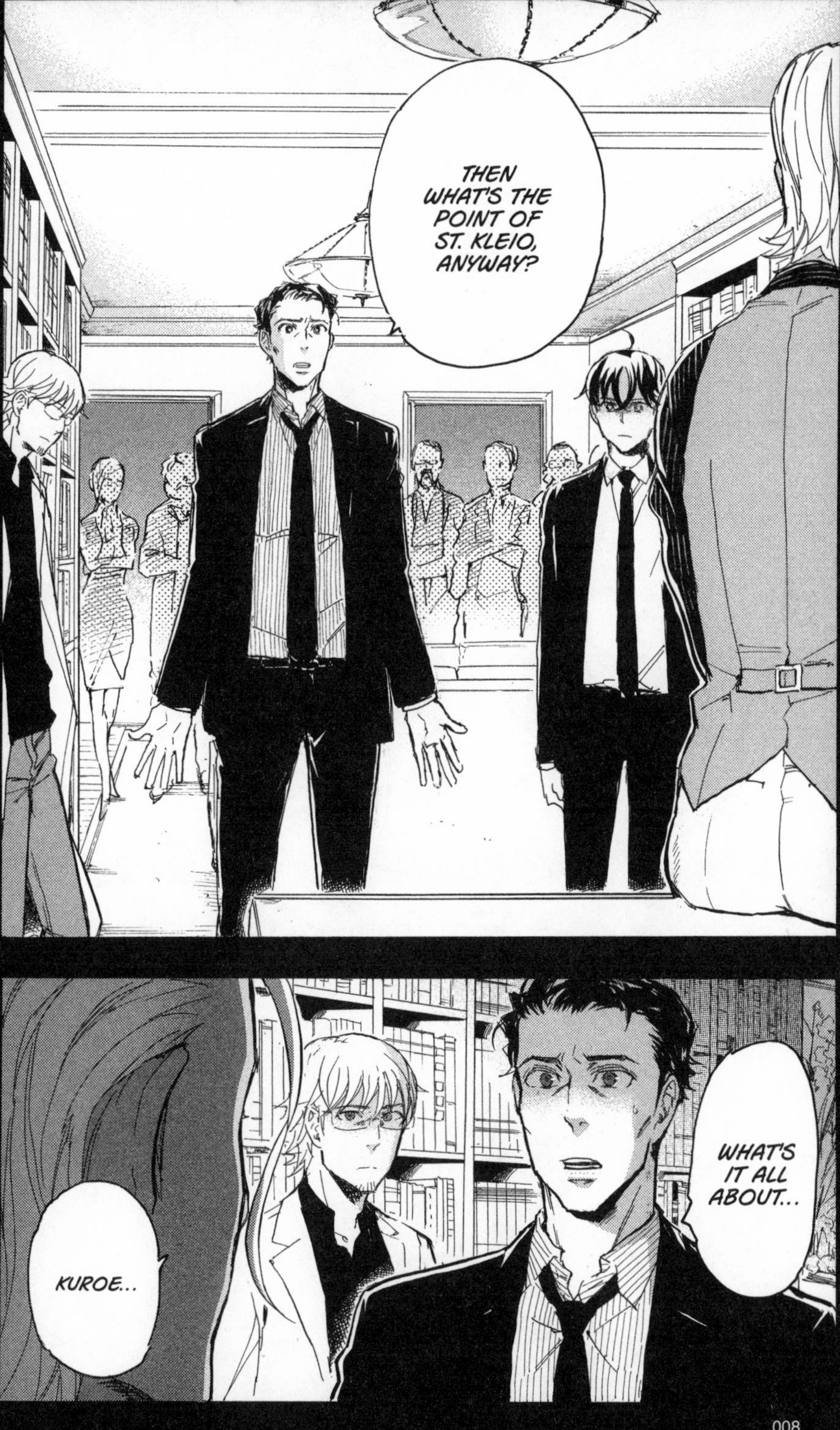
THEN WHAT'S THE POINT OF ST. KLEIO, ANYWAY?
WHAT'S IT ALL ABOUT...
KUROE...

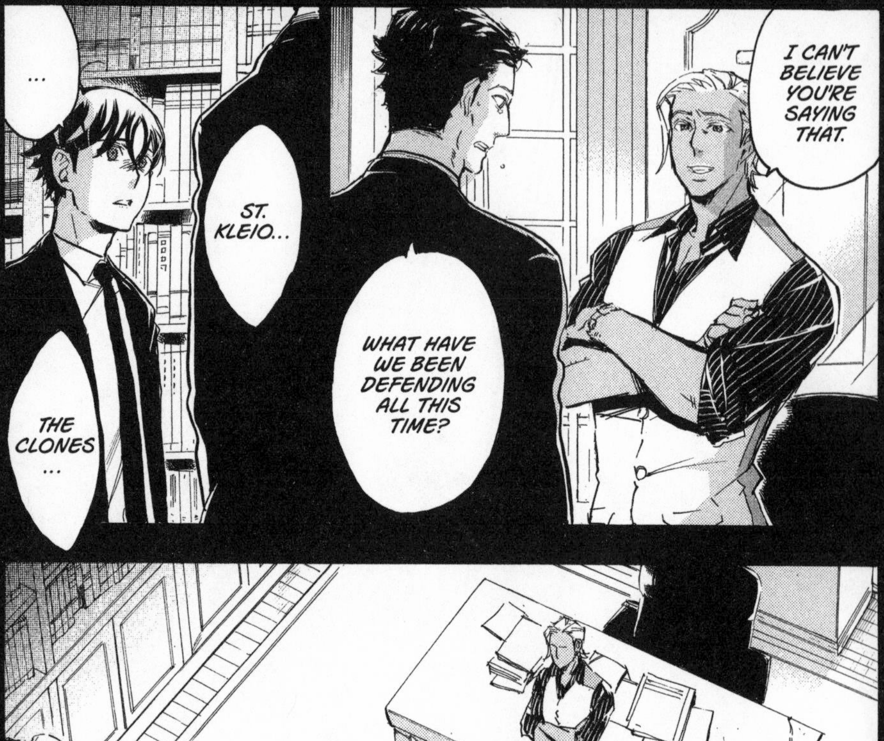
I CAN'T BELIEVE YOU'RE SAYING THAT.
WHAT HAVE WE BEEN DEFENDING ALL THIS TIME?
...
ST. KLEIO...
THE CLONES ...
I'M...SO SORRY.

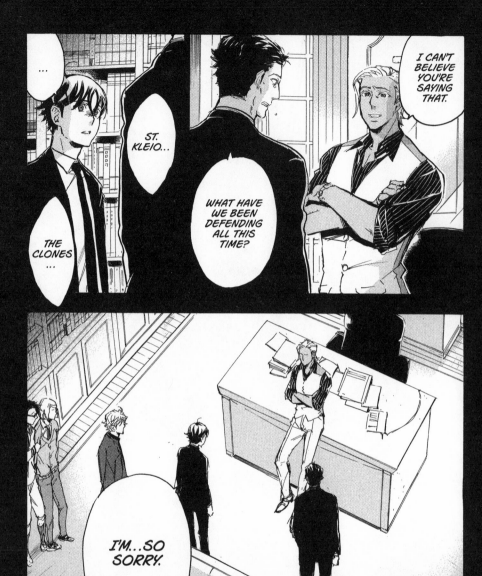

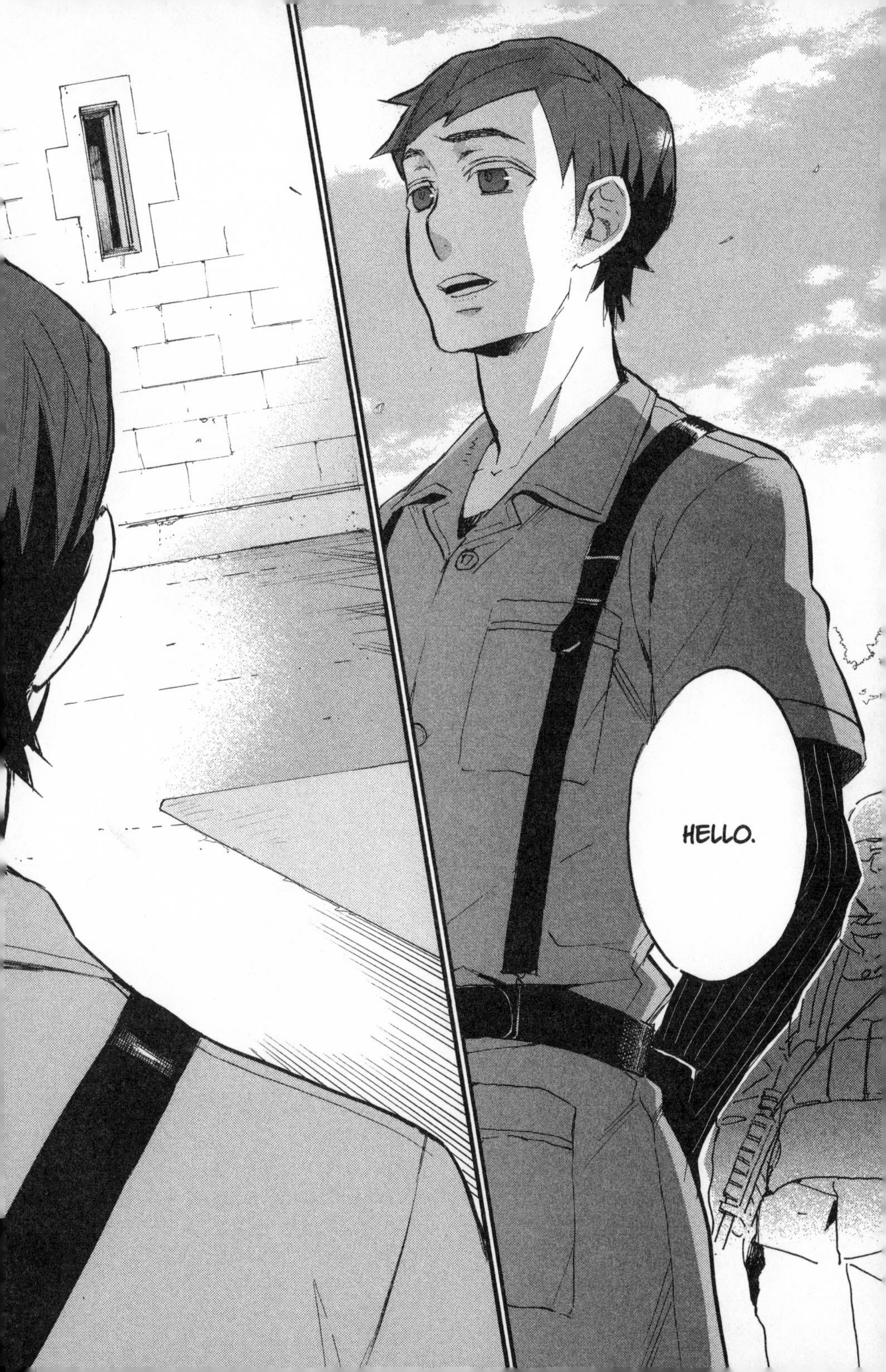
HELLO.

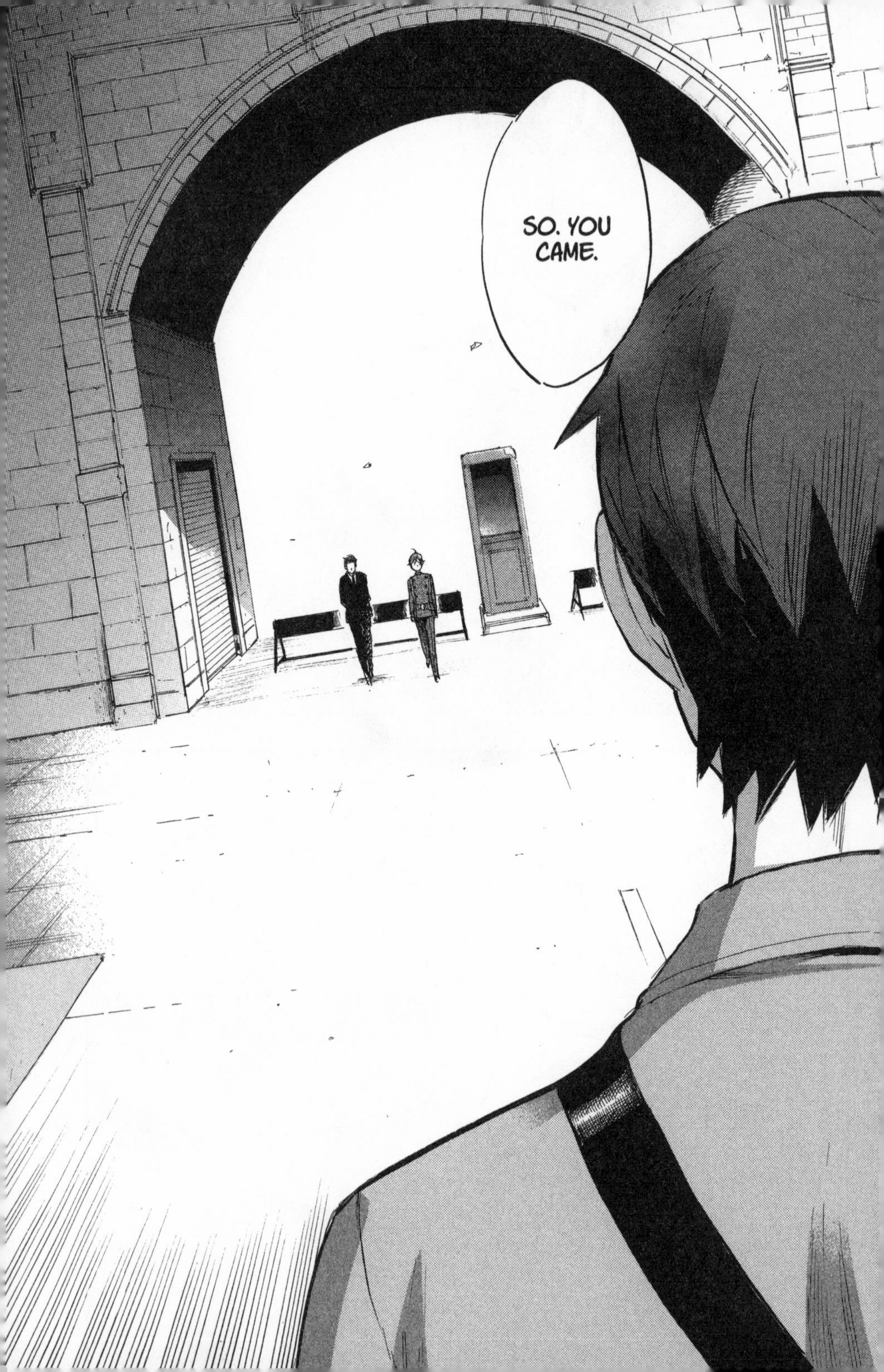
SO. YOU CAME.

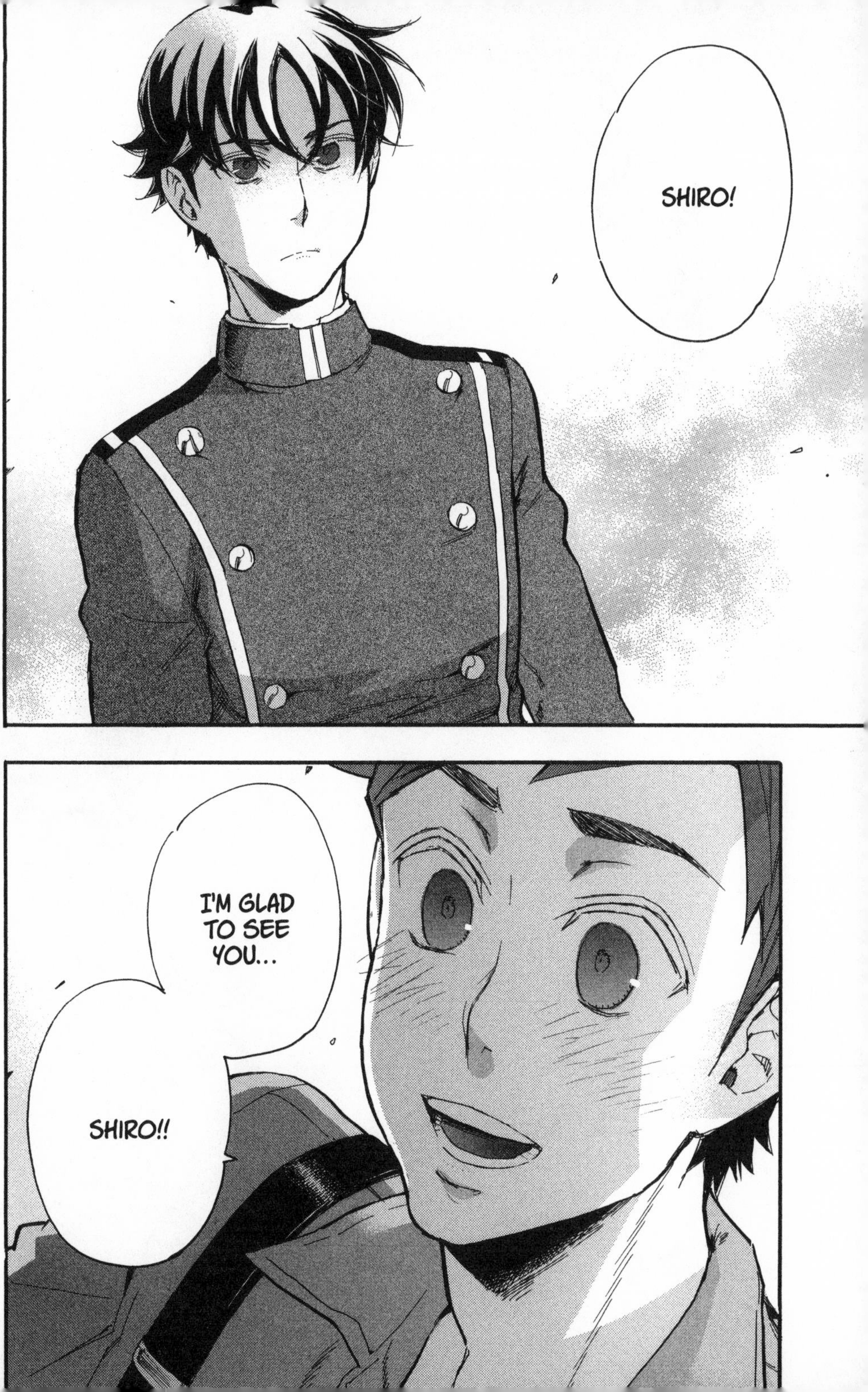
SHIRO!
I'M GLAD TO SEE YOU...
SHIRO!!

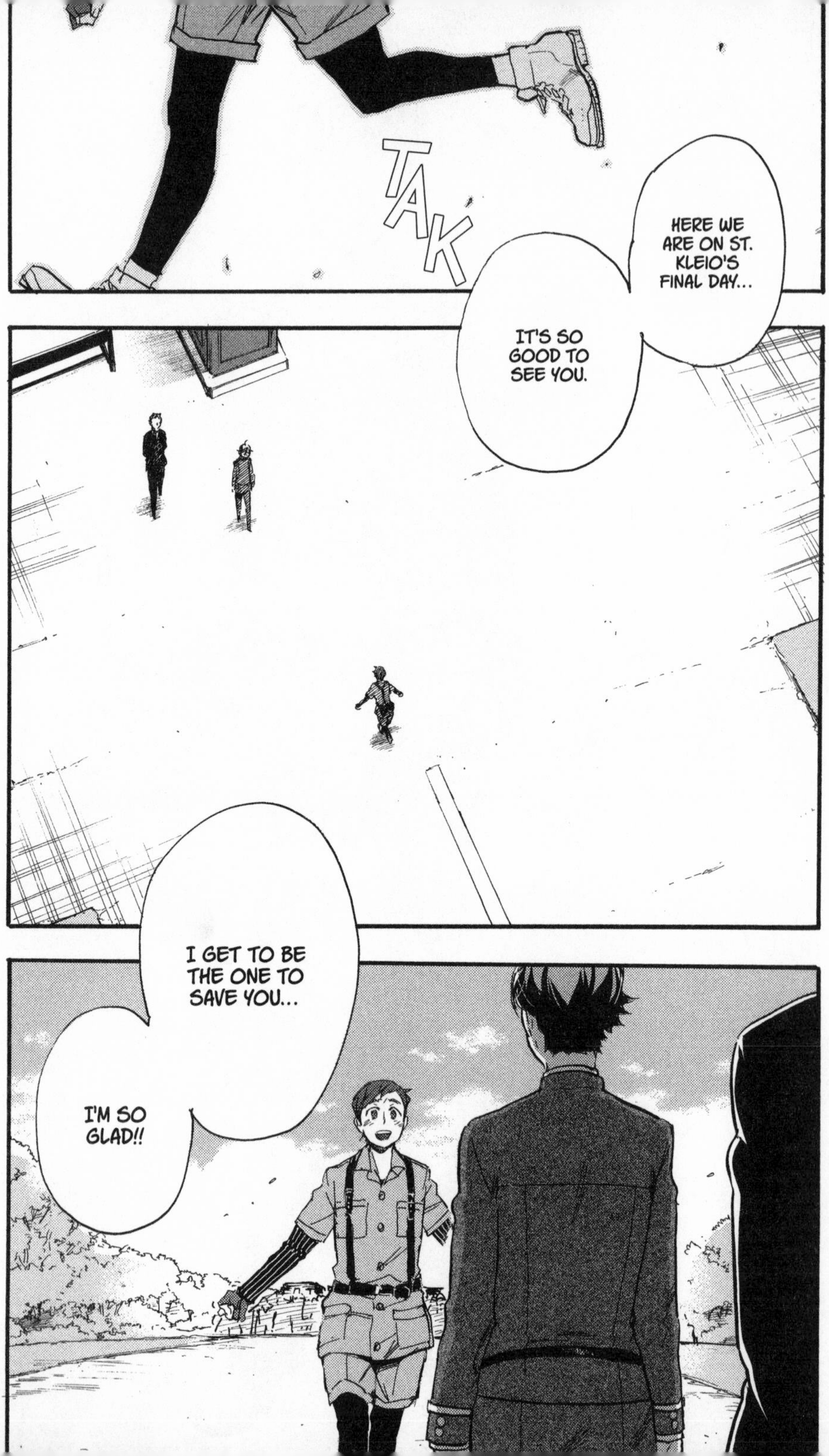
TAK
HERE WE ARE ON ST. KLEIO'S FINAL DAY...
IT'S SO GOOD TO SEE YOU.
I GET TO BE THE ONE TO SAVE YOU...
I'M SO GLAD!!

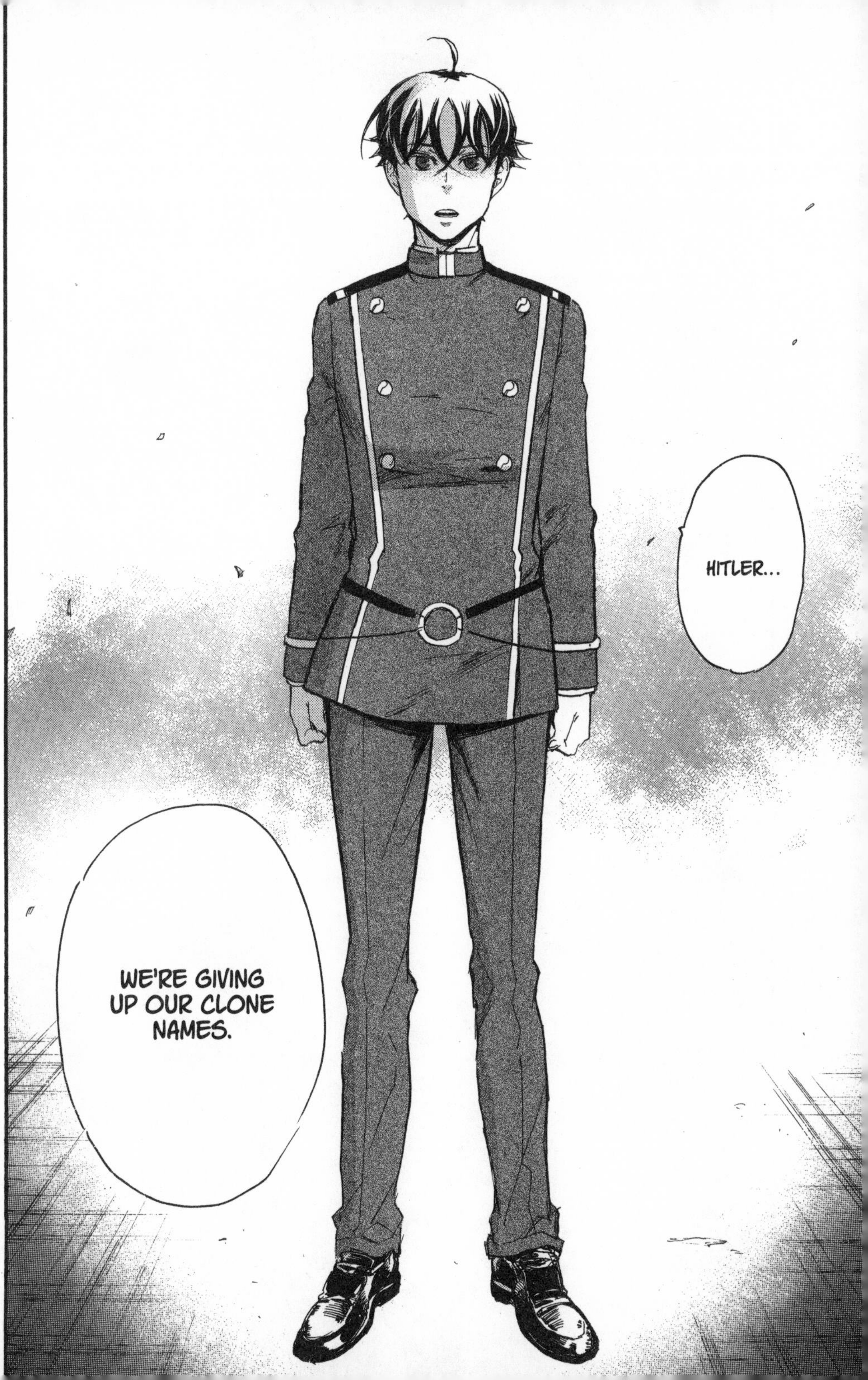
HITLER...
WE'RE GIVING UP OUR CLONE NAMES.

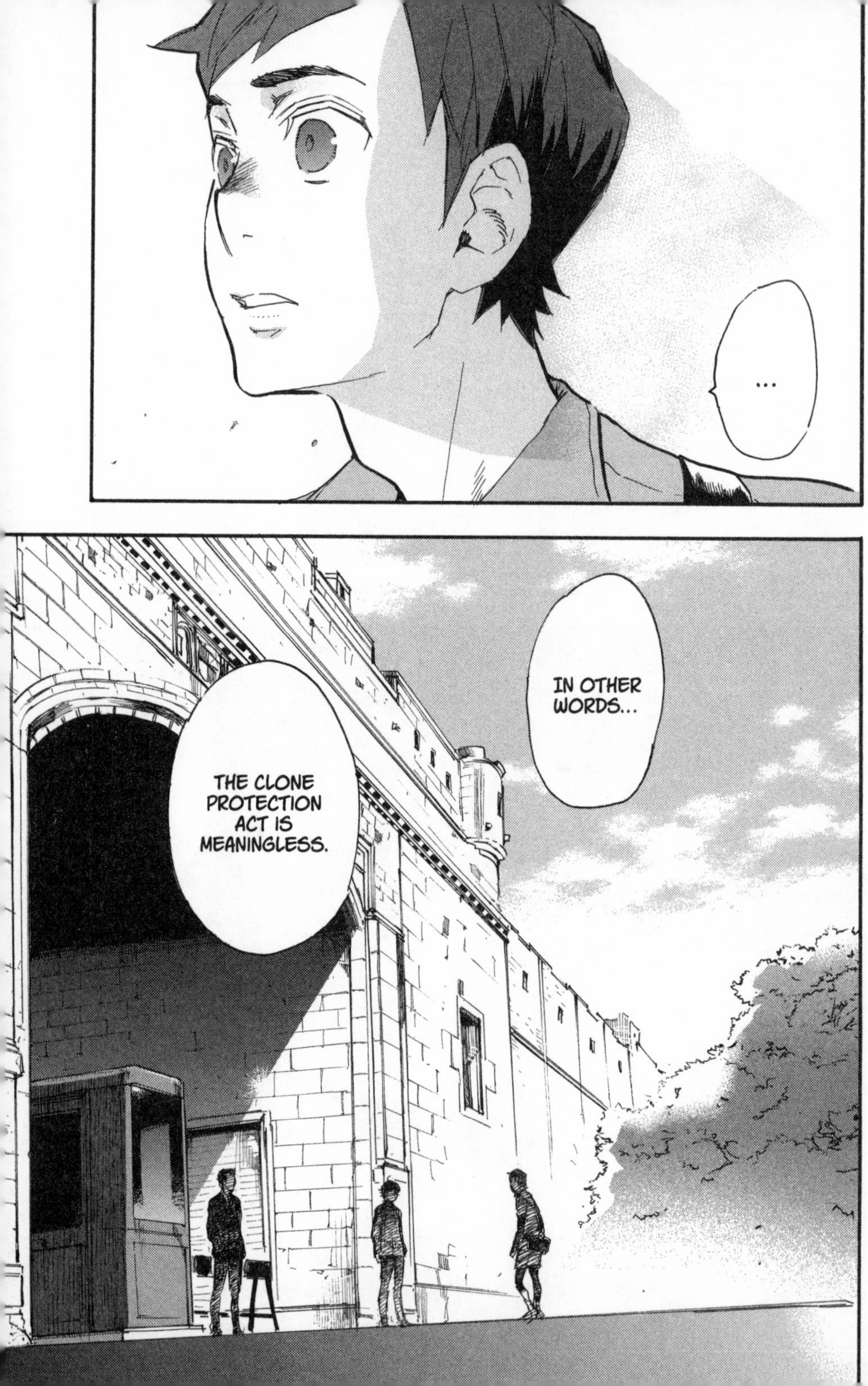
...
IN OTHER WORDS...
THE CLONE PROTECTION ACT IS MEANINGLESS.

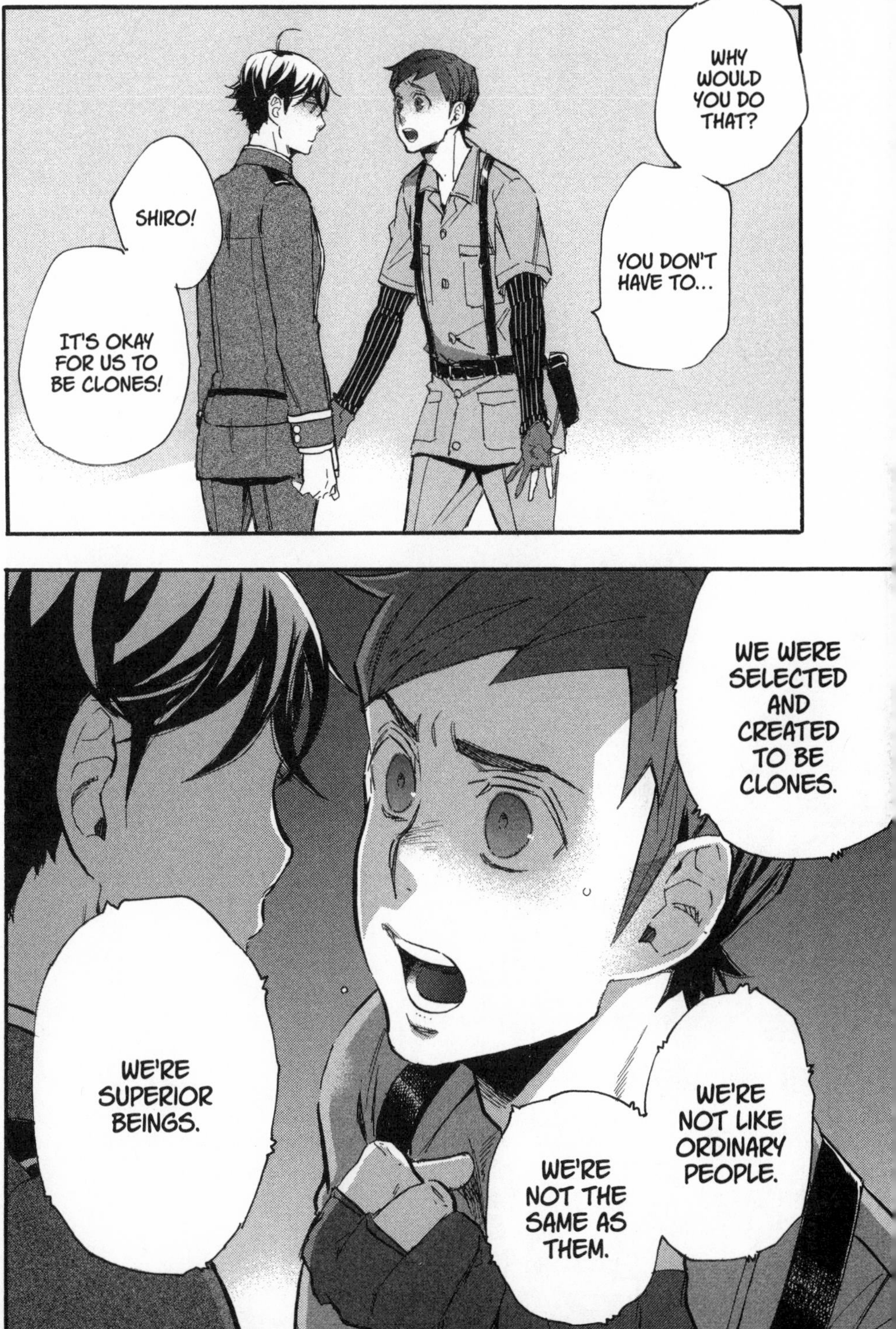
WHY WOULD YOU DO THAT?
YOU DON'T HAVE TO...
SHIRO!
IT'S OKAY FOR US TO BE CLONES!
WE WERE SELECTED AND CREATED TO BE CLONES.
WE'RE NOT LIKE ORDINARY PEOPLE.
WE'RE NOT THE SAME AS THEM.
WE'RE SUPERIOR BEINGS.

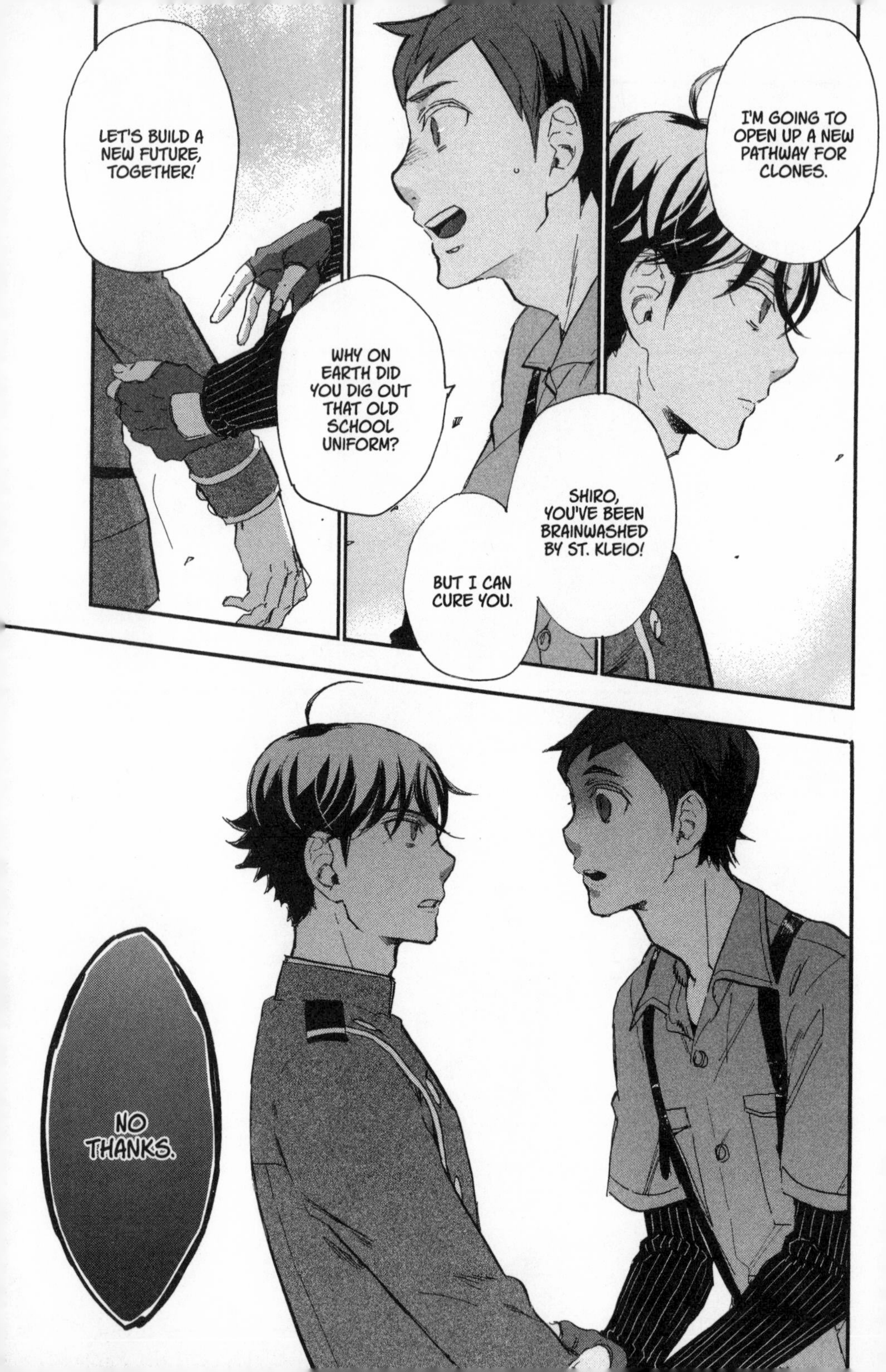
I'M GOING TO OPEN UP A NEW PATHWAY FOR CLONES.
WHY ON EARTH DID YOU DIG OUT THAT OLD SCHOOL UNIFORM?
SHIRO, YOU'VE BEEN BRAINWASHED BY ST. KLEIO!
BUT I CAN CURE YOU.
LET'S BUILD A NEW FUTURE, TOGETHER!
NO THANKS.

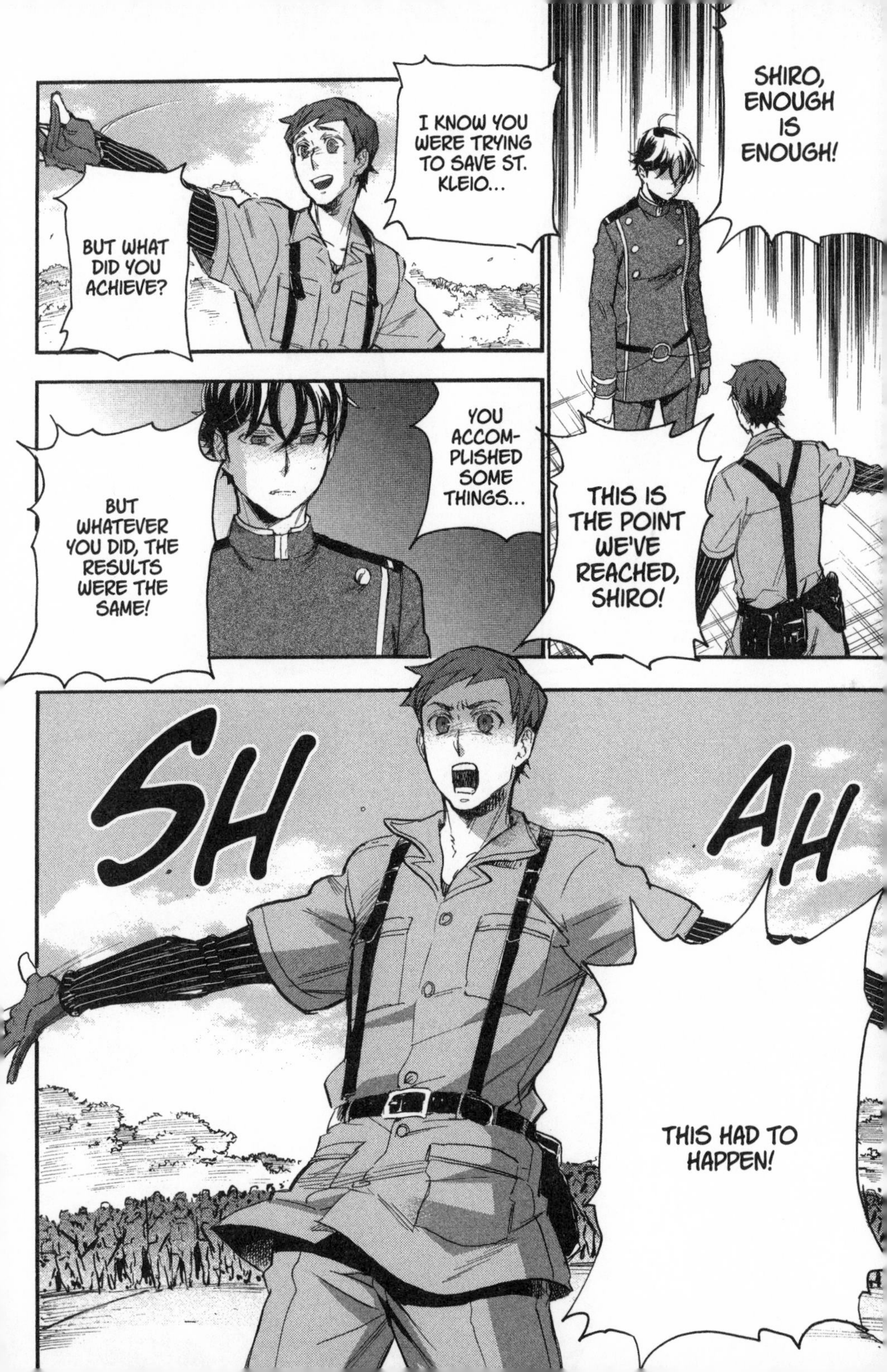
SHIRO, ENOUGH IS ENOUGH!
THIS IS THE POINT WE'VE REACHED, SHIRO!
I KNOW YOU WERE TRYING TO SAVE ST. KLEIO...
BUT WHAT DID YOU ACHIEVE?
YOU ACCOMPLISHED SOME THINGS...
BUT WHATEVER YOU DID, THE RESULTS WERE THE SAME!
SH AH
THIS HAD TO HAPPEN!

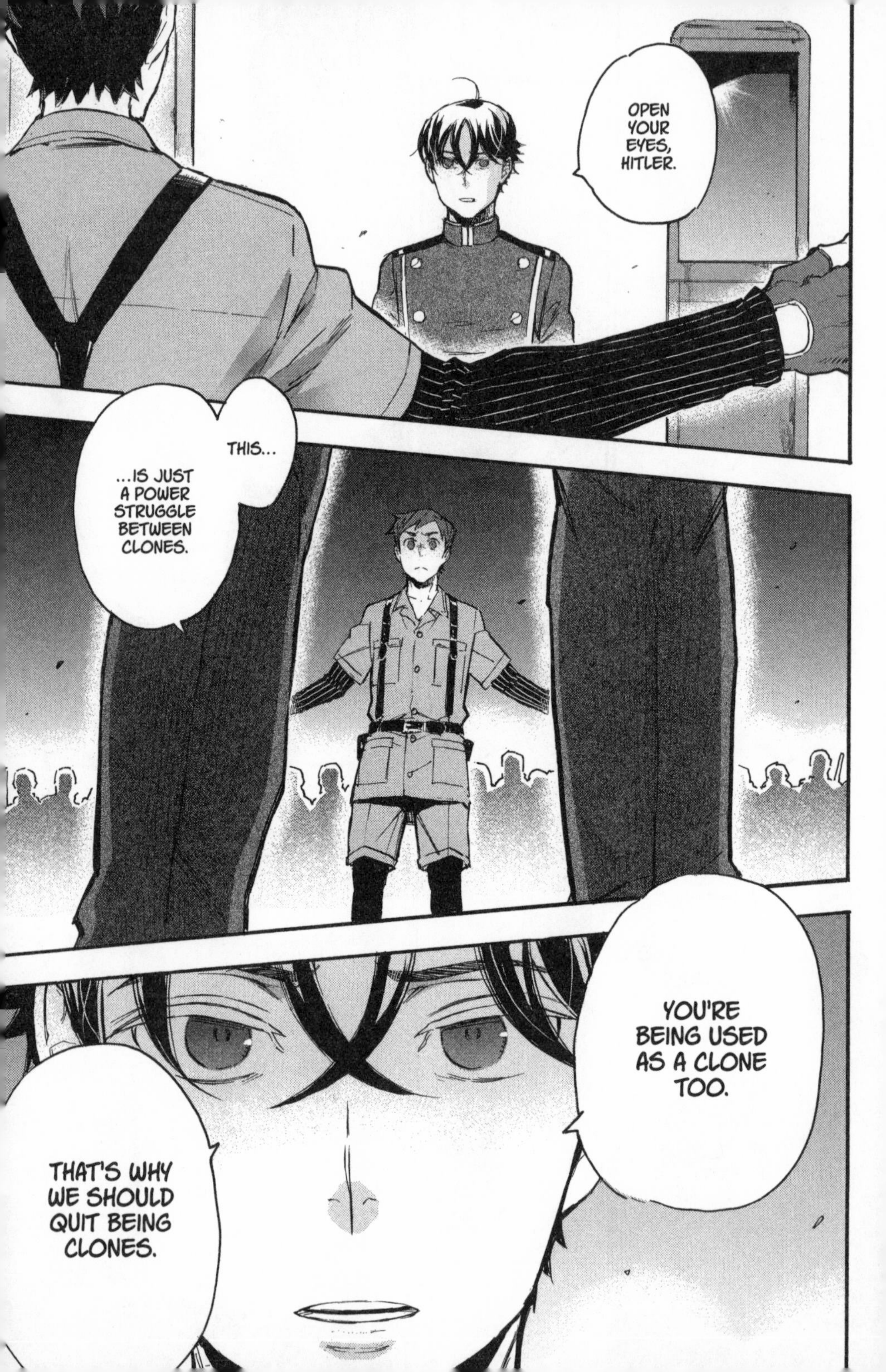
OPEN YOUR EYES, HITLER.
THIS...
...IS JUST A POWER STRUGGLE BETWEEN CLONES.
YOU'RE BEING USED AS A CLONE TOO.
THAT'S WHY WE SHOULD QUIT BEING CLONES.

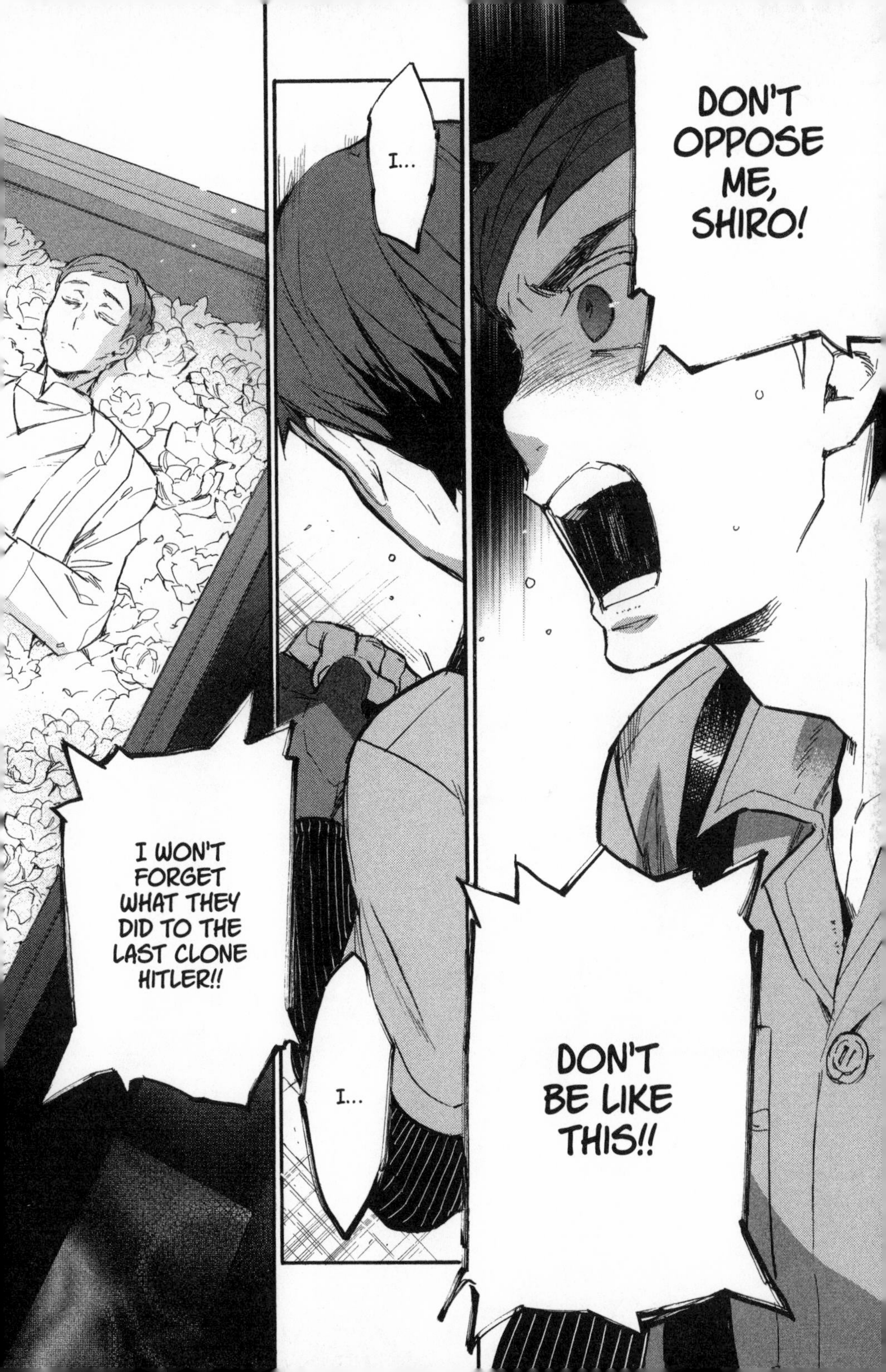
DON'T OPPOSE ME, SHIRO!
DON'T BE LIKE THIS!!
I...
I...
I WON'T FORGET WHAT THEY DID TO THE LAST CLONE HITLER!!

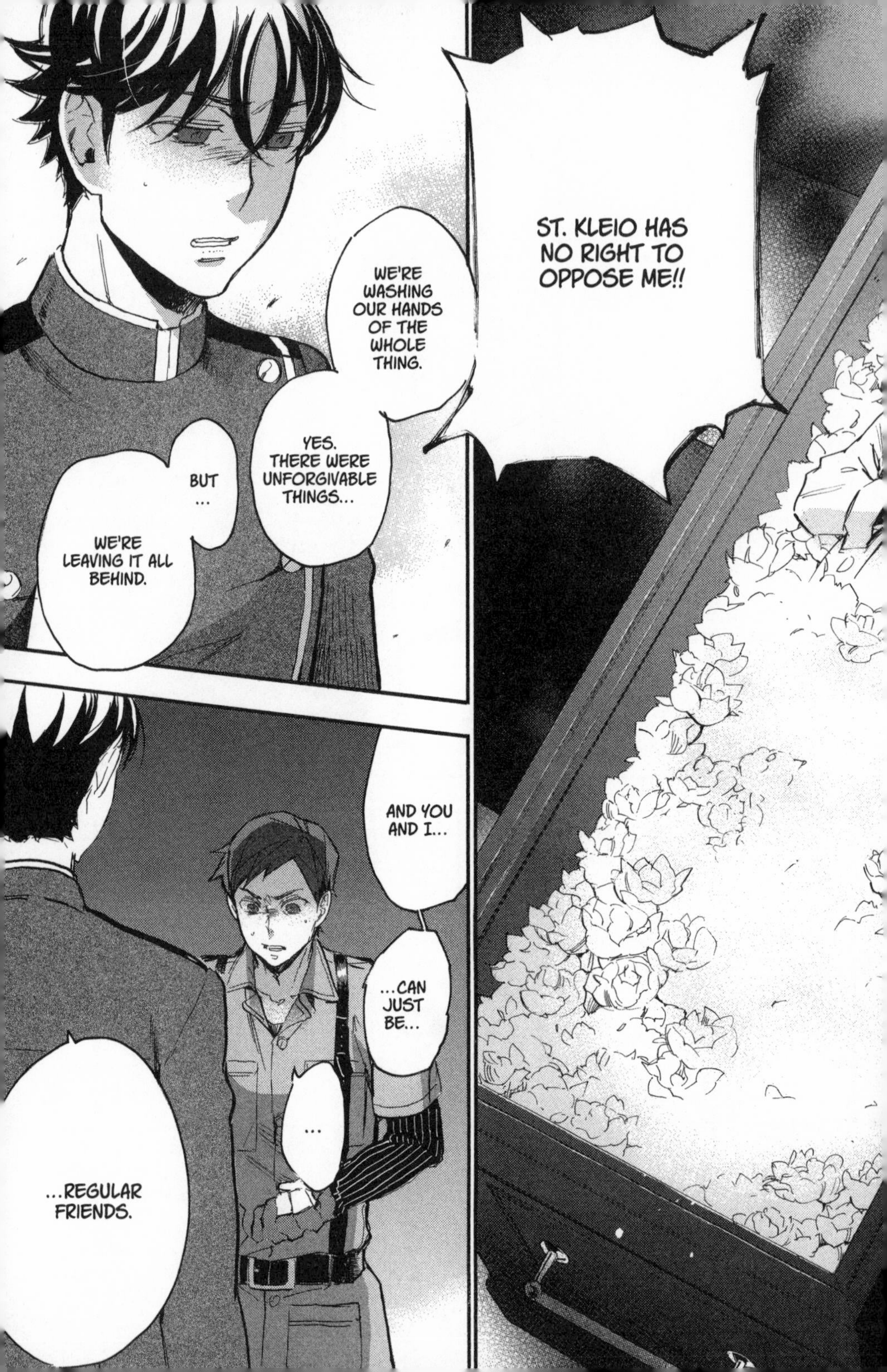
ST. KLEIO HAS NO RIGHT TO OPPOSE ME!!
WE'RE WASHING OUR HANDS OF THE WHOLE THING.
YES. THERE WERE UNFORGIVABLE THINGS...
BUT ...
WE'RE LEAVING IT ALL BEHIND.
AND YOU AND I...
...CAN JUST BE...
...
...REGULAR FRIENDS.

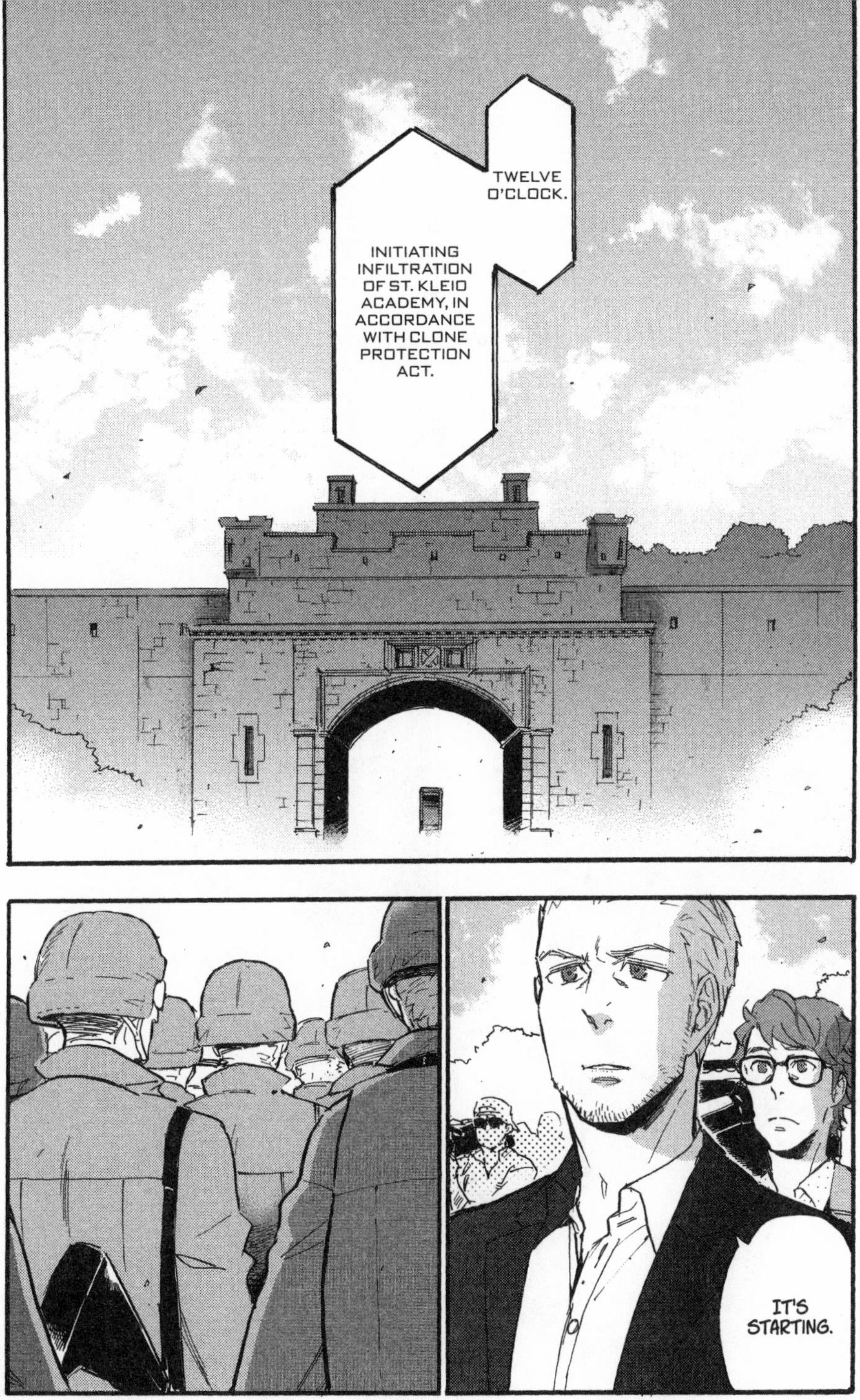
TWELVE O'CLOCK.
INITIATING INFILTRATION OF ST. KLEIO ACADEMY, IN ACCORDANCE WITH CLONE PROTECTION ACT.
IT'S STARTING.

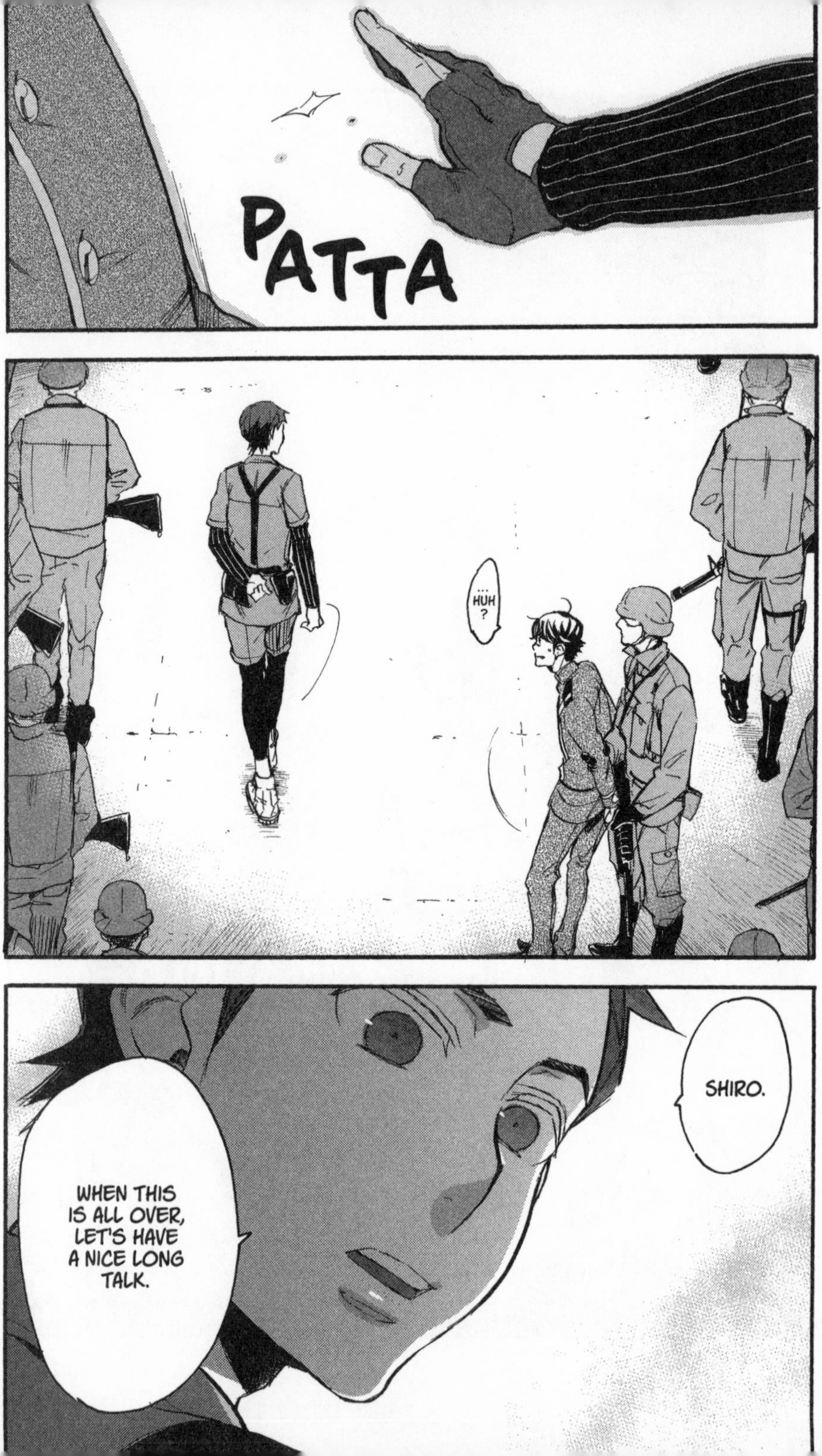
PATTA
...HUH?
SHIRO.
WHEN THIS IS ALL OVER, LET'S HAVE A NICE LONG TALK.

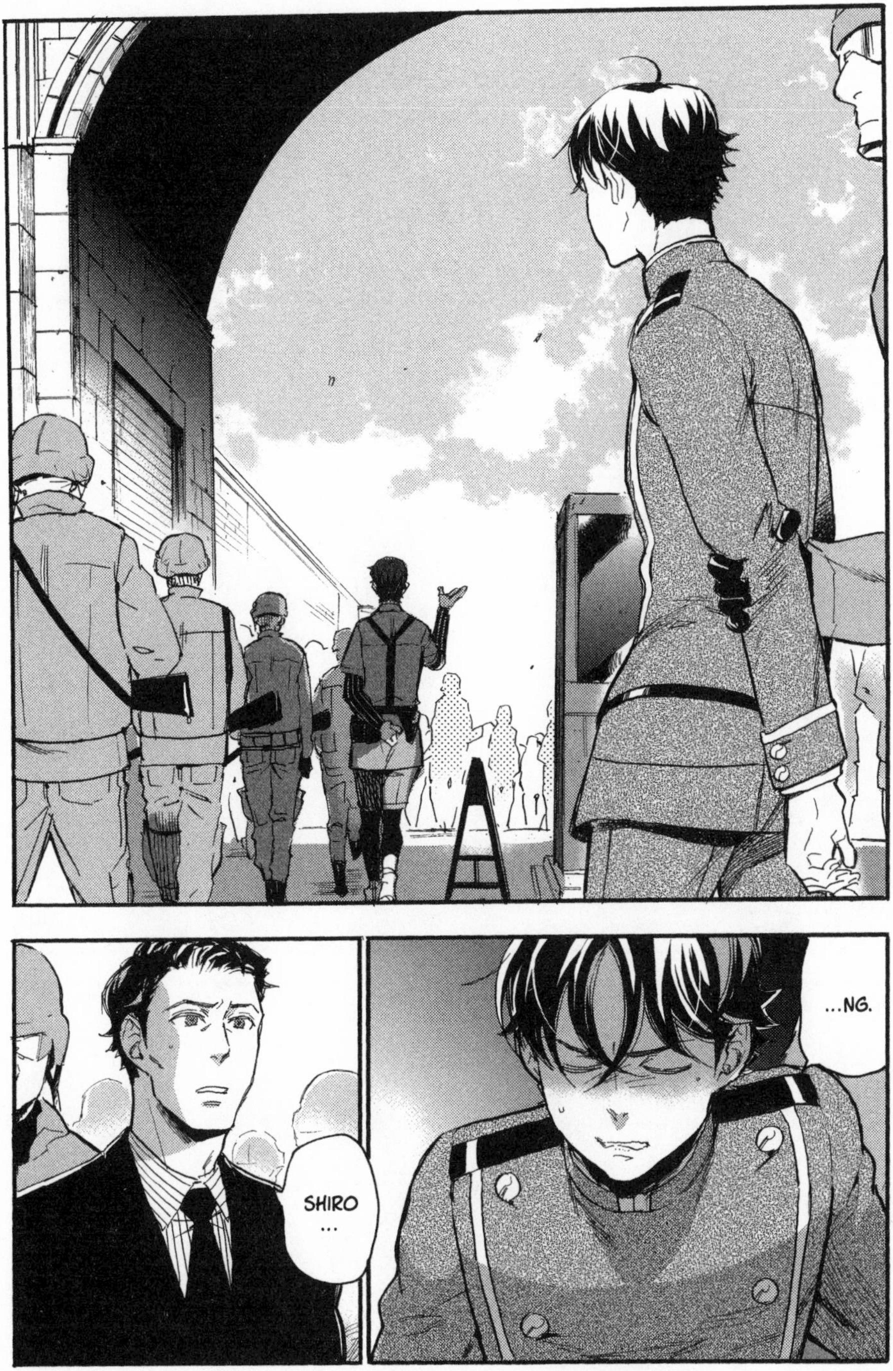
...NG.
SHIRO ...

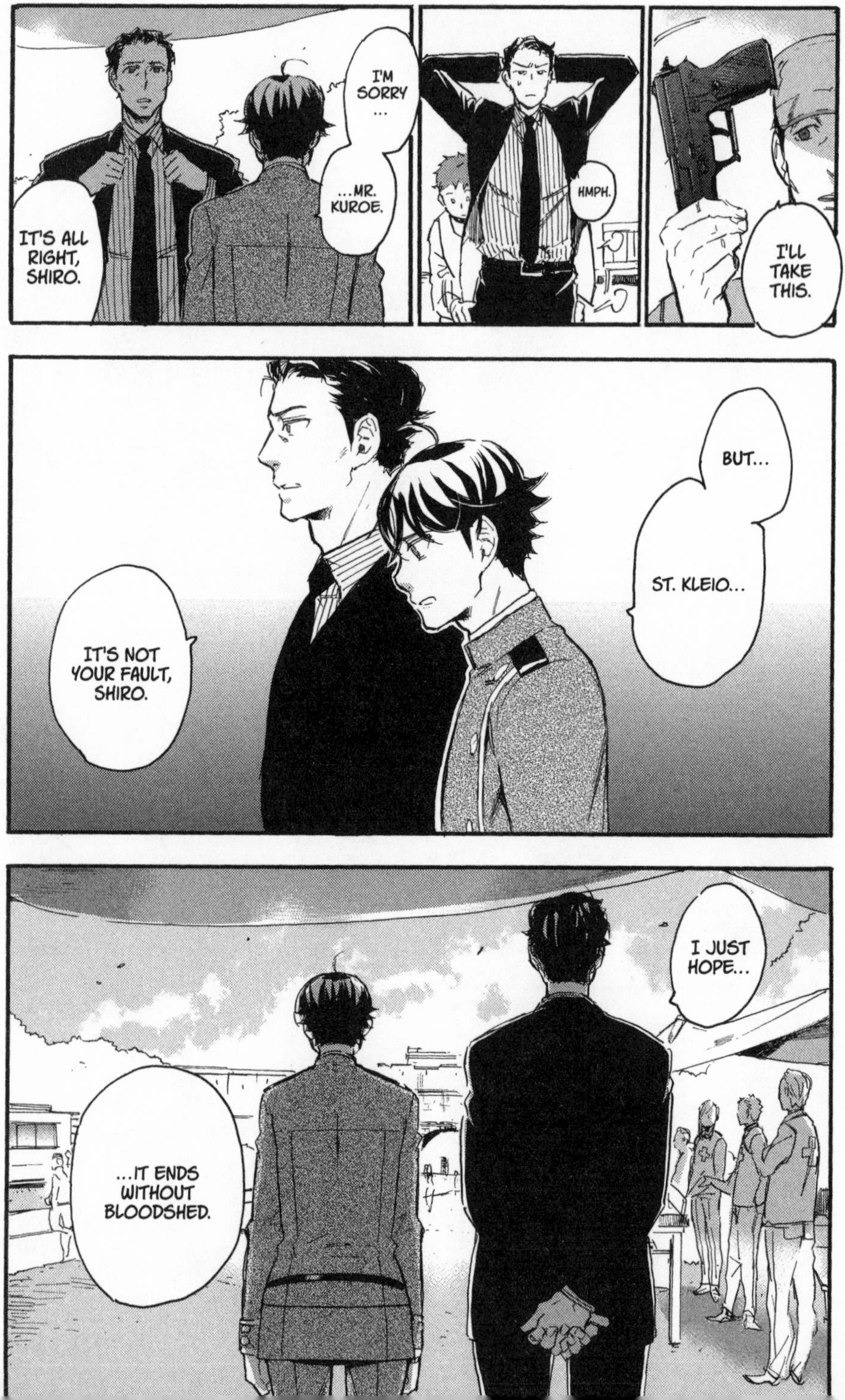
I'LL TAKE THIS.
HMPH.
I'M SORRY ...
...MR. KUROE.
IT'S ALL RIGHT, SHIRO.
BUT...
ST. KLEIO...
IT'S NOT YOUR FAULT, SHIRO.
I JUST HOPE...
...IT ENDS WITHOUT BLOODSHED.

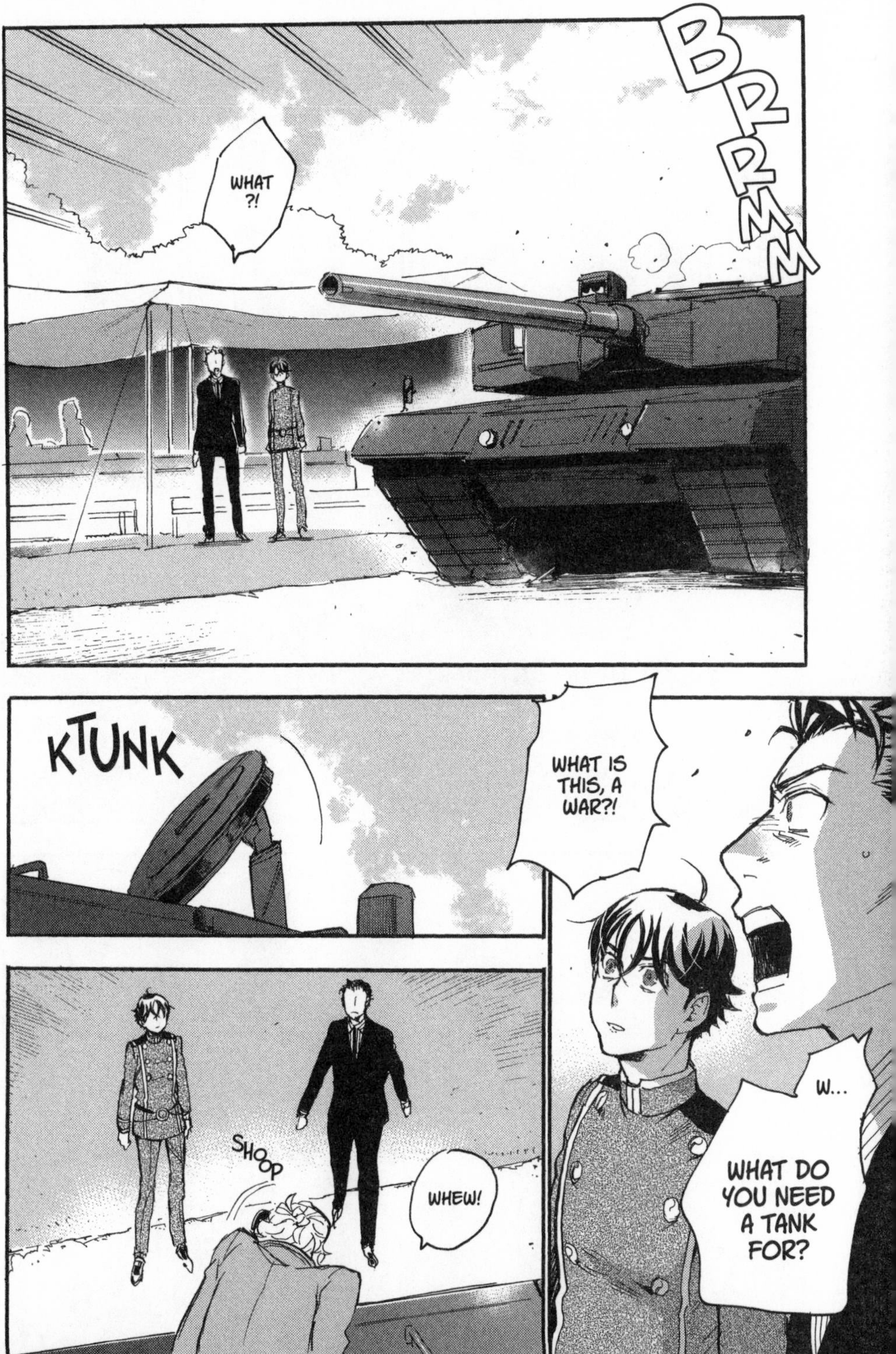
BRRMM
WHAT ?!
WHAT IS THIS, A WAR?!
W...
WHAT DO YOU NEED A TANK FOR?
KTUNK
SHOOP
WHEW!

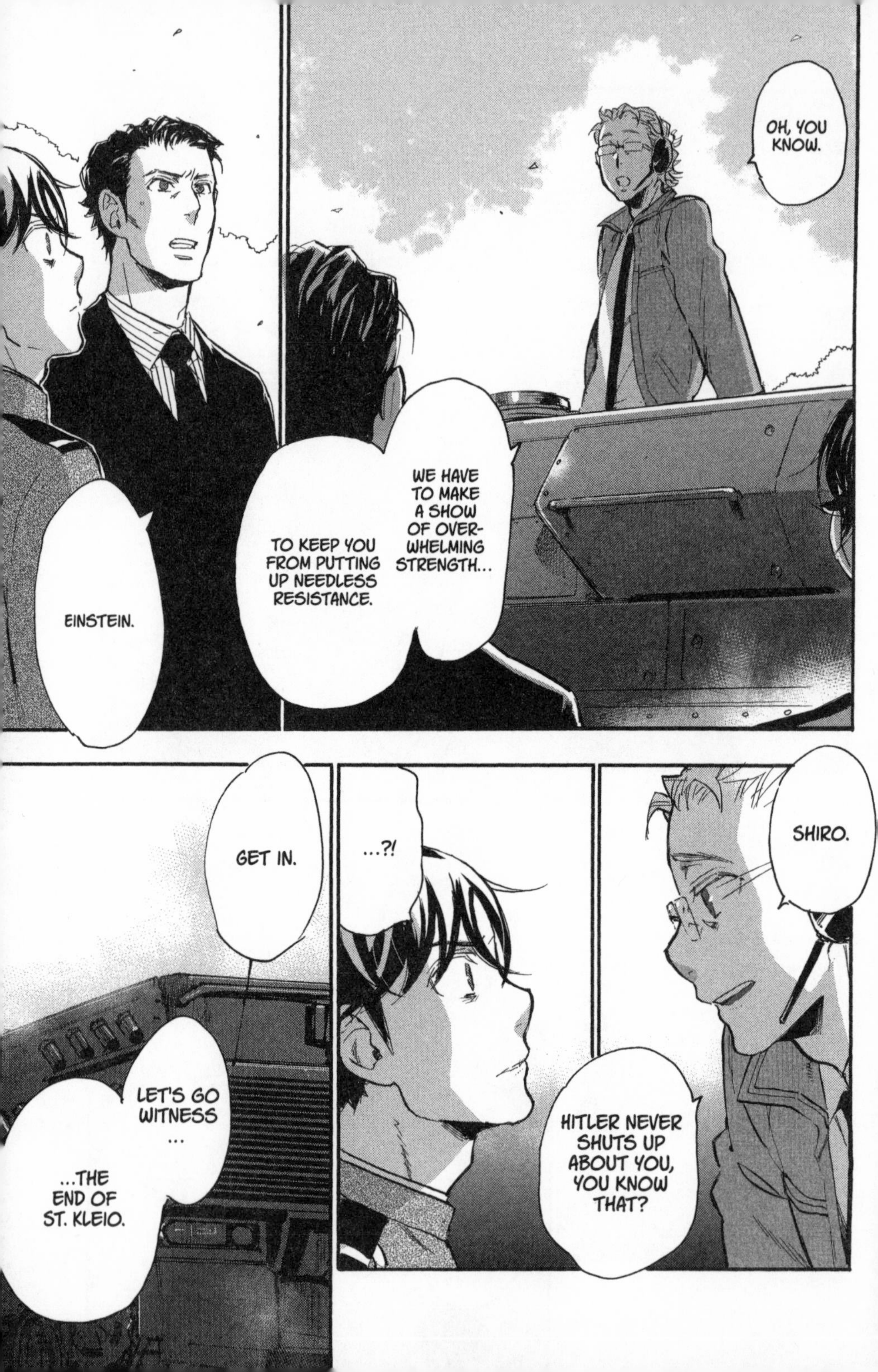
OH, YOU KNOW.
WE HAVE TO MAKE A SHOW OF OVER-WHELMING STRENGTH...
TO KEEP YOU FROM PUTTING UP NEEDLESS RESISTANCE.
EINSTEIN.
SHIRO.
HITLER NEVER SHUTS UP ABOUT YOU, YOU KNOW THAT?
...?!
GET IN.
LET'S GO WITNESS ...
...THE END OF ST. KLEIO.

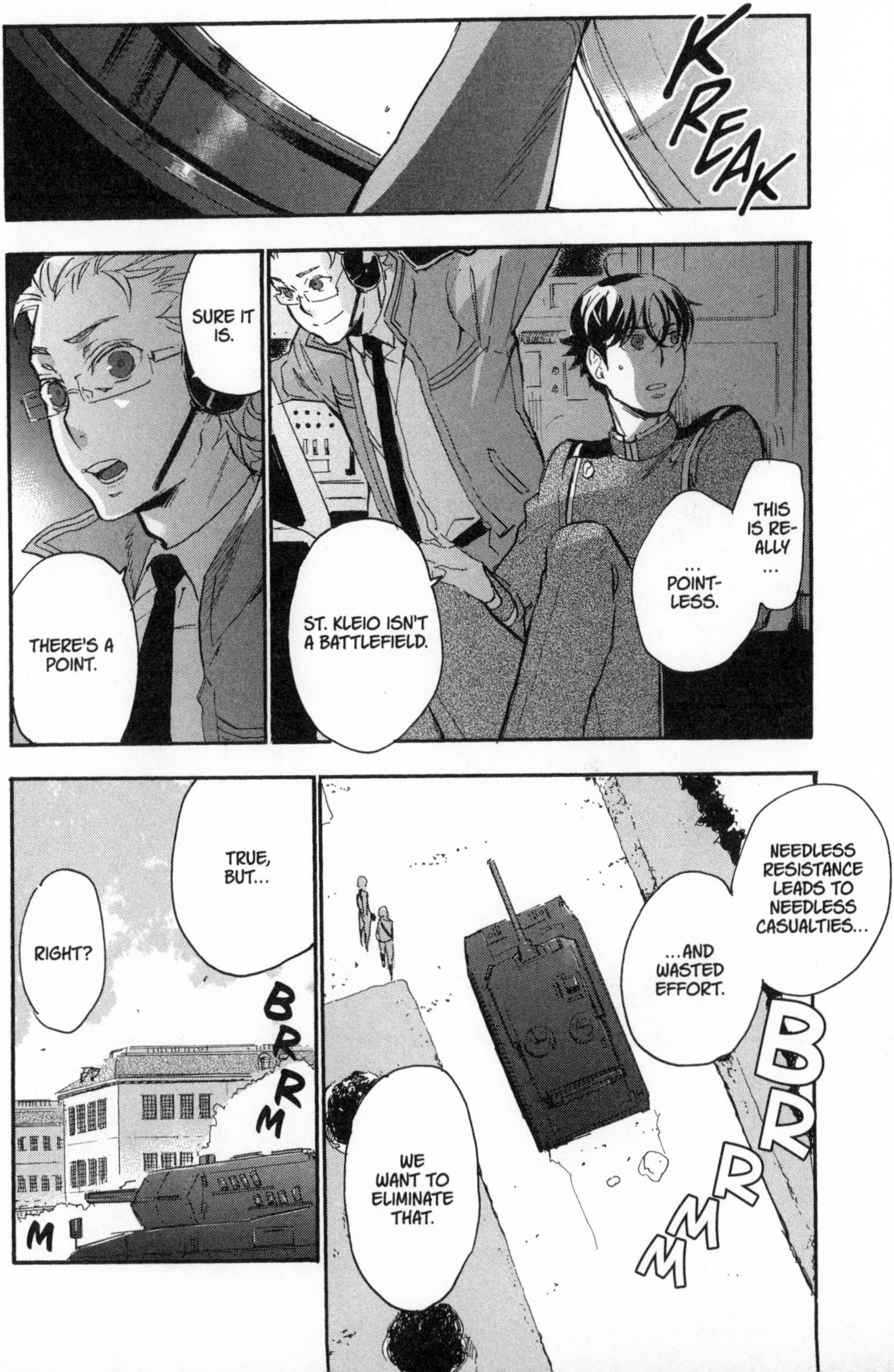
KREAK
THIS IS RE-ALLY...
...POINT-LESS.
ST. KLEIO ISN'T A BATTLEFIELD.
SURE IT IS.
THERE'S A POINT.
NEEDLESS RESISTANCE LEADS TO NEEDLESS CASUALTIES...
...AND WASTED EFFORT.
BRRMMM
WE WANT TO ELIMINATE THAT.
TRUE, BUT...
RIGHT?
BRRMM

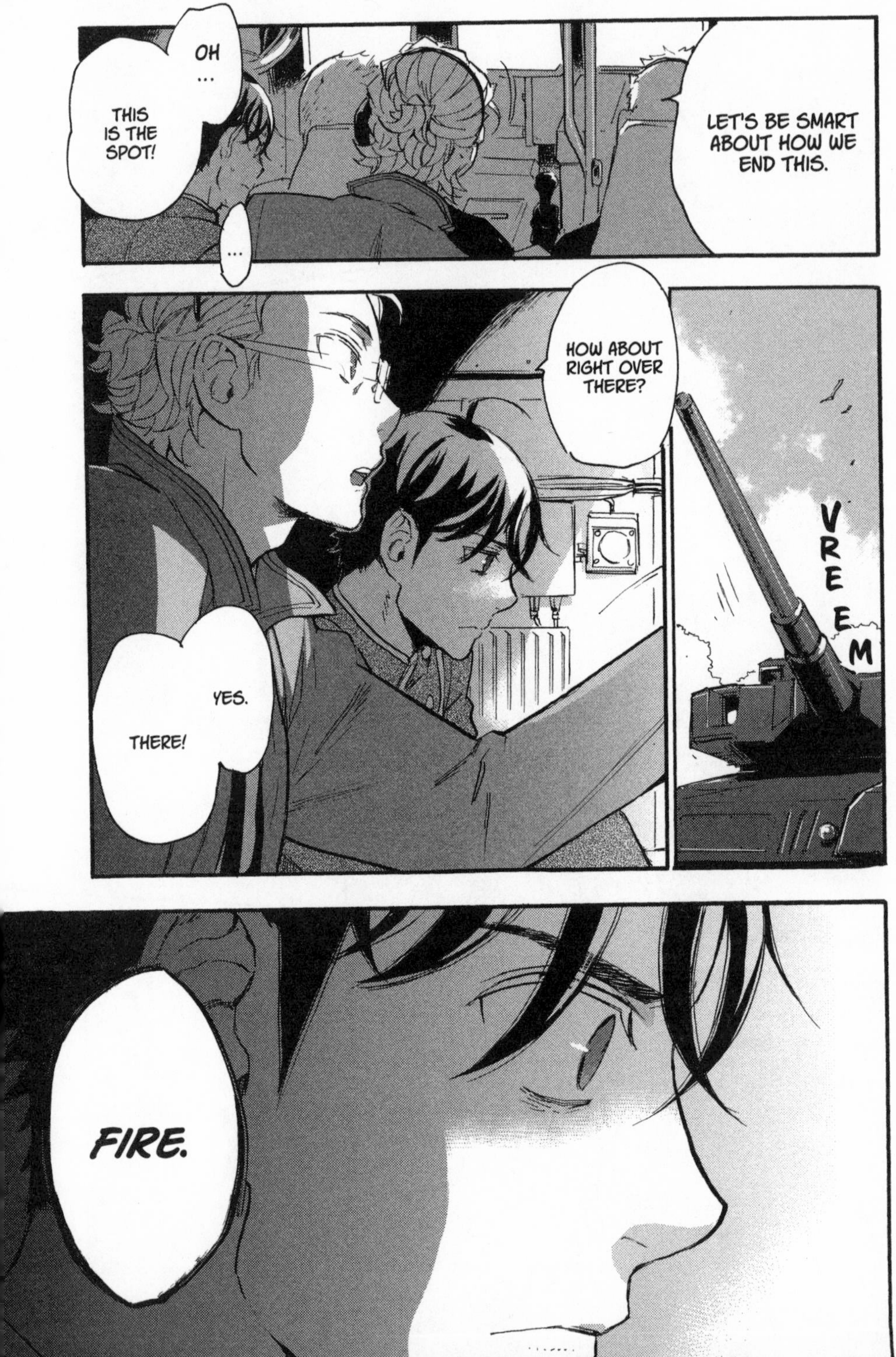
LET'S BE SMART ABOUT HOW WE END THIS.
OH ...
THIS IS THE SPOT!
...
VREEEM
HOW ABOUT RIGHT OVER THERE?
YES.
THERE!
FIRE.

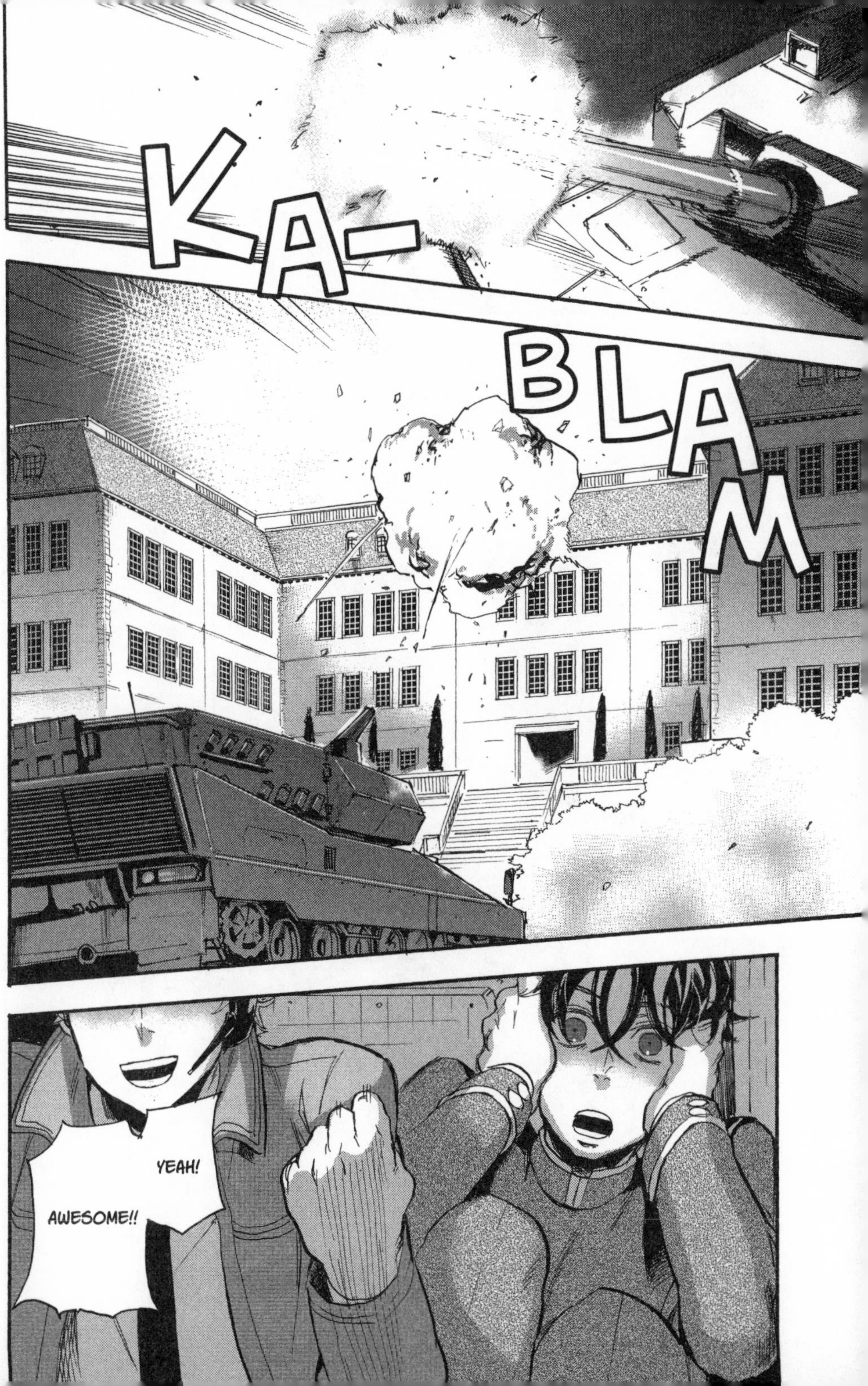
KA-
BLAM
YEAH!
AWESOME!!

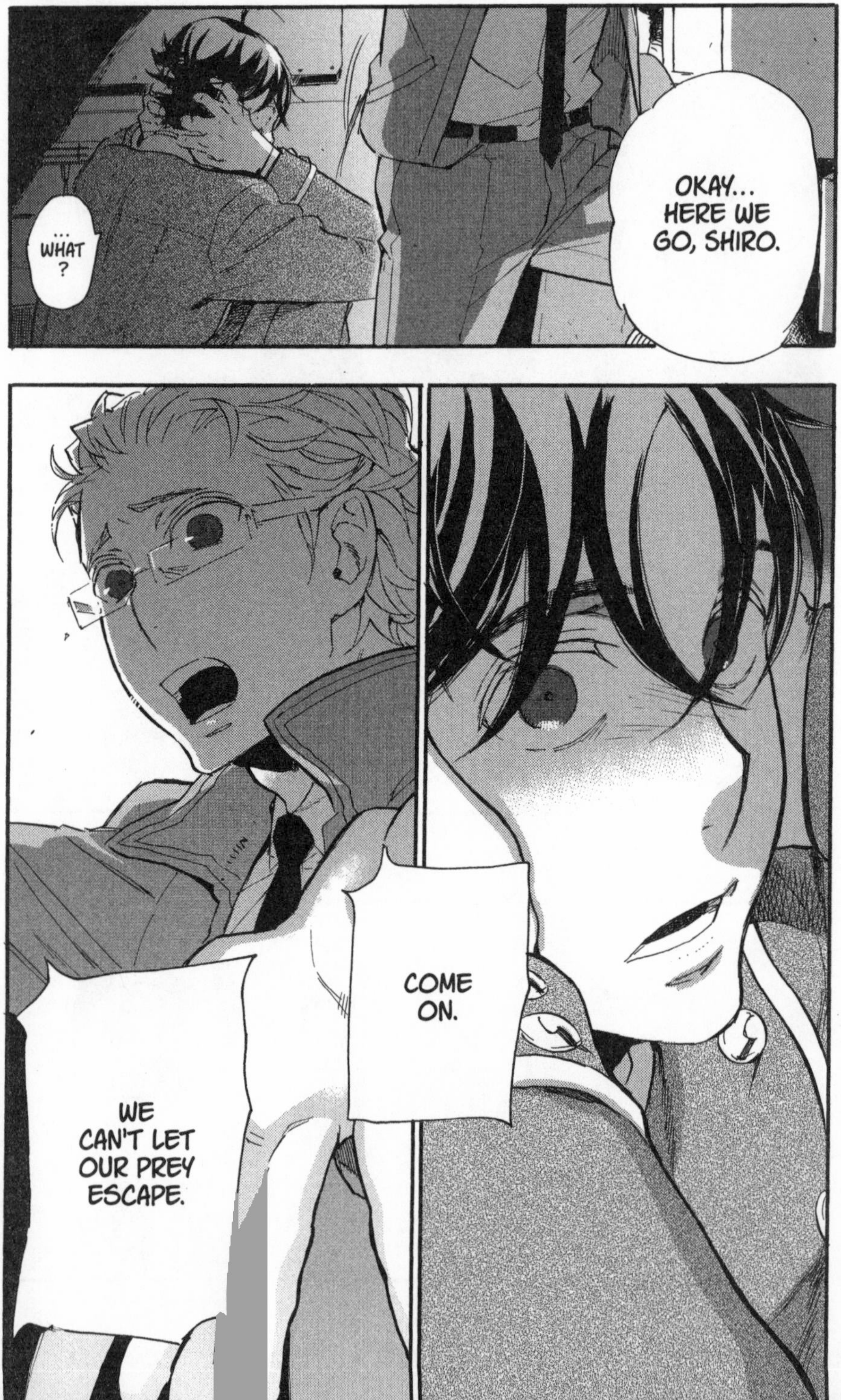
OKAY... HERE WE GO, SHIRO.
...WHAT?
COME ON.
WE CAN'T LET OUR PREY ESCAPE.

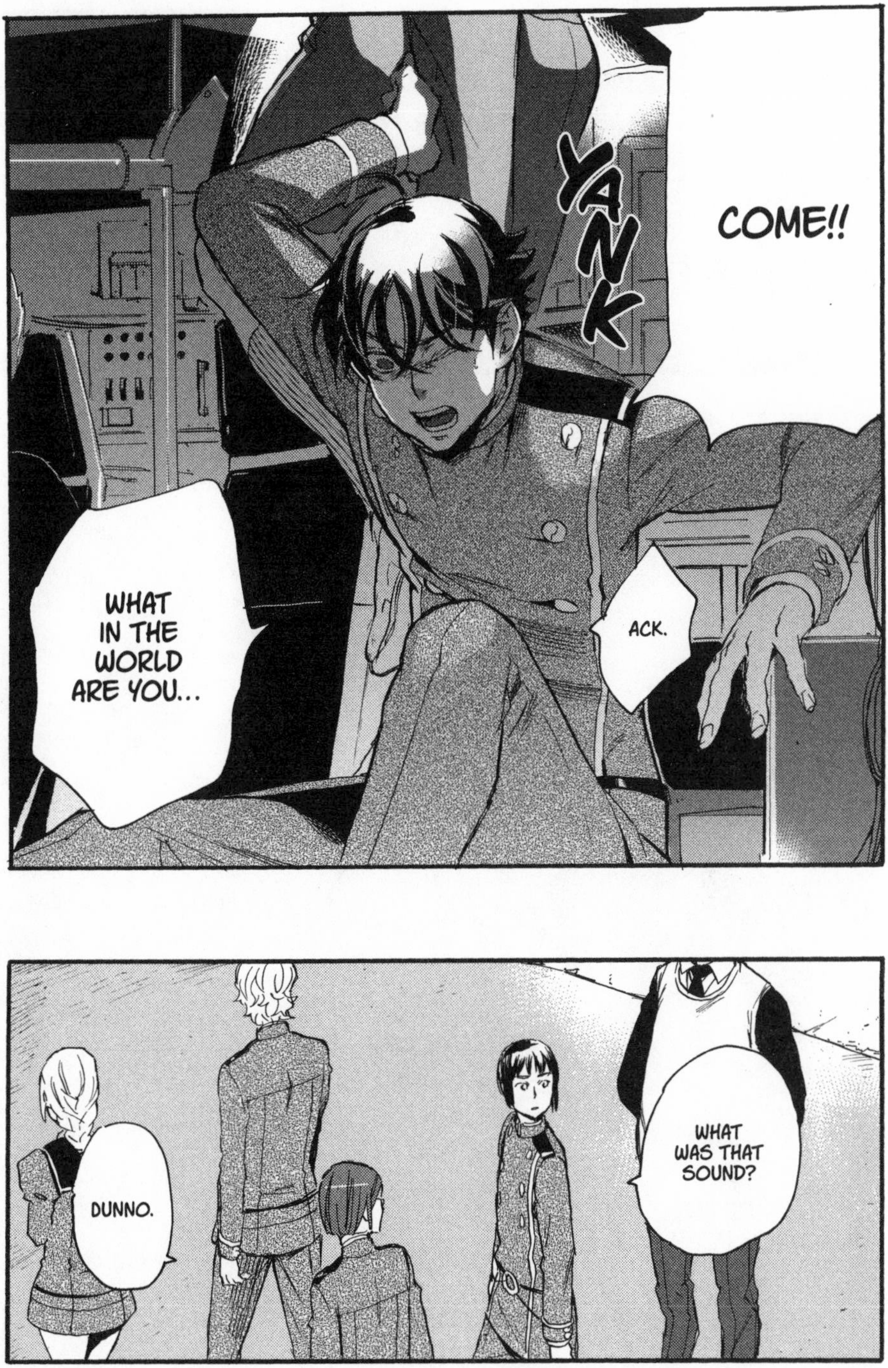
COME!!
YANK
ACK.
WHAT IN THE WORLD ARE YOU...
WHAT WAS THAT SOUND?
DUNNO.

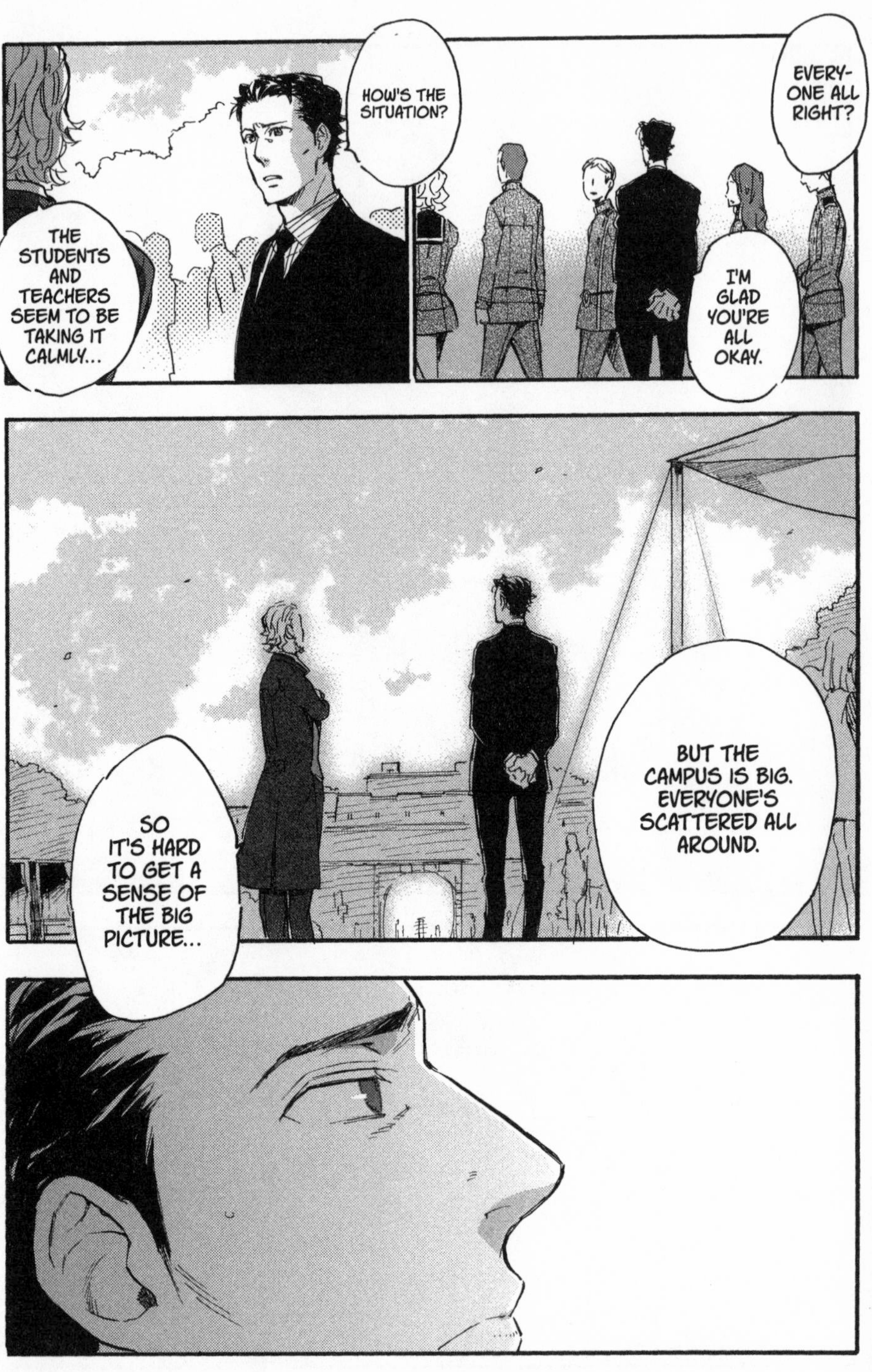
EVERY-ONE ALL RIGHT?
I'M GLAD YOU'RE ALL OKAY.
HOW'S THE SITUATION?
THE STUDENTS AND TEACHERS SEEM TO BE TAKING IT CALMLY...
BUT THE CAMPUS IS BIG. EVERYONE'S SCATTERED ALL AROUND.
SO IT'S HARD TO GET A SENSE OF THE BIG PICTURE...

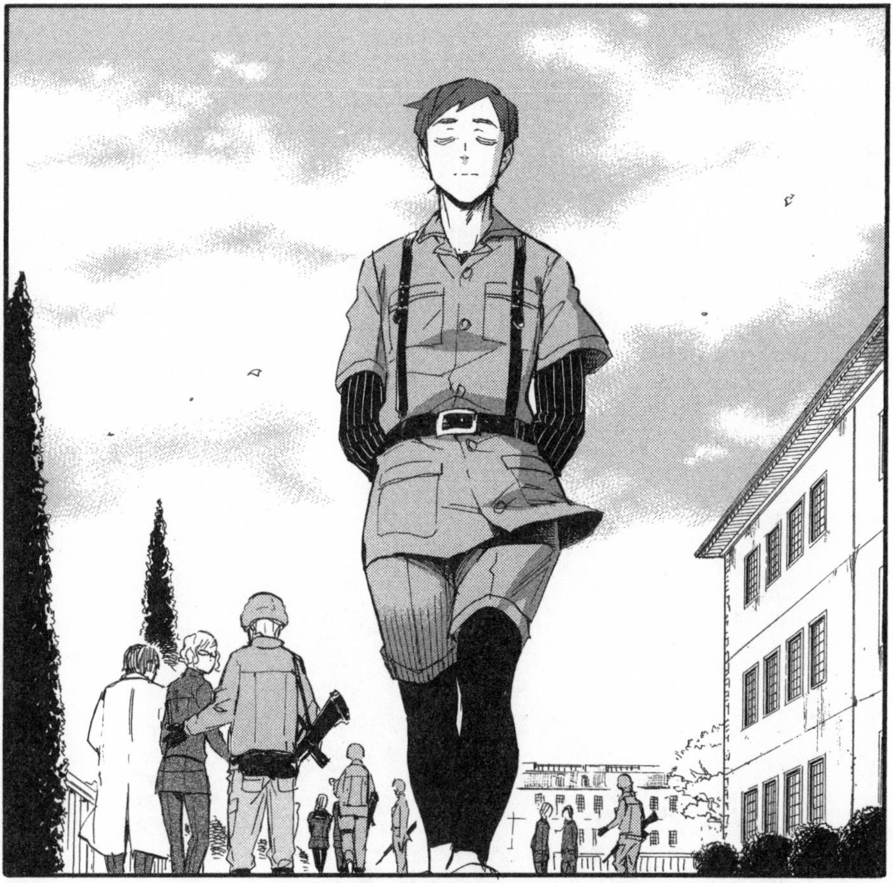

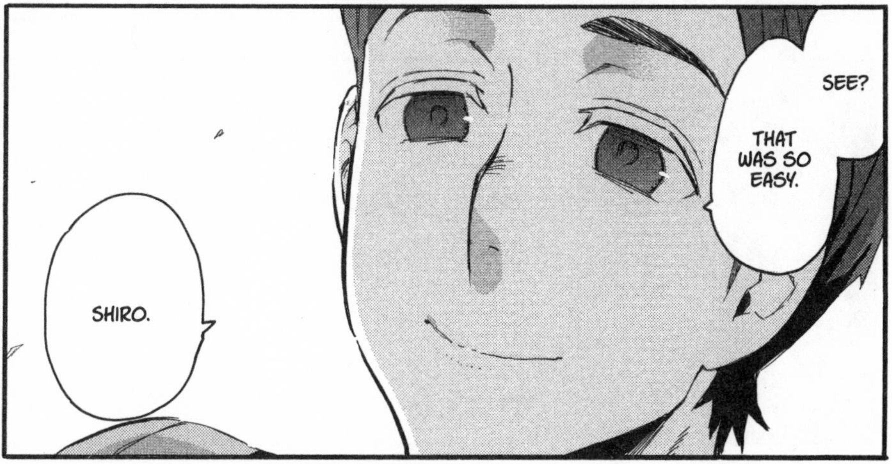
SEE?
THAT WAS SO EASY.
SHIRO.

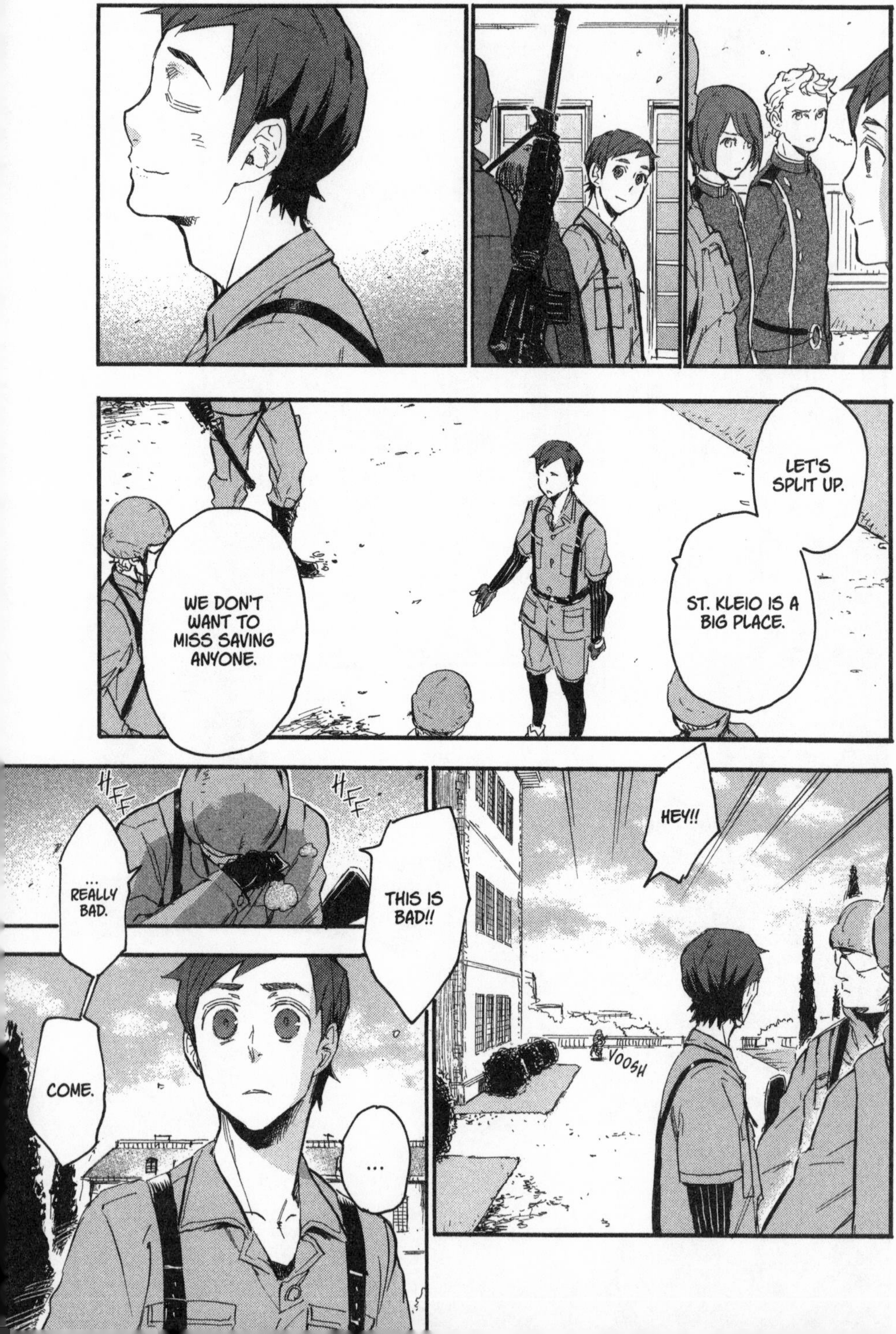
LET'S SPLIT UP.
ST. KLEIO IS A BIG PLACE.
WE DON'T WANT TO MISS SAVING ANYONE.
HEY!!
VOOSH
HFF
HFF
THIS IS BAD!!
... REALLY BAD.
...
COME.

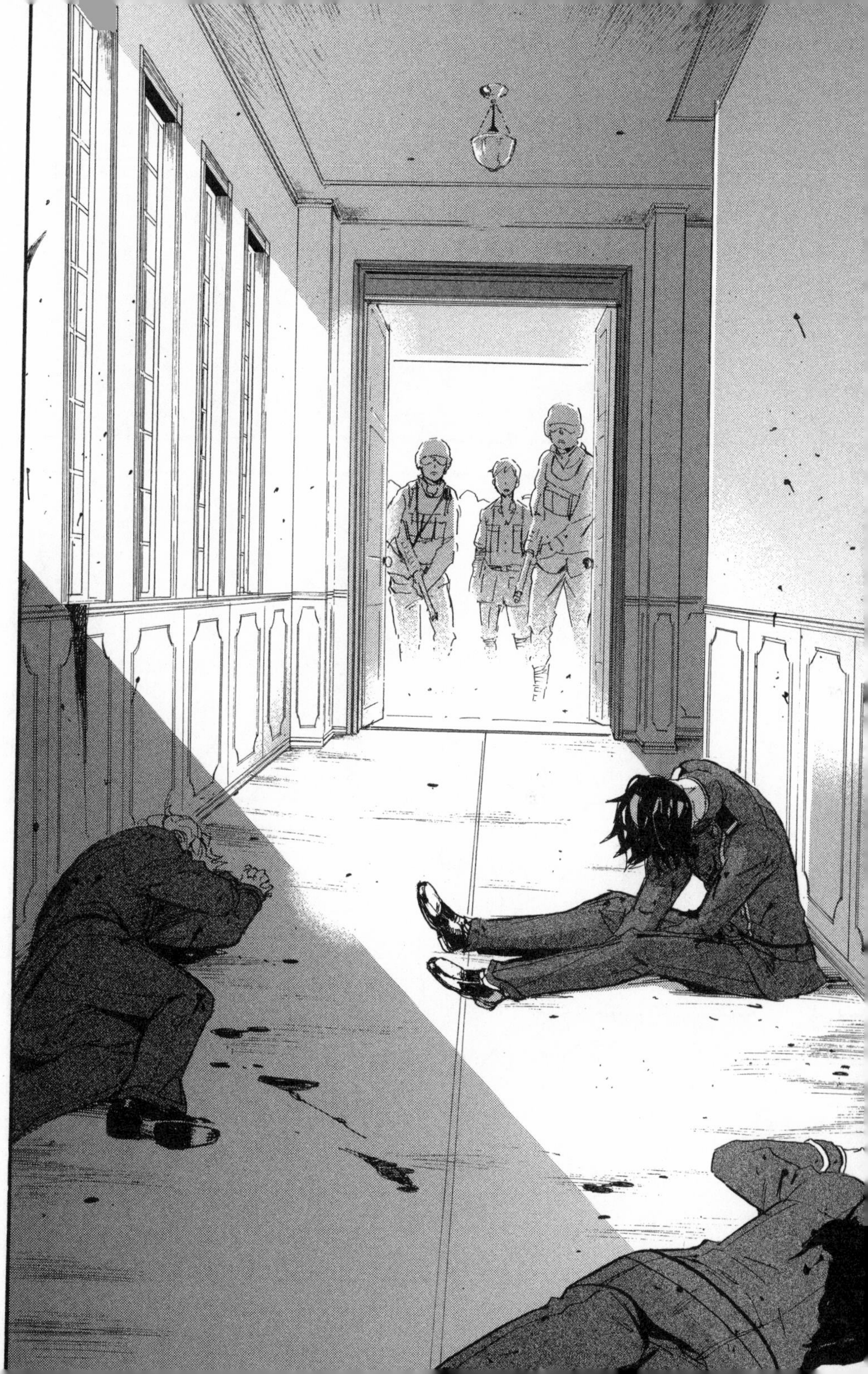

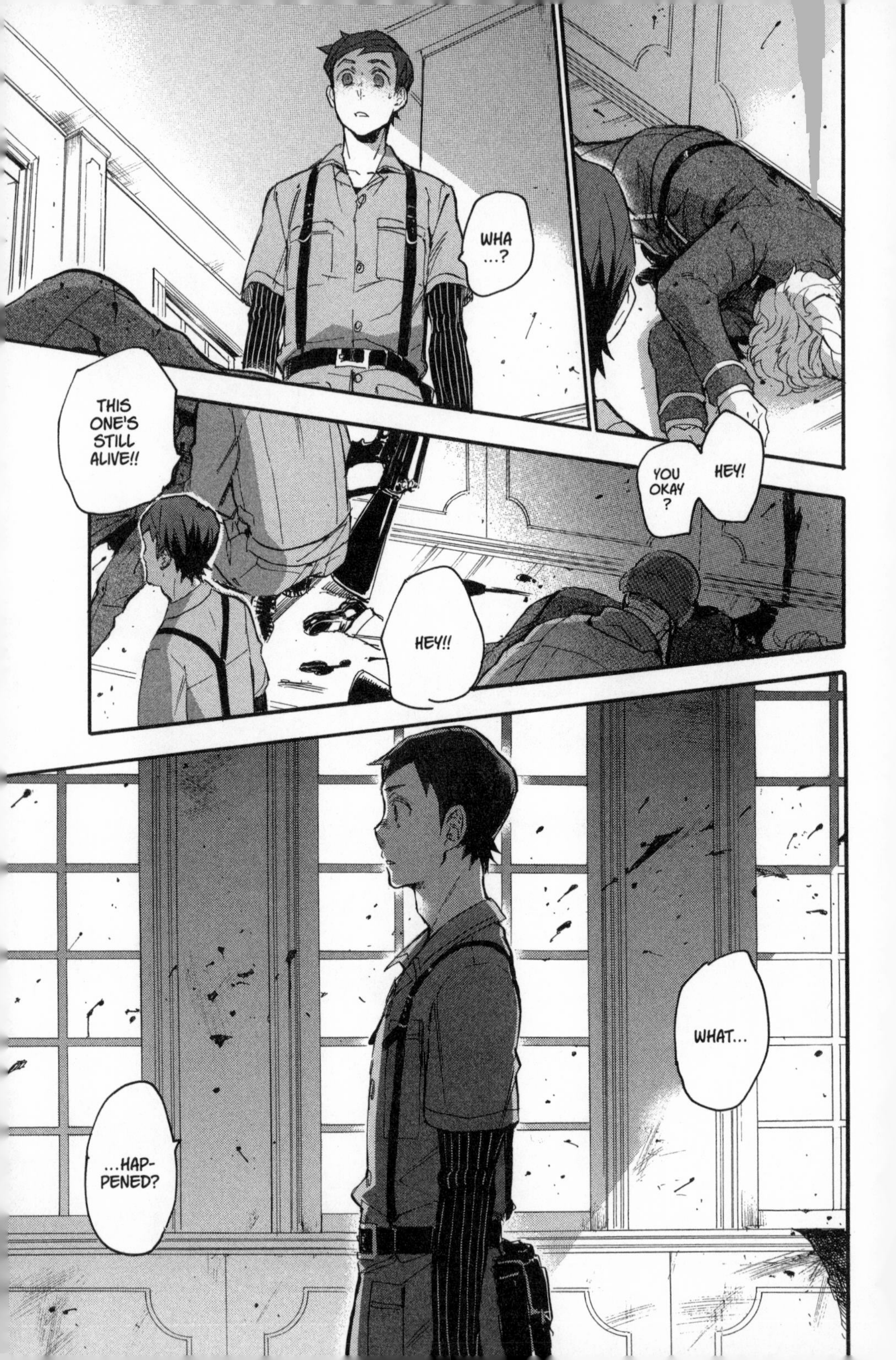
WHA ...?
HEY!
YOU OKAY?
THIS ONE'S STILL ALIVE!!
HEY!!
WHAT...
...HAP-PENED?

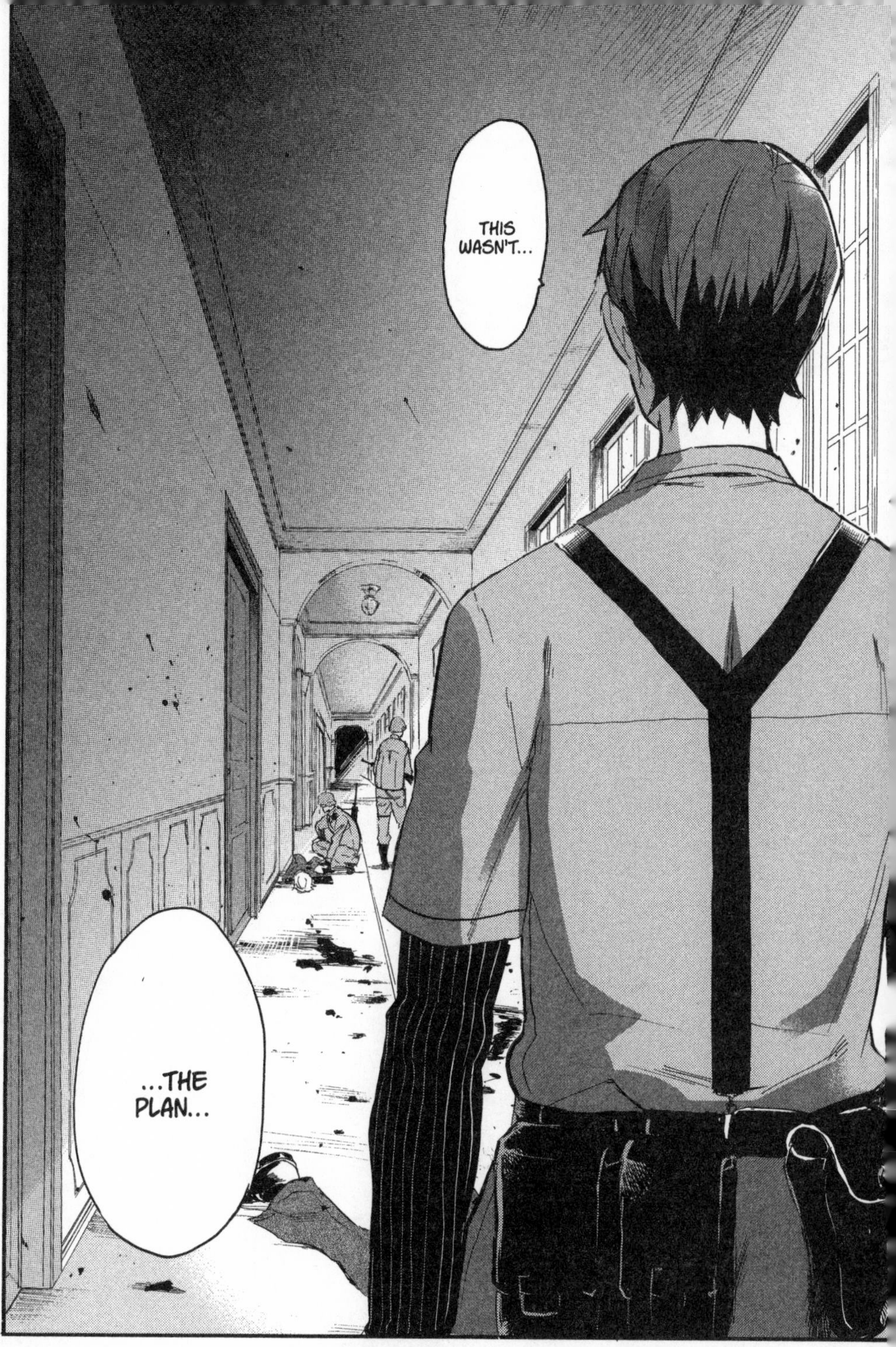
THIS WASN'T...
...THE PLAN...

CHAPTER sixty-eight

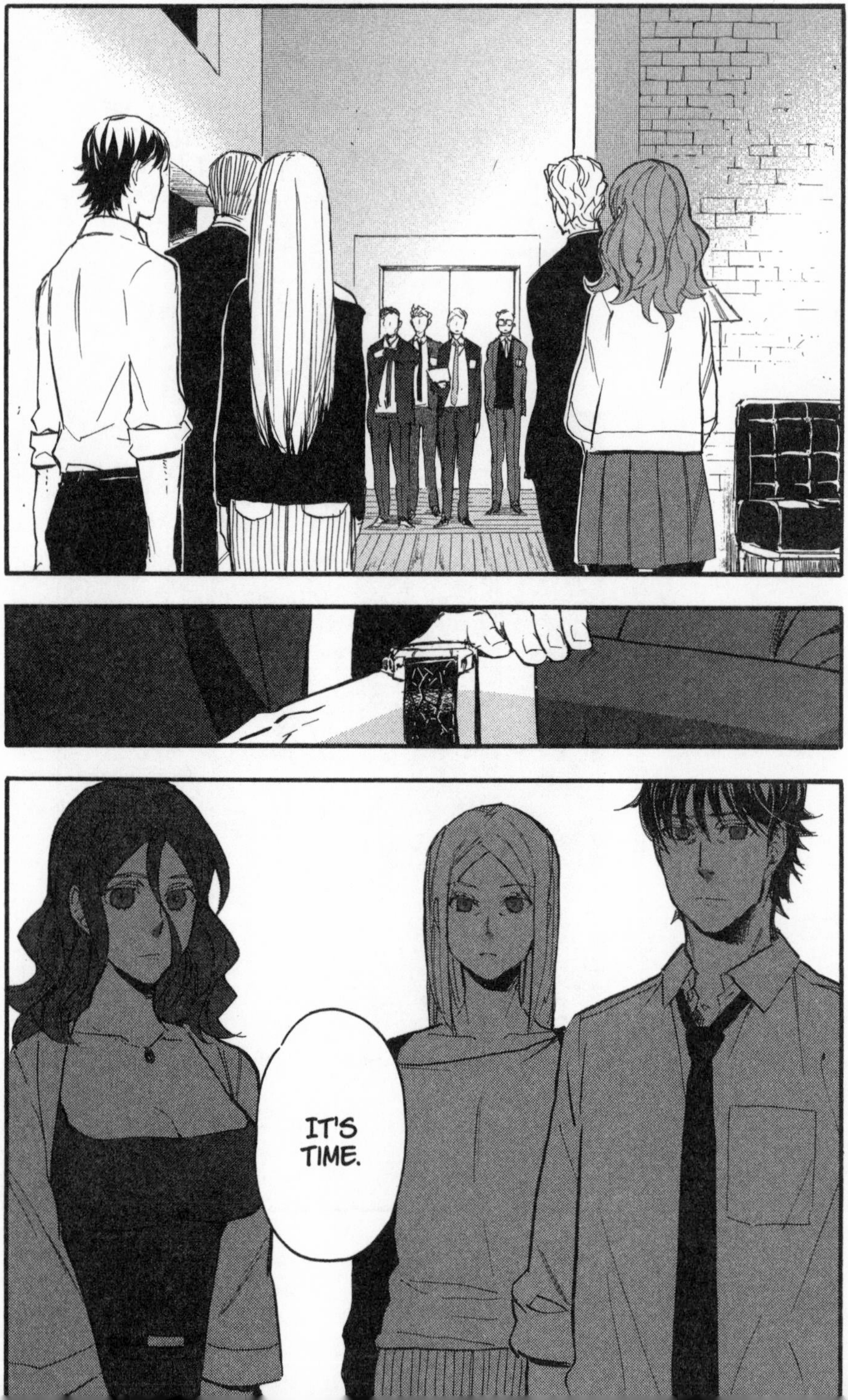
IT'S TIME.

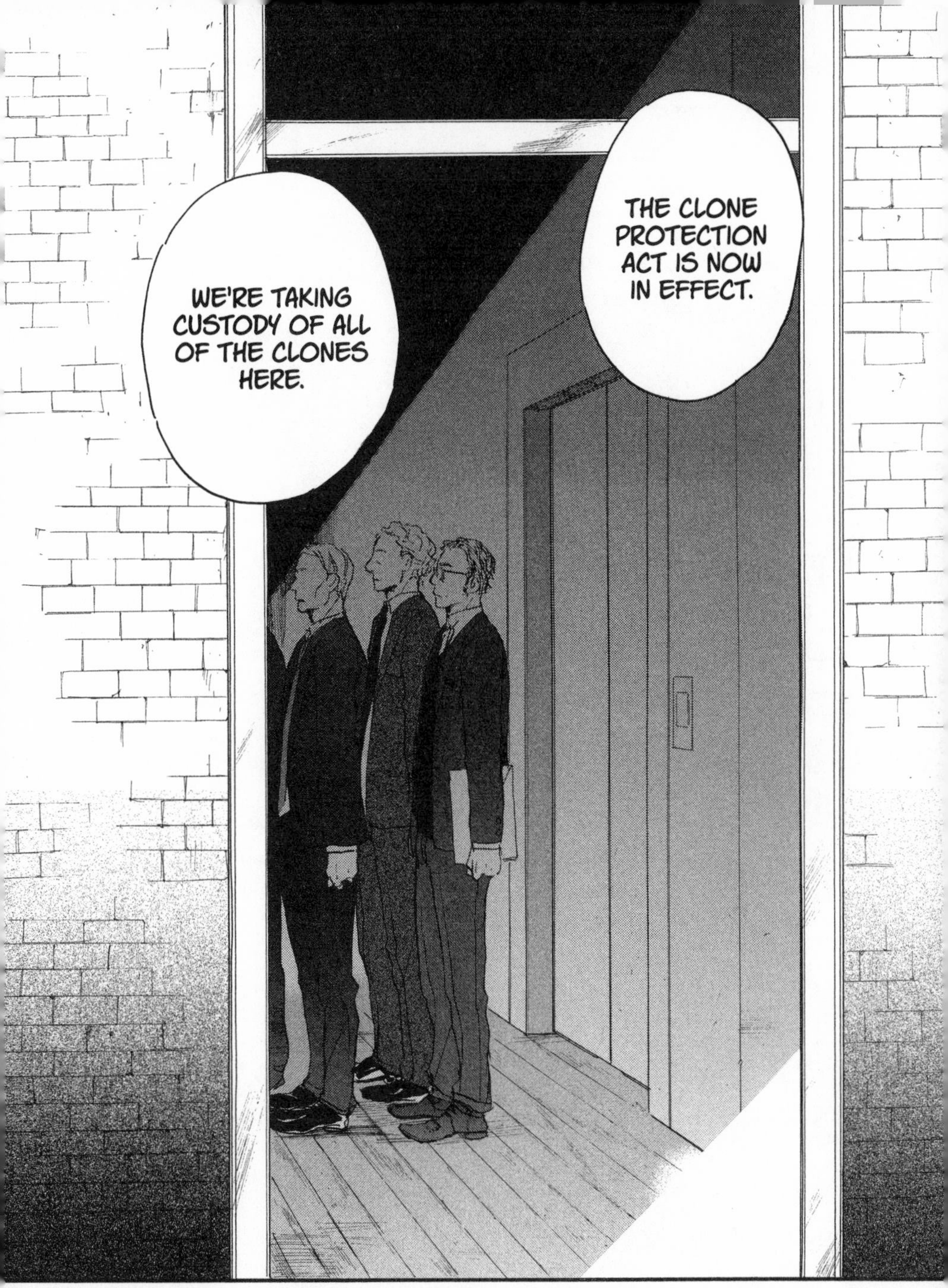
THE CLONE PROTECTION ACT IS NOW IN EFFECT.
WE'RE TAKING CUSTODY OF ALL OF THE CLONES HERE.

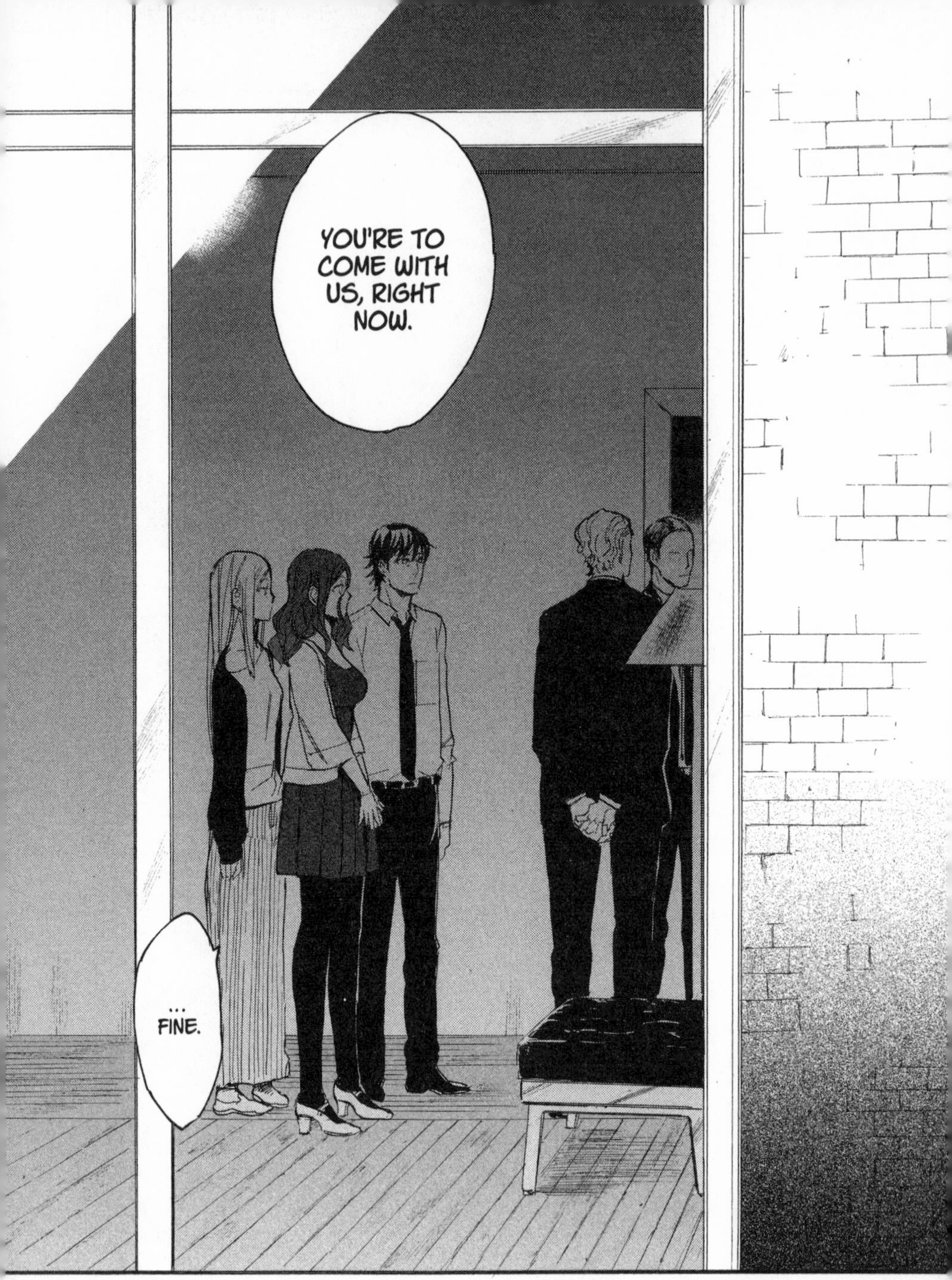
YOU'RE TO COME WITH US, RIGHT NOW.
... FINE.

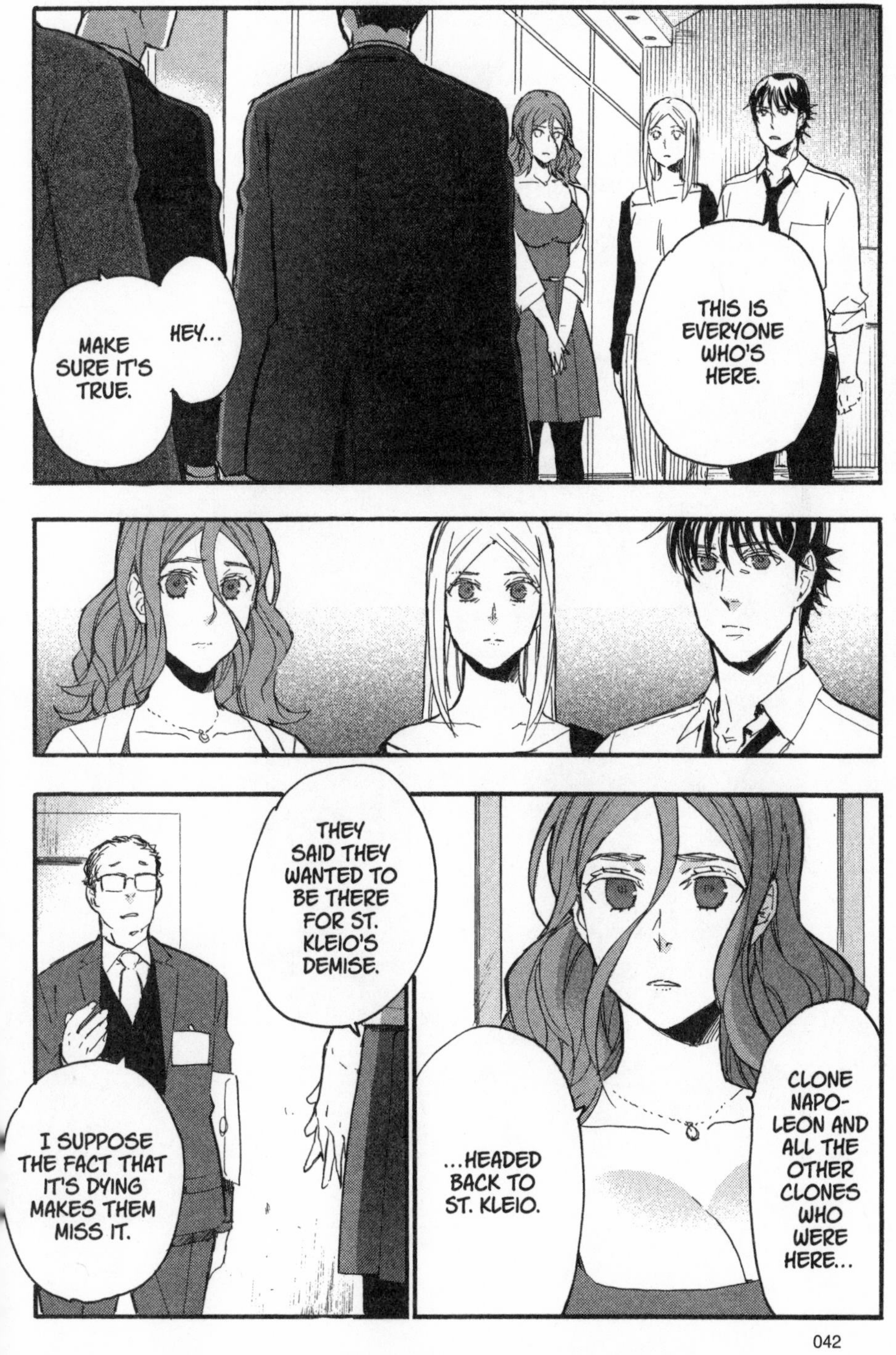
THIS IS EVERYONE WHO'S HERE.
HEY...
MAKE SURE IT'S TRUE.
CLONE NAPO-LEON AND ALL THE OTHER CLONES WHO WERE HERE...
...HEADED BACK TO ST. KLEIO.
THEY SAID THEY WANTED TO BE THERE FOR ST. KLEIO'S DEMISE.
I SUPPOSE THE FACT THAT IT'S DYING MAKES THEM MISS IT.

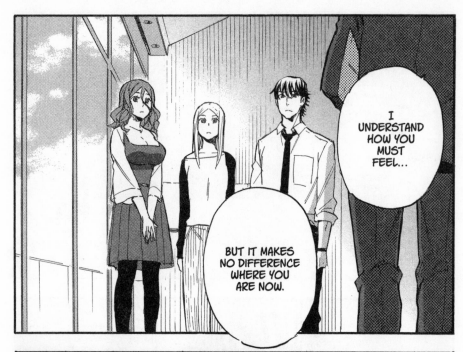

I UNDERSTAND HOW YOU MUST FEEL...

BUT IT MAKES NO DIFFERENCE WHERE YOU ARE NOW.

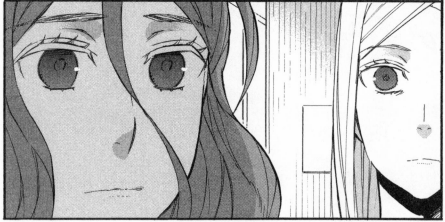

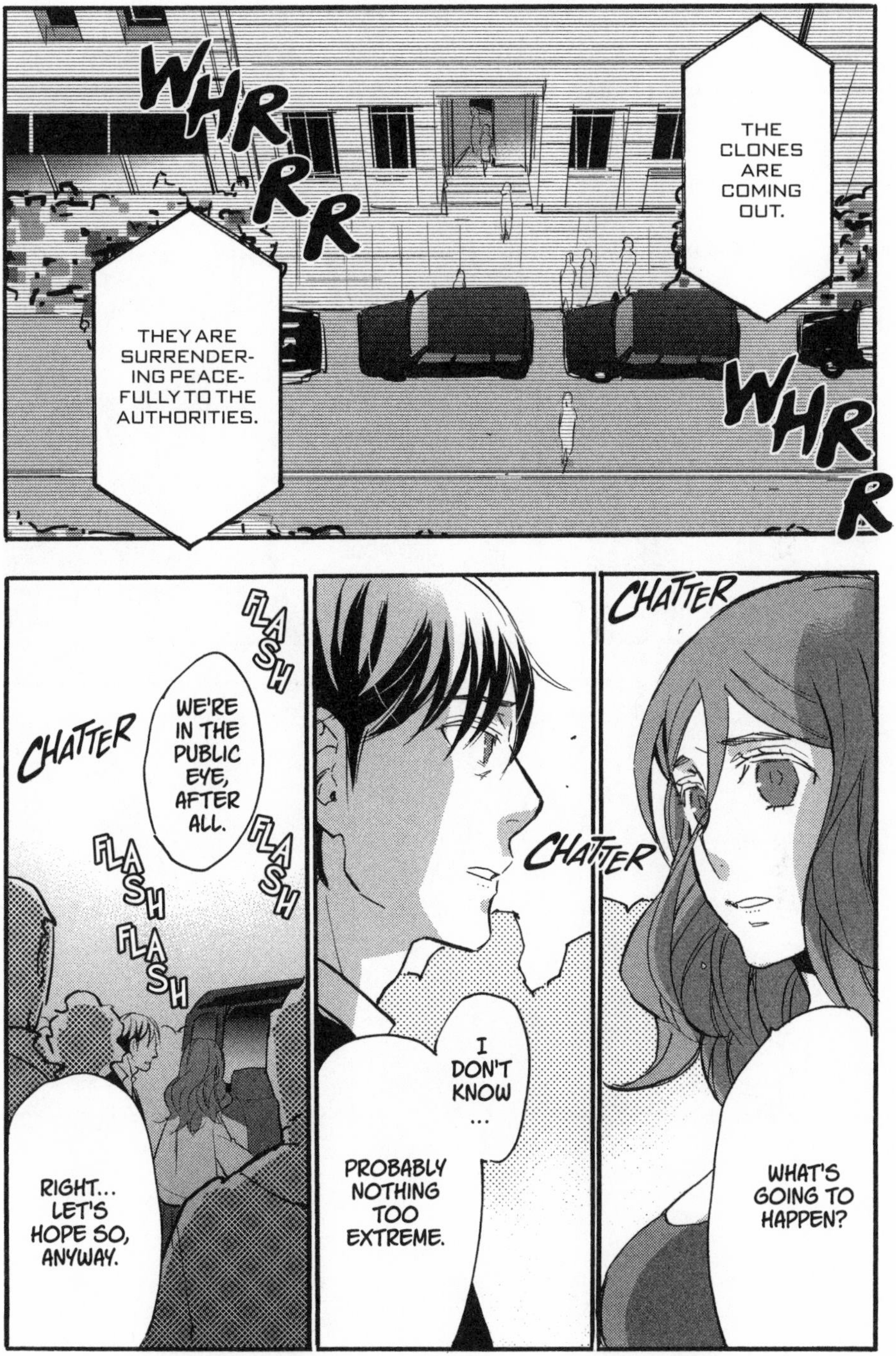
WHRRR
THE CLONES ARE COMING OUT.
THEY ARE SURRENDERING PEACEFULLY TO THE AUTHORITIES.
WHRR
CHATTER
WHAT'S GOING TO HAPPEN?
CHATTER
I DON'T KNOW...
PROBABLY NOTHING TOO EXTREME.
FLASH
WE'RE IN THE PUBLIC EYE, AFTER ALL.
CHATTER
FLASH
FLASH
FLASH
RIGHT... LET'S HOPE SO, ANYWAY.

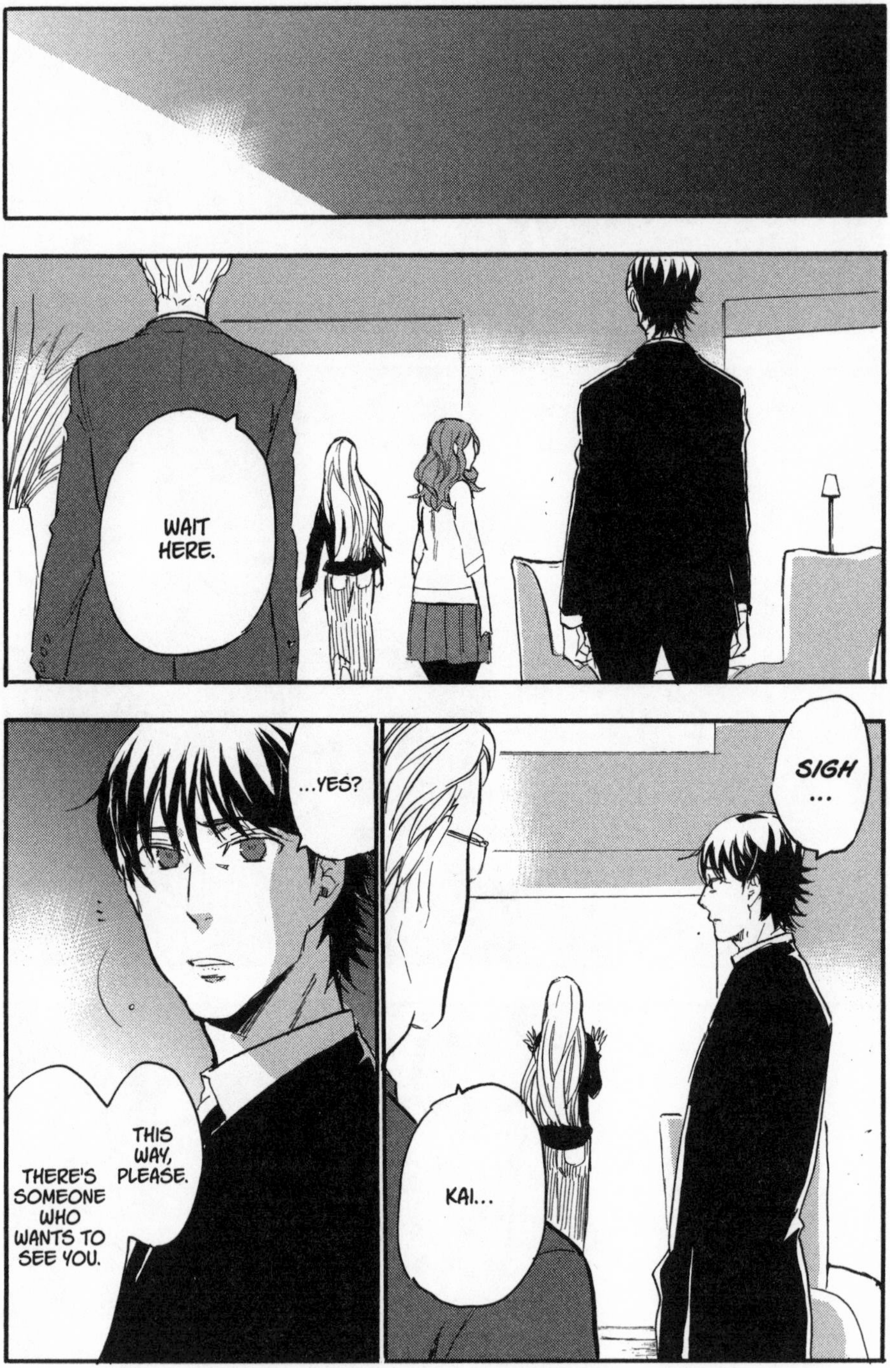
WAIT HERE.
SIGH ...
KAI...
...YES?
THIS WAY, PLEASE.
THERE'S SOMEONE WHO WANTS TO SEE YOU.

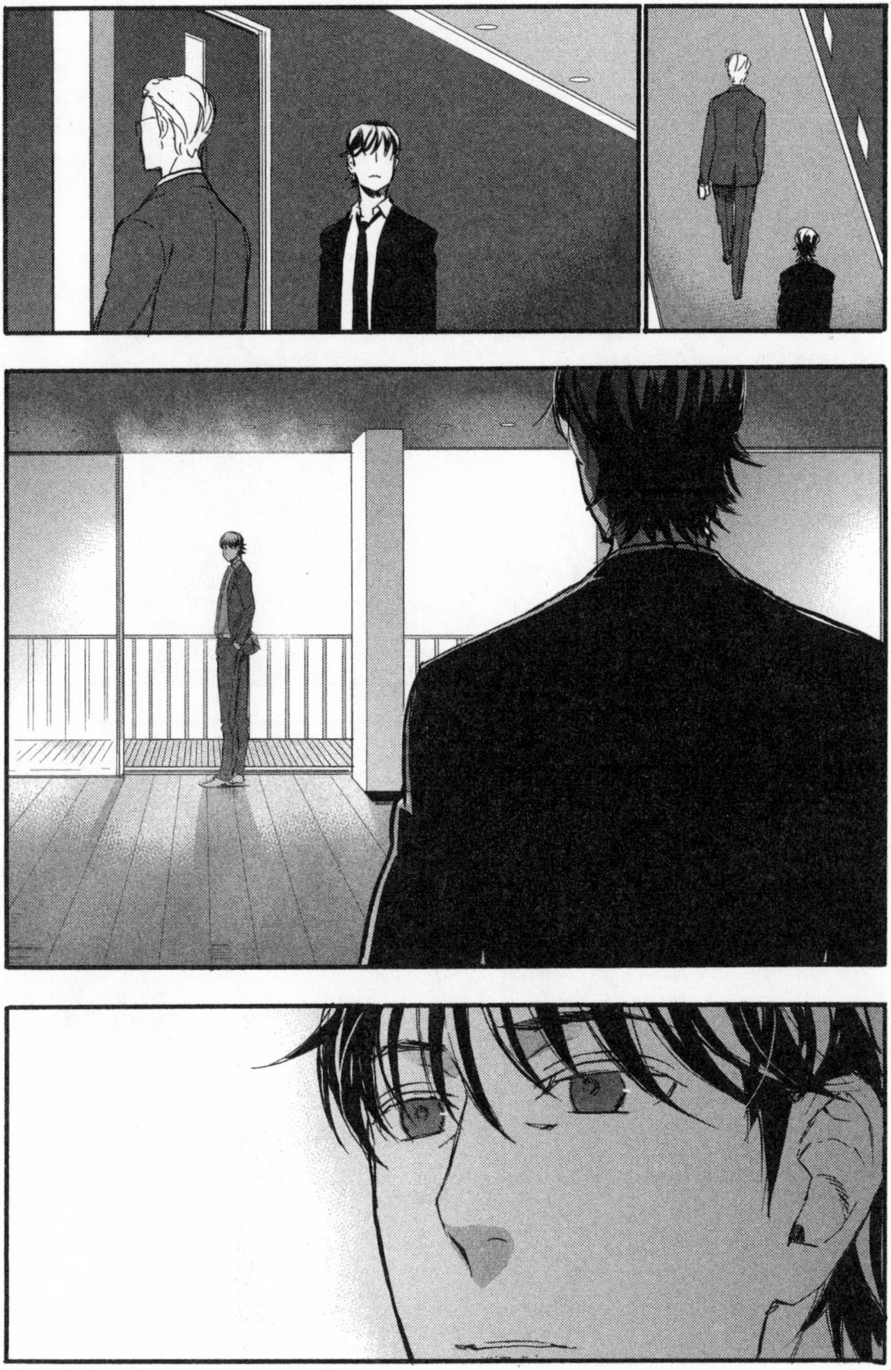

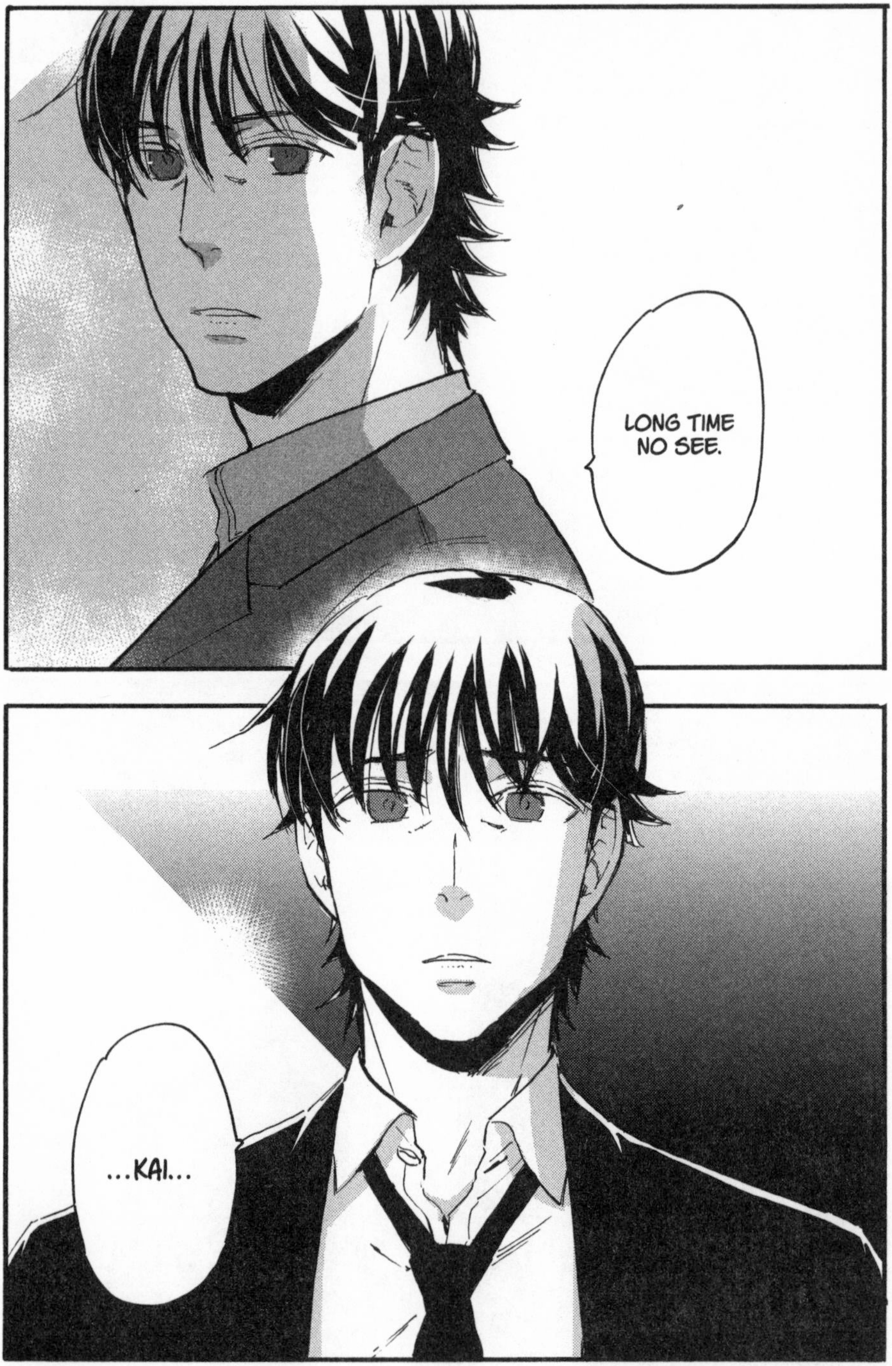
LONG TIME NO SEE.
...KAI...

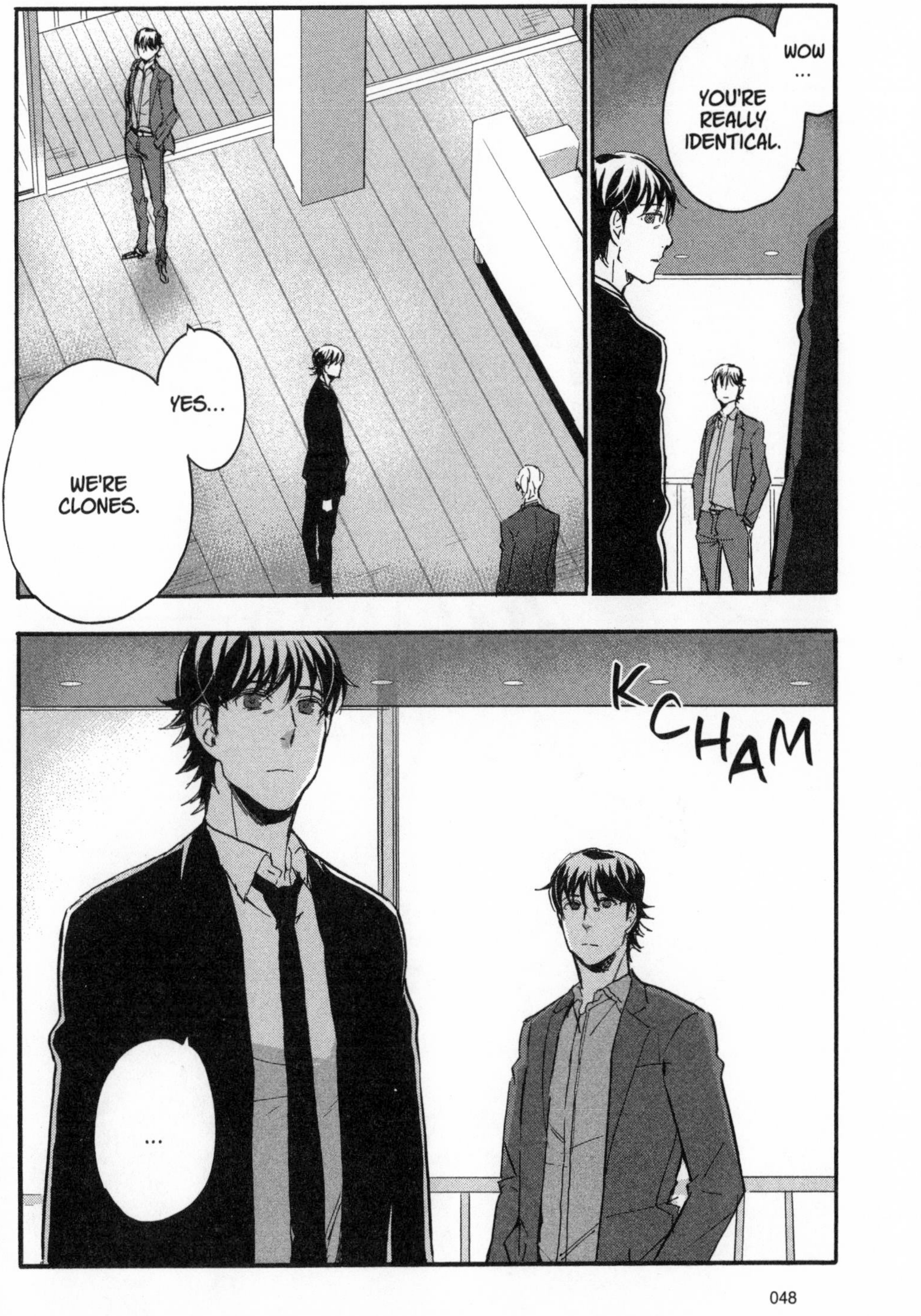
WOW ...
YOU'RE REALLY IDENTICAL.
YES...
WE'RE CLONES.
KCHAM
...

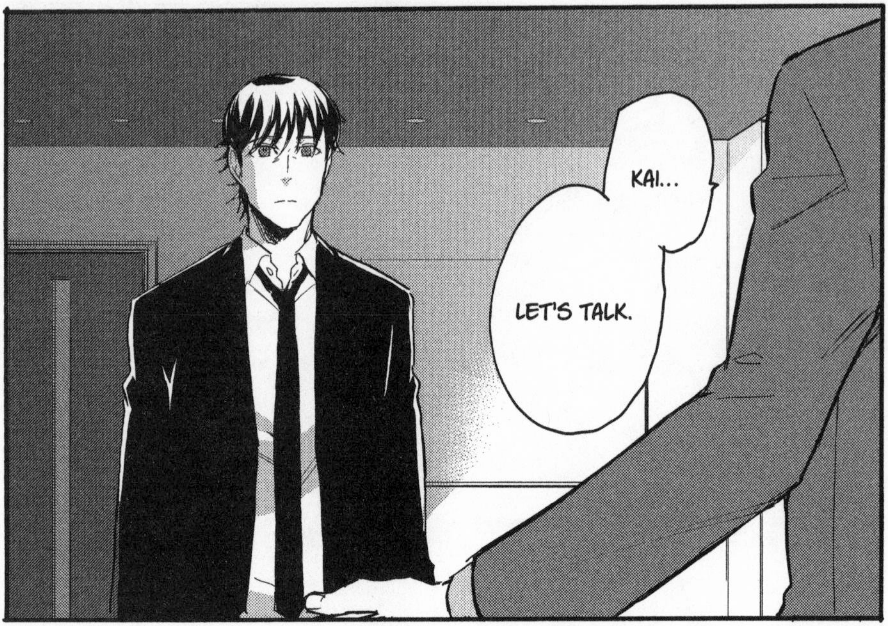
KAI...
LET'S TALK.

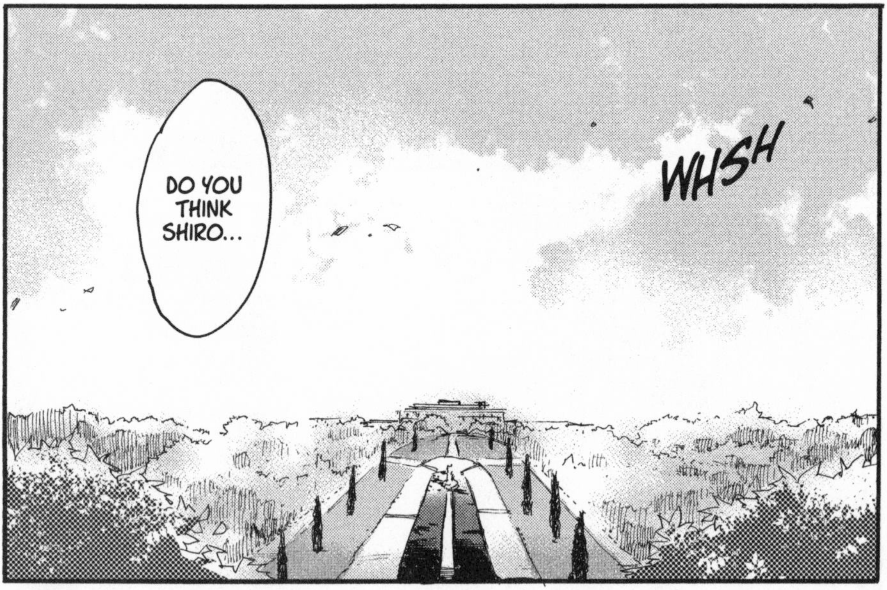
WHSH
DO YOU THINK SHIRO...

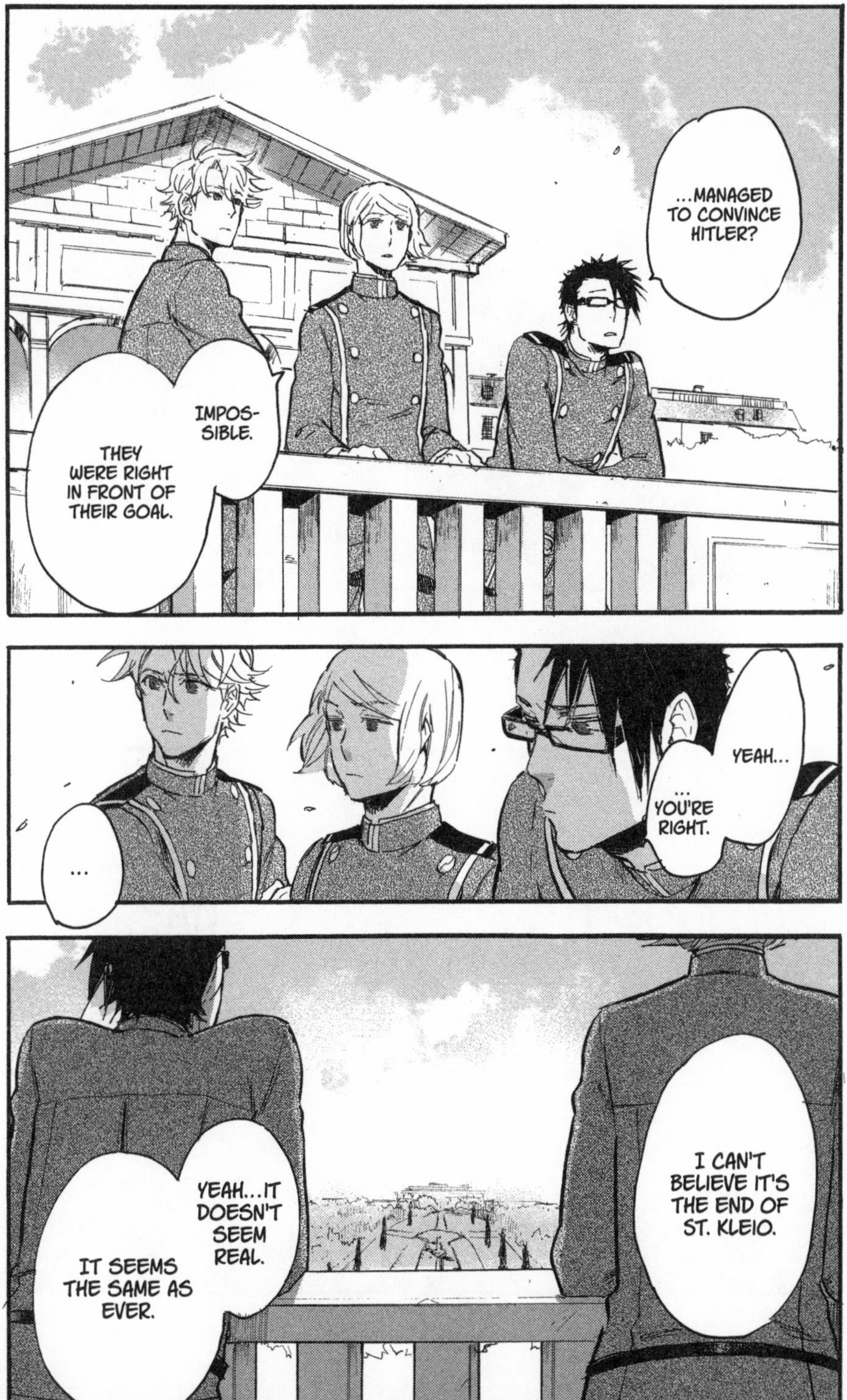
...MANAGED TO CONVINCE HITLER?
IMPOS-SIBLE.
THEY WERE RIGHT IN FRONT OF THEIR GOAL.
YEAH...
...YOU'RE RIGHT.
...
I CAN'T BELIEVE IT'S THE END OF ST. KLEIO.
YEAH...IT DOESN'T SEEM REAL.
IT SEEMS THE SAME AS EVER.

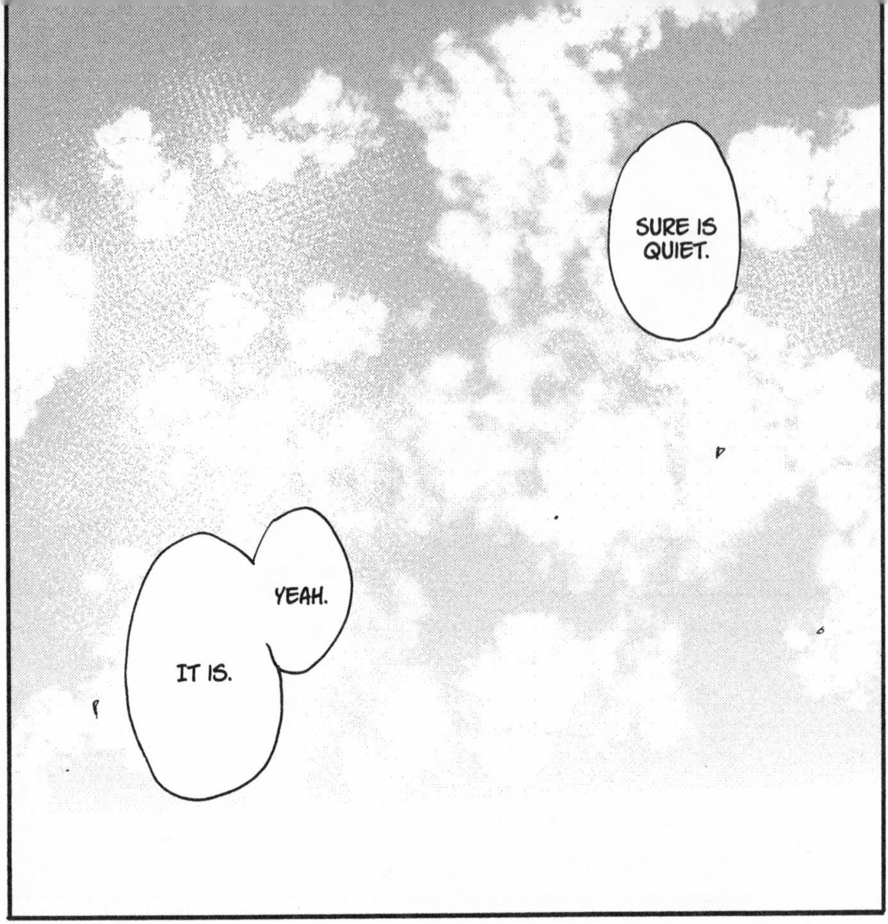
SURE IS QUIET.
YEAH.
IT IS.
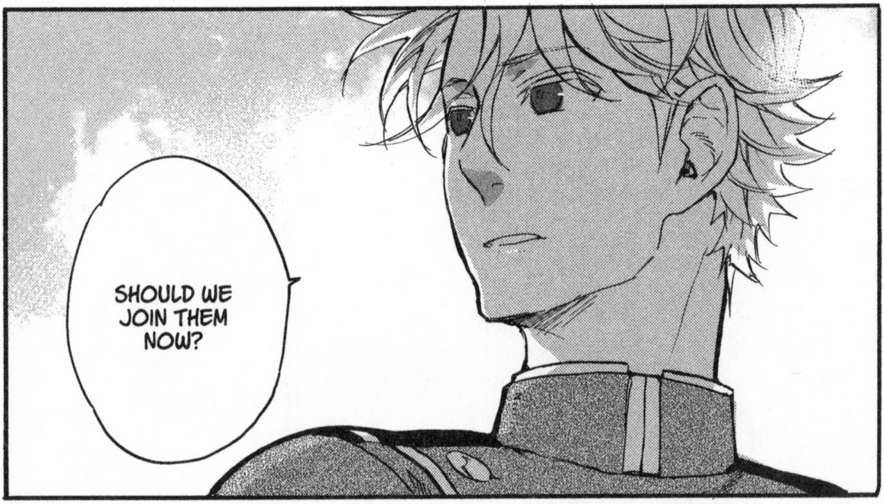
SHOULD WE JOIN THEM NOW?

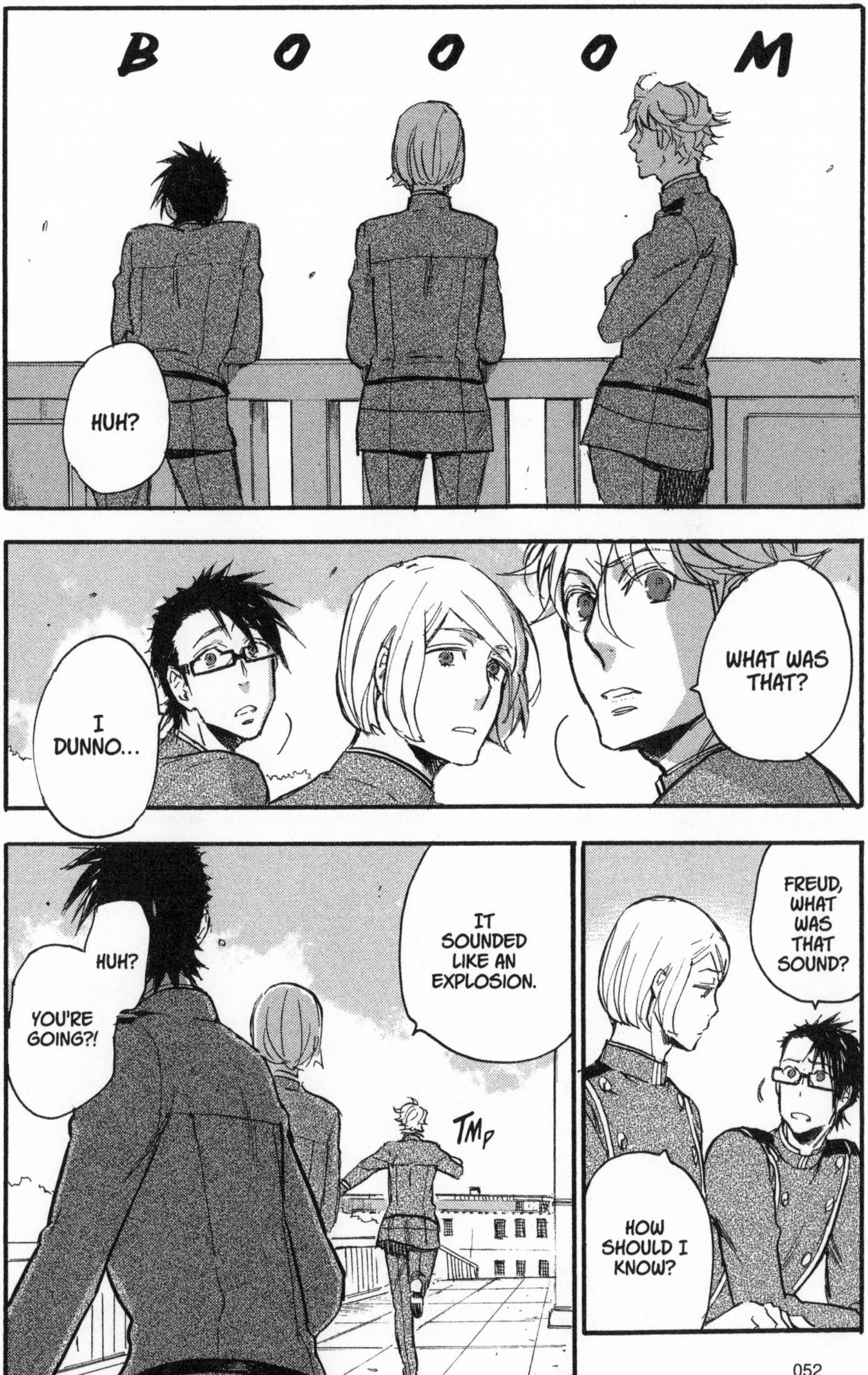
B O O O M
HUH?
WHAT WAS THAT?
I DUNNO...
FREUD, WHAT WAS THAT SOUND?
HOW SHOULD I KNOW?
IT SOUNDED LIKE AN EXPLOSION.
TMP
HUH?
YOU'RE GOING?!

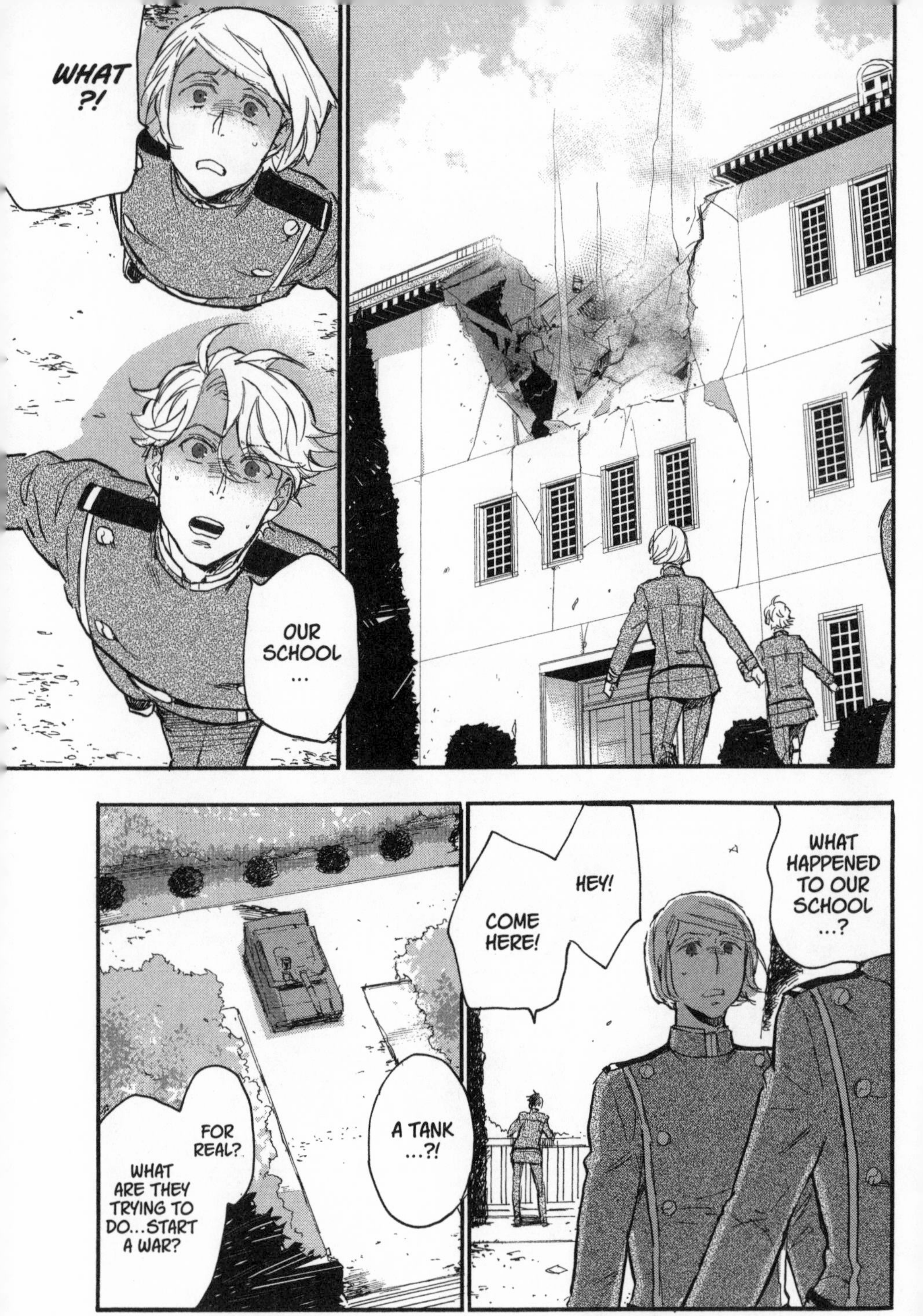
WHAT ?!
OUR SCHOOL ...
WHAT HAPPENED TO OUR SCHOOL ...?
HEY!
COME HERE!
A TANK ...?!
FOR REAL?
WHAT ARE THEY TRYING TO DO...START A WAR?

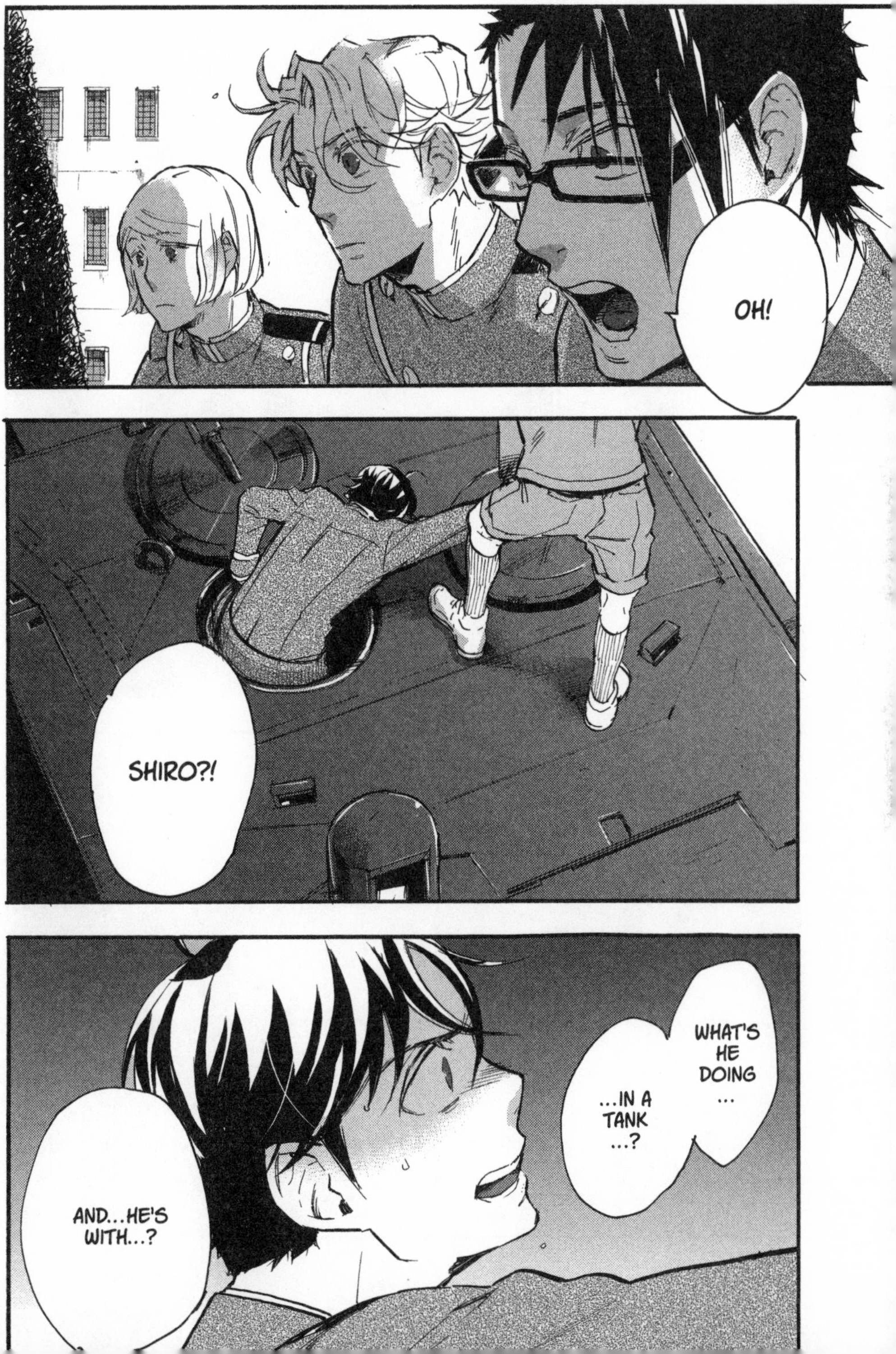

OH!
SHIRO?!
WHAT'S HE DOING …
…IN A TANK …?
AND…HE'S WITH…?

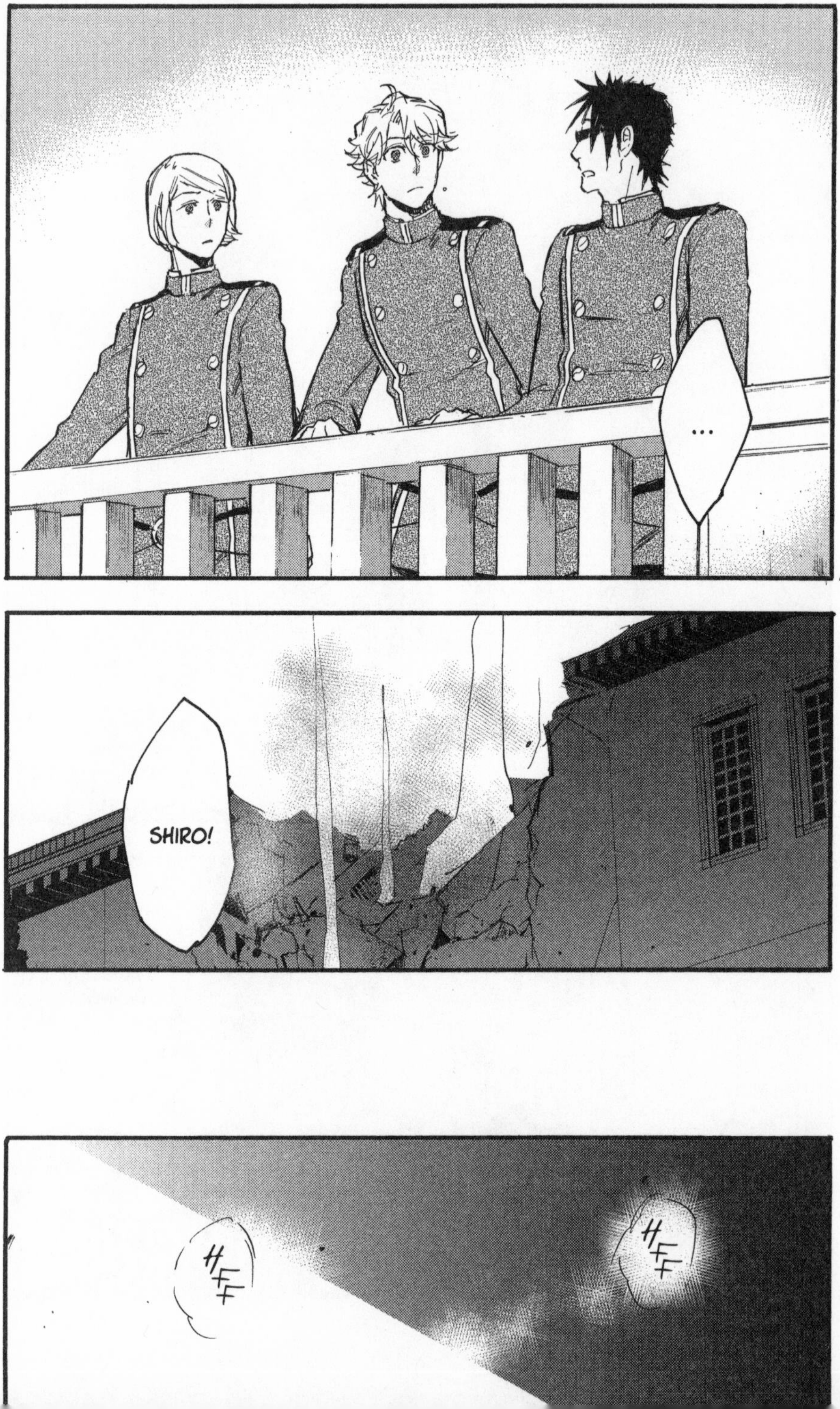
...
SHIRO!
HFF
HFF

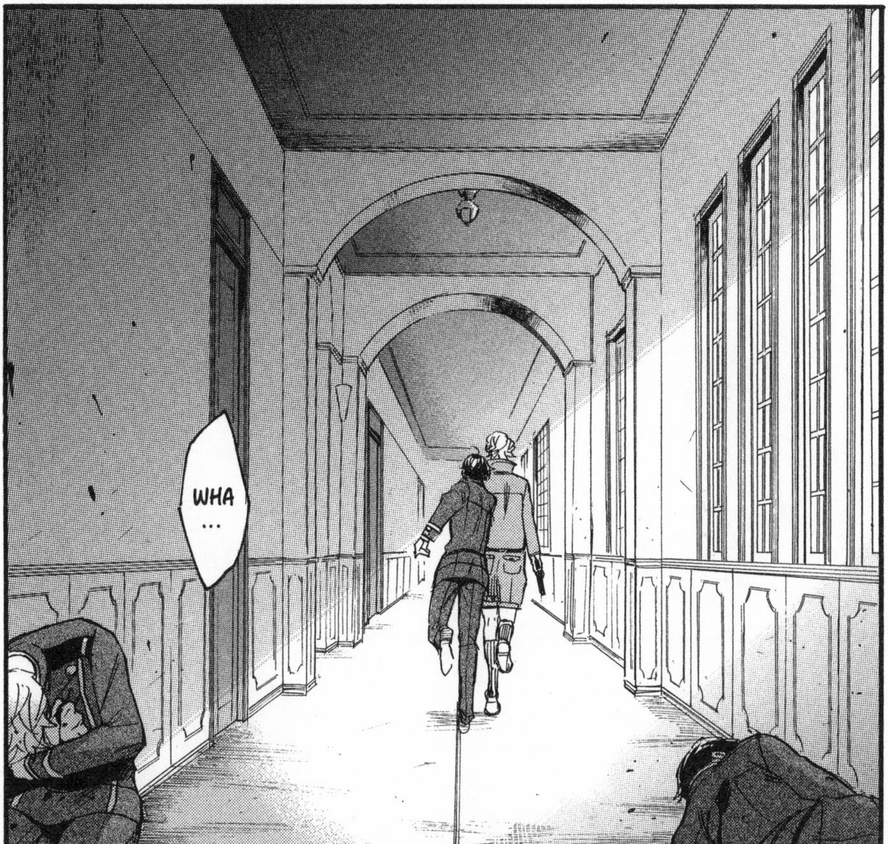
WHA...

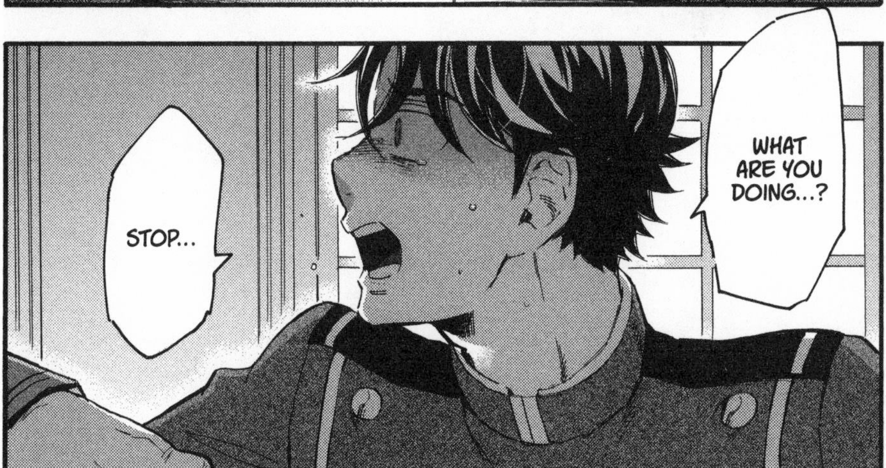
WHAT ARE YOU DOING...?
STOP...

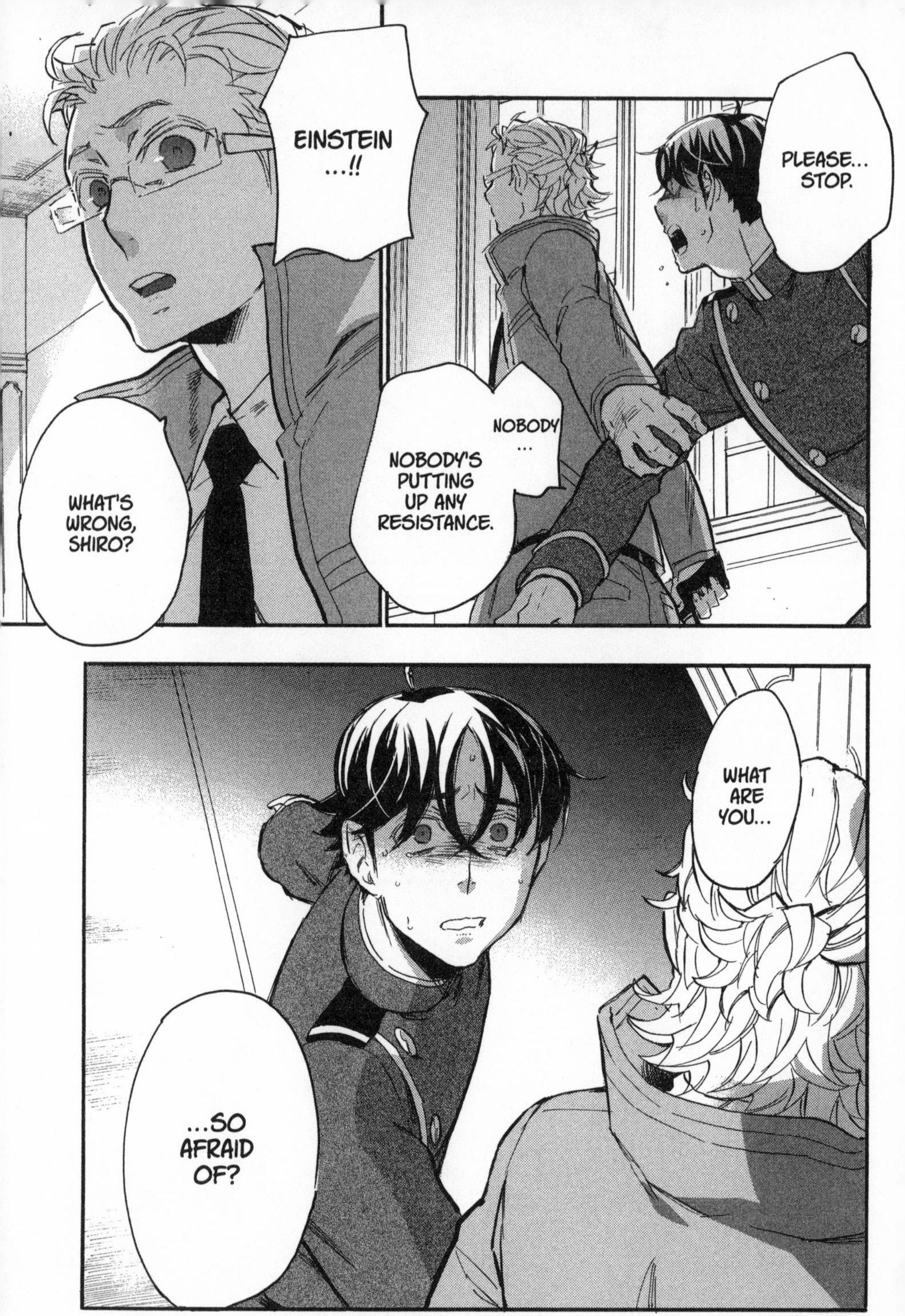
PLEASE... STOP.
NOBODY ...
NOBODY'S PUTTING UP ANY RESISTANCE.
EINSTEIN ...!!
WHAT'S WRONG, SHIRO?
WHAT ARE YOU...
...SO AFRAID OF?

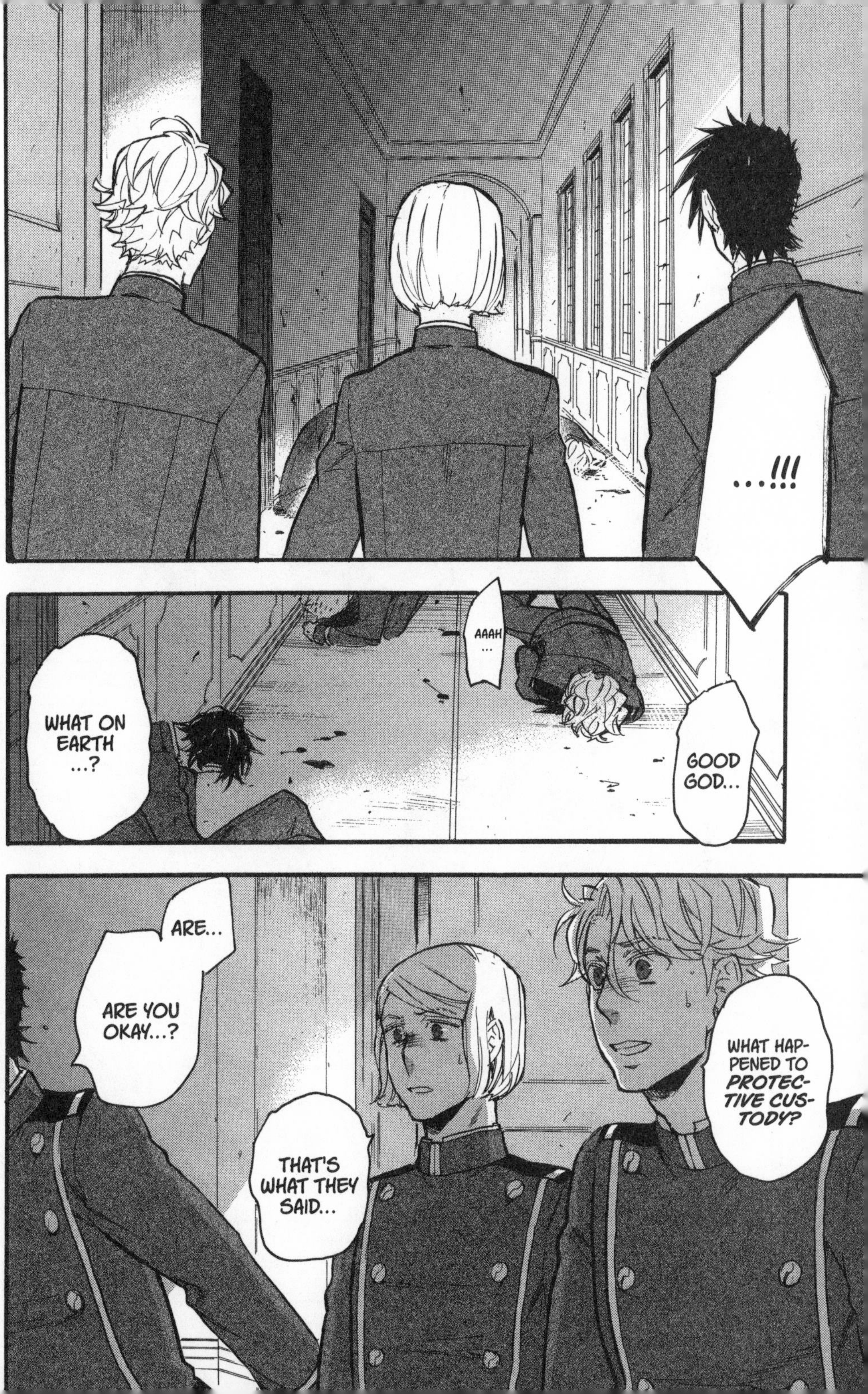

...!!!
GOOD GOD...
AAAH ...
WHAT ON EARTH ...?
WHAT HAPPENED TO *PROTECTIVE CUSTODY*?
THAT'S WHAT THEY SAID...
ARE...
ARE YOU OKAY...?

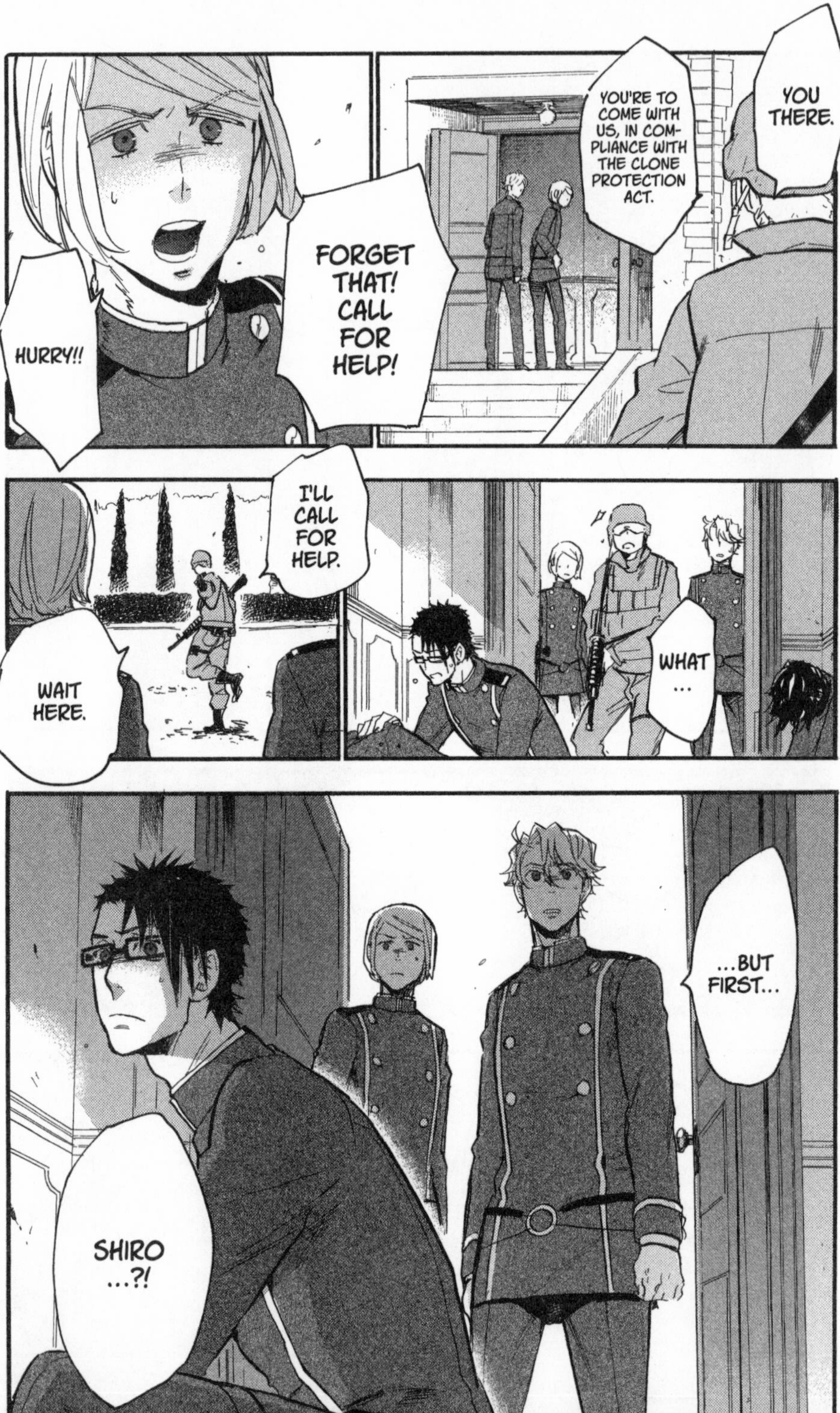
YOU THERE.
YOU'RE TO COME WITH US, IN COMPLIANCE WITH THE CLONE PROTECTION ACT.
FORGET THAT! CALL FOR HELP!
HURRY!!
WHAT ...
I'LL CALL FOR HELP.
WAIT HERE.
...BUT FIRST...
SHIRO ...?!

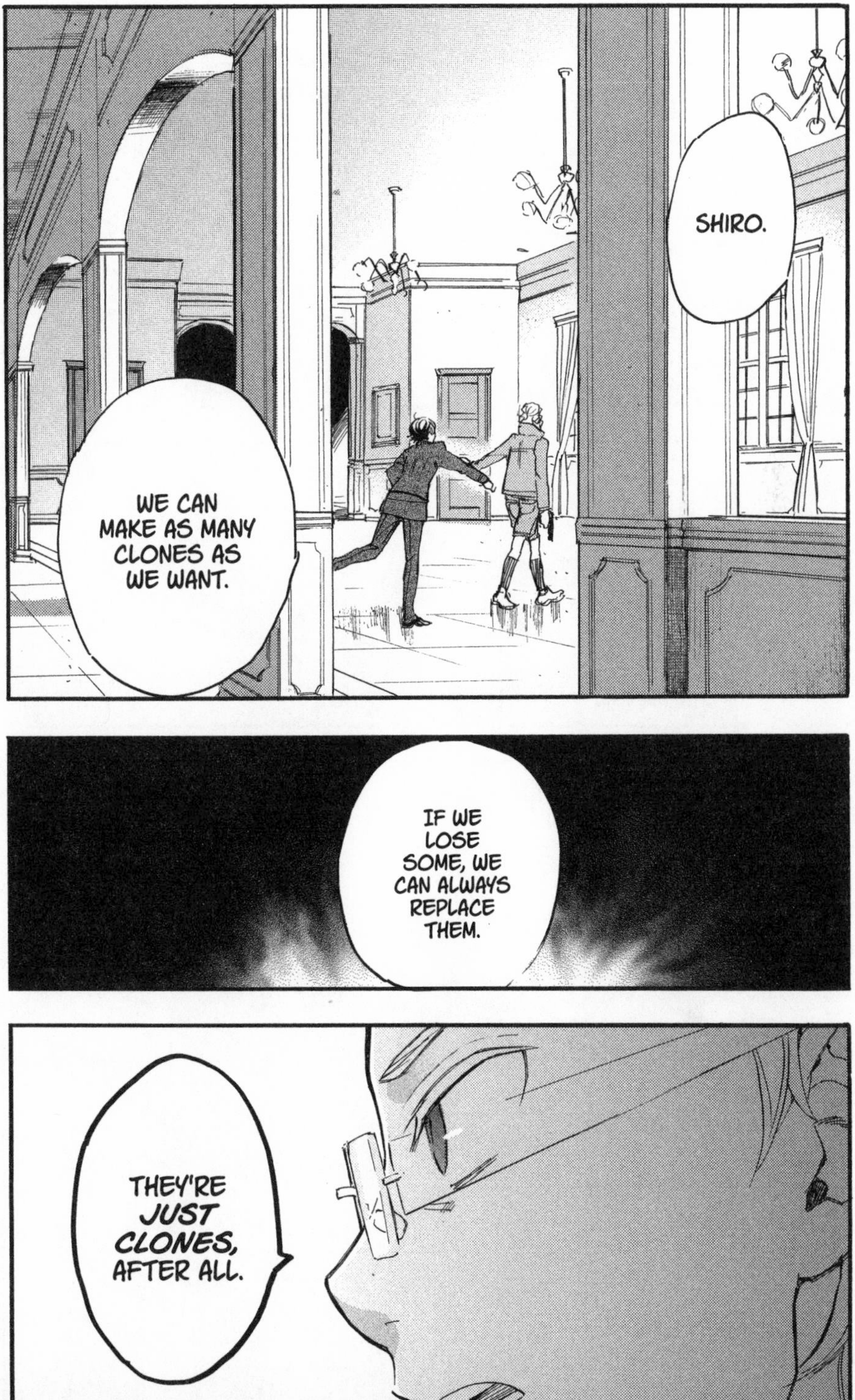
SHIRO.
WE CAN MAKE AS MANY CLONES AS WE WANT.
IF WE LOSE SOME, WE CAN ALWAYS REPLACE THEM.
THEY'RE *JUST CLONES*, AFTER ALL.

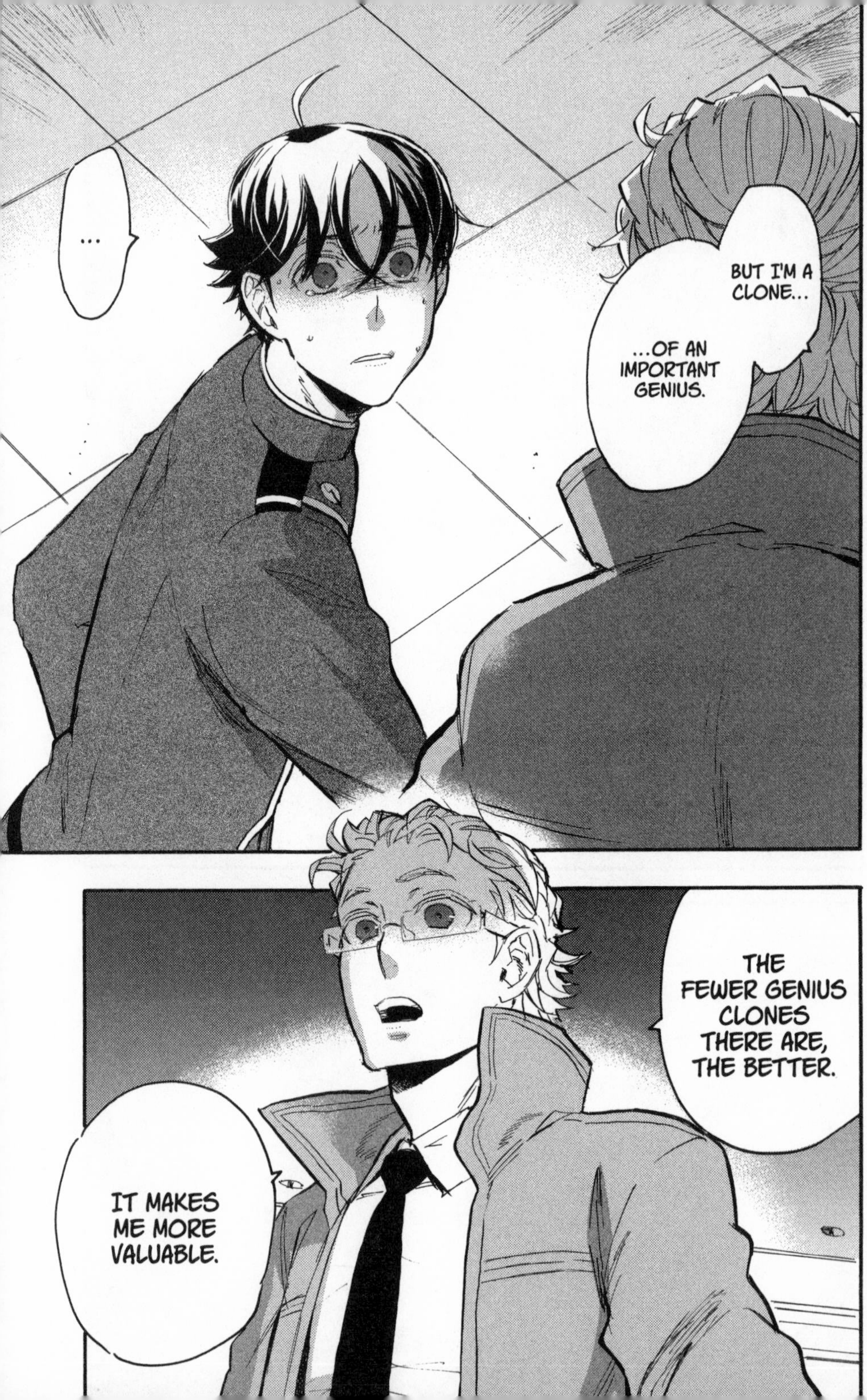
BUT I'M A CLONE...
...OF AN IMPORTANT GENIUS.
...
THE FEWER GENIUS CLONES THERE ARE, THE BETTER.
IT MAKES ME MORE VALUABLE.

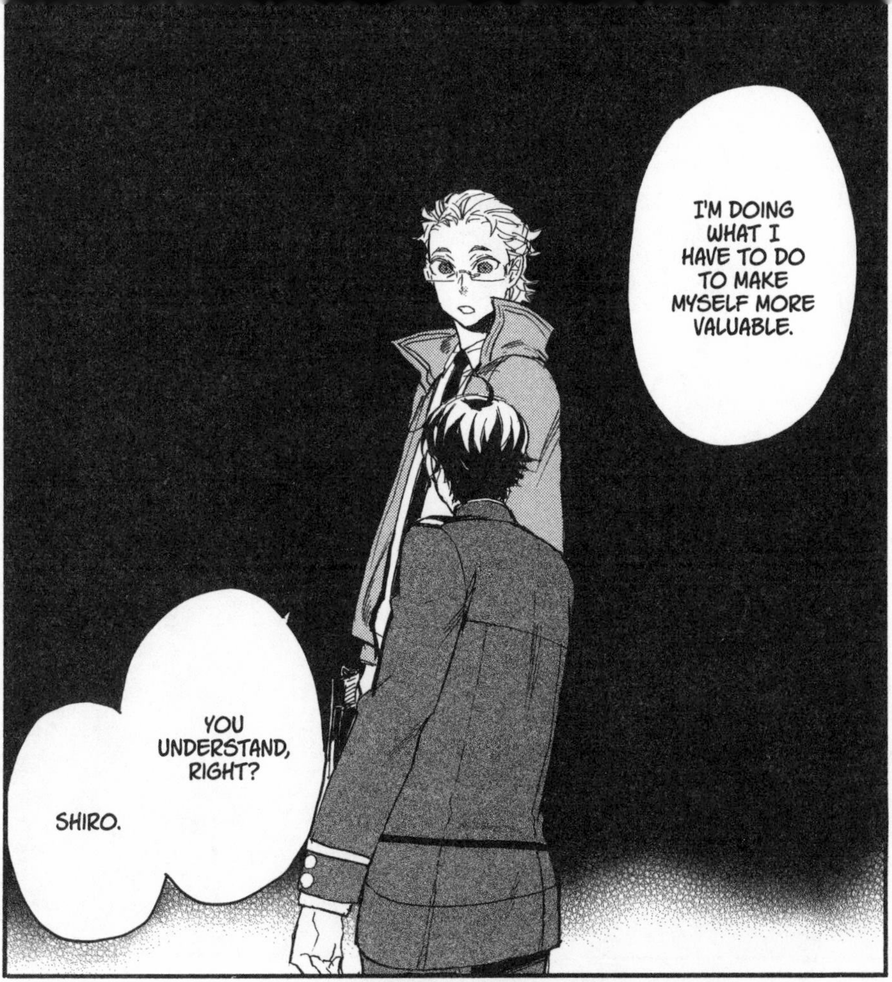
I'M DOING WHAT I HAVE TO DO TO MAKE MYSELF MORE VALUABLE.
YOU UNDERSTAND, RIGHT?
SHIRO.
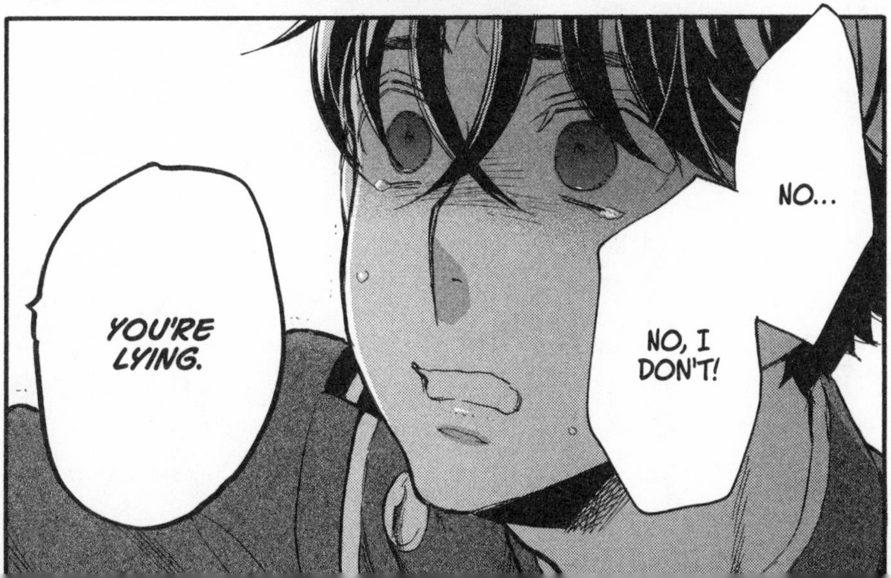
NO...
NO, I DON'T!
YOU'RE LYING.

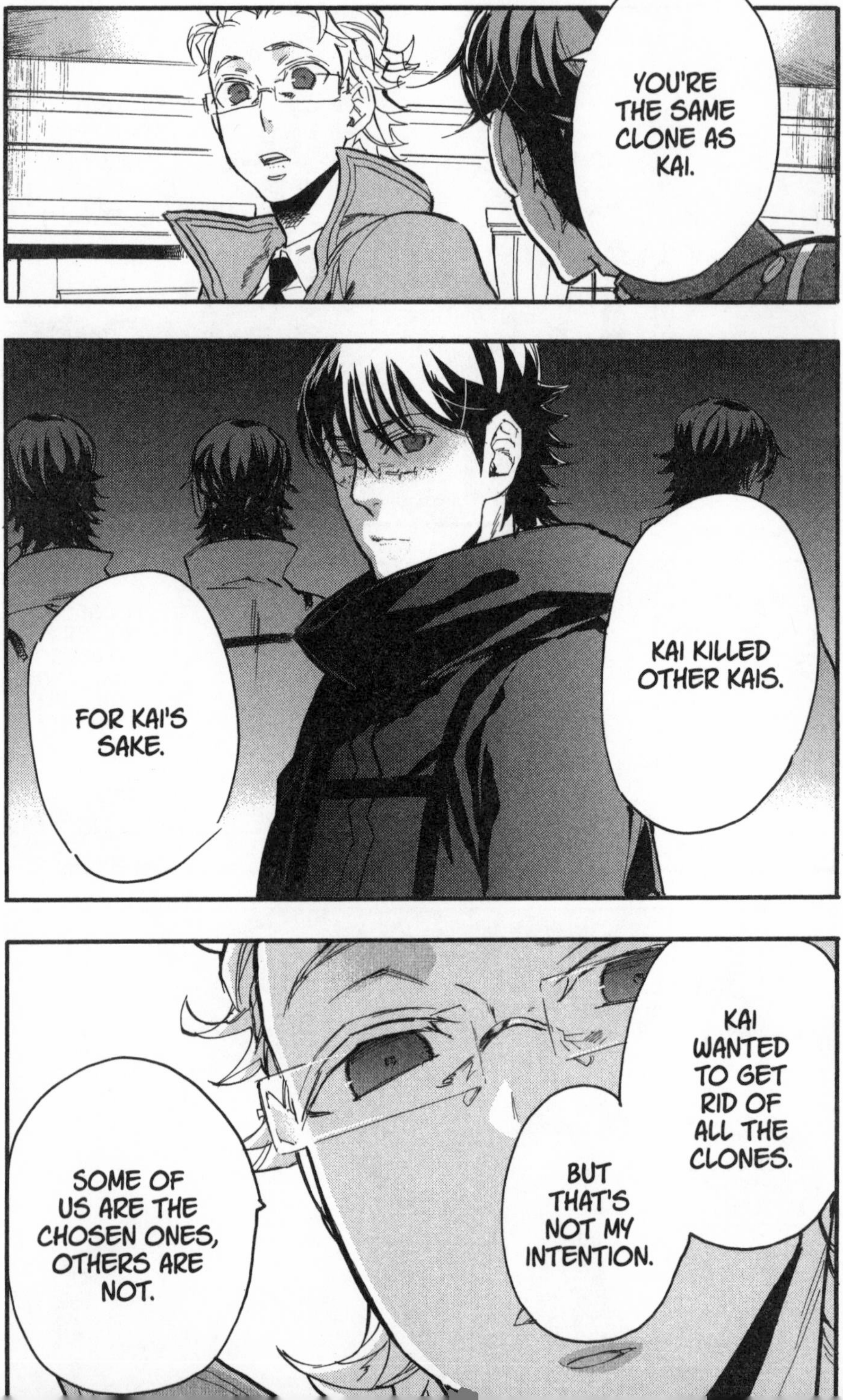
YOU'RE THE SAME CLONE AS KAI.
KAI KILLED OTHER KAIS.
FOR KAI'S SAKE.
KAI WANTED TO GET RID OF ALL THE CLONES.
BUT THAT'S NOT MY INTENTION.
SOME OF US ARE THE CHOSEN ONES, OTHERS ARE NOT.

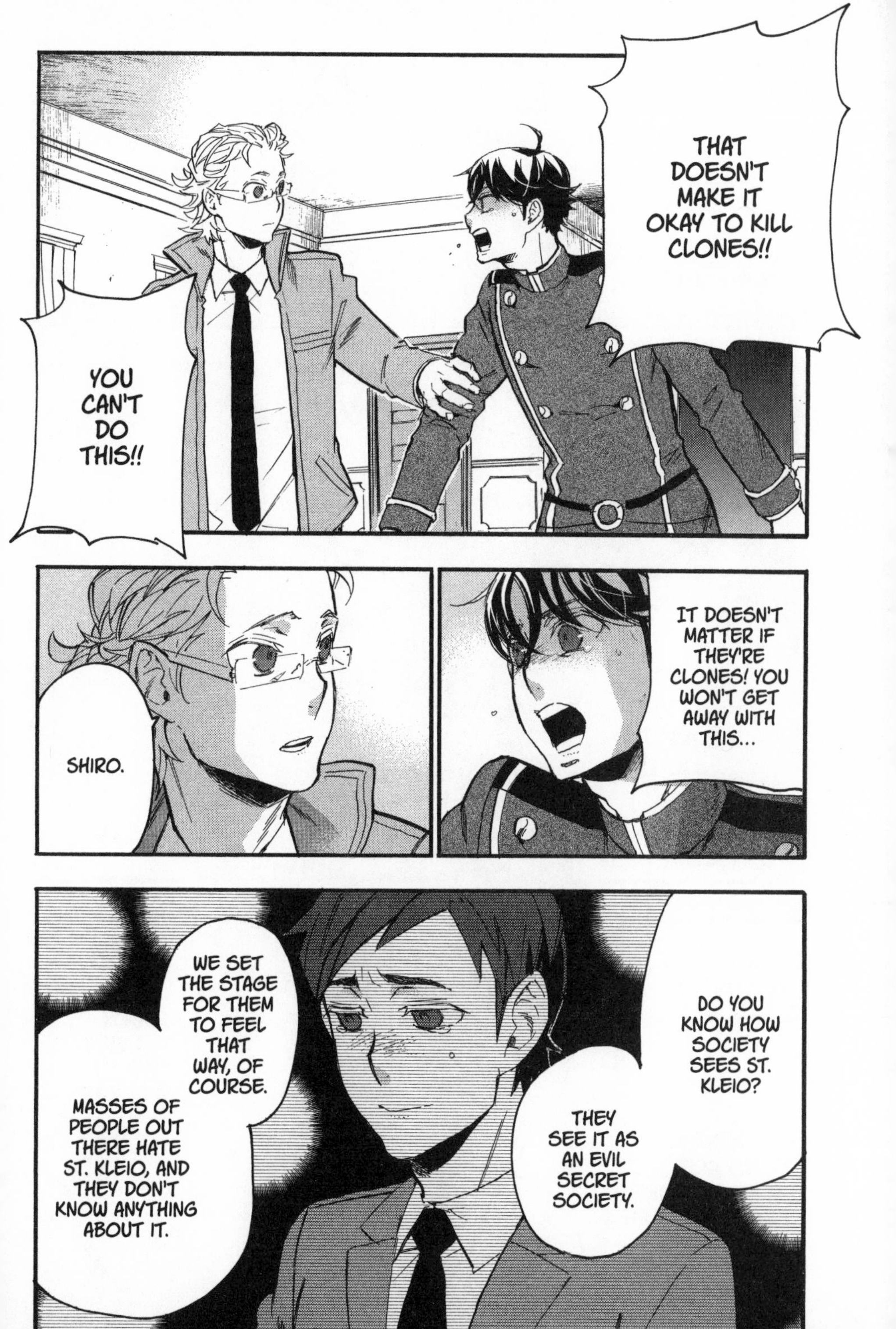
THAT DOESN'T MAKE IT OKAY TO KILL CLONES!!
YOU CAN'T DO THIS!!
IT DOESN'T MATTER IF THEY'RE CLONES! YOU WON'T GET AWAY WITH THIS...
SHIRO.
DO YOU KNOW HOW SOCIETY SEES ST. KLEIO?
THEY SEE IT AS AN EVIL SECRET SOCIETY.
MASSES OF PEOPLE OUT THERE HATE ST. KLEIO, AND THEY DON'T KNOW ANYTHING ABOUT IT.
WE SET THE STAGE FOR THEM TO FEEL THAT WAY, OF COURSE.

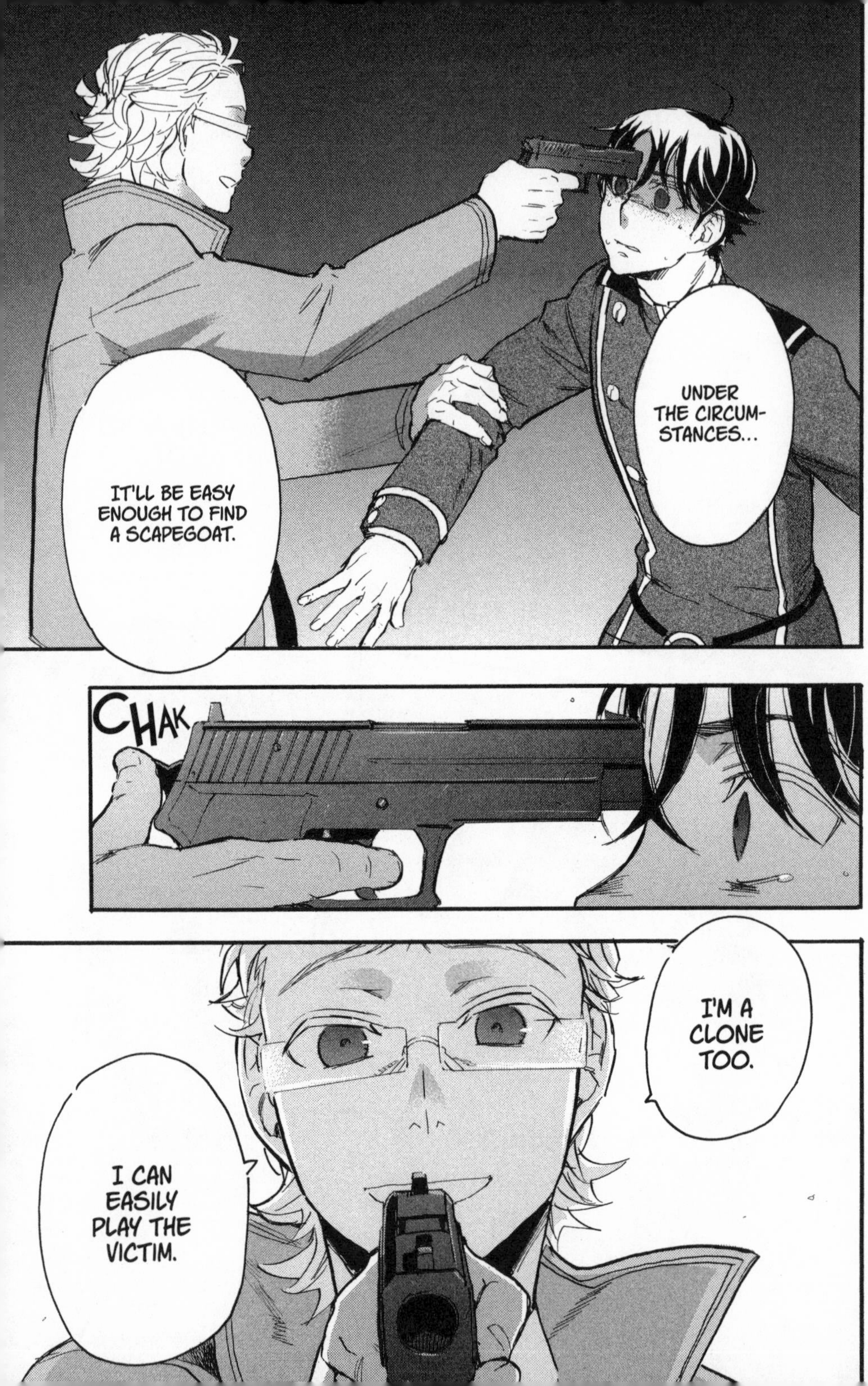
UNDER THE CIRCUM-STANCES...
IT'LL BE EASY ENOUGH TO FIND A SCAPEGOAT.
CHAK
I'M A CLONE TOO.
I CAN EASILY PLAY THE VICTIM.

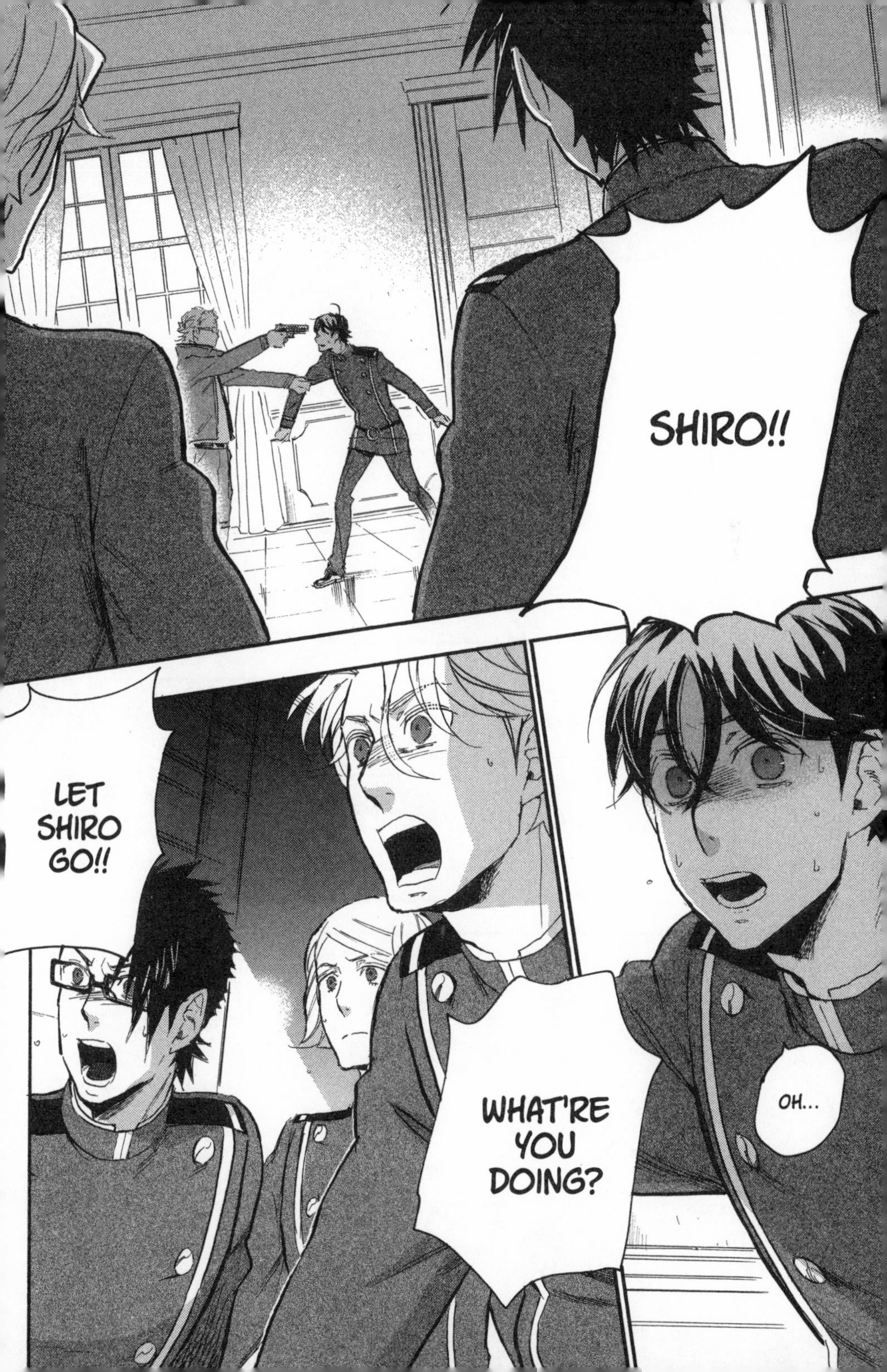
SHIRO!!
OH...
WHAT'RE YOU DOING?
LET SHIRO GO!!

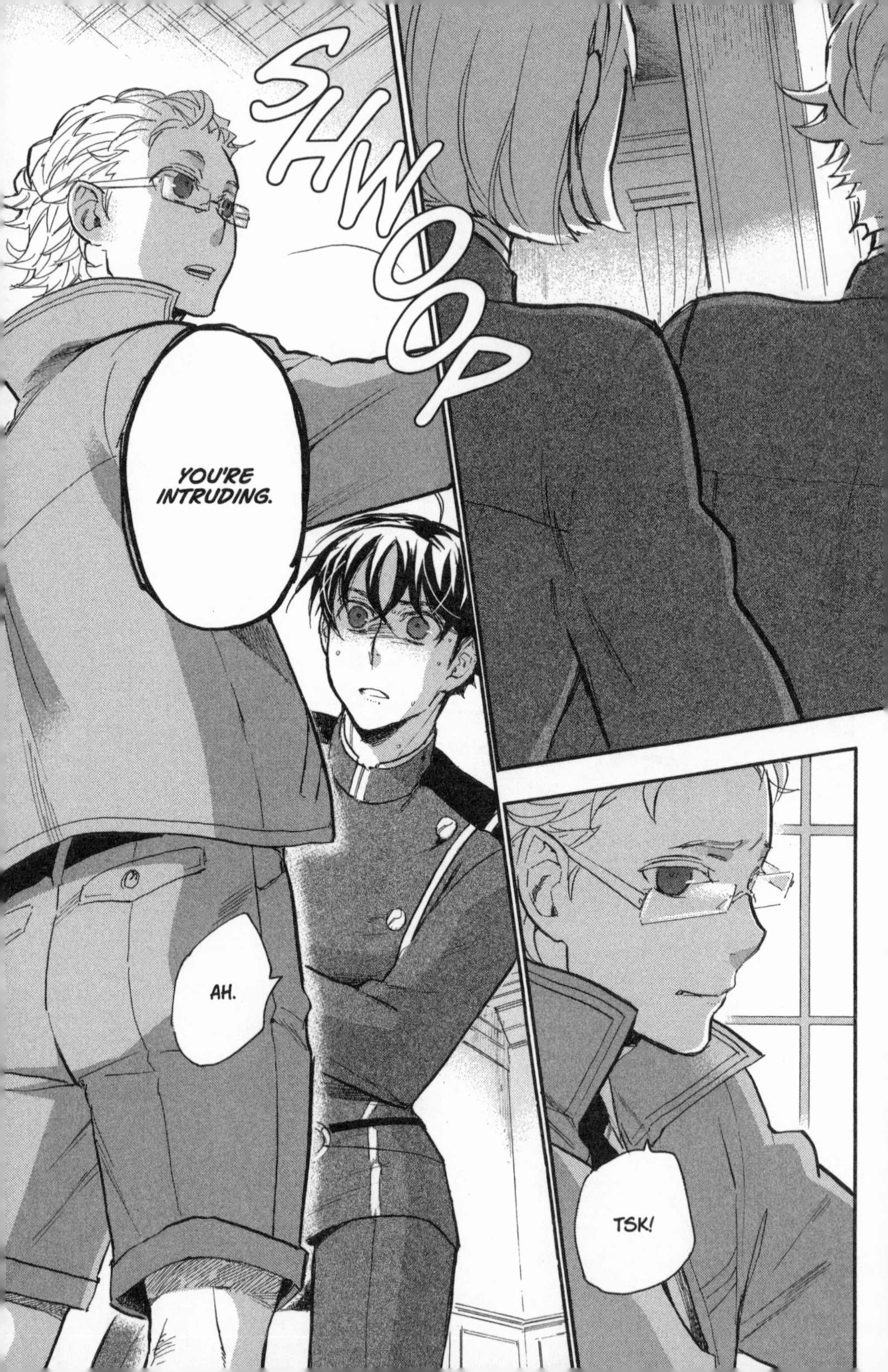
SHWOOP
TSK!
YOU'RE INTRUDING.
AH.

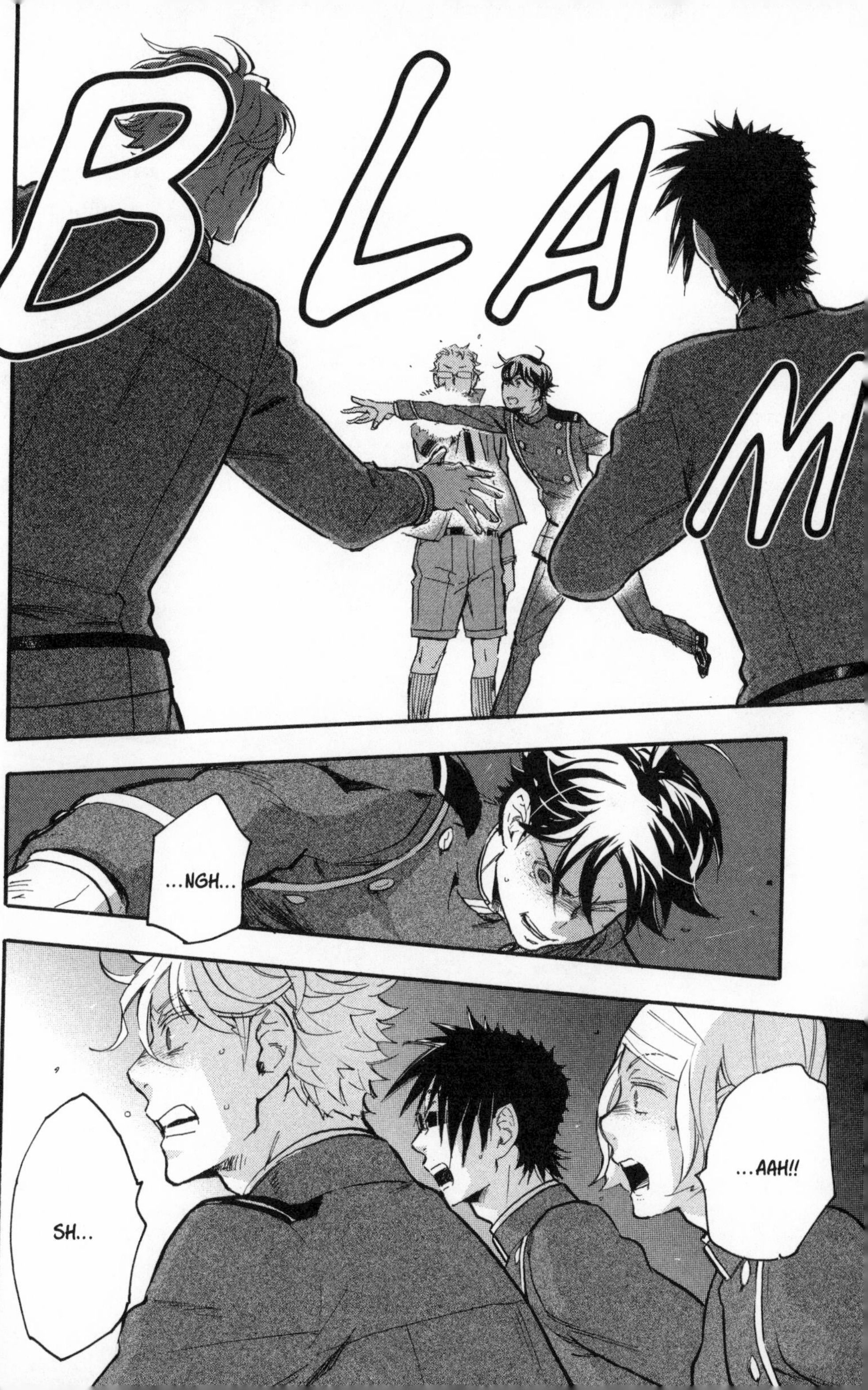
BLAM
...NGH...
...AAH!!
SH...

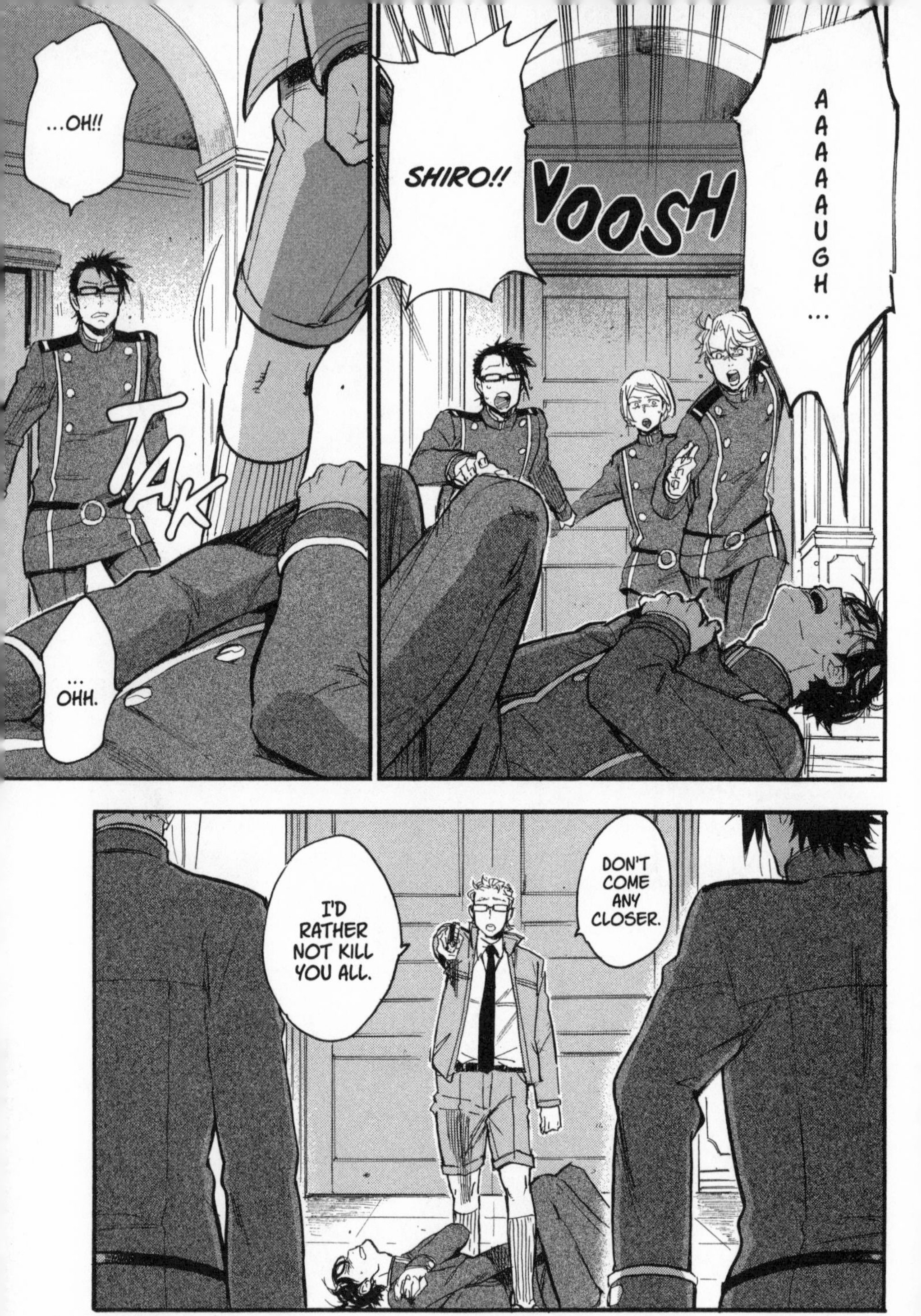
AAAAAAUGH...
VOOSH
SHIRO!!
...OH!!
TAK
...OHH.
DON'T COME ANY CLOSER.
I'D RATHER NOT KILL YOU ALL.

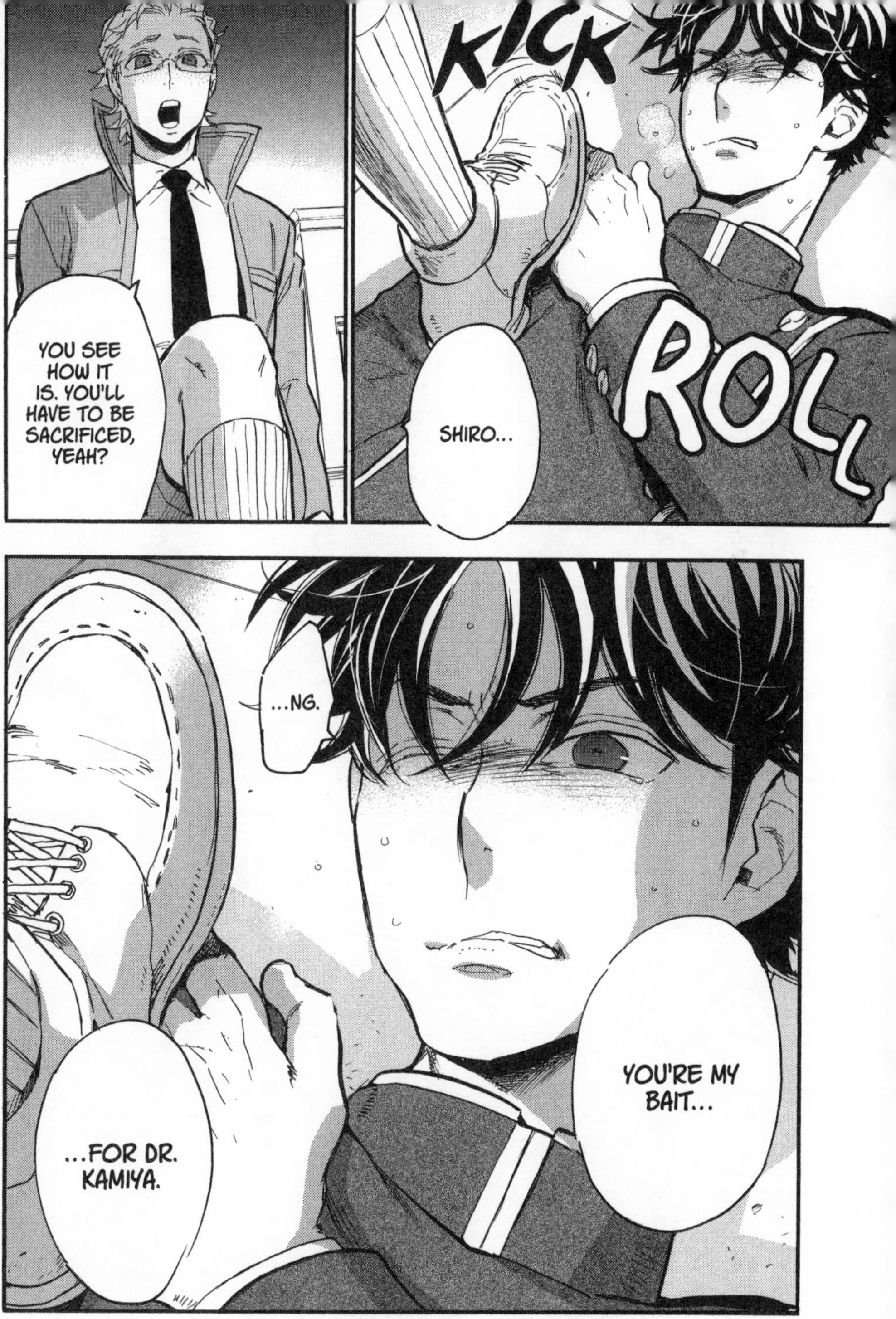
KICK
ROLL
SHIRO...
YOU SEE HOW IT IS. YOU'LL HAVE TO BE SACRIFICED, YEAH?
...NG.
YOU'RE MY BAIT...
...FOR DR. KAMIYA.

CHAPTER sixty-nine

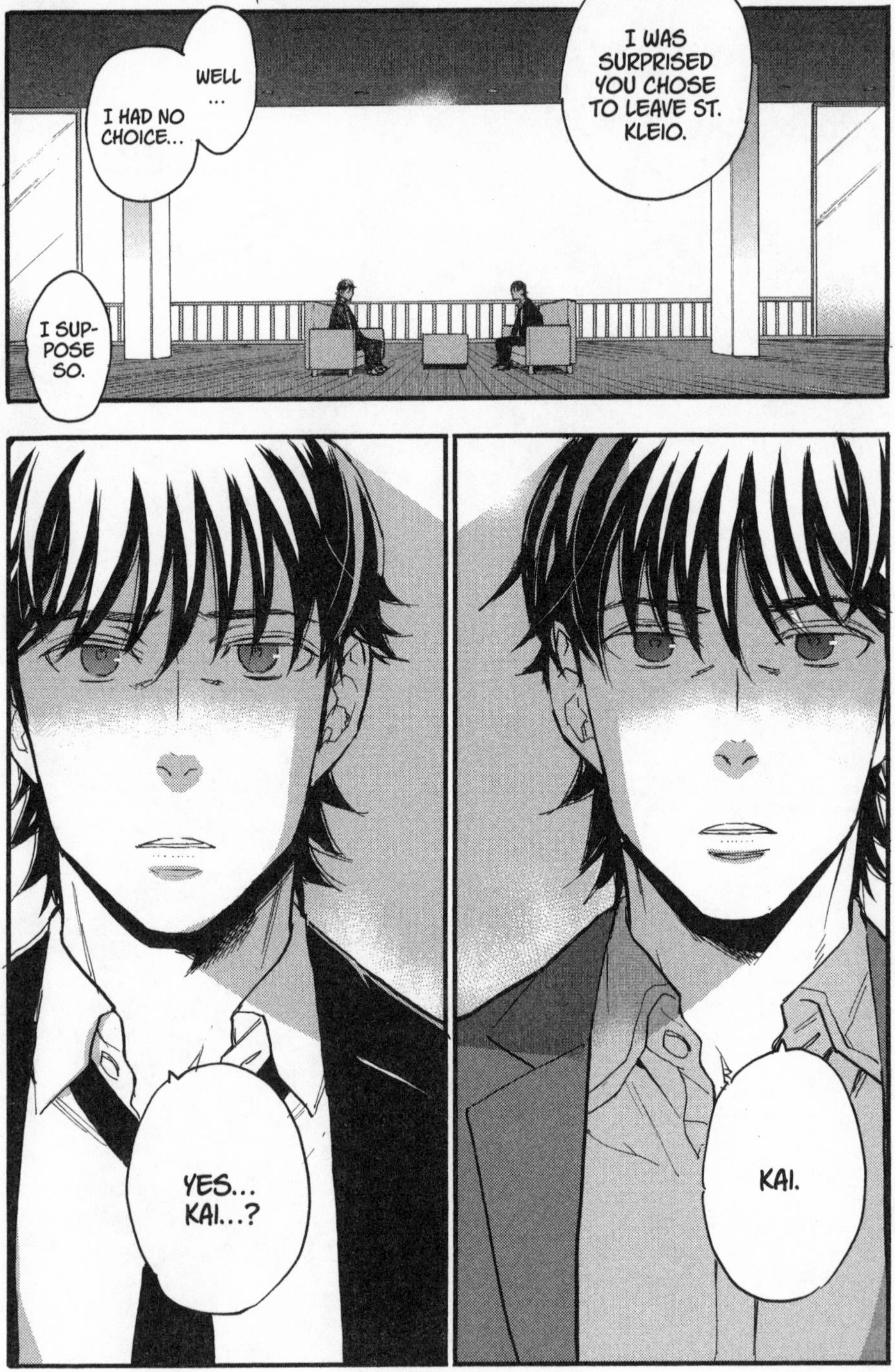
I WAS SURPRISED YOU CHOSE TO LEAVE ST. KLEIO.
WELL ...
I HAD NO CHOICE...
I SUP-POSE SO.
KAI.
YES... KAI...?

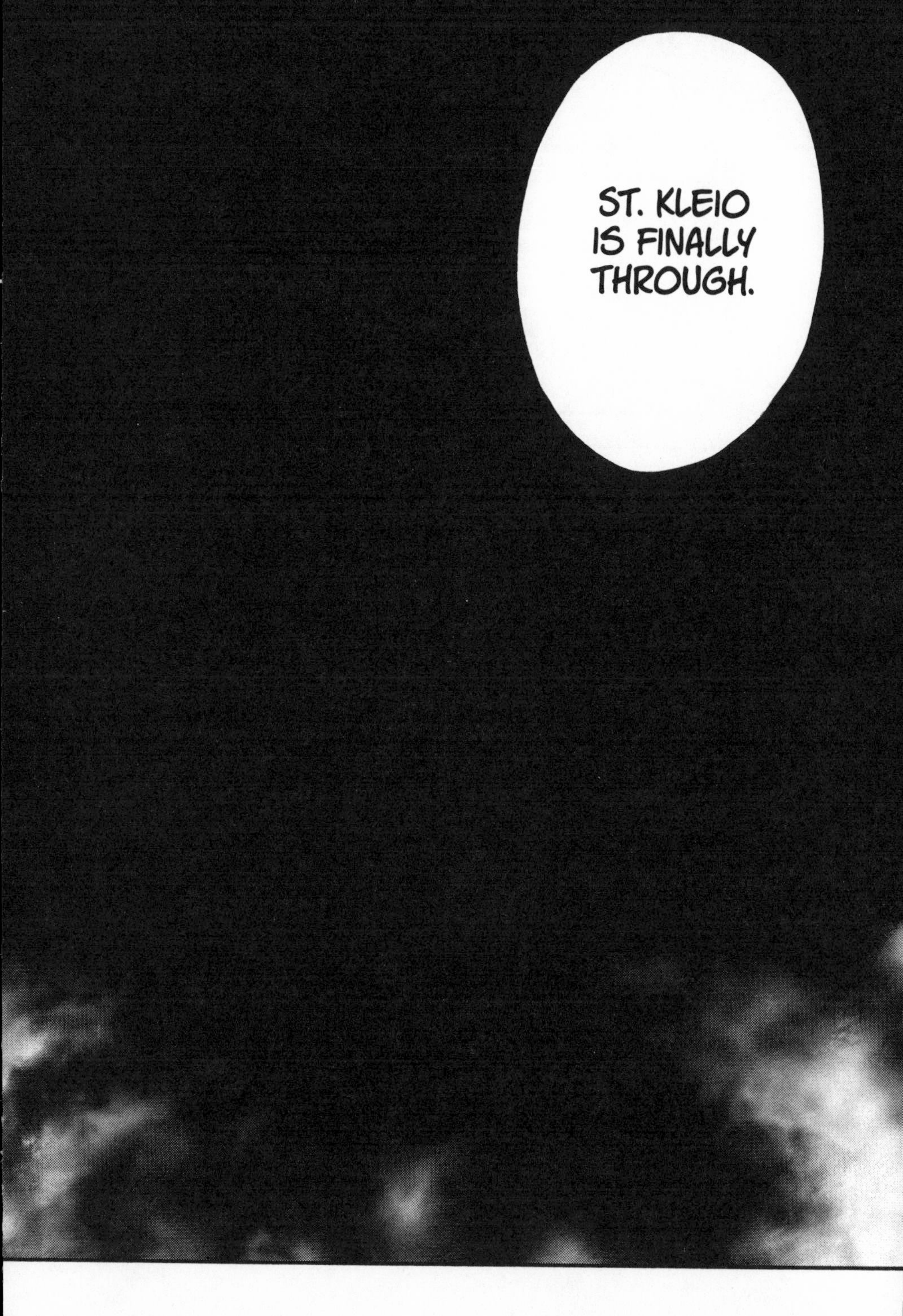
ST. KLEIO IS FINALLY THROUGH.

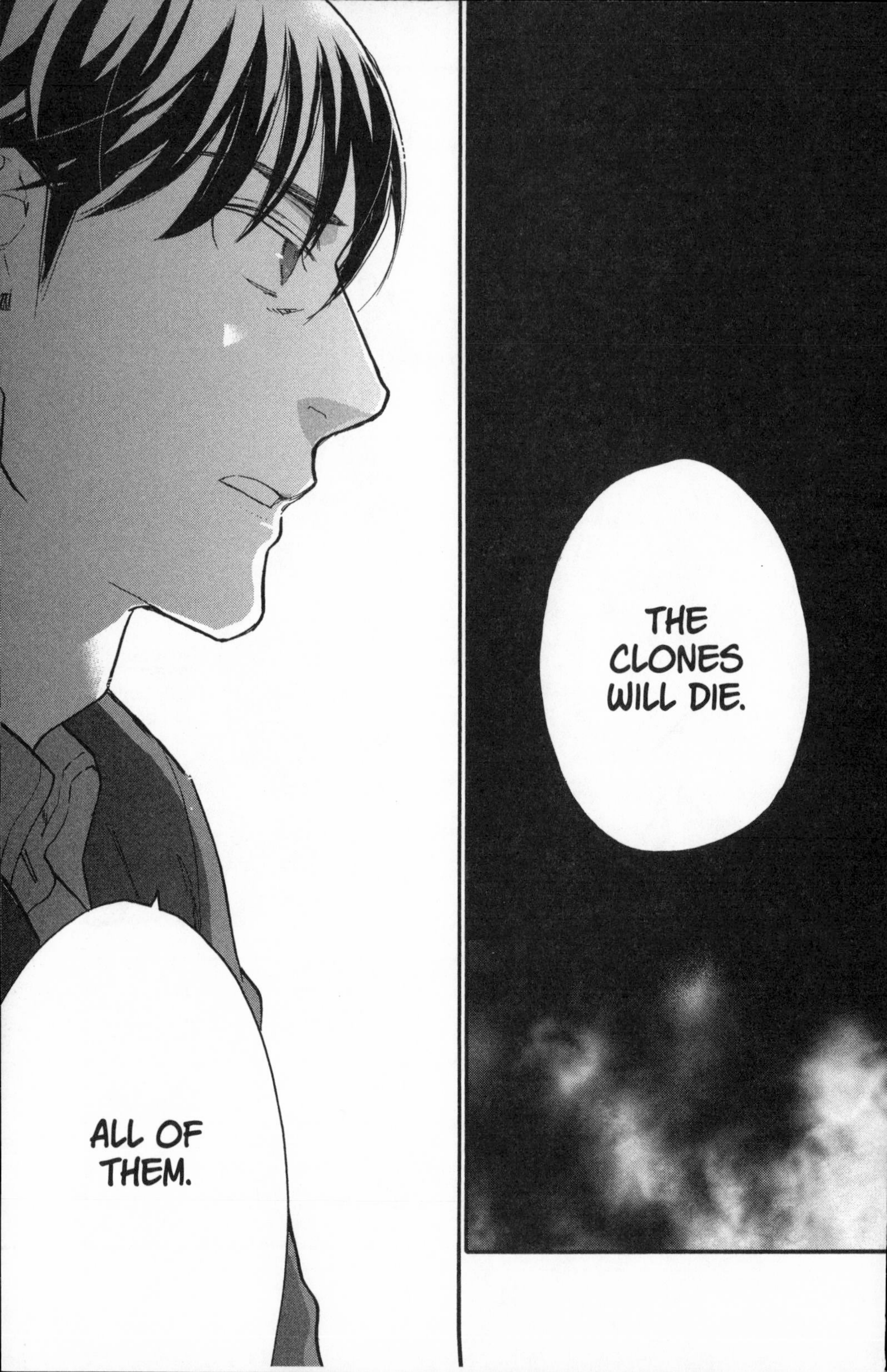
THE CLONES WILL DIE.
ALL OF THEM.

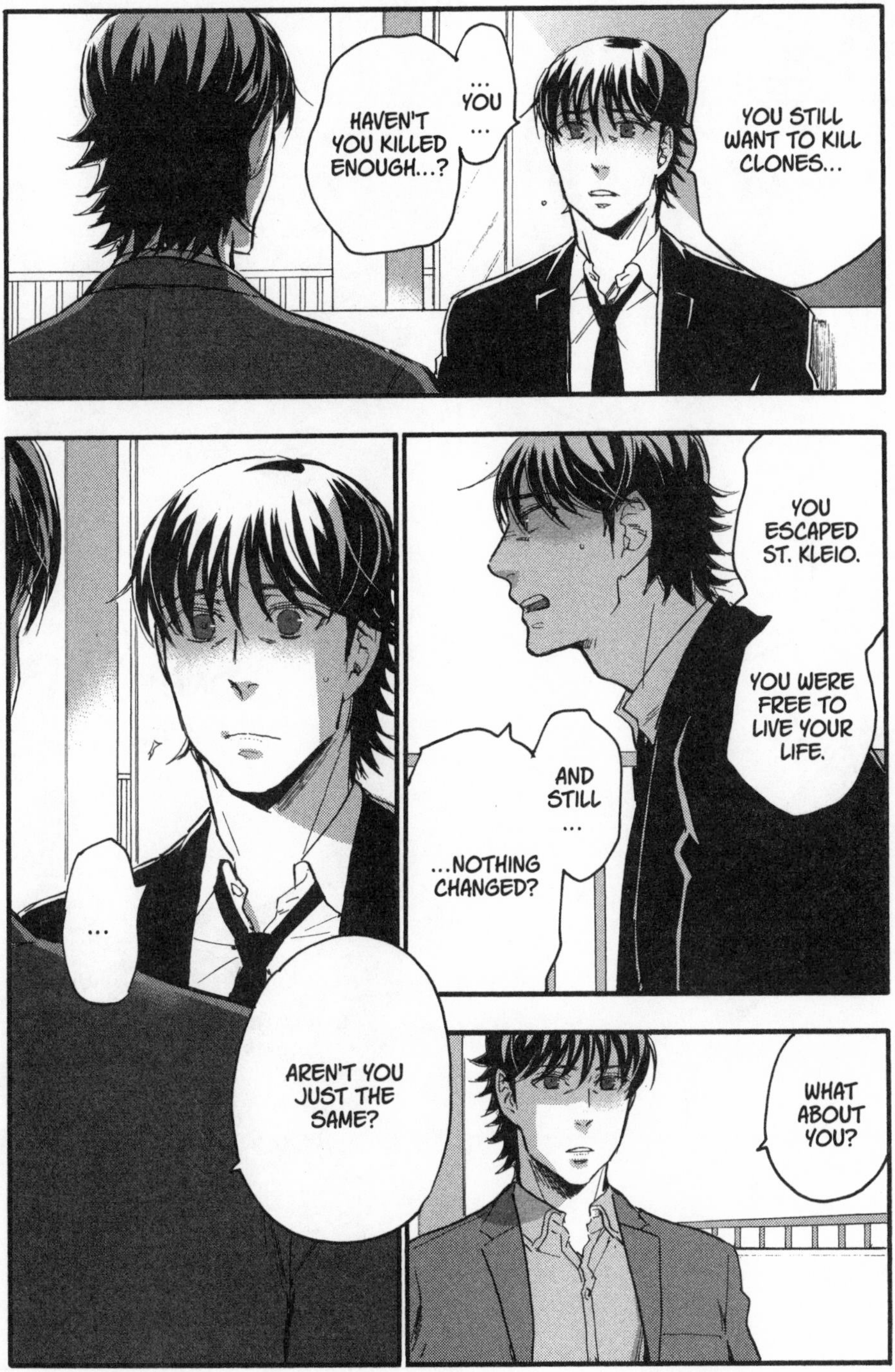
YOU STILL WANT TO KILL CLONES...
... YOU ...
HAVEN'T YOU KILLED ENOUGH...?
YOU ESCAPED ST. KLEIO.
YOU WERE FREE TO LIVE YOUR LIFE.
AND STILL ...
...NOTHING CHANGED?
WHAT ABOUT YOU?
...
AREN'T YOU JUST THE SAME?

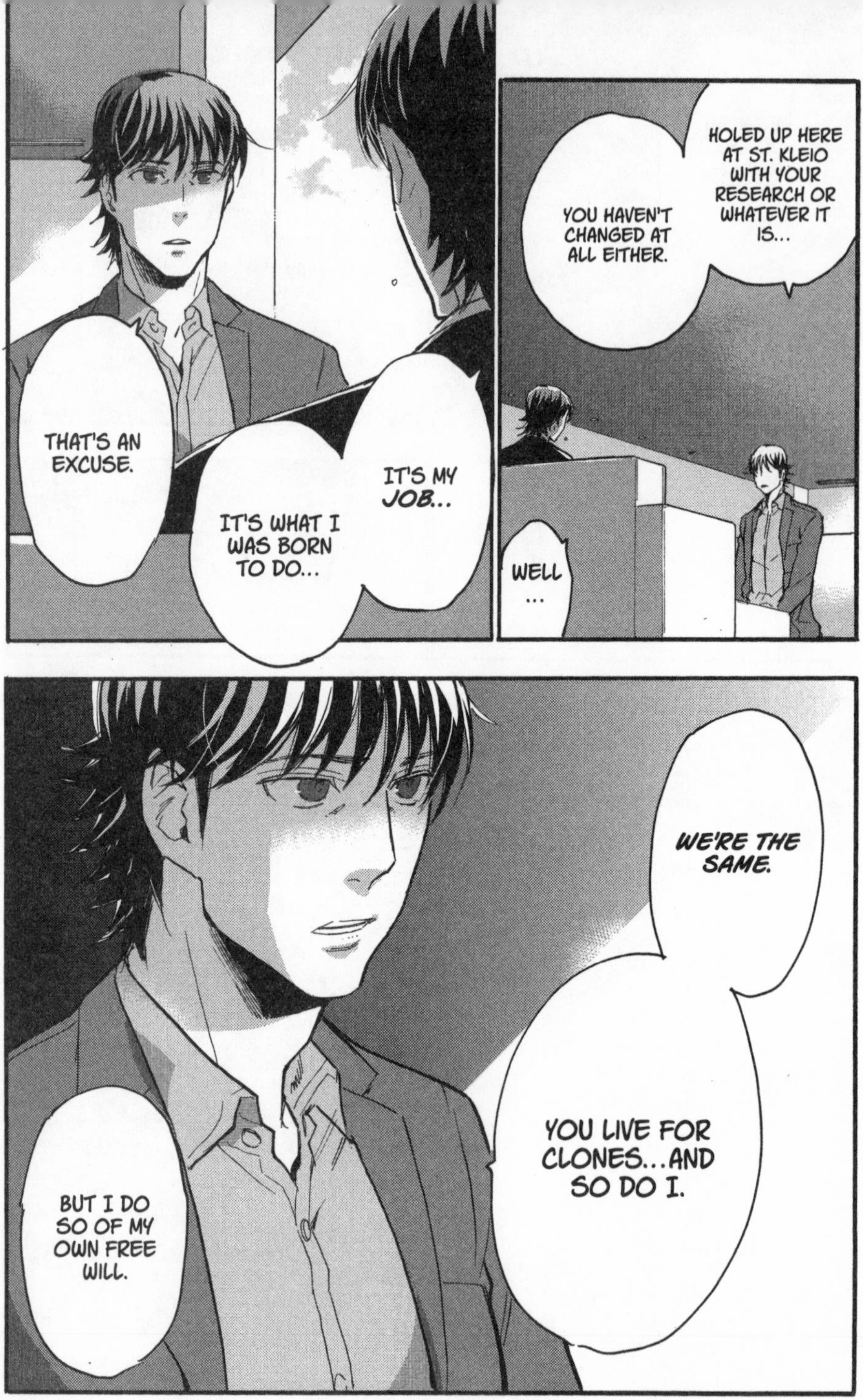

HOLED UP HERE AT ST. KLEIO WITH YOUR RESEARCH OR WHATEVER IT IS...
YOU HAVEN'T CHANGED AT ALL EITHER.
WELL ...
IT'S MY *JOB*...
IT'S WHAT I WAS BORN TO DO...
THAT'S AN EXCUSE.
WE'RE THE SAME.
YOU LIVE FOR CLONES...AND SO DO I.
BUT I DO SO OF MY OWN FREE WILL.

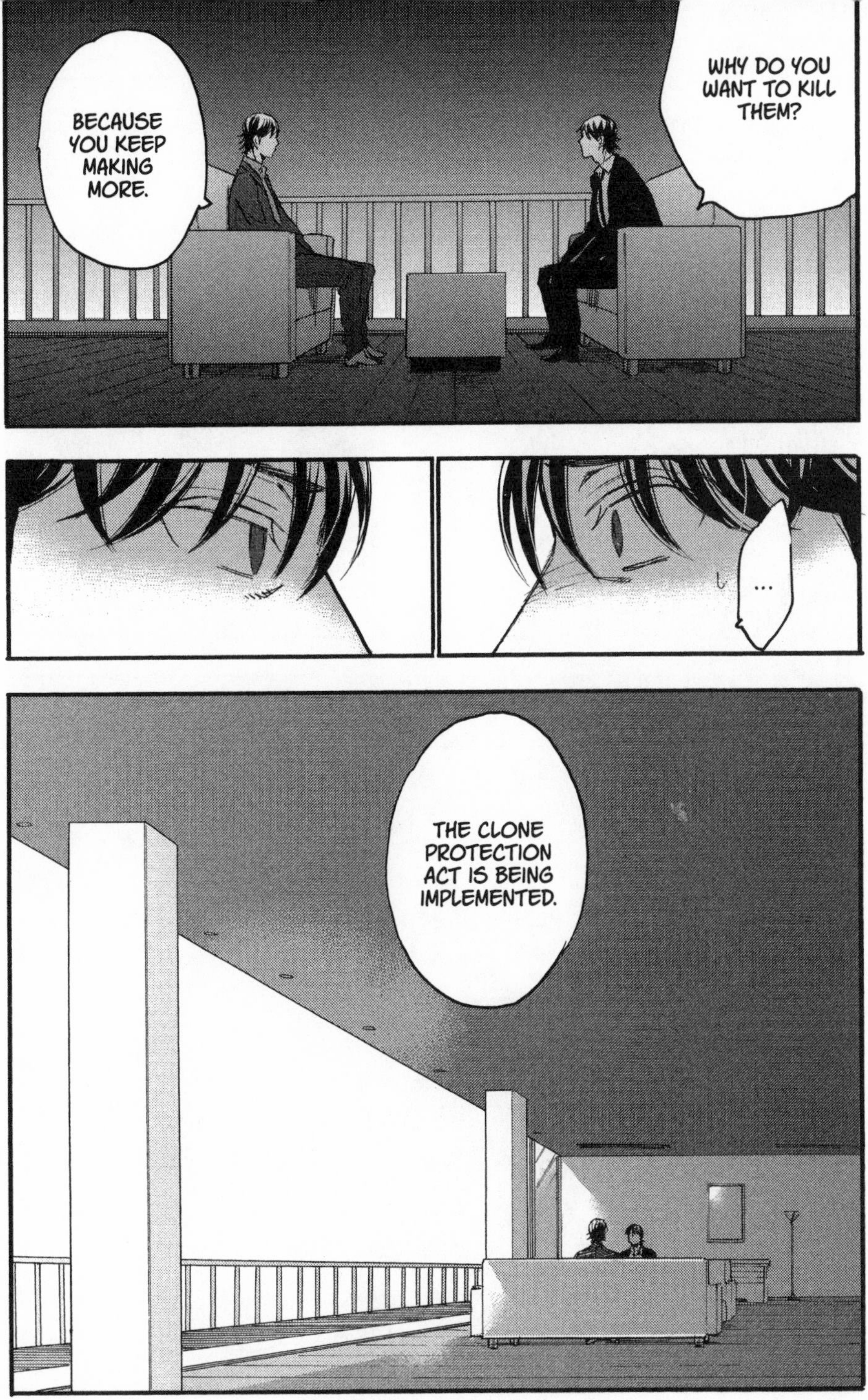
WHY DO YOU WANT TO KILL THEM?
BECAUSE YOU KEEP MAKING MORE.
...
THE CLONE PROTECTION ACT IS BEING IMPLEMENTED.

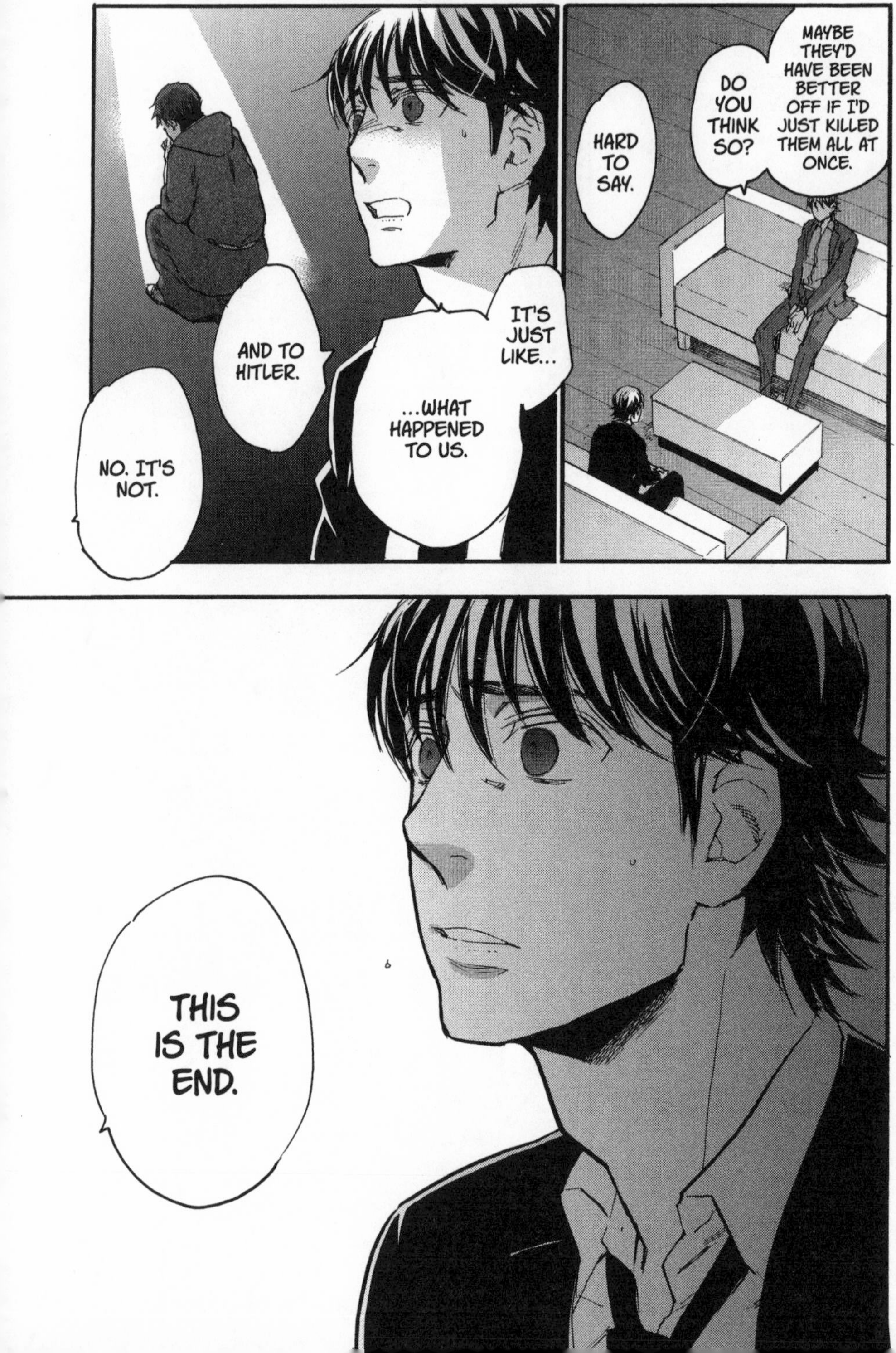
MAYBE THEY'D HAVE BEEN BETTER OFF IF I'D JUST KILLED THEM ALL AT ONCE.
DO YOU THINK SO?
HARD TO SAY.
IT'S JUST LIKE...
...WHAT HAPPENED TO US.
AND TO HITLER.
NO. IT'S NOT.
THIS IS THE END.

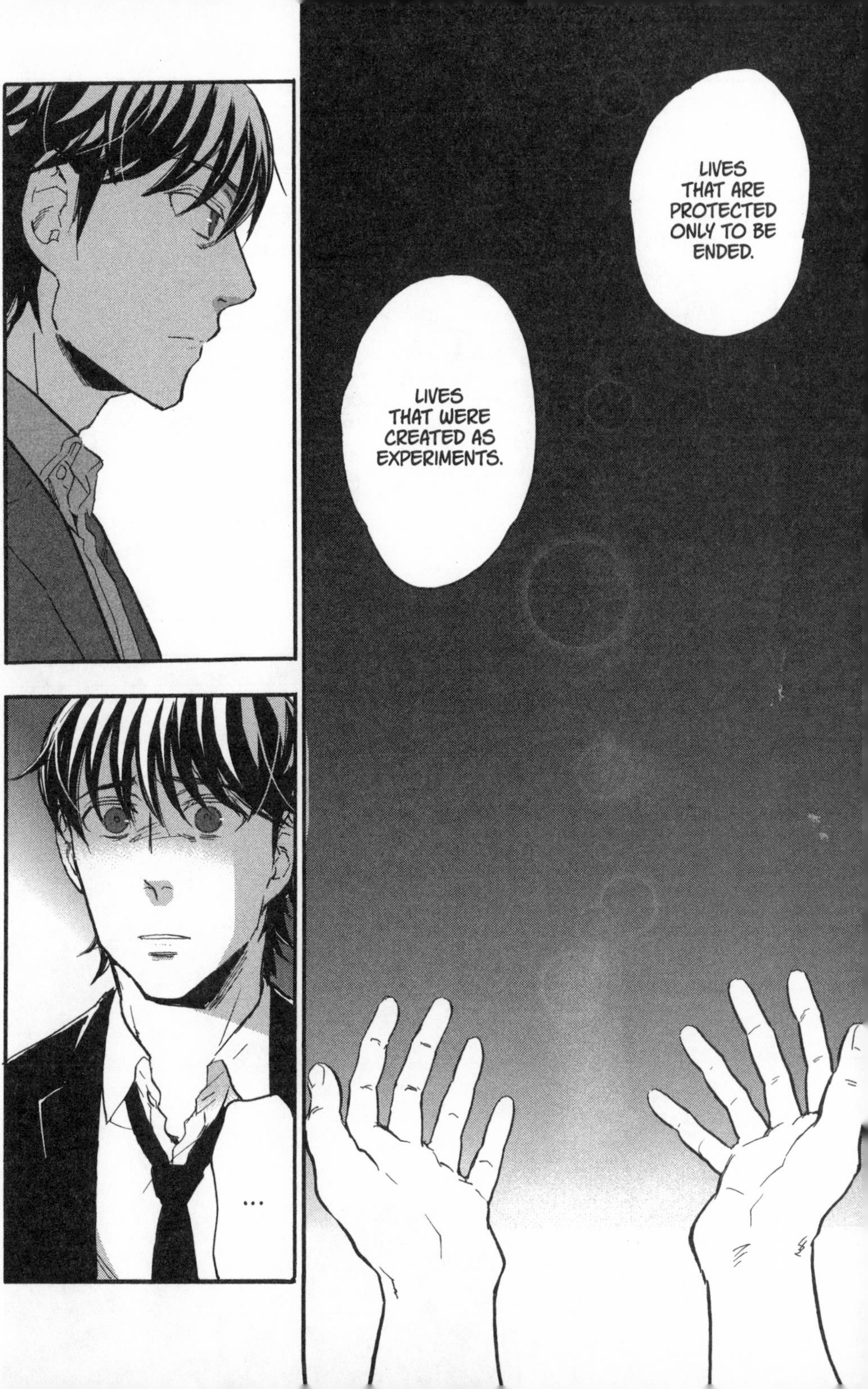
LIVES THAT ARE PROTECTED ONLY TO BE ENDED.
LIVES THAT WERE CREATED AS EXPERIMENTS.
...

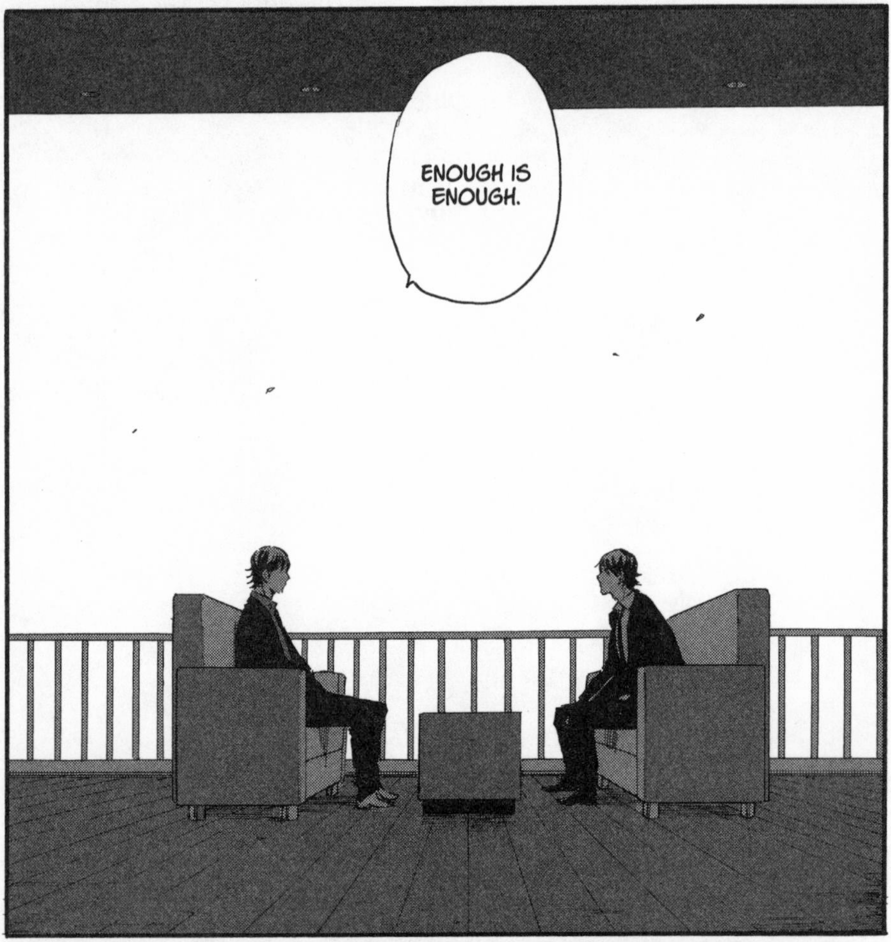
ENOUGH IS ENOUGH.
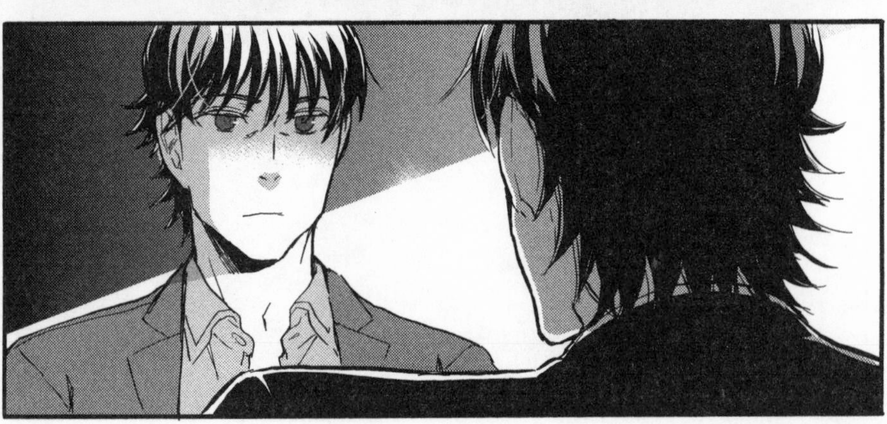

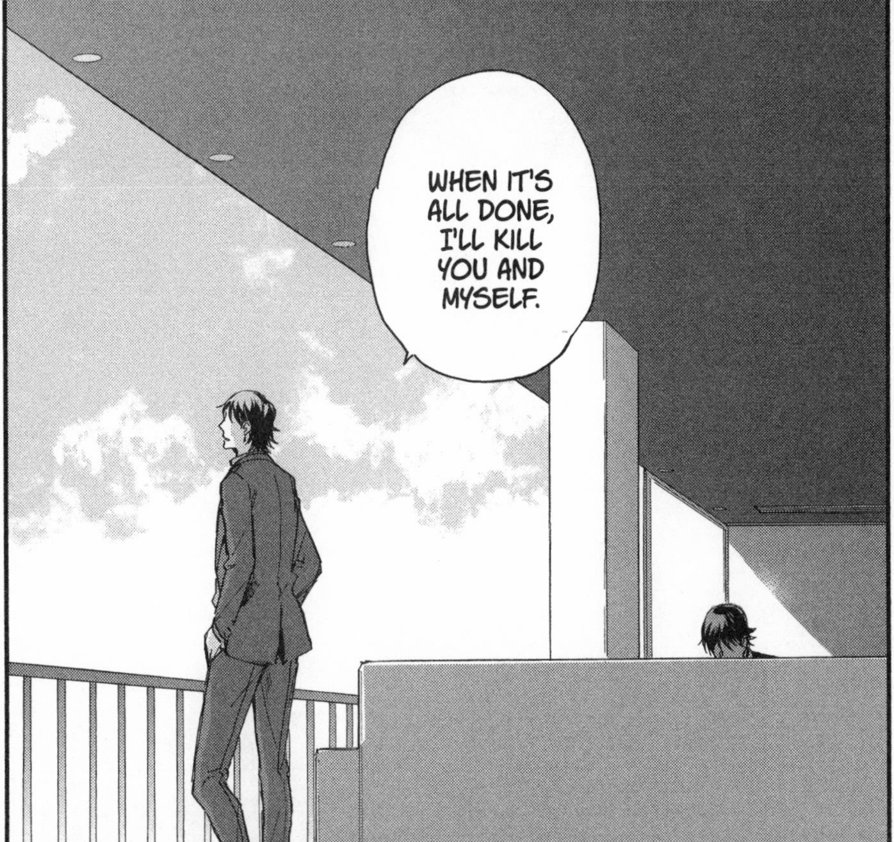
WHEN IT'S ALL DONE, I'LL KILL YOU AND MYSELF.
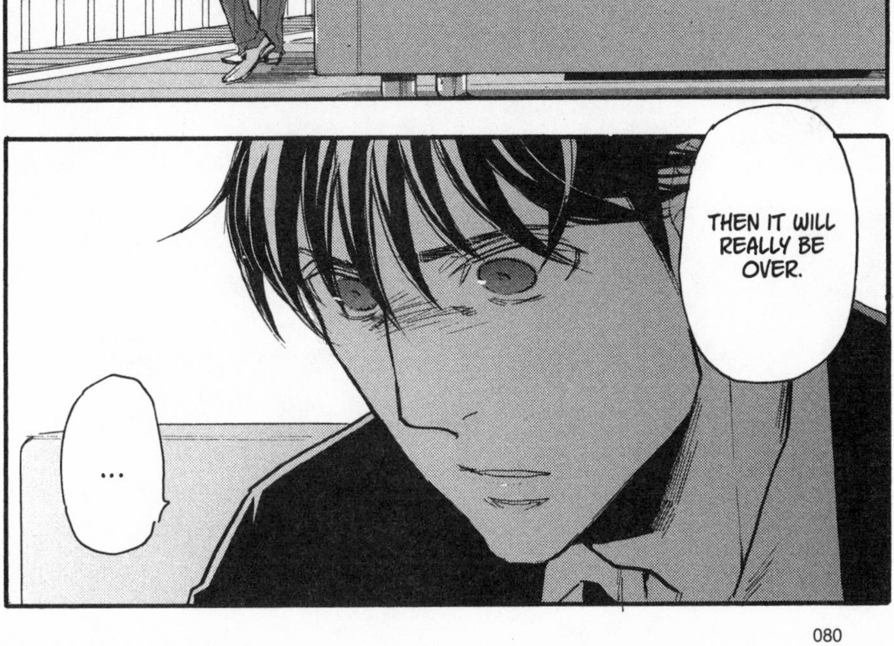
THEN IT WILL REALLY BE OVER.
...

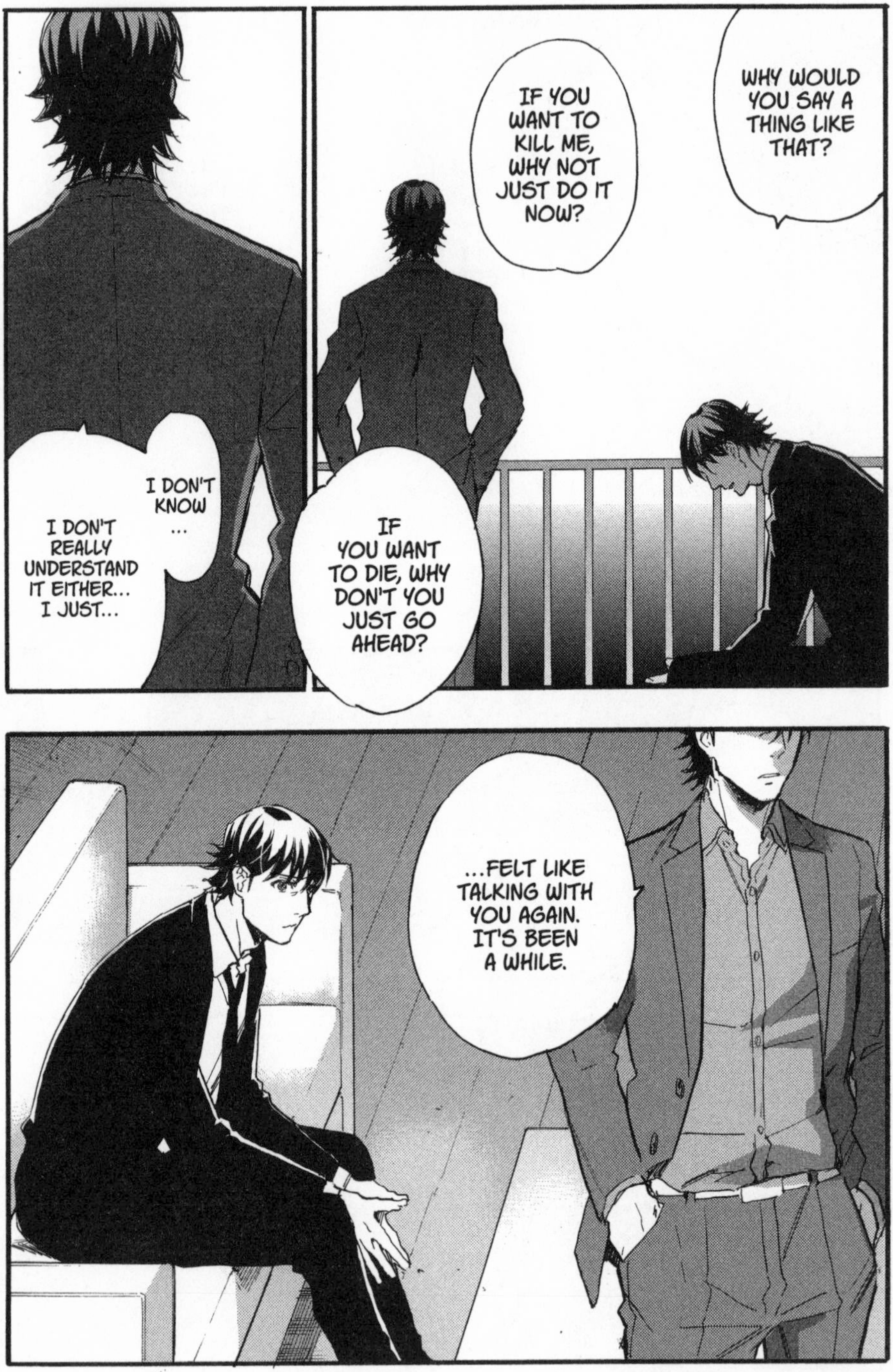
WHY WOULD YOU SAY A THING LIKE THAT?
IF YOU WANT TO KILL ME, WHY NOT JUST DO IT NOW?
IF YOU WANT TO DIE, WHY DON'T YOU JUST GO AHEAD?
I DON'T KNOW ...
I DON'T REALLY UNDERSTAND IT EITHER... I JUST...
...FELT LIKE TALKING WITH YOU AGAIN. IT'S BEEN A WHILE.

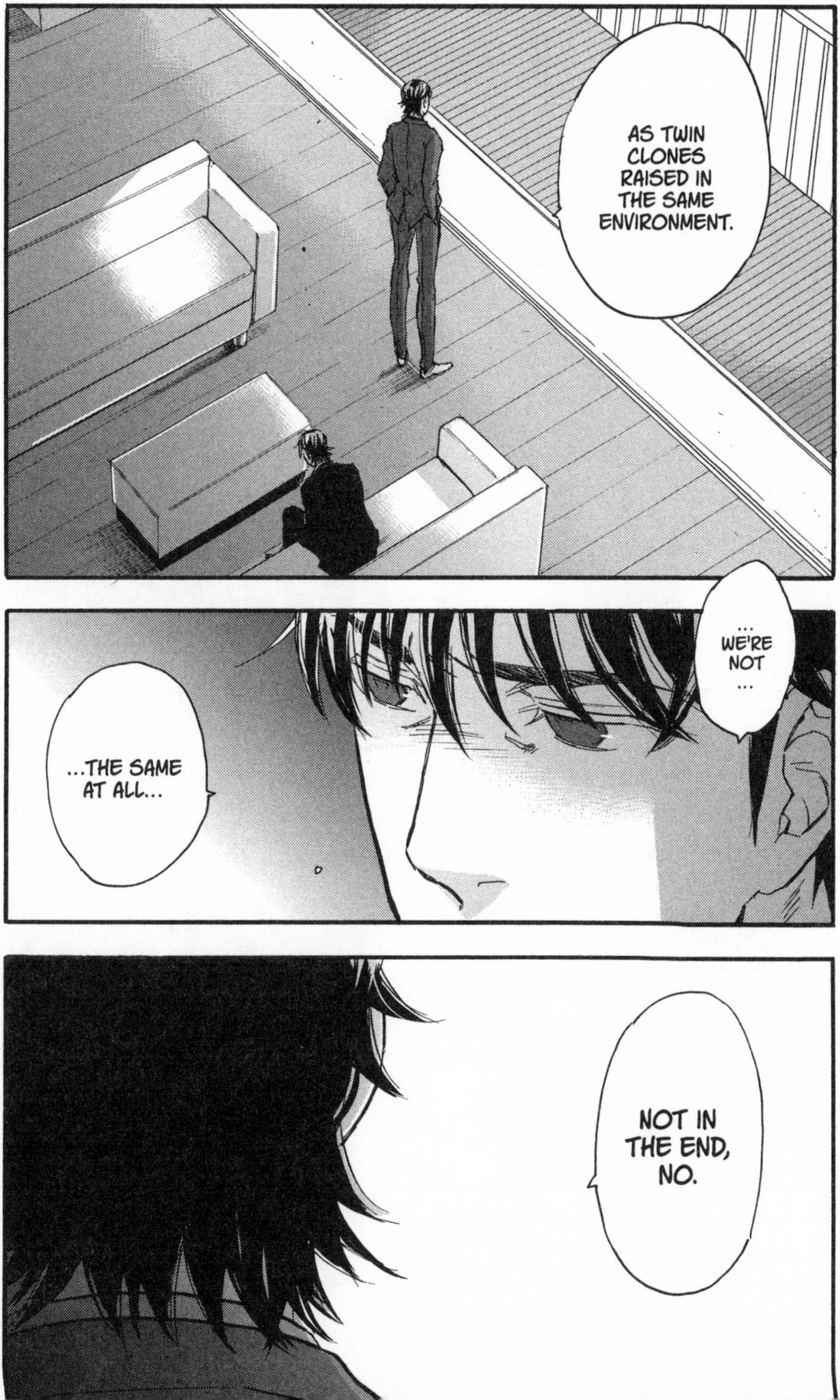
AS TWIN CLONES RAISED IN THE SAME ENVIRONMENT.
...WE'RE NOT...
...THE SAME AT ALL...
NOT IN THE END, NO.

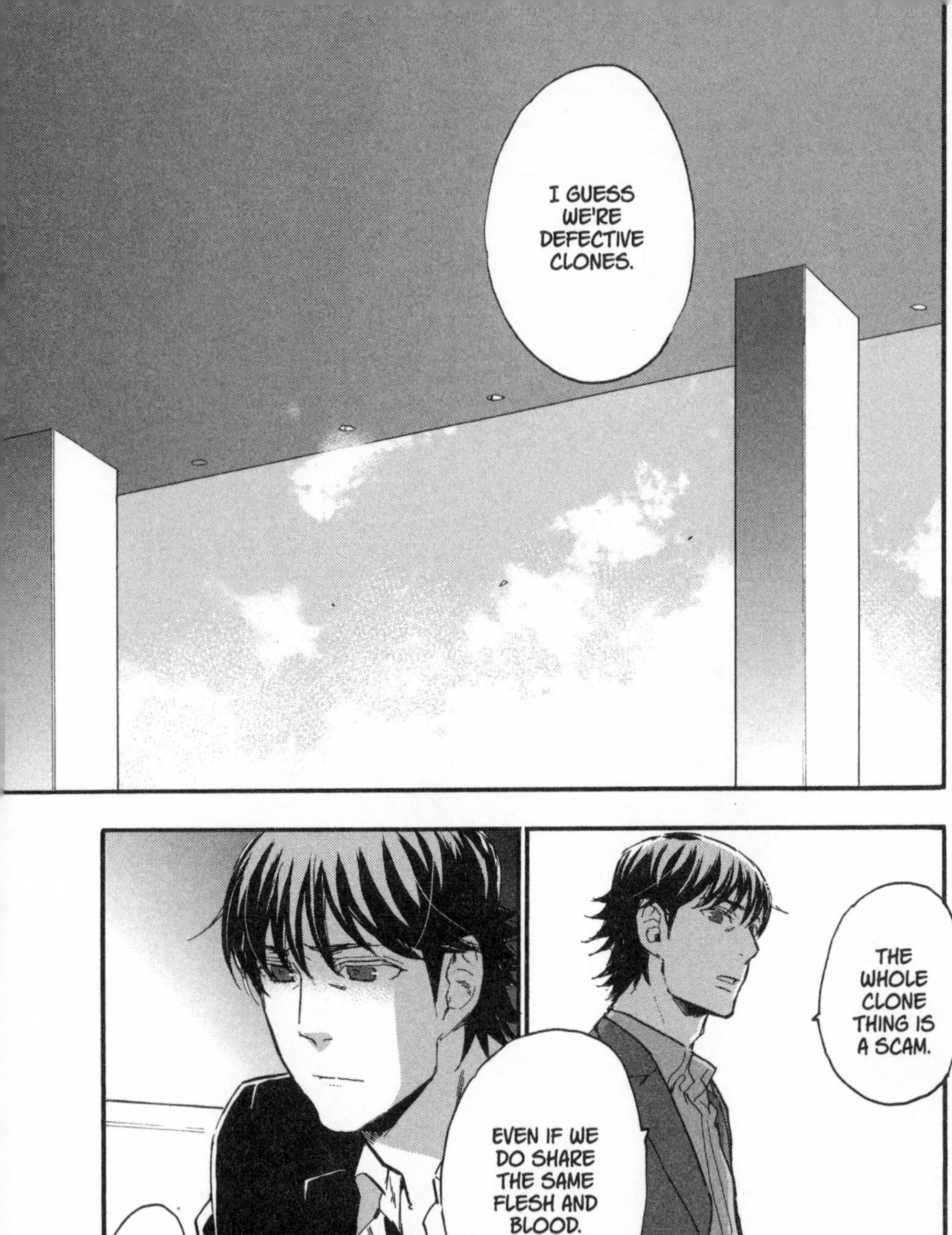
I GUESS WE'RE DEFECTIVE CLONES.
THE WHOLE CLONE THING IS A SCAM.
EVEN IF WE DO SHARE THE SAME FLESH AND BLOOD.
...

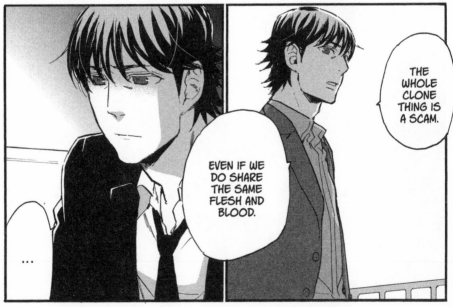

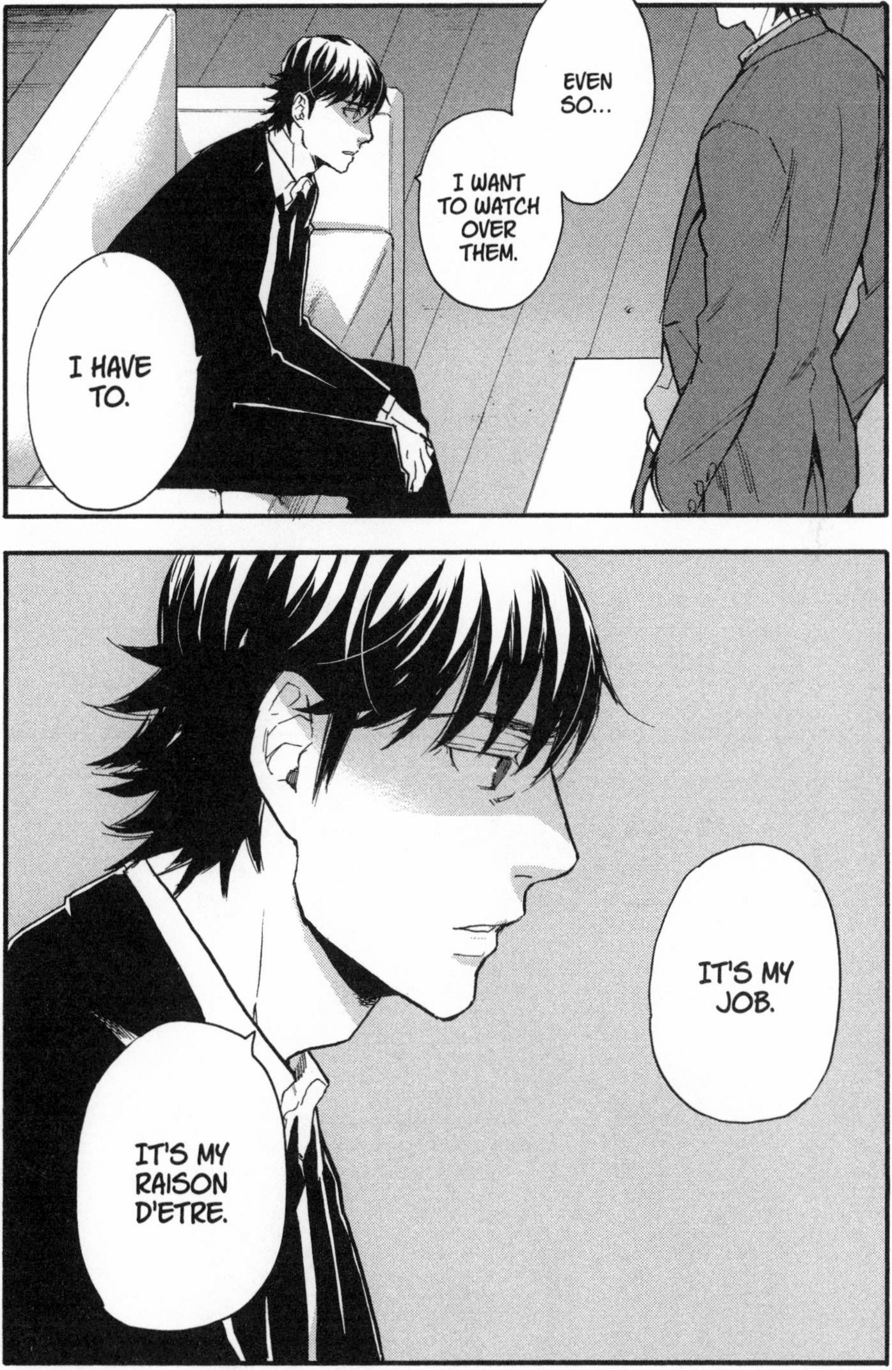
EVEN SO...
I WANT TO WATCH OVER THEM.
I HAVE TO.
IT'S MY JOB.
IT'S MY RAISON D'ETRE.

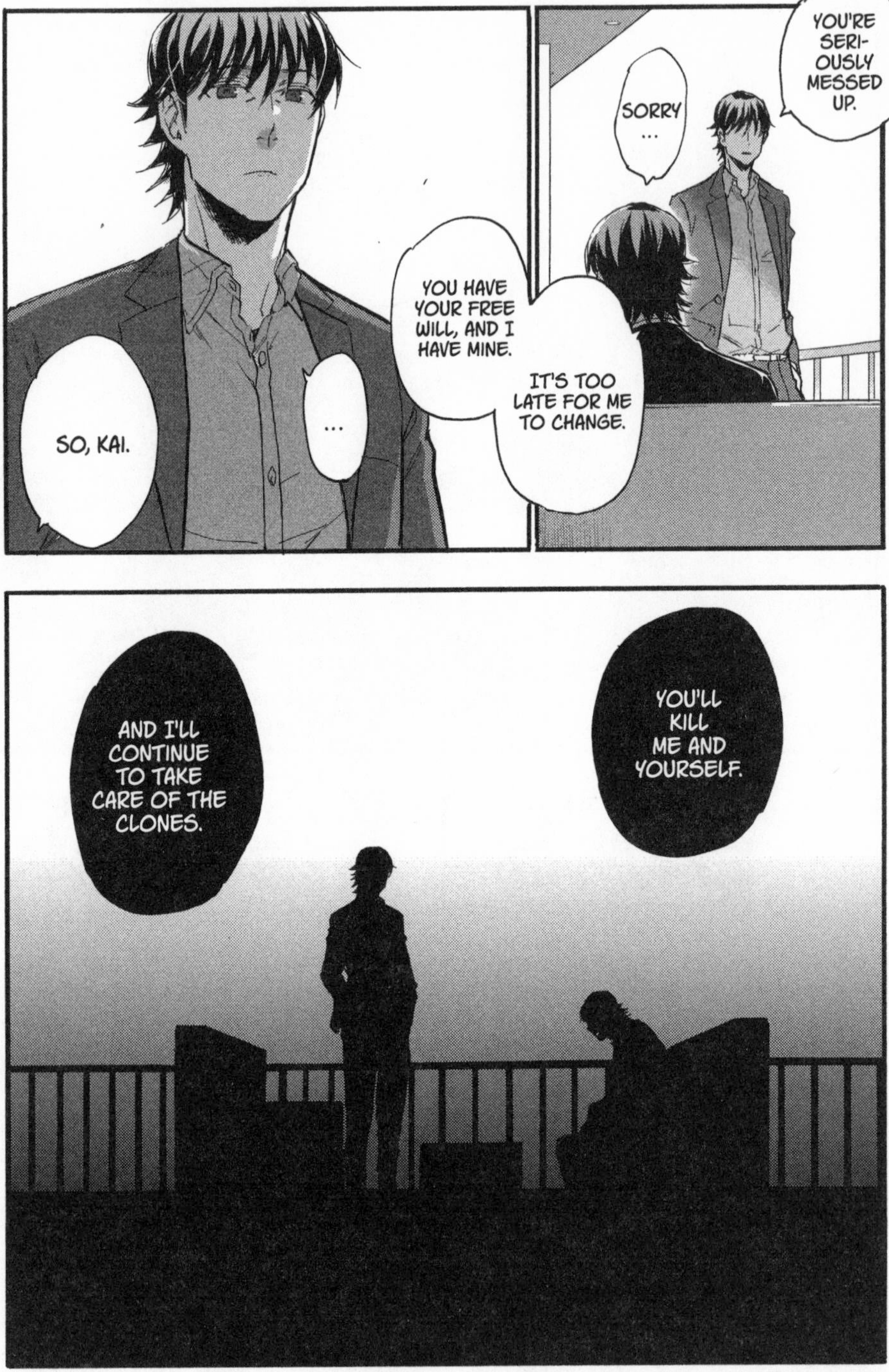
YOU'RE SERI-OUSLY MESSED UP.
SORRY ...
YOU HAVE YOUR FREE WILL, AND I HAVE MINE.
IT'S TOO LATE FOR ME TO CHANGE.
...
SO, KAI.
YOU'LL KILL ME AND YOURSELF.
AND I'LL CONTINUE TO TAKE CARE OF THE CLONES.

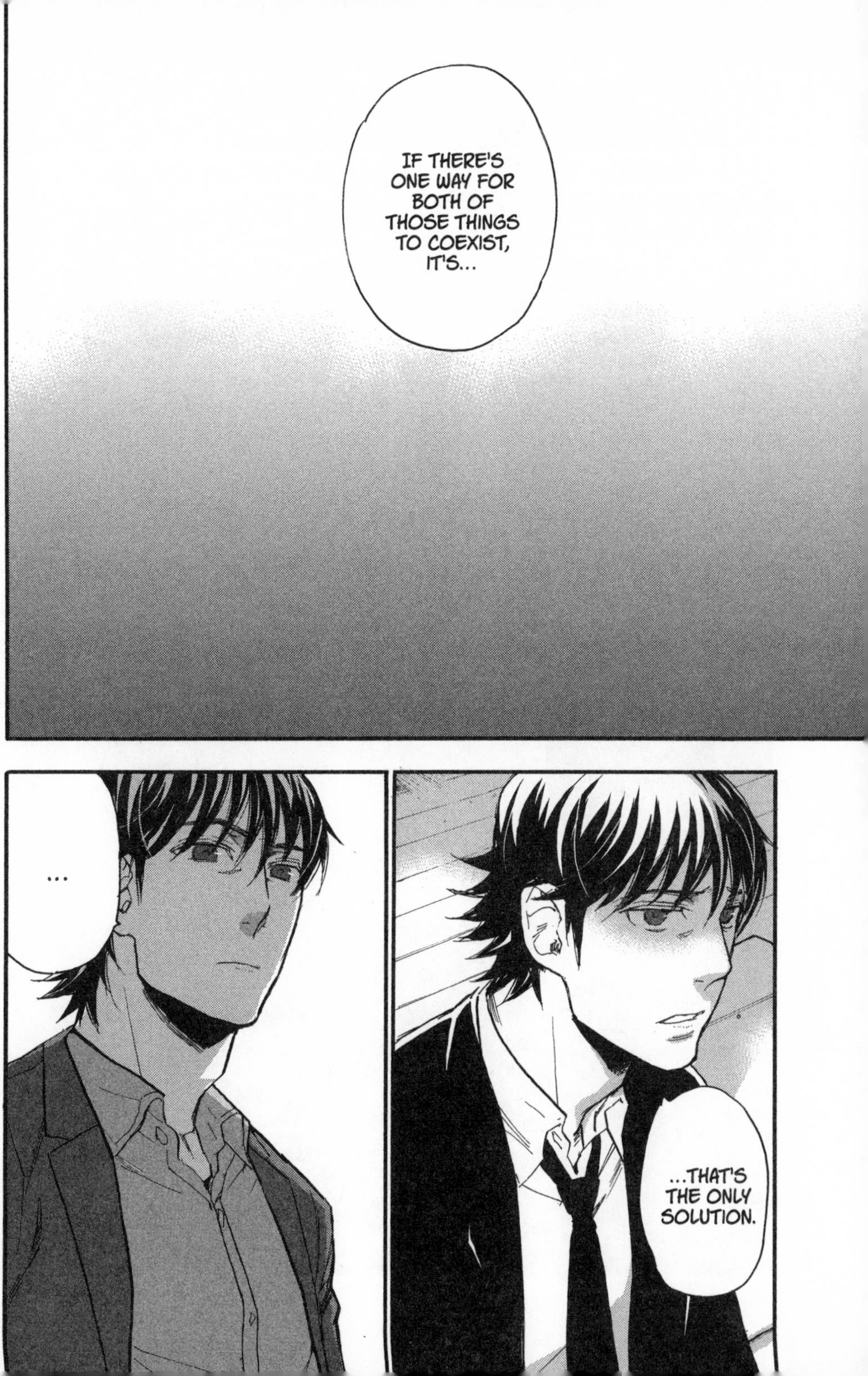
IF THERE'S ONE WAY FOR BOTH OF THOSE THINGS TO COEXIST, IT'S...
...THAT'S THE ONLY SOLUTION.
...

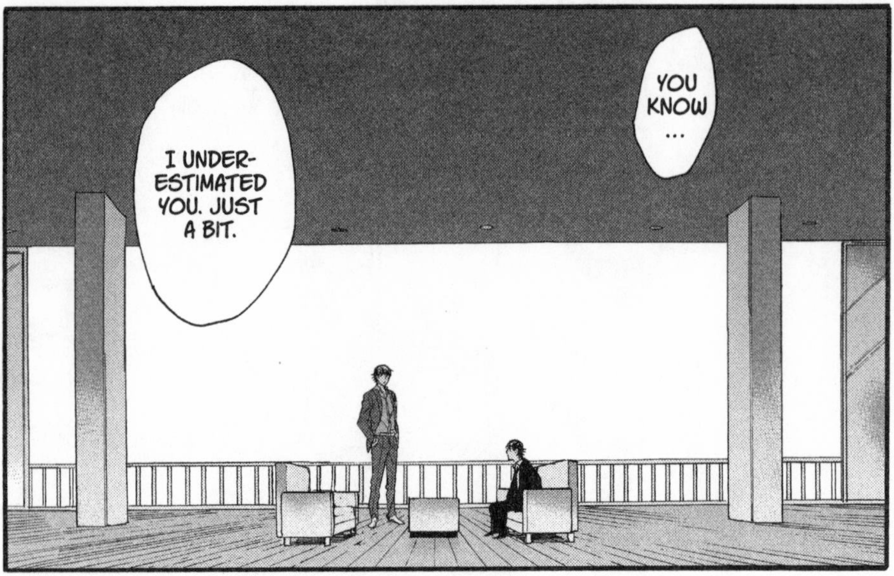
YOU KNOW ...
I UNDER-ESTIMATED YOU. JUST A BIT.

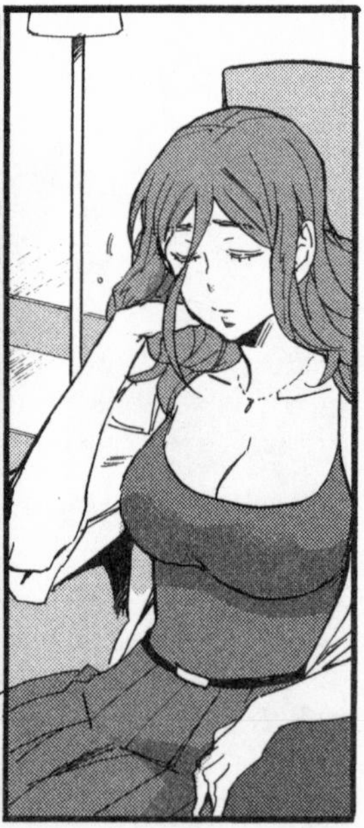

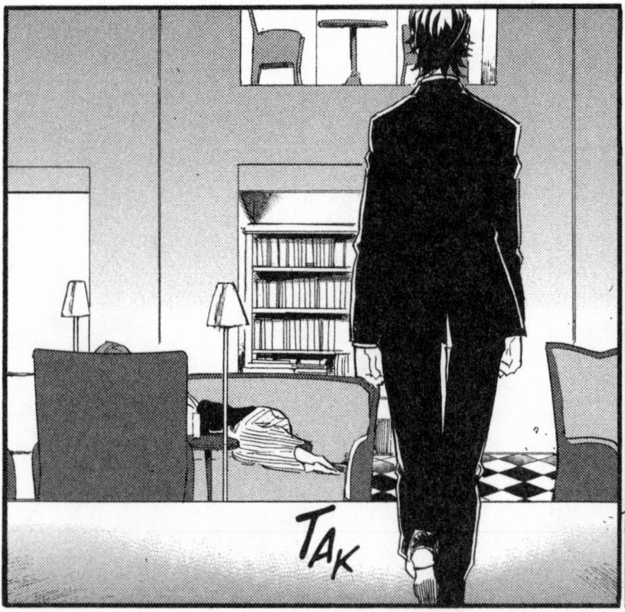
TAK

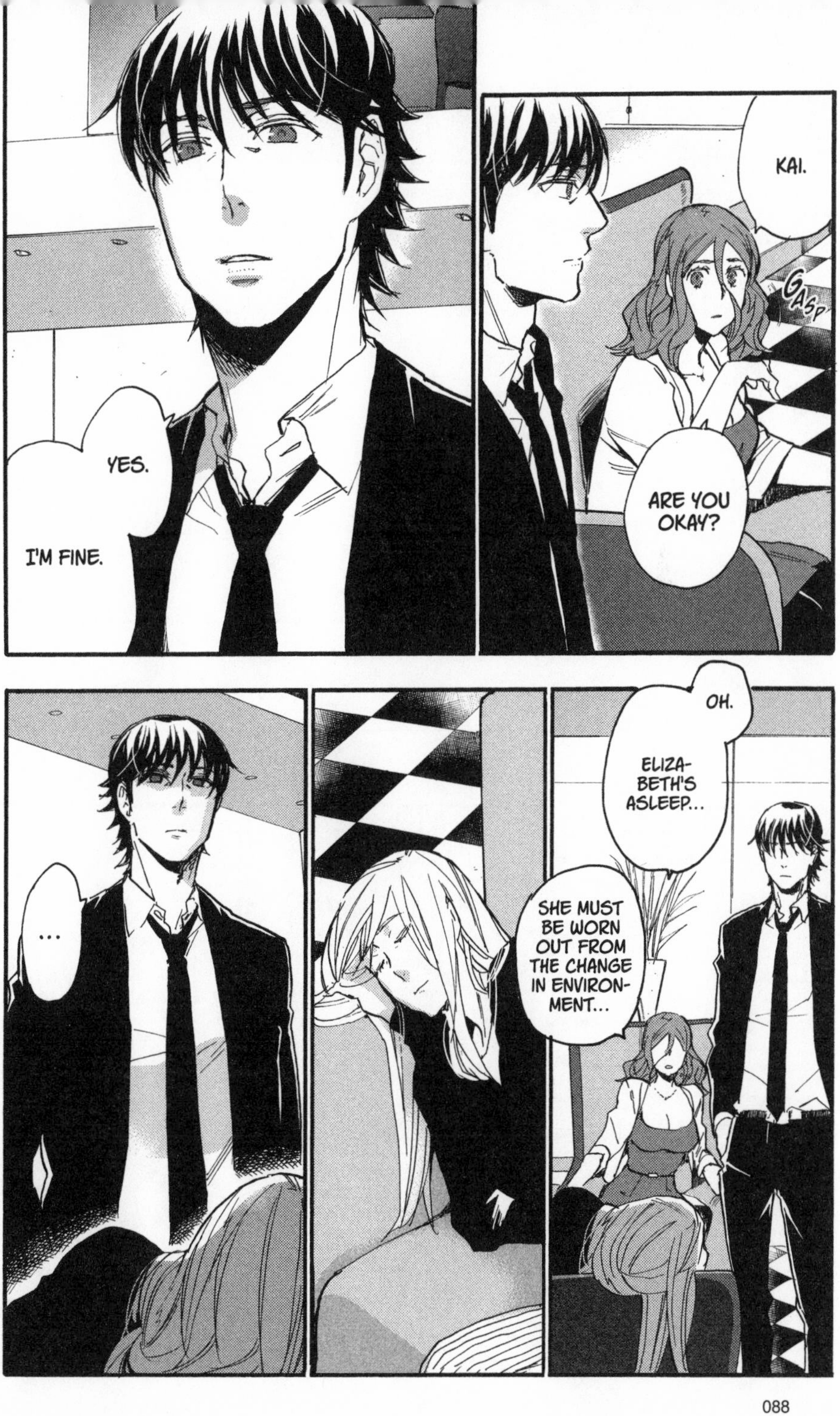
KAI.
GASP
ARE YOU OKAY?
YES.
I'M FINE.
OH.
ELIZA-BETH'S ASLEEP...
SHE MUST BE WORN OUT FROM THE CHANGE IN ENVIRON-MENT...
...

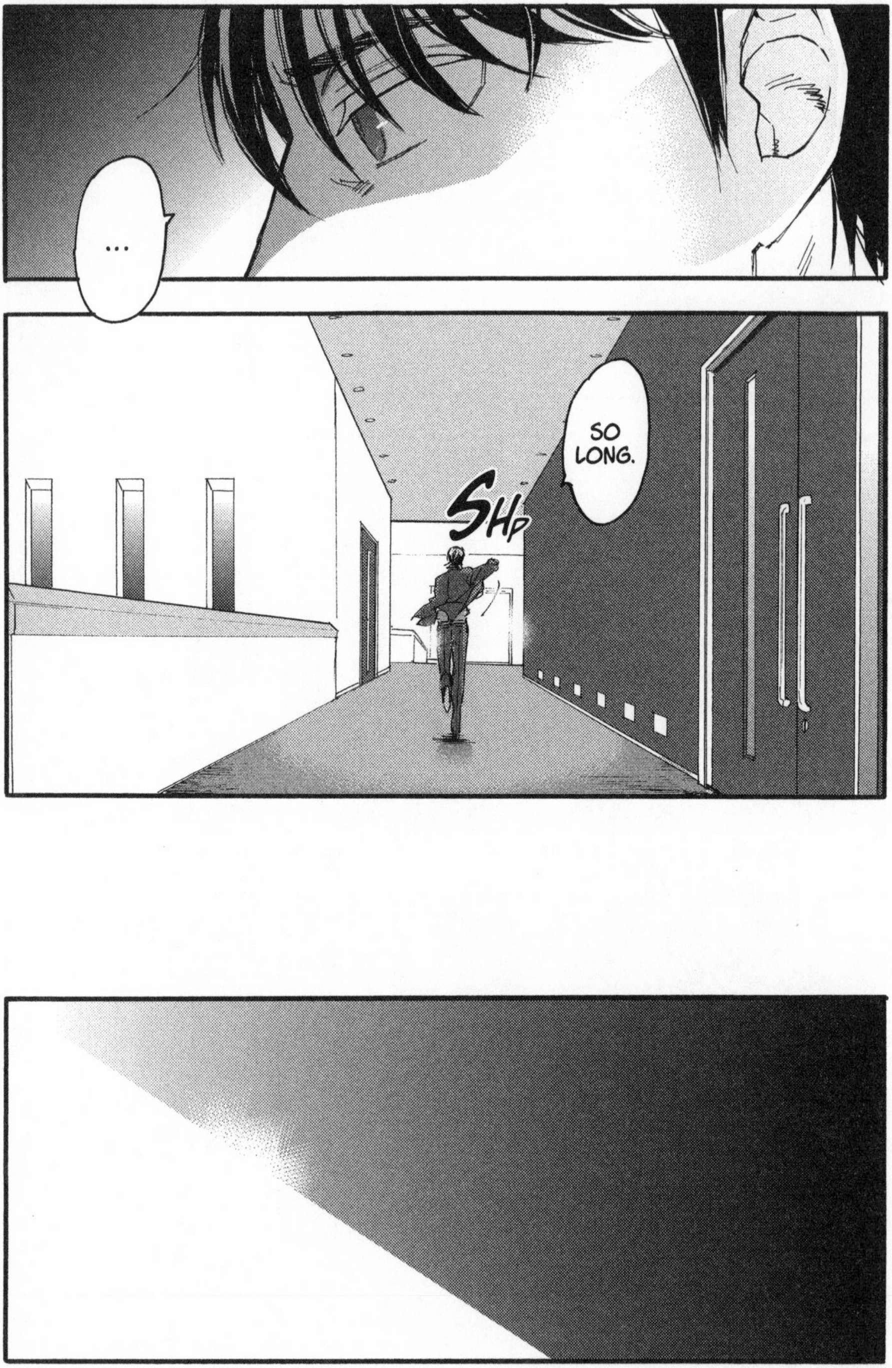
...
SO LONG.
SHp

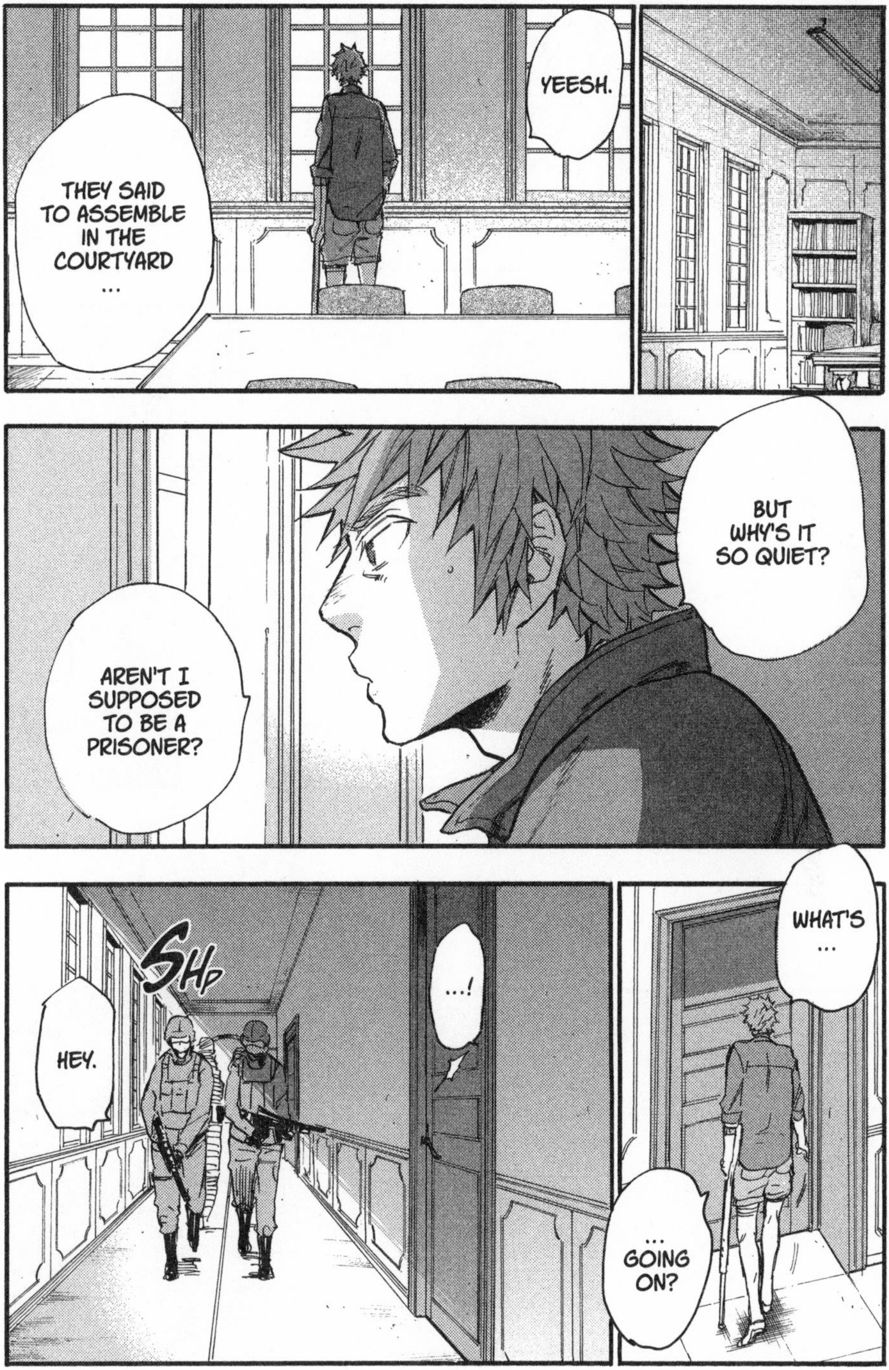
YEESH.
THEY SAID TO ASSEMBLE IN THE COURTYARD ...
BUT WHY'S IT SO QUIET?
AREN'T I SUPPOSED TO BE A PRISONER?
WHAT'S ...
... GOING ON?
...!
SHP
HEY.

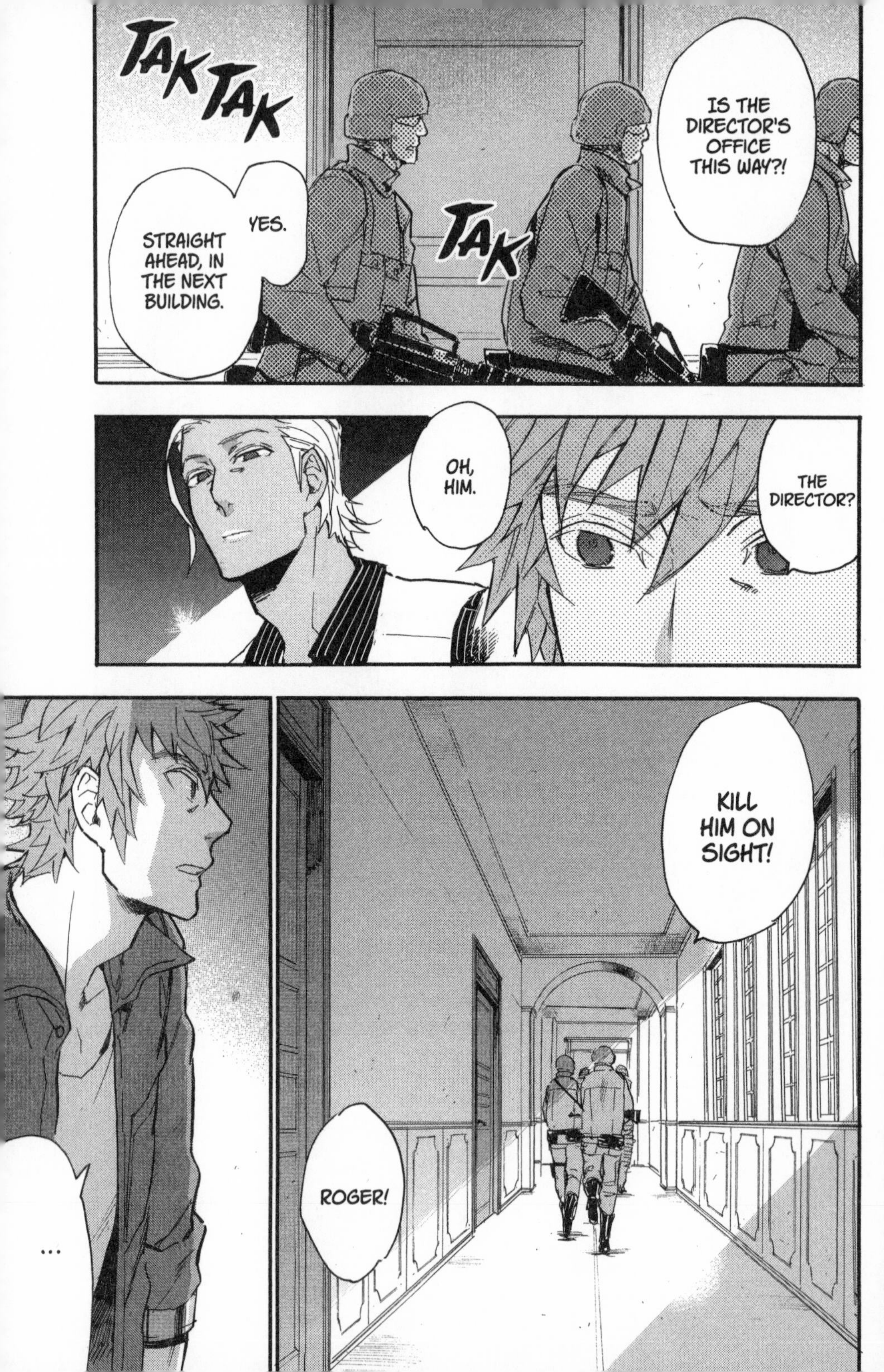
IS THE DIRECTOR'S OFFICE THIS WAY?!
TAK TAK
TAK
YES.
STRAIGHT AHEAD, IN THE NEXT BUILDING.
THE DIRECTOR?
OH, HIM.
KILL HIM ON SIGHT!
ROGER!
...

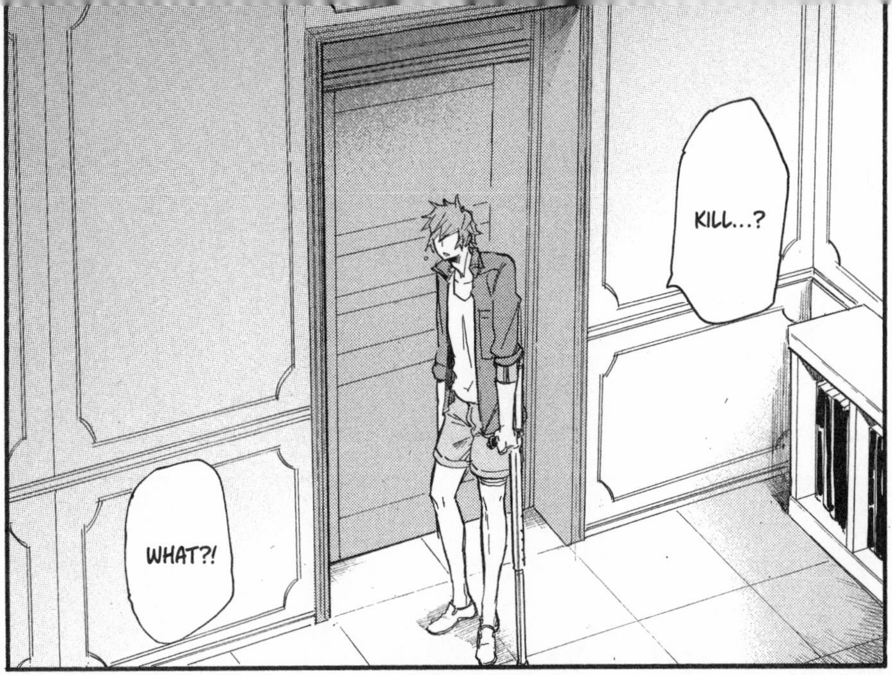
KILL...?
WHAT?!
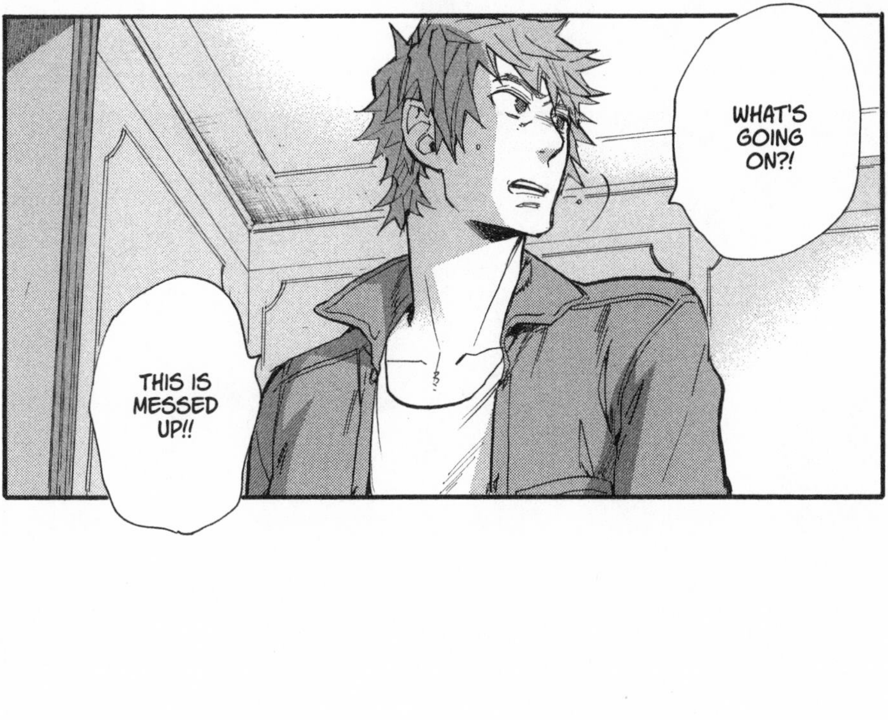
WHAT'S GOING ON?!
THIS IS MESSED UP!!

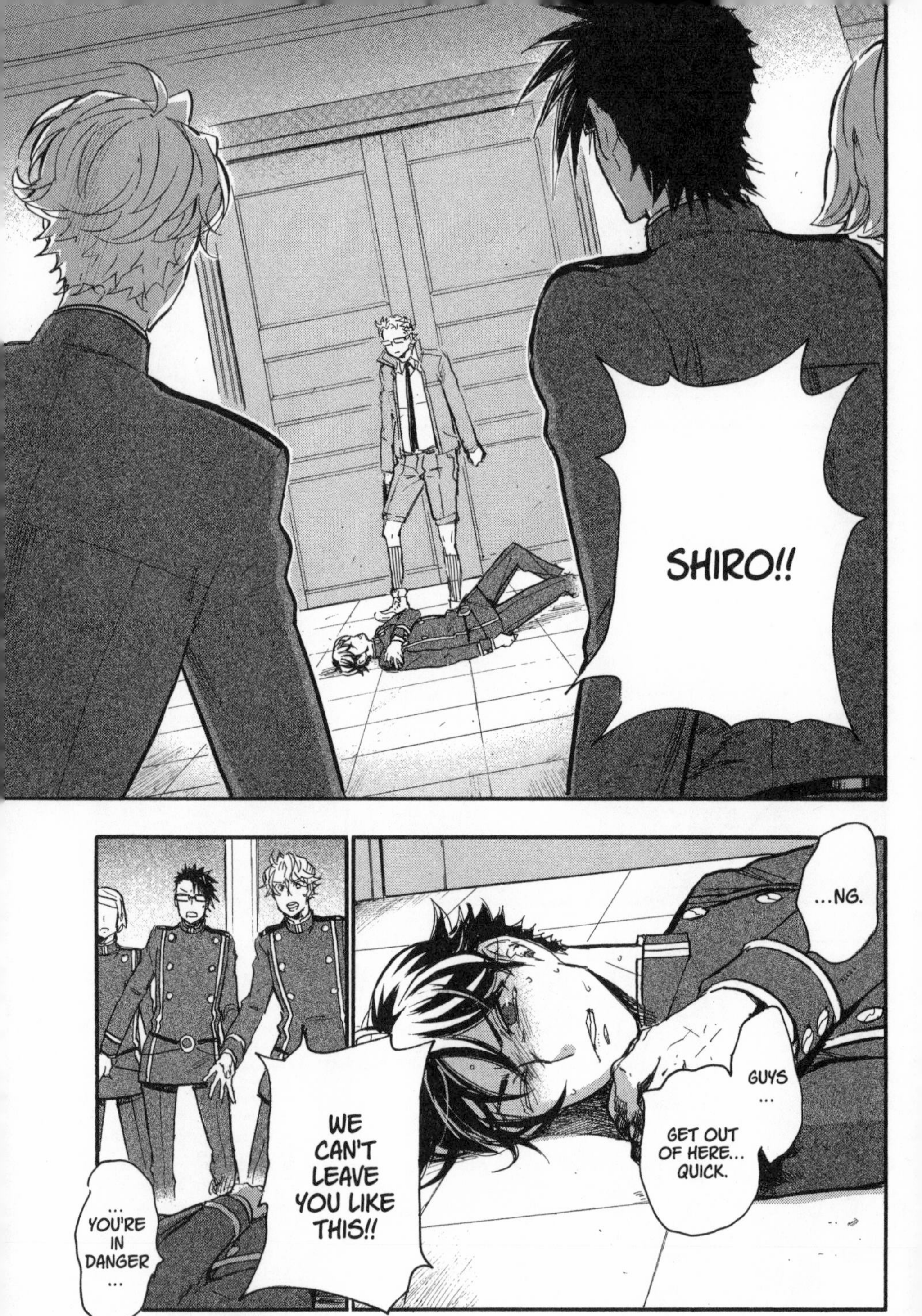
SHIRO!!
...NG.
GUYS ...
GET OUT OF HERE... QUICK.
WE CAN'T LEAVE YOU LIKE THIS!!
... YOU'RE IN DANGER ...

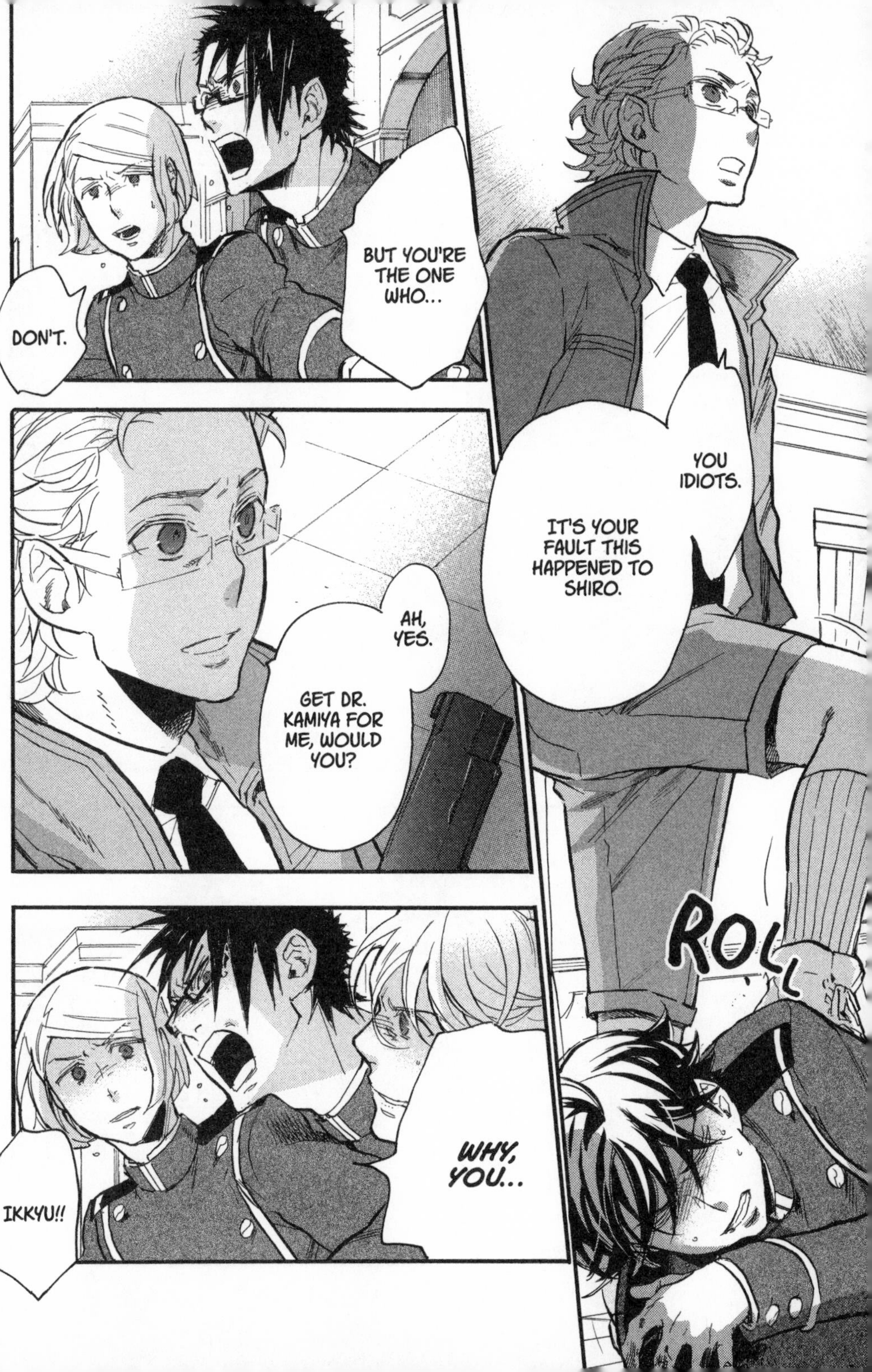
YOU IDIOTS.
IT'S YOUR FAULT THIS HAPPENED TO SHIRO.
ROLL
BUT YOU'RE THE ONE WHO...
DON'T.
AH, YES.
GET DR. KAMIYA FOR ME, WOULD YOU?
WHY, YOU...
IKKYU!!

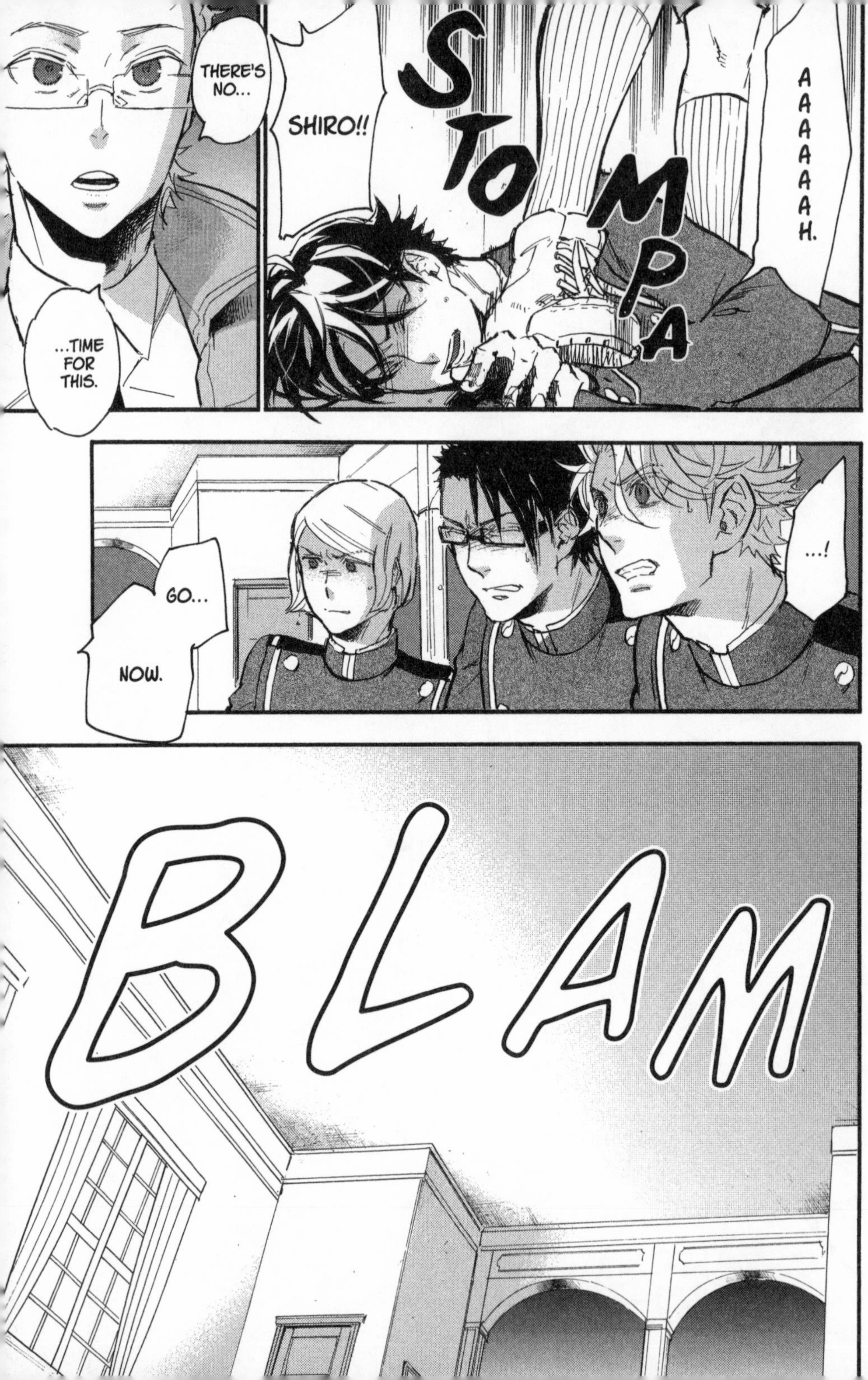
AAAAAAAH.
STOMPA
SHIRO!!
THERE'S NO...
...TIME FOR THIS.
...!
GO...
NOW.
BLAM

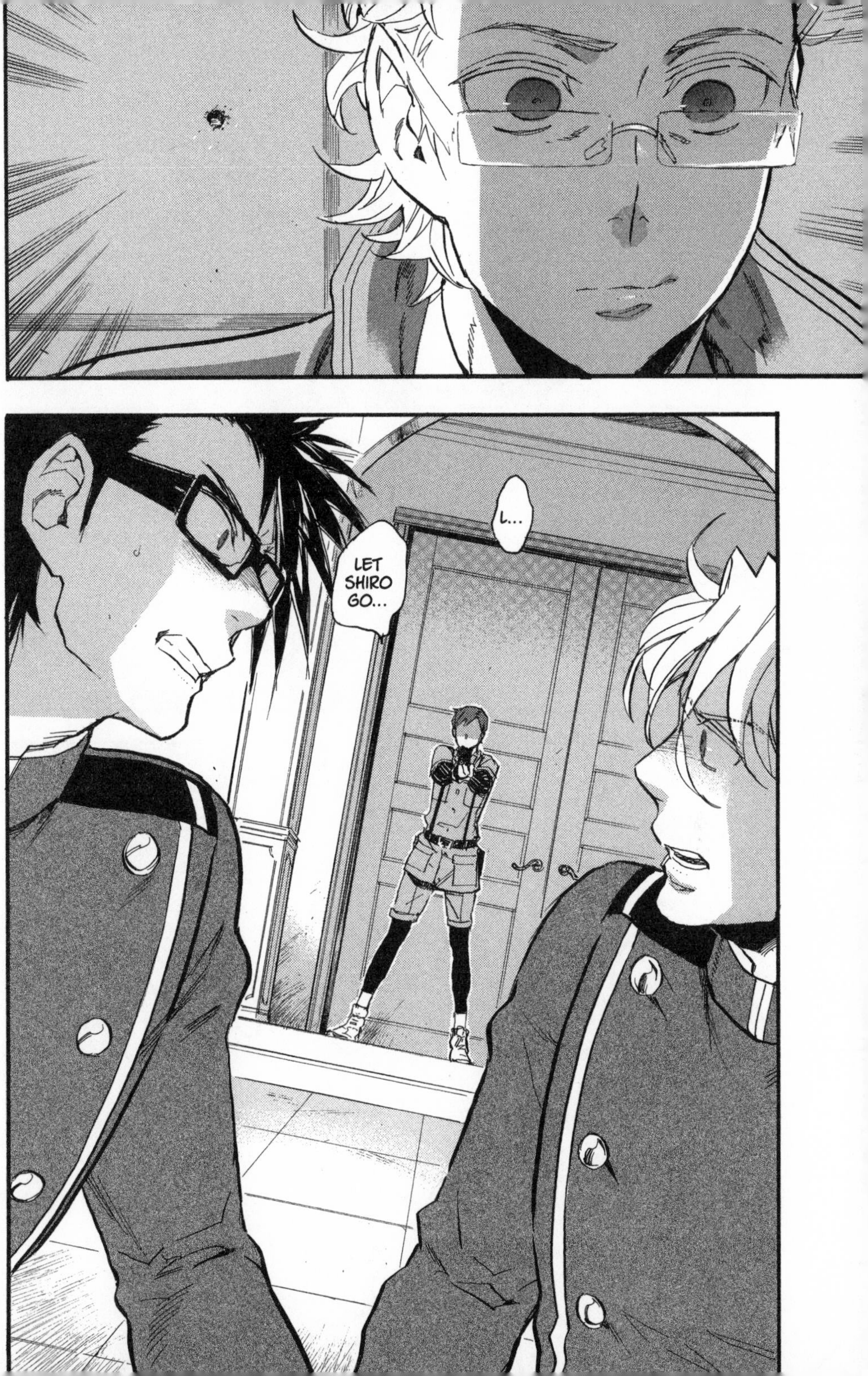
I...
LET SHIRO GO...

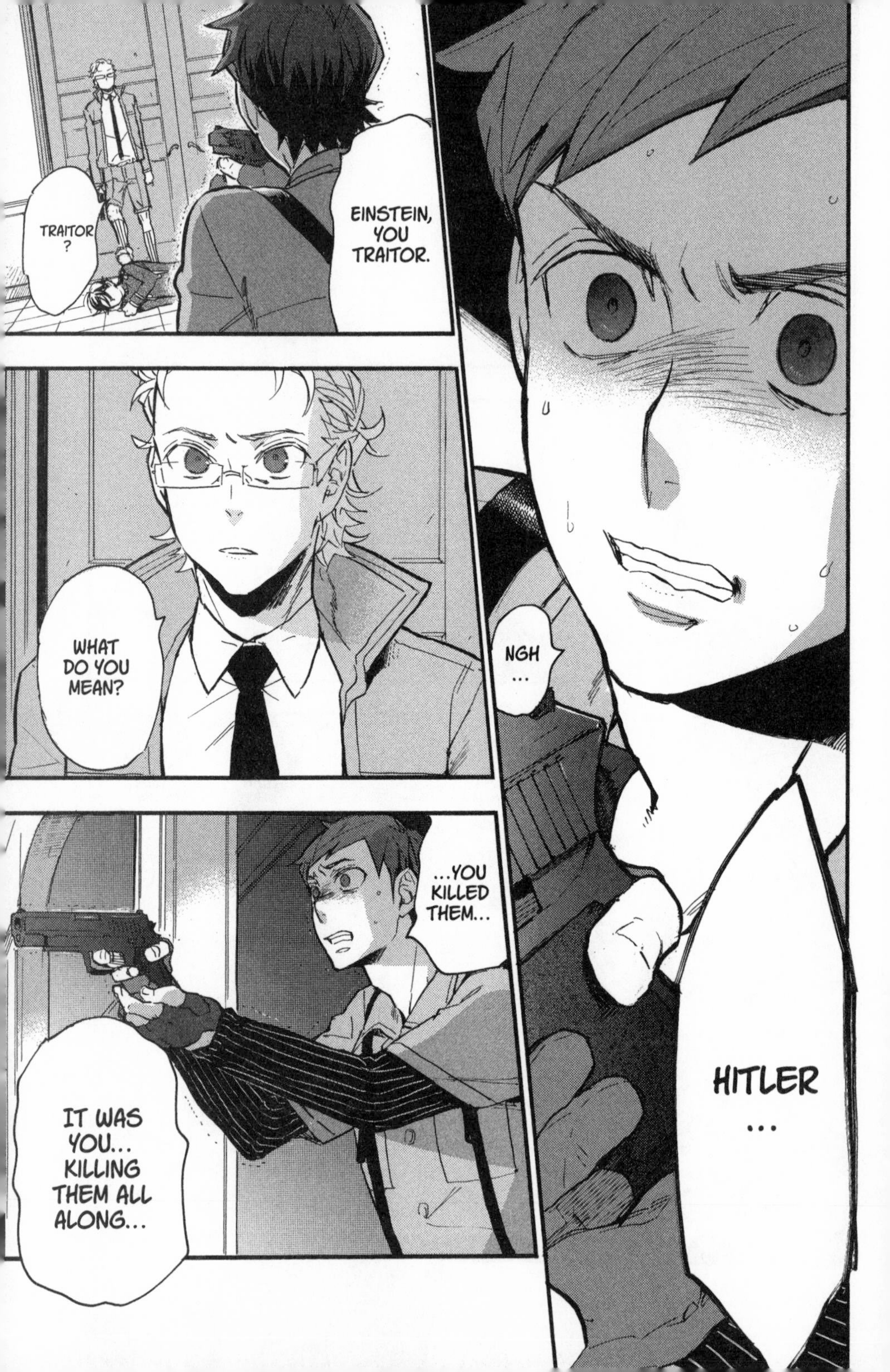
NGH...
HITLER...
EINSTEIN, YOU TRAITOR.
TRAITOR?
WHAT DO YOU MEAN?
...YOU KILLED THEM...
IT WAS YOU... KILLING THEM ALL ALONG...

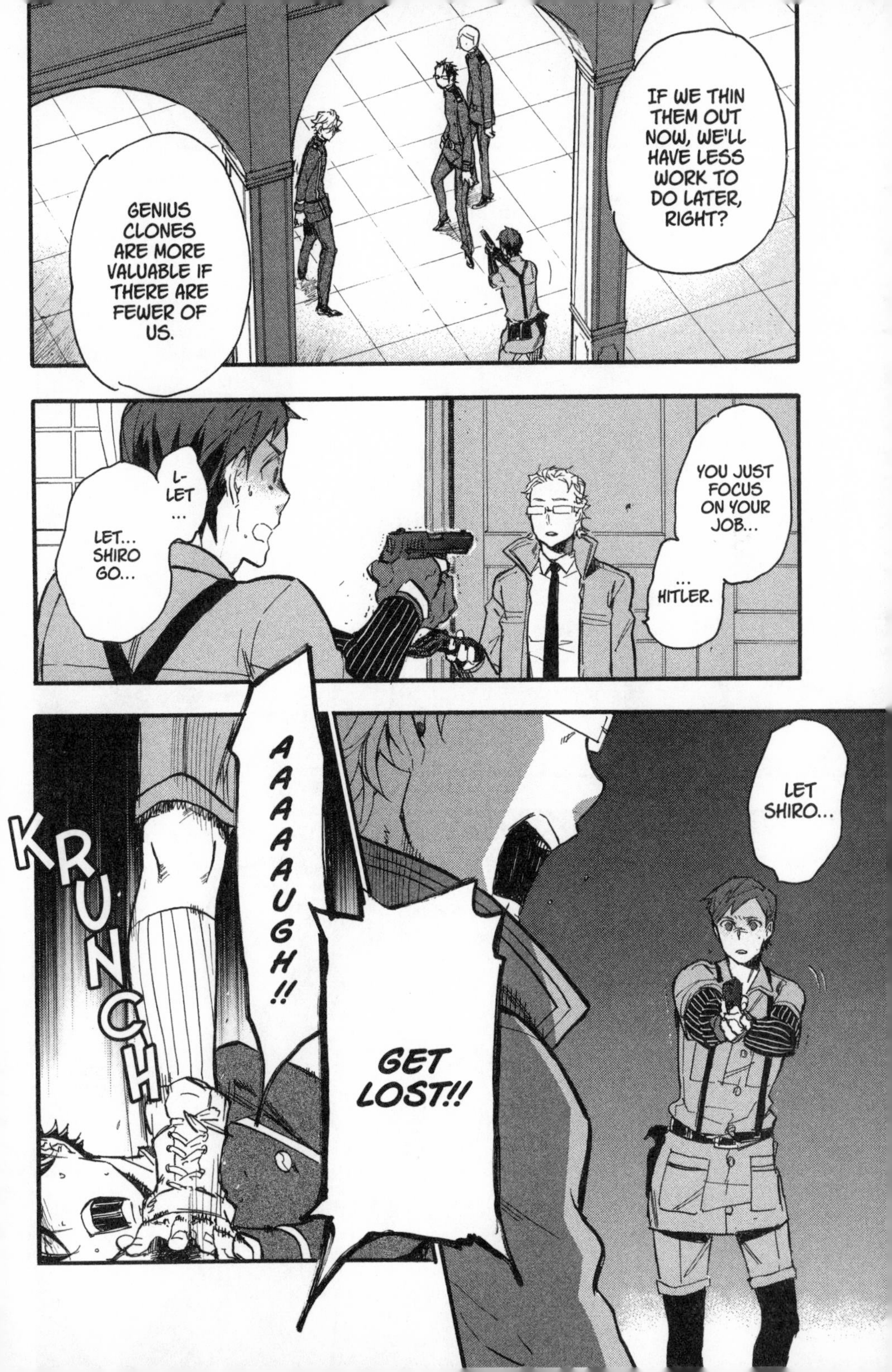
IF WE THIN THEM OUT NOW, WE'LL HAVE LESS WORK TO DO LATER, RIGHT?
GENIUS CLONES ARE MORE VALUABLE IF THERE ARE FEWER OF US.
YOU JUST FOCUS ON YOUR JOB...
... HITLER.
L-LET...
LET... SHIRO GO...
LET SHIRO...
AAAAAUGH!!
GET LOST!!
KRUNCH

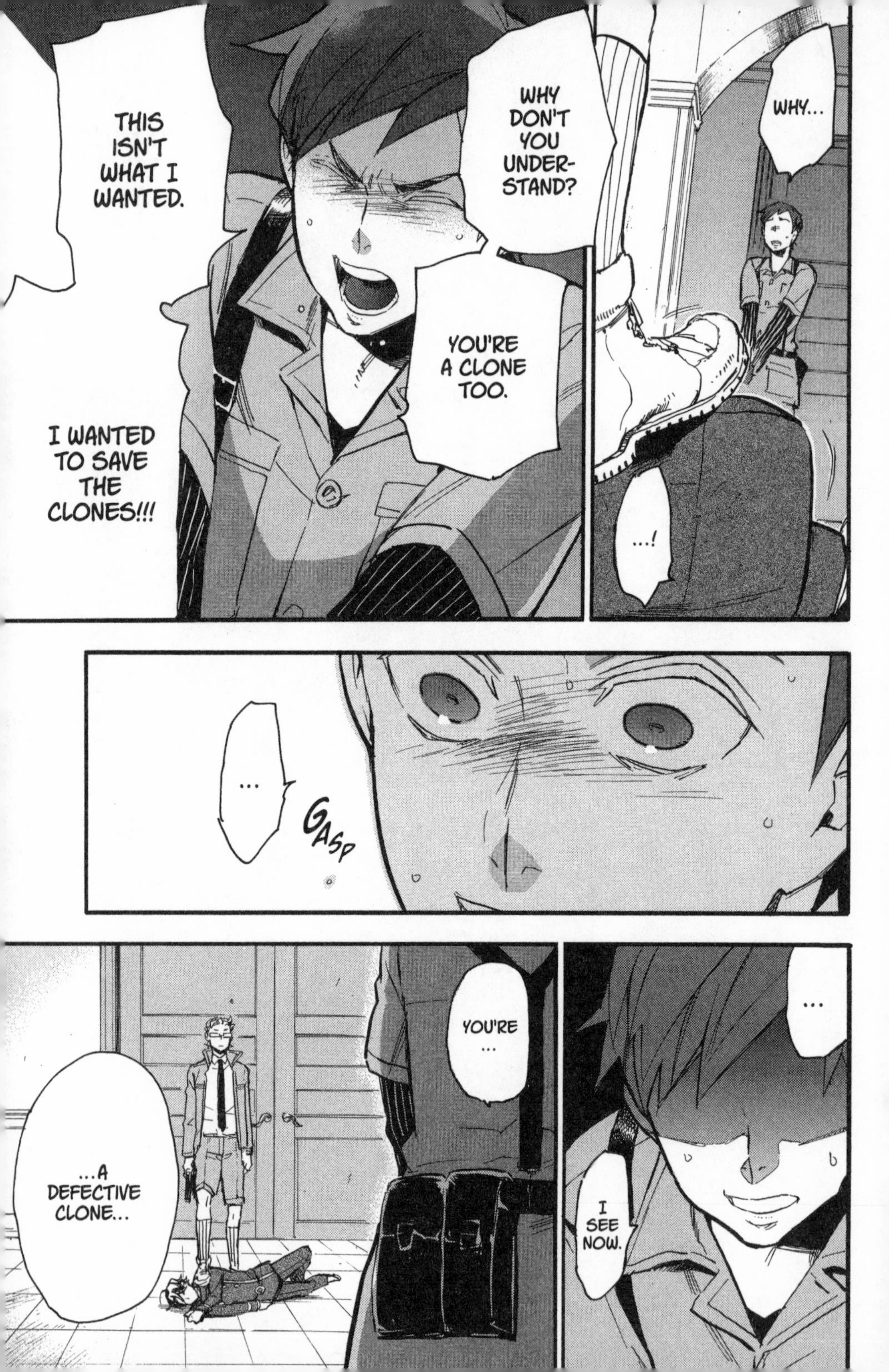
WHY...
...!
WHY DON'T YOU UNDERSTAND?
THIS ISN'T WHAT I WANTED.
YOU'RE A CLONE TOO.
I WANTED TO SAVE THE CLONES!!!
...
GASP
...
I SEE NOW.
YOU'RE ...
...A DEFECTIVE CLONE...

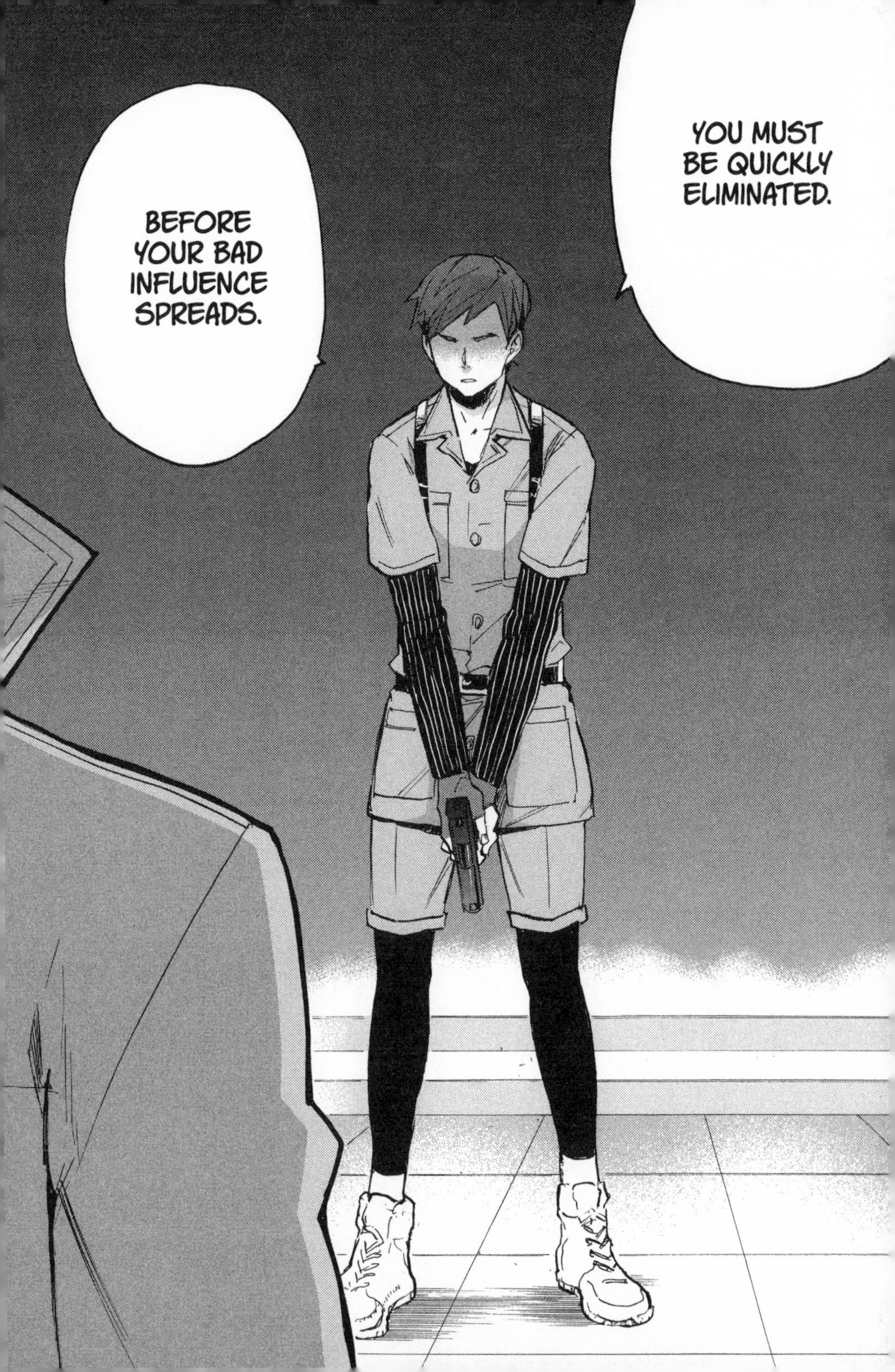
YOU MUST BE QUICKLY ELIMINATED.
BEFORE YOUR BAD INFLUENCE SPREADS.

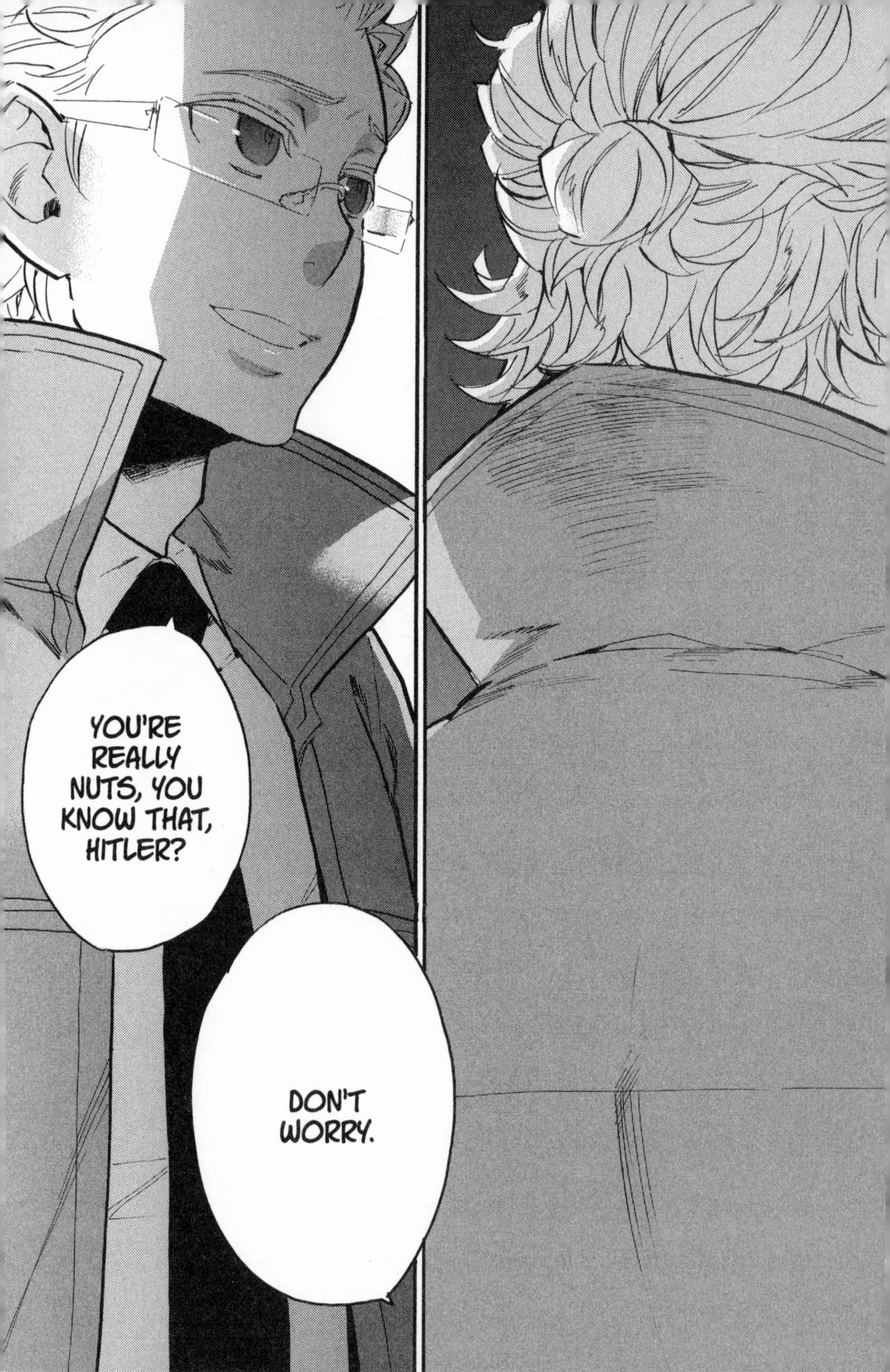
YOU'RE REALLY NUTS, YOU KNOW THAT, HITLER?
DON'T WORRY.

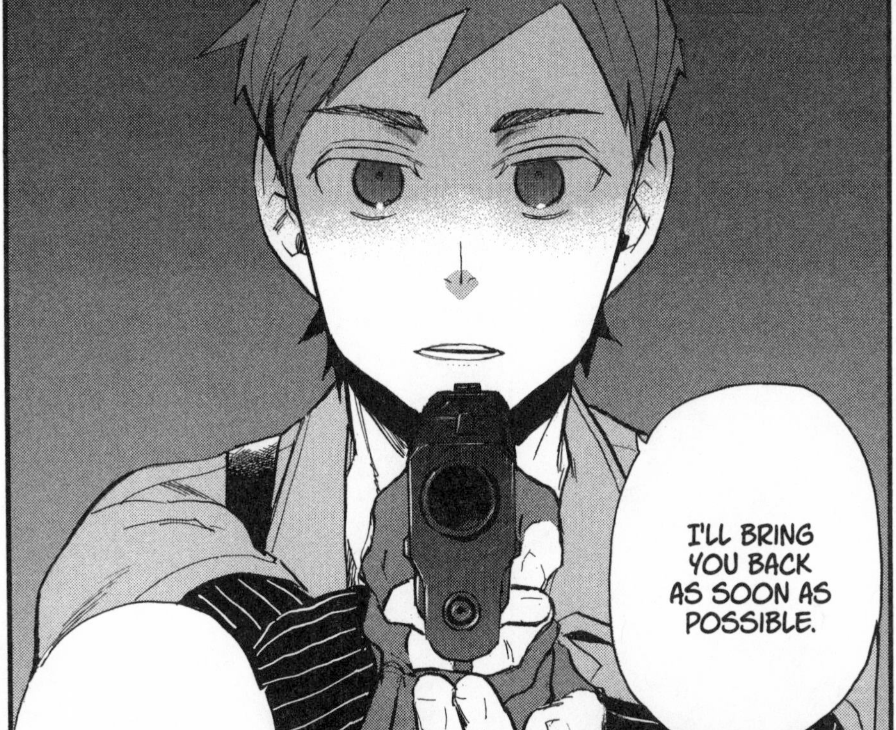
I'LL BRING YOU BACK AS SOON AS POSSIBLE.
LET'S START OVER, EINSTEIN.

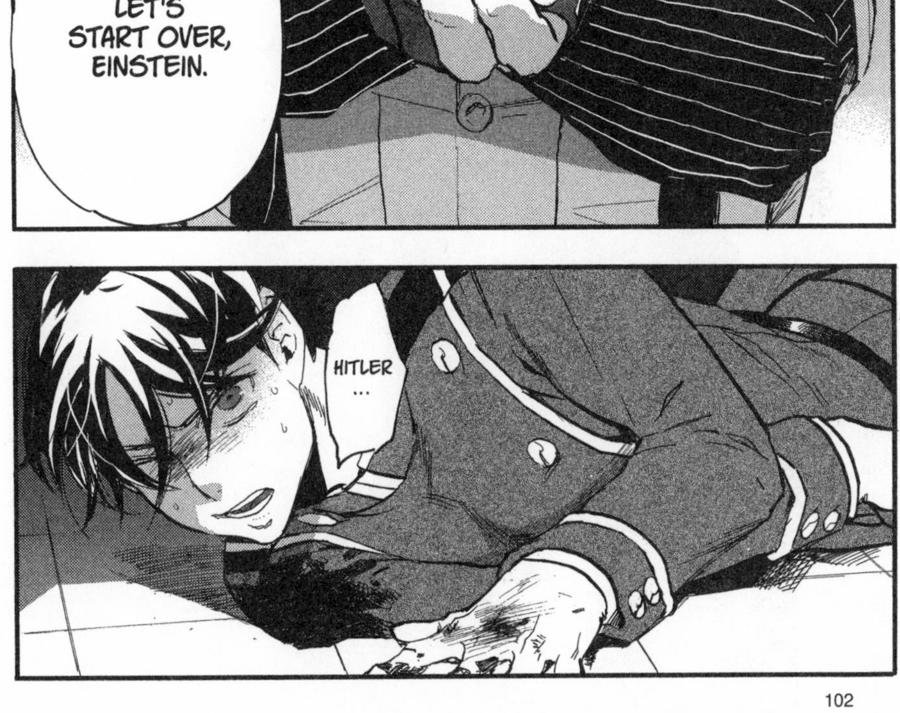
HITLER ...

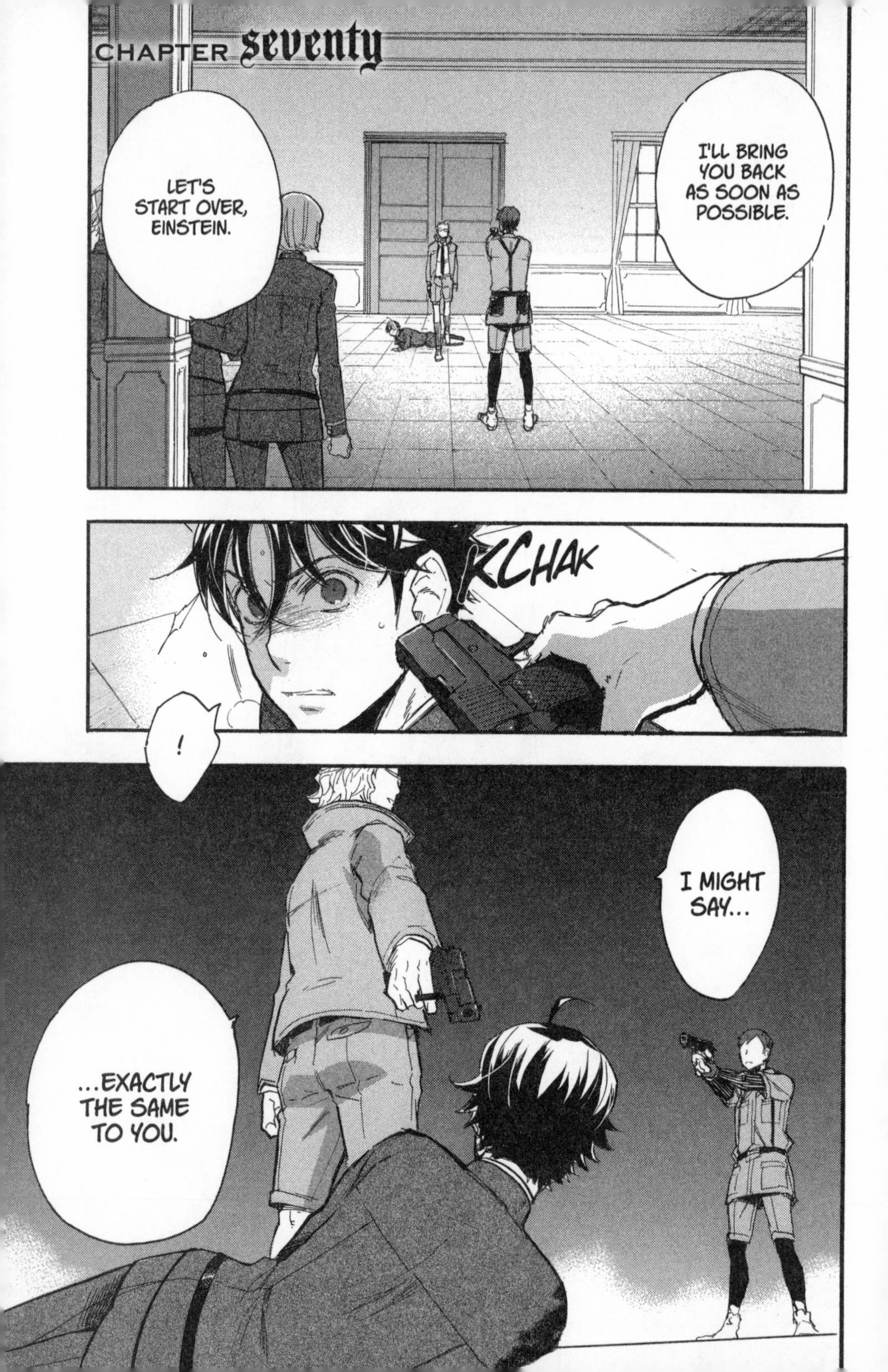
CHAPTER seventy
I'LL BRING YOU BACK AS SOON AS POSSIBLE.
LET'S START OVER, EINSTEIN.
KCHAK
!
I MIGHT SAY...
...EXACTLY THE SAME TO YOU.

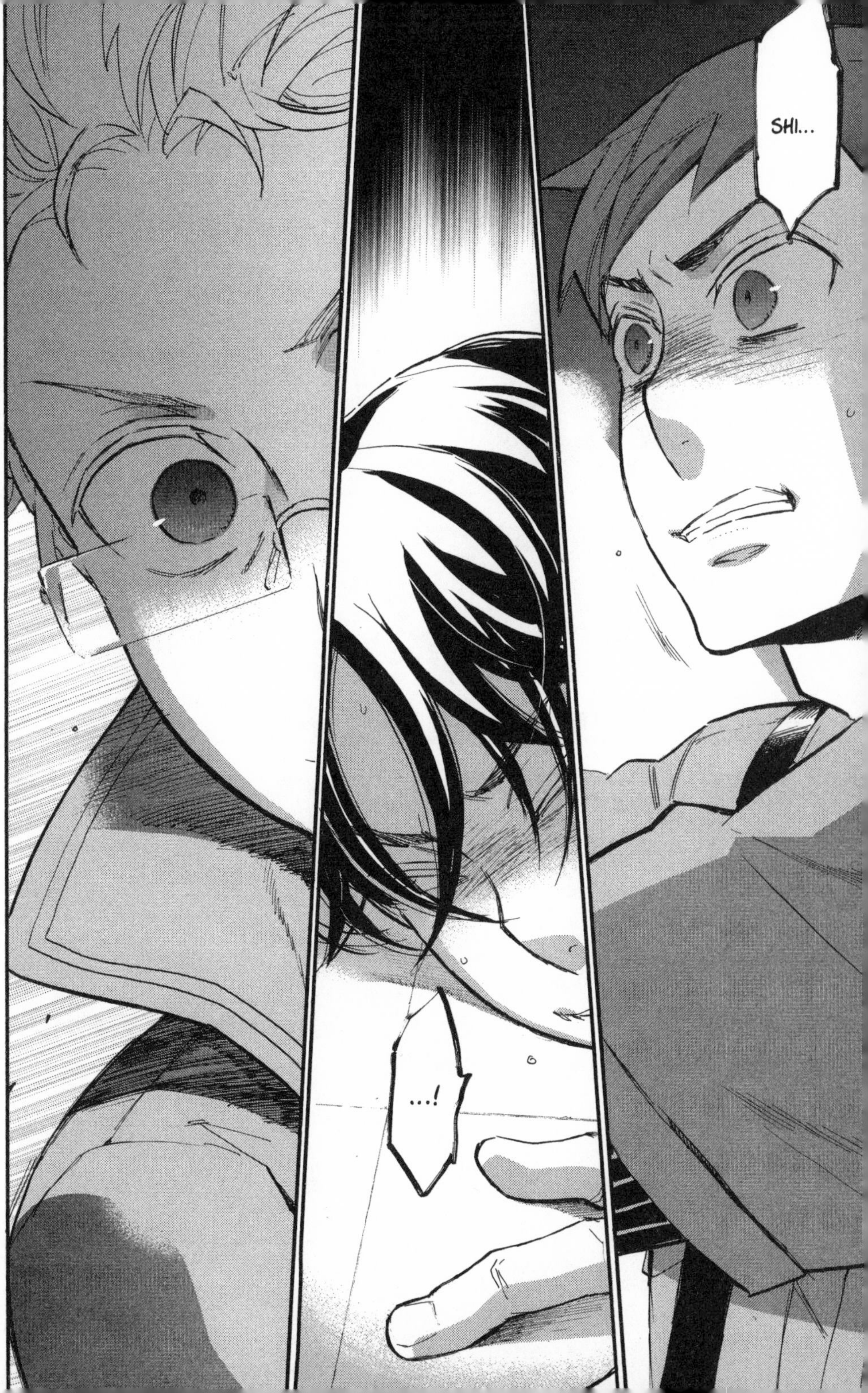
SHI...
...!

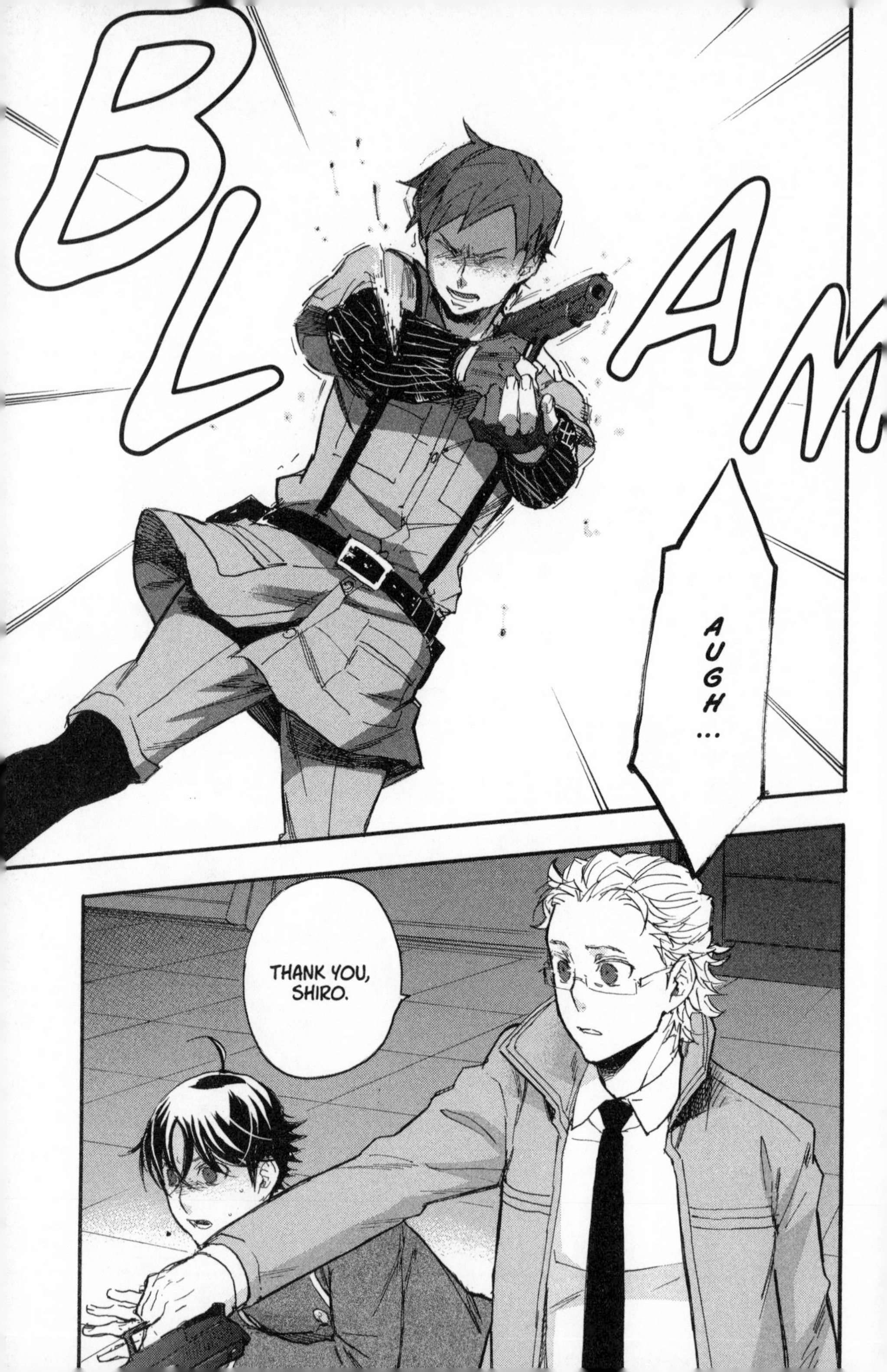
BLAM
AUGH...
THANK YOU, SHIRO.

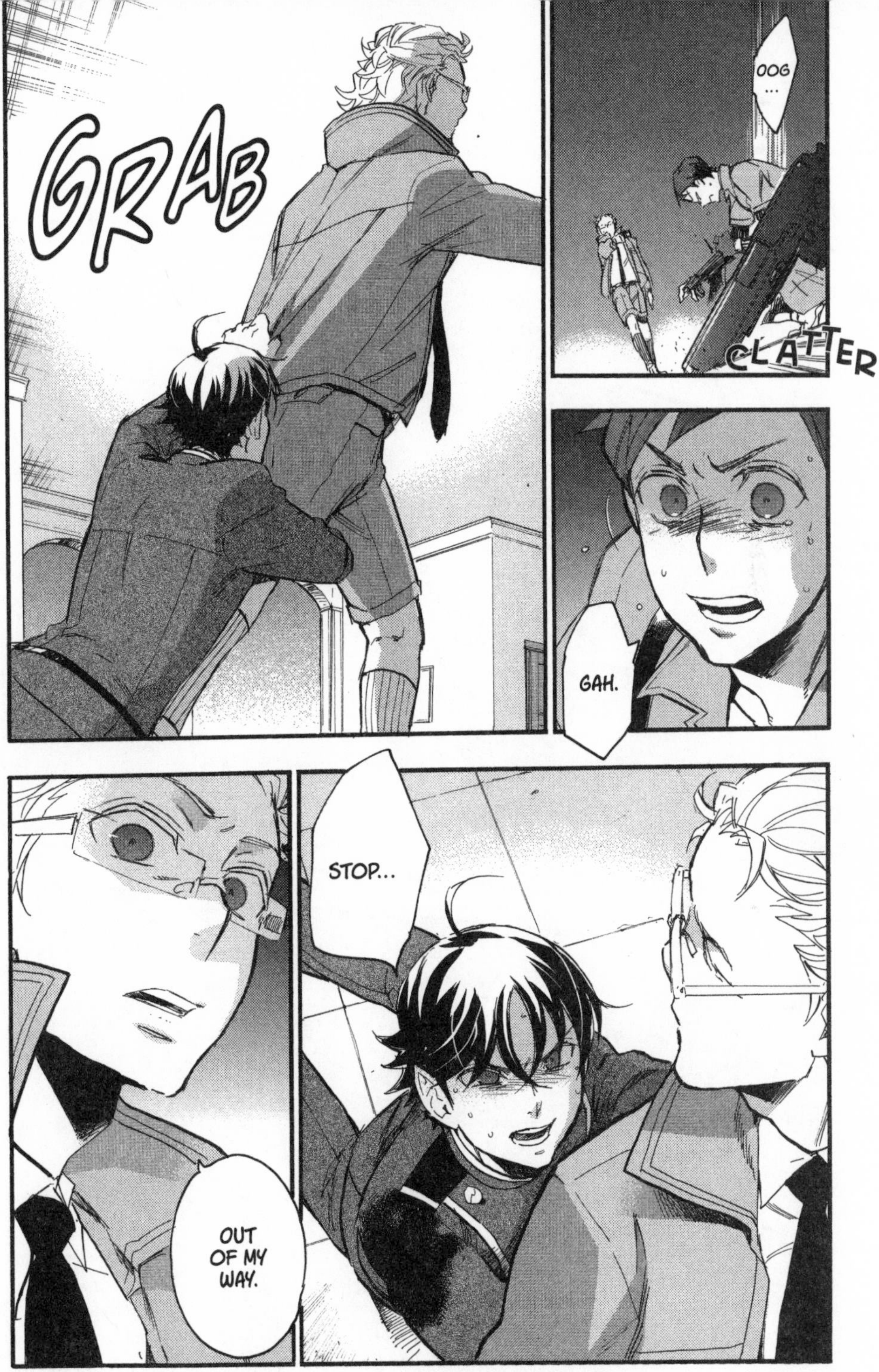
OOG ...
CLATTER
GAH.
GRAB
STOP...
OUT OF MY WAY.

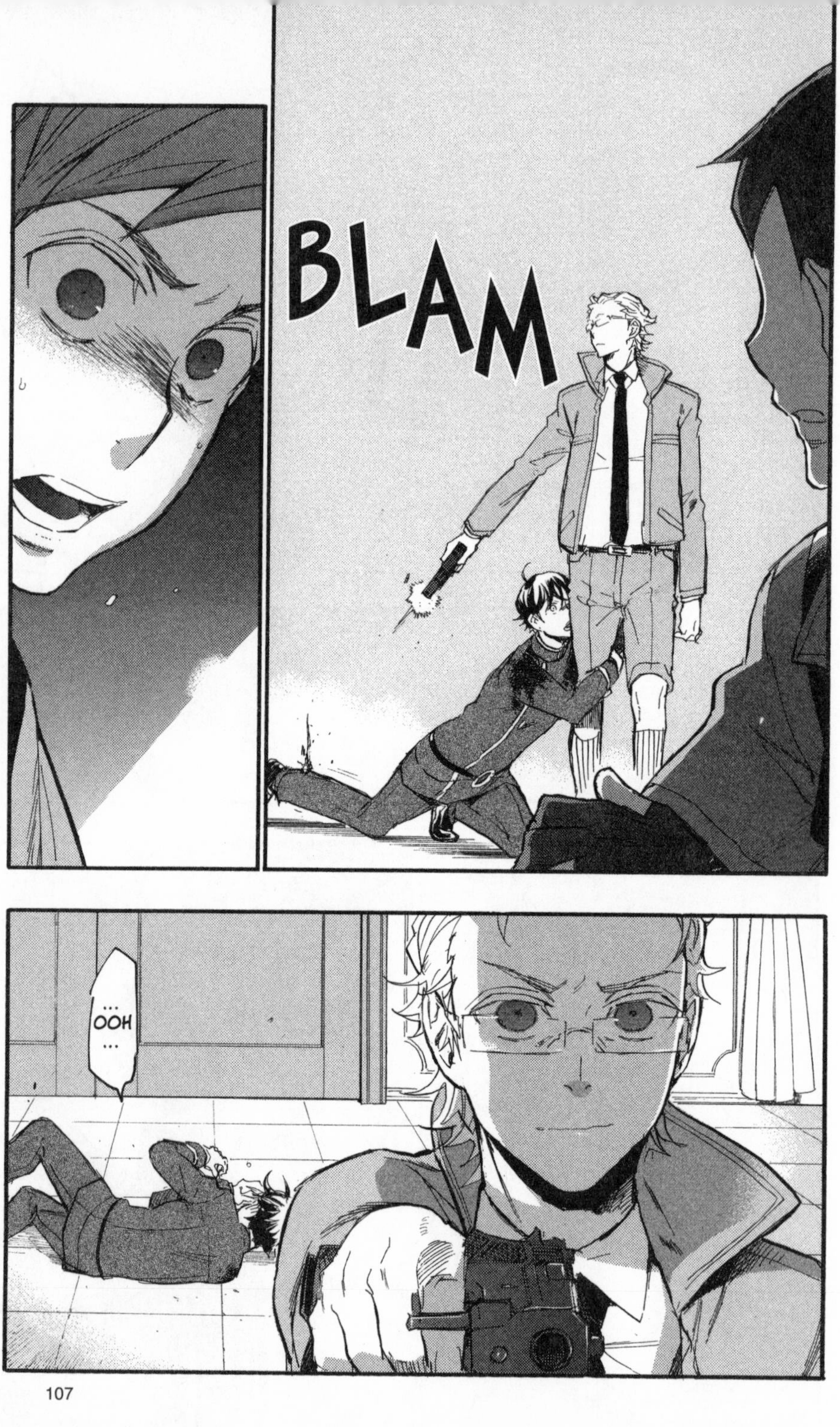
BLAM
...OOH...

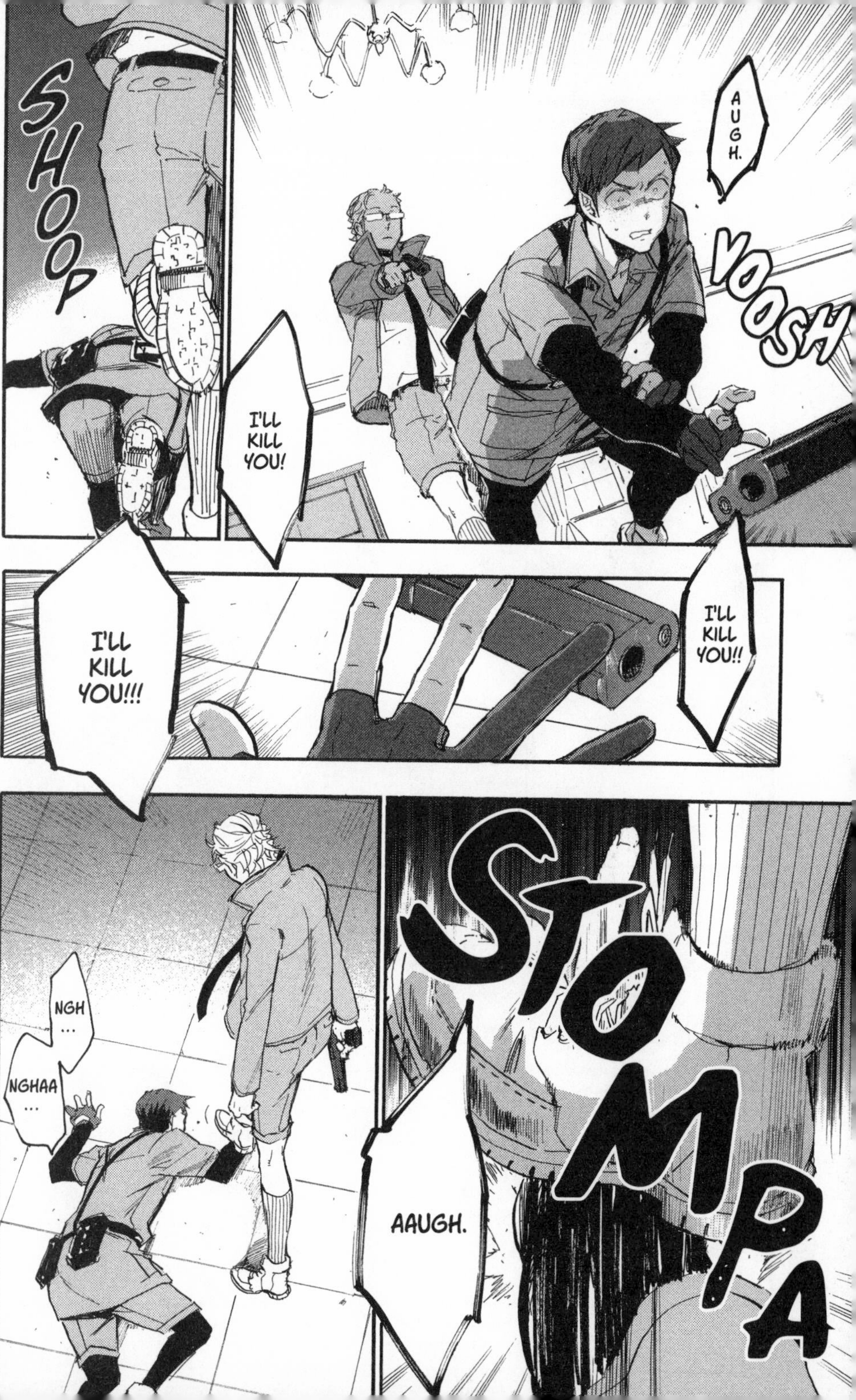
AUGH.
VOOSH
I'LL KILL YOU!
SHOOP
I'LL KILL YOU!!
I'LL KILL YOU!!!
STOMPA
AAUGH.
NGH…
NGHAA…

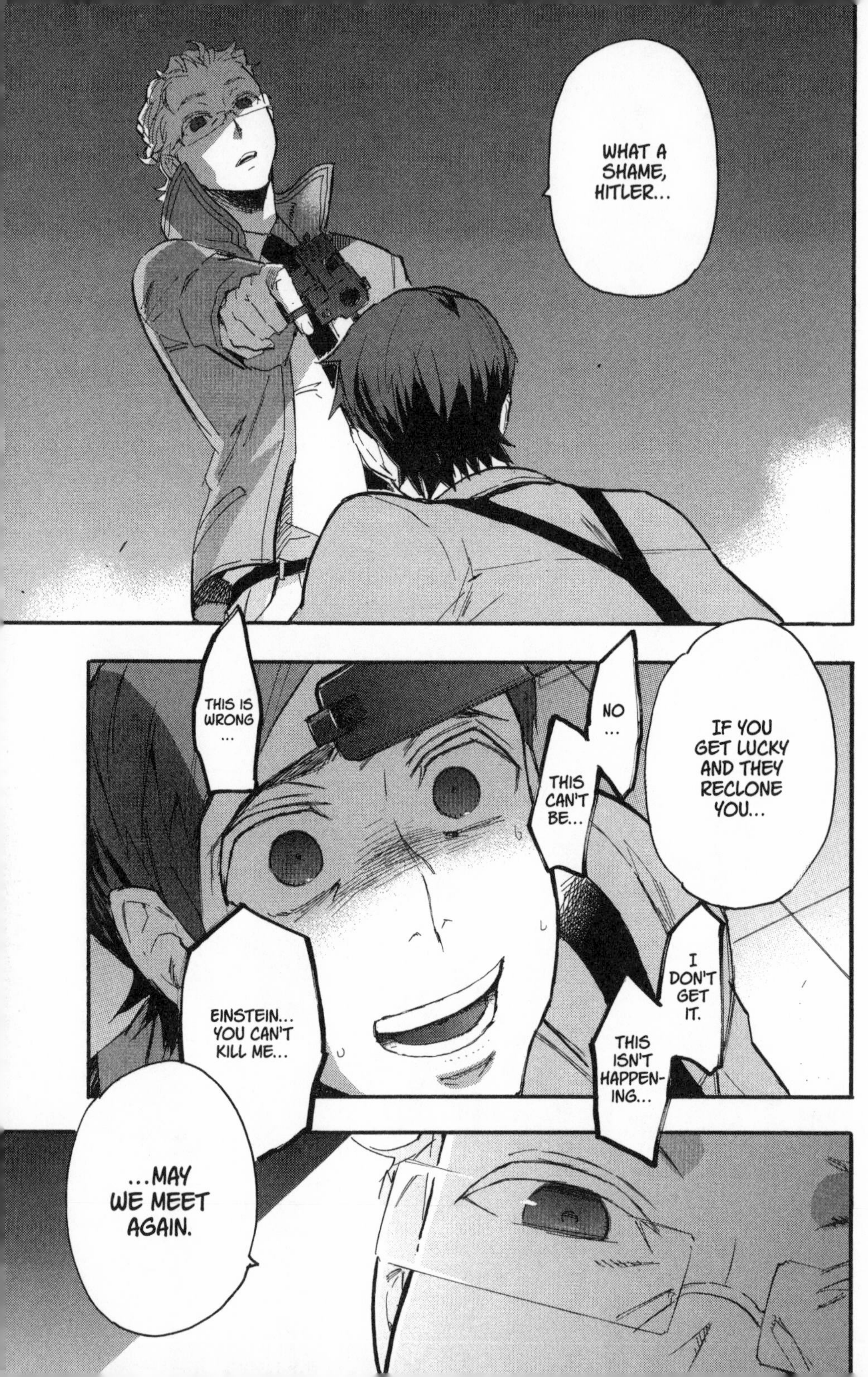
WHAT A SHAME, HITLER...
IF YOU GET LUCKY AND THEY RECLONE YOU...
NO...
THIS CAN'T BE...
THIS IS WRONG...
I DON'T GET IT.
THIS ISN'T HAPPEN-ING...
EINSTEIN... YOU CAN'T KILL ME...
...MAY WE MEET AGAIN.

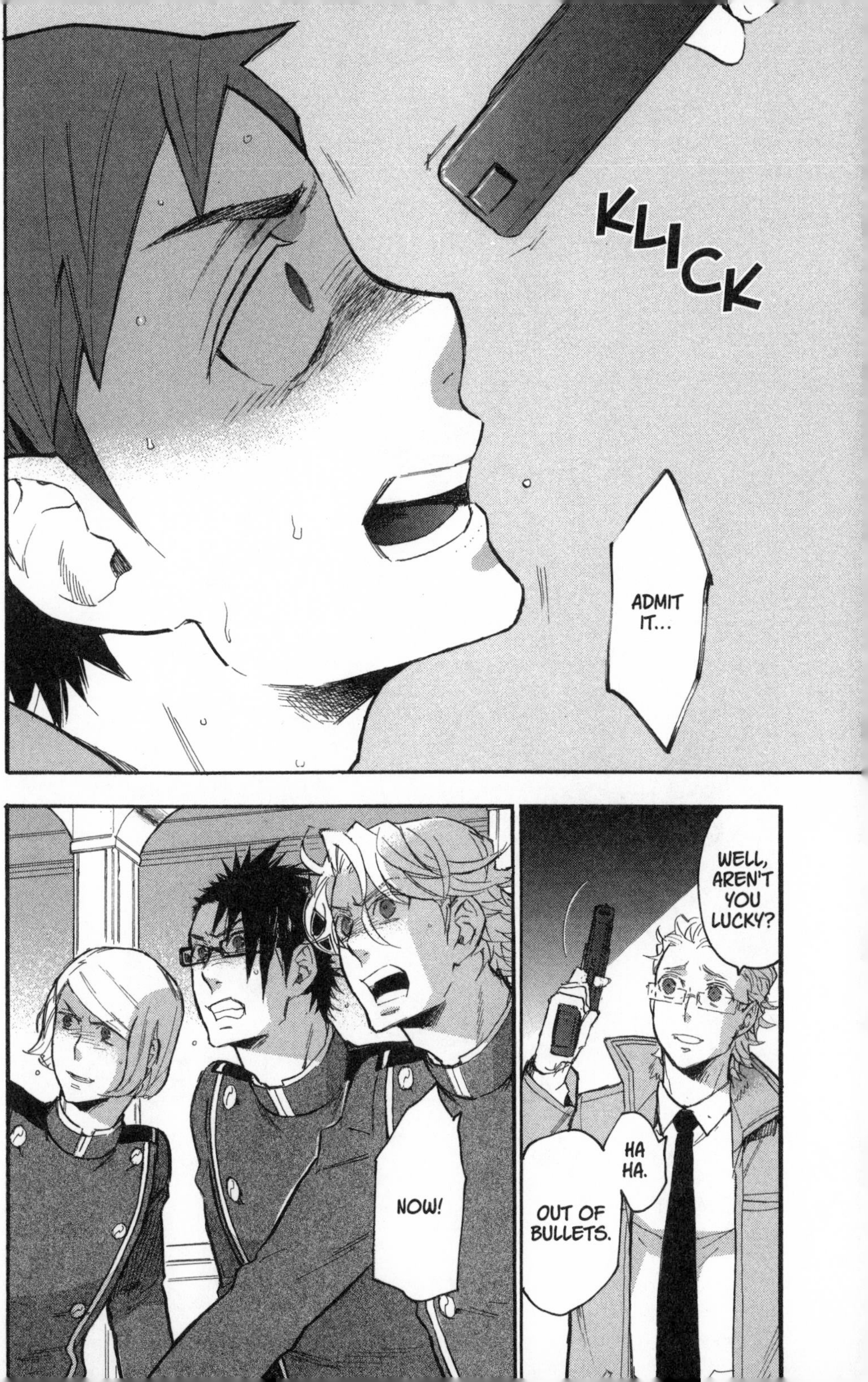
KLICK
ADMIT IT...
WELL, AREN'T YOU LUCKY?
HA HA.
OUT OF BULLETS.
NOW!

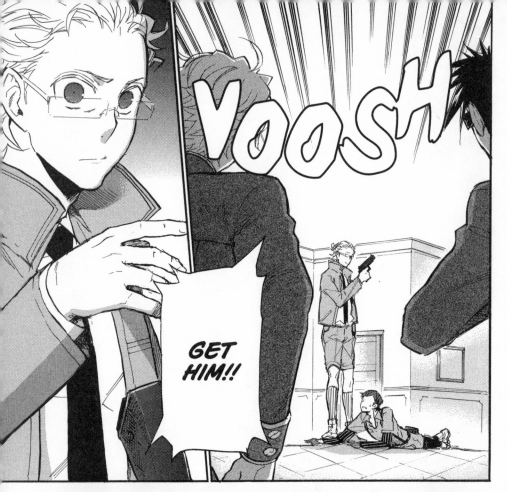

VOOSH

GET HIM!!

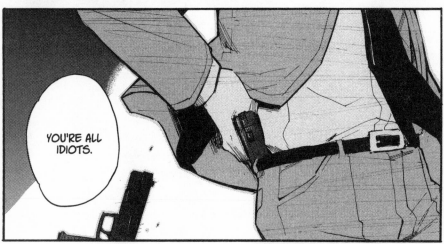

YOU'RE ALL IDIOTS.

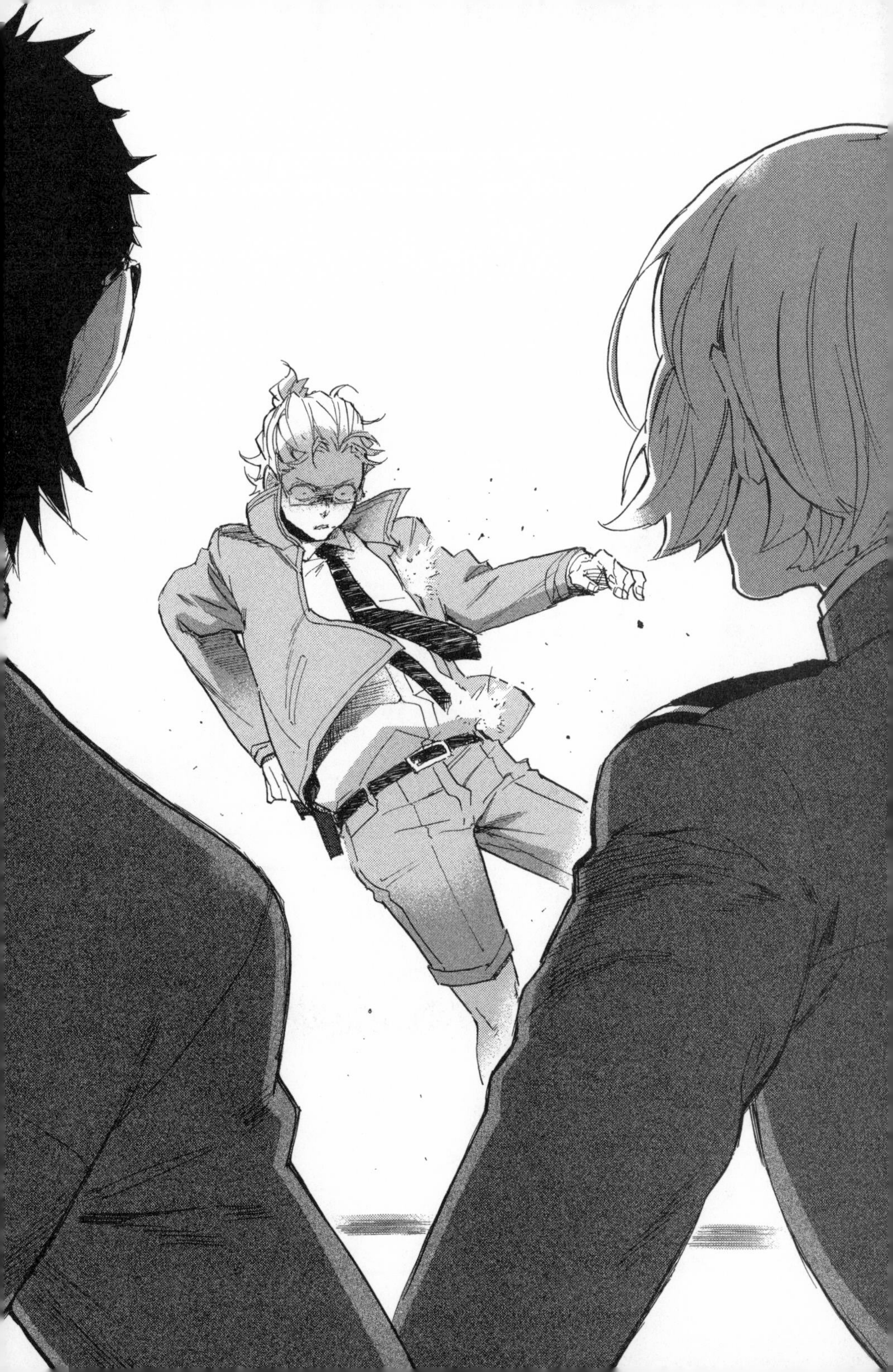

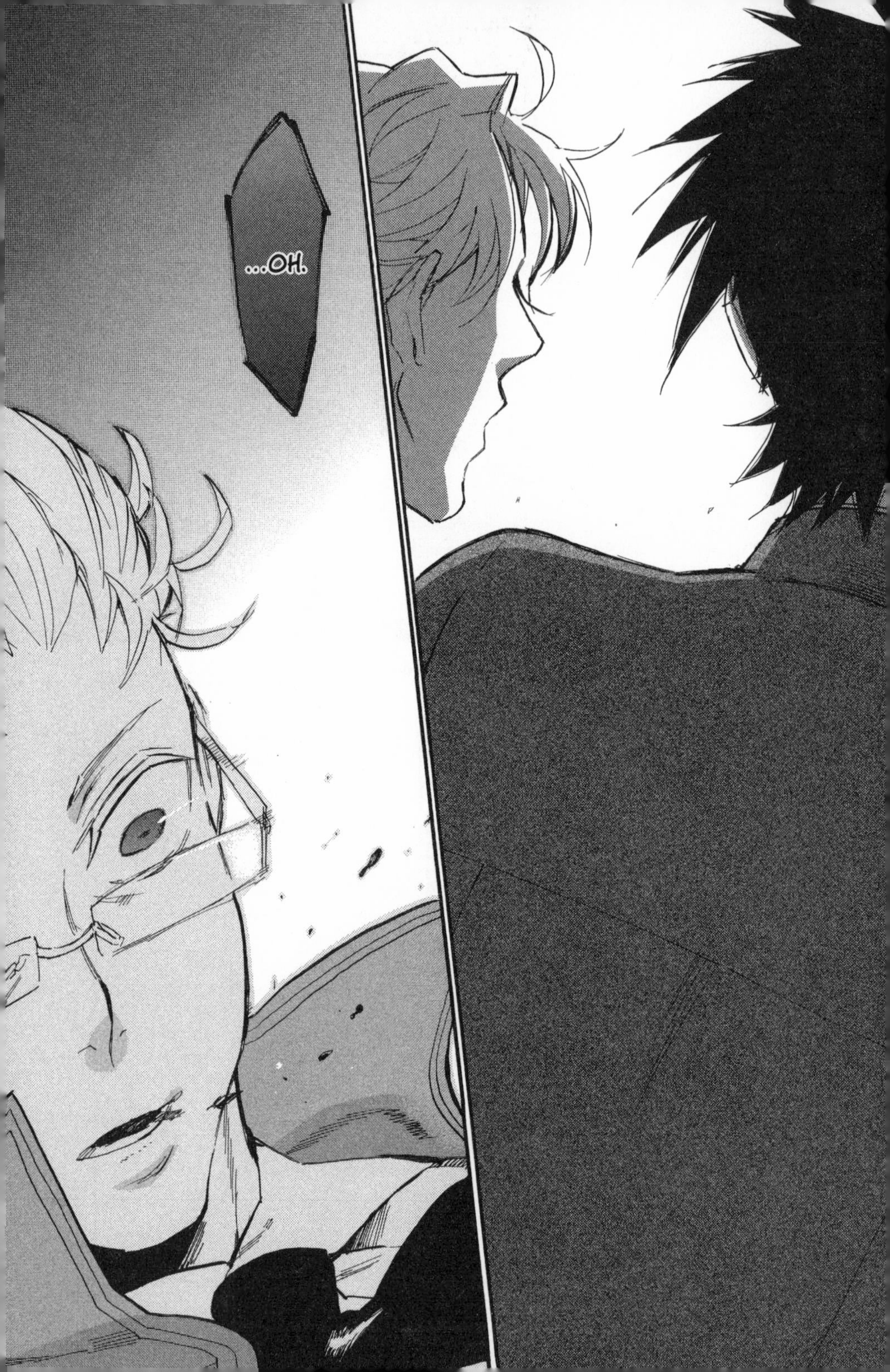
...OH.

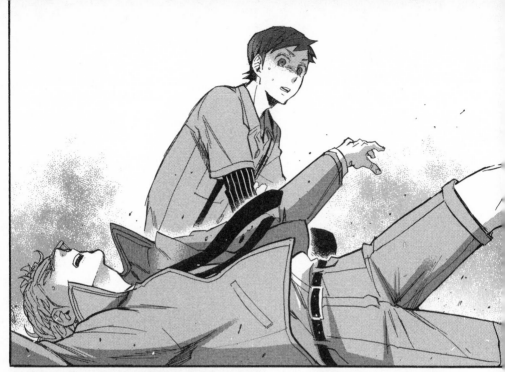

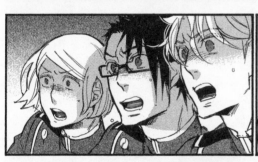

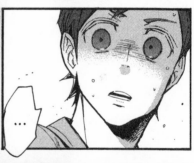

...

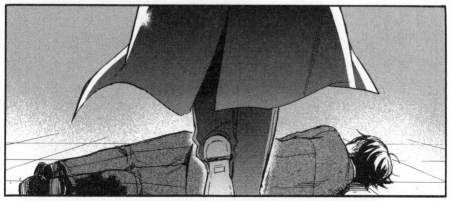

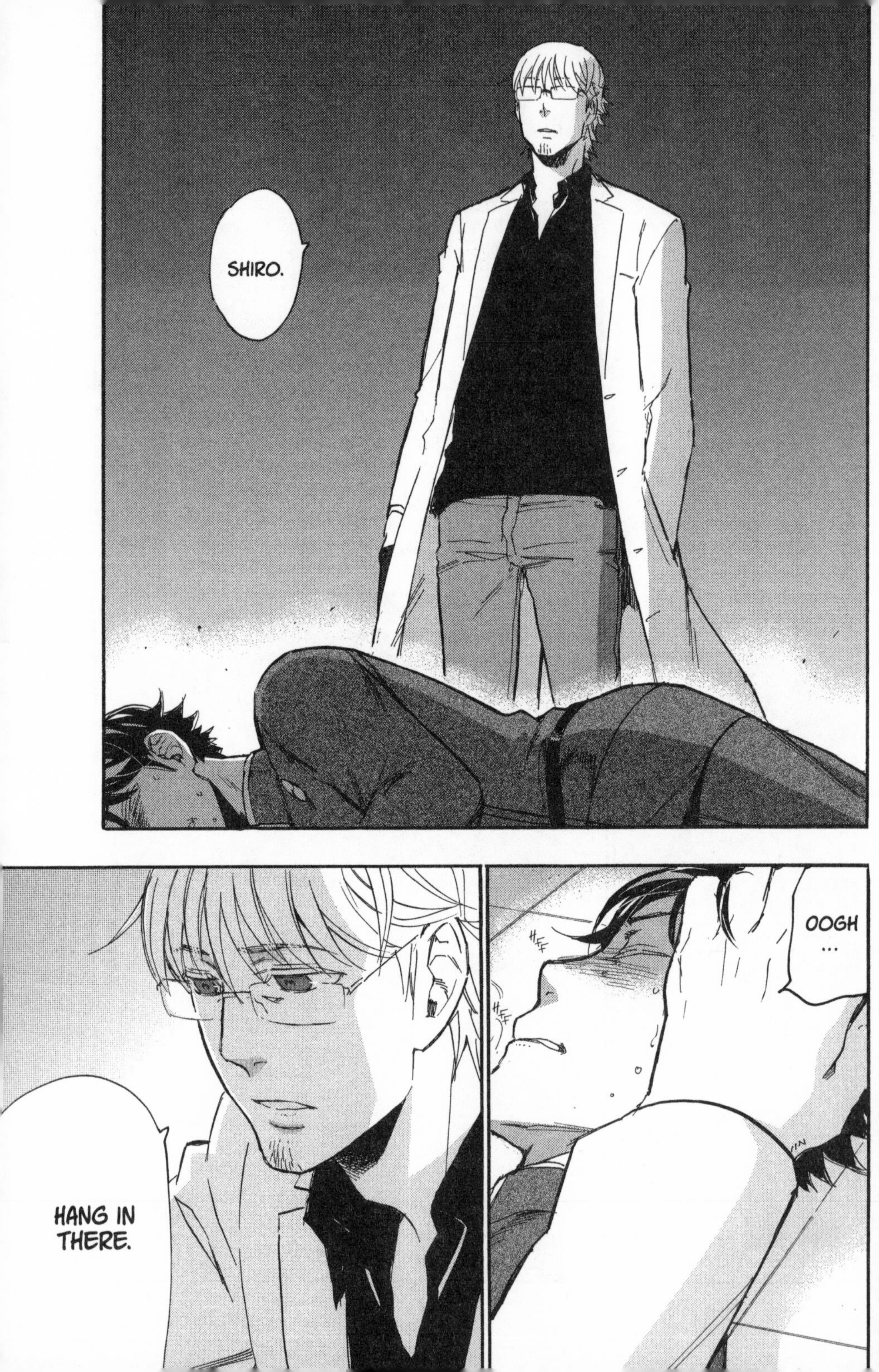
SHIRO.
OOGH ...
HEF
HEF
HANG IN THERE.

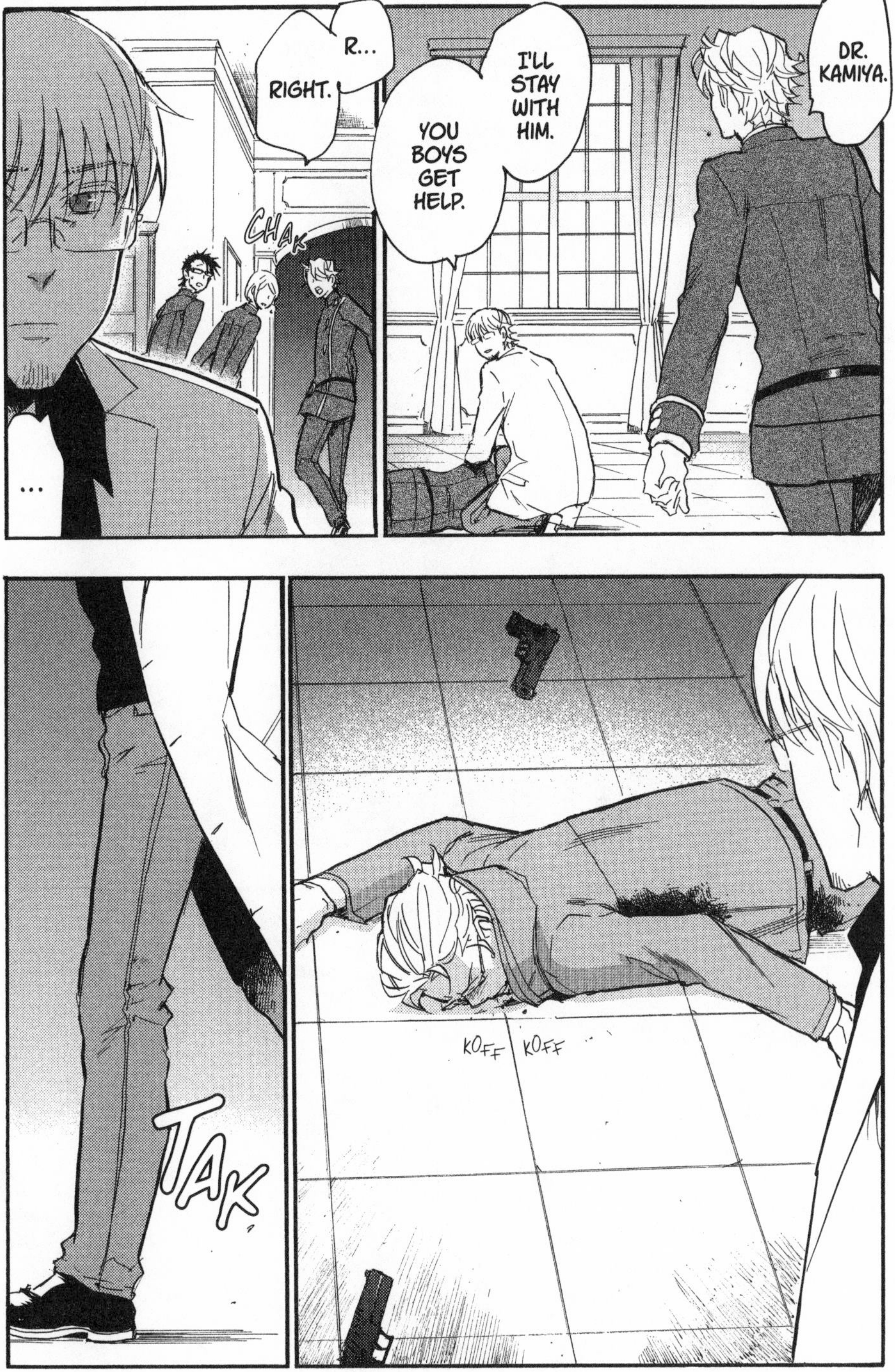
DR. KAMIYA.
I'LL STAY WITH HIM.
YOU BOYS GET HELP.
R...
RIGHT.
CHAK
...
KOFF KOFF
TAK

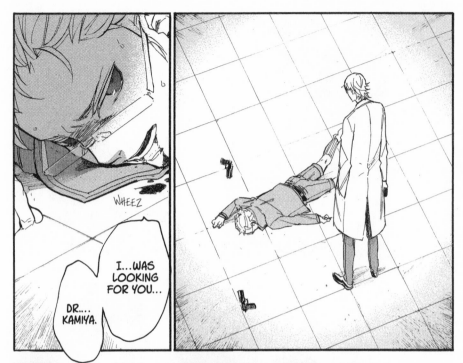

WHEEZ

I...WAS LOOKING FOR YOU...

DR.... KAMIYA.

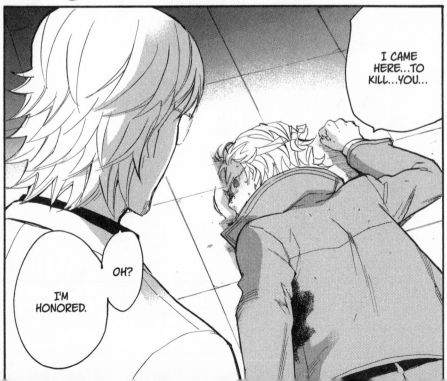

I CAME HERE...TO KILL...YOU...

OH?

I'M HONORED.

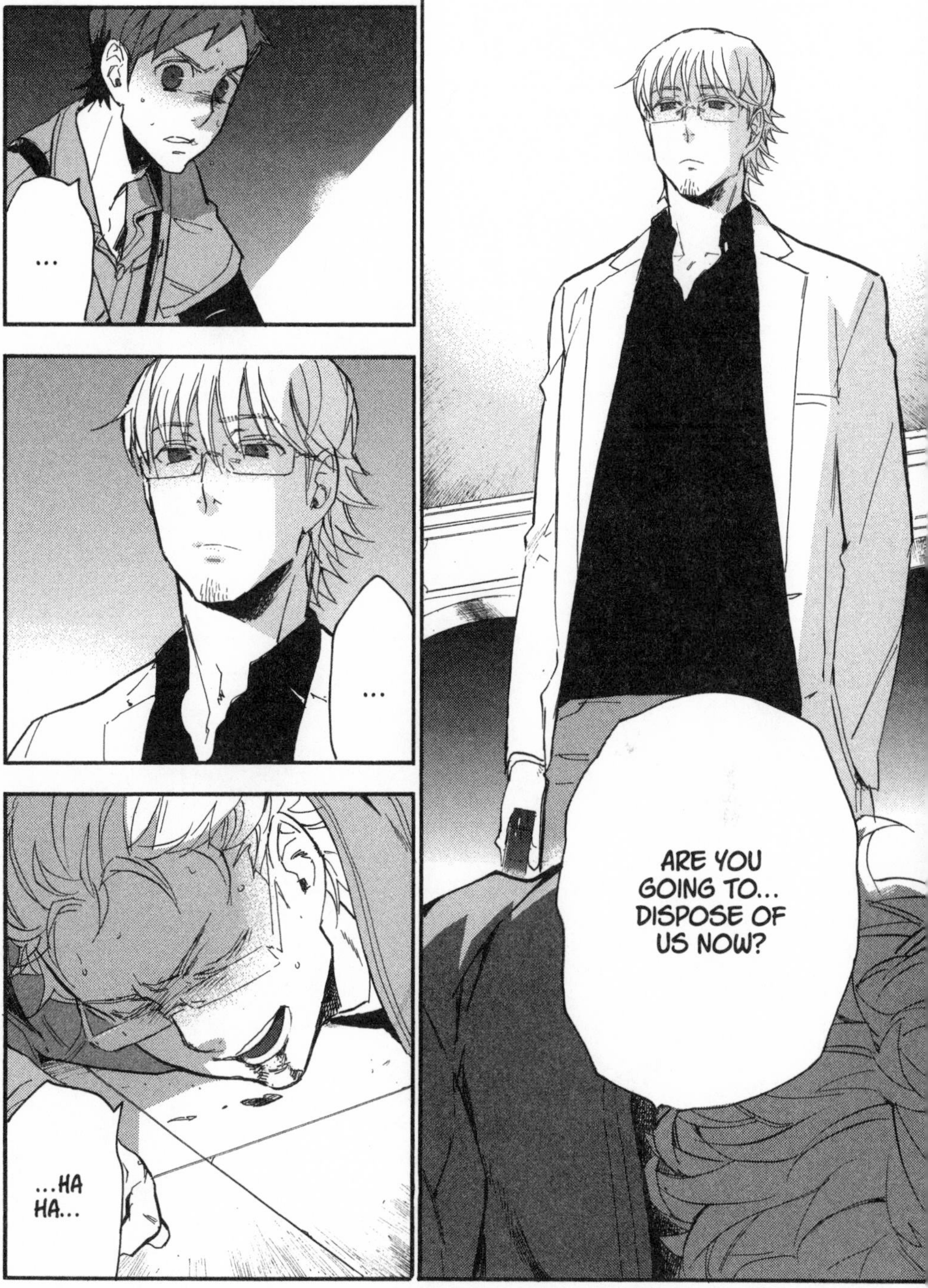
ARE YOU GOING TO... DISPOSE OF US NOW?
...
...
...HA HA...

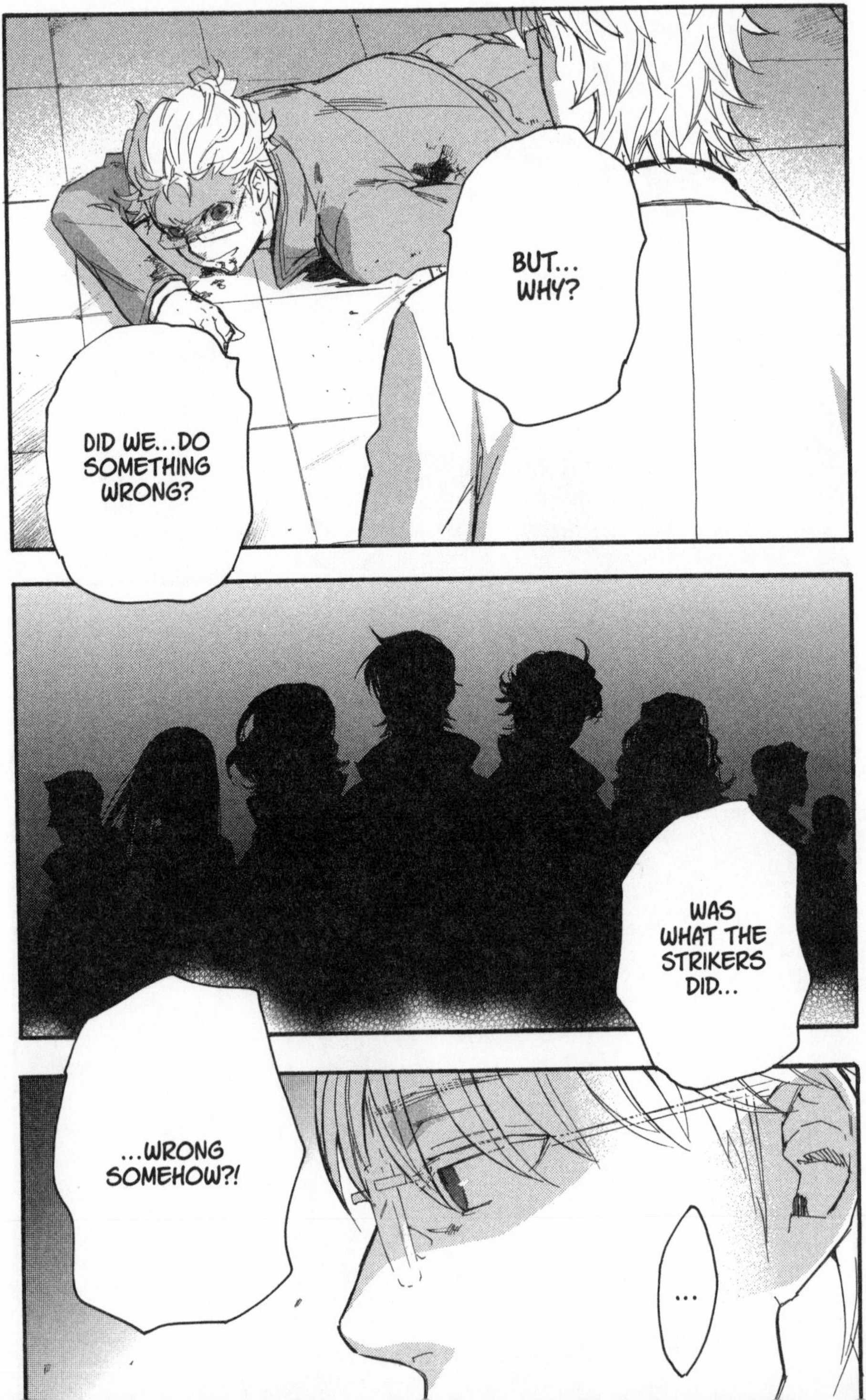
BUT... WHY?
DID WE...DO SOMETHING WRONG?
WAS WHAT THE STRIKERS DID...
...WRONG SOMEHOW?!
...

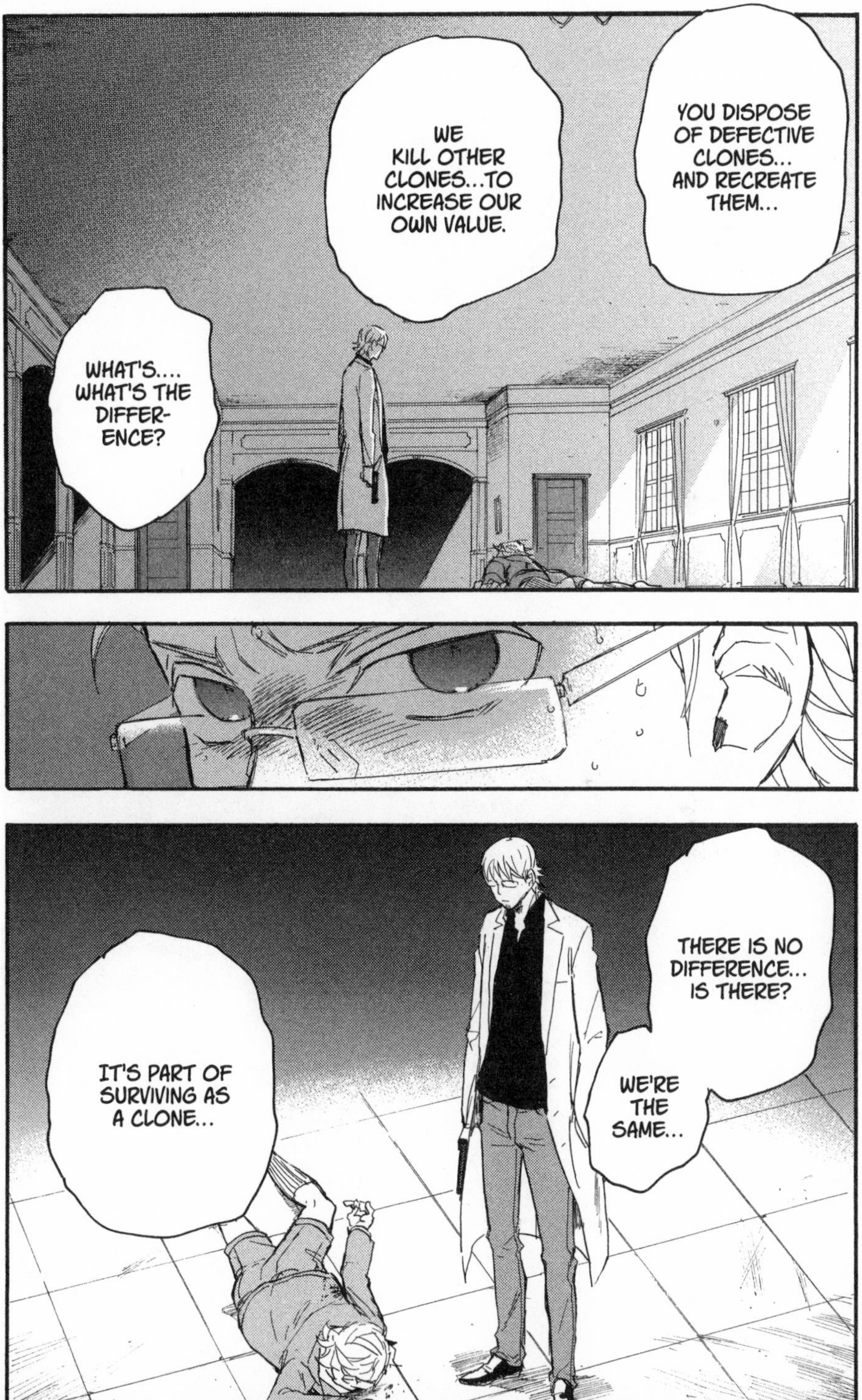
YOU DISPOSE OF DEFECTIVE CLONES... AND RECREATE THEM...
WE KILL OTHER CLONES...TO INCREASE OUR OWN VALUE.
WHAT'S.... WHAT'S THE DIFFER- ENCE?
THERE IS NO DIFFERENCE... IS THERE?
WE'RE THE SAME...
IT'S PART OF SURVIVING AS A CLONE...

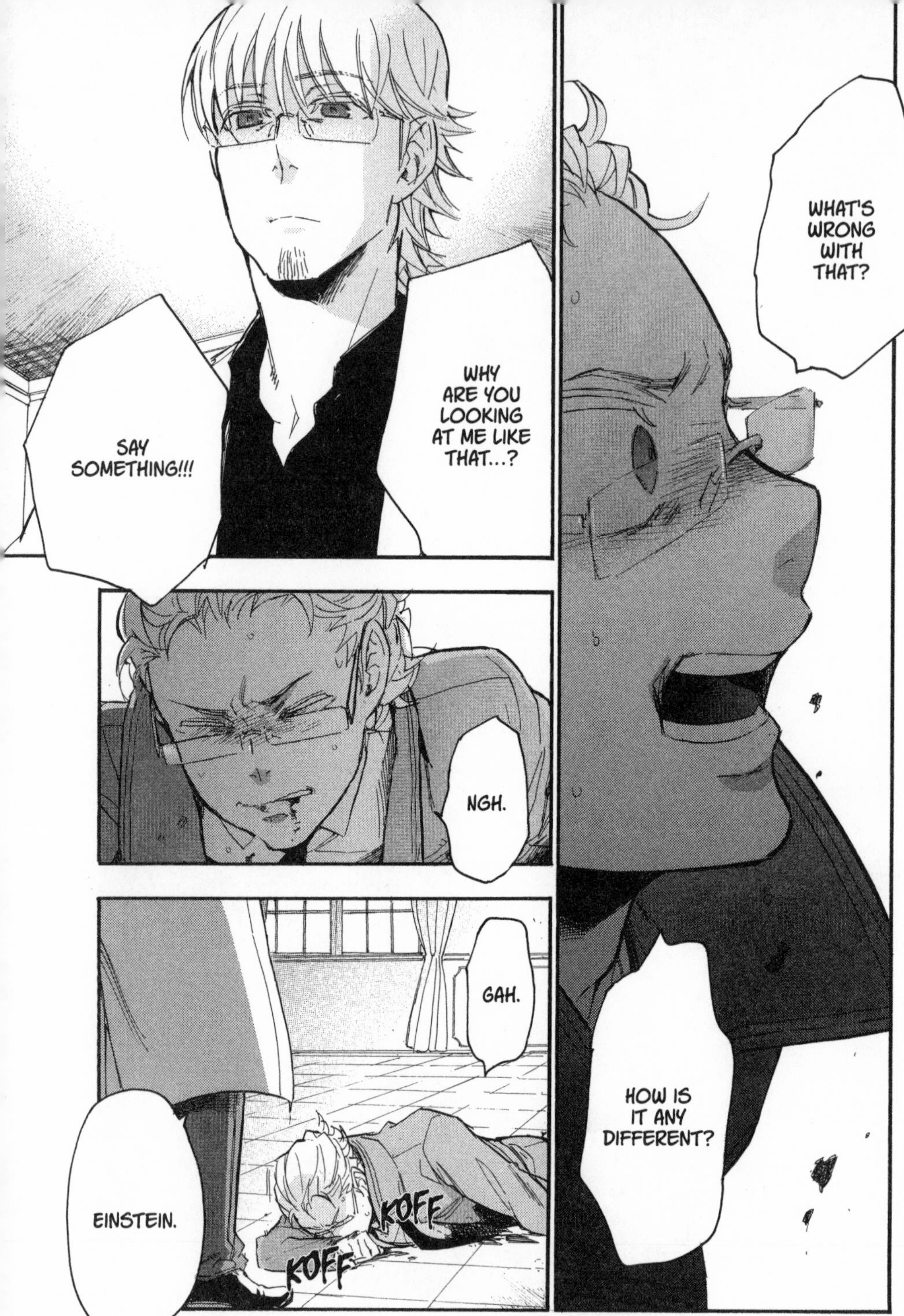
WHAT'S WRONG WITH THAT?
HOW IS IT ANY DIFFERENT?
WHY ARE YOU LOOKING AT ME LIKE THAT...?
SAY SOMETHING!!!
NGH.
GAH.
KOFF
KOFF
EINSTEIN.

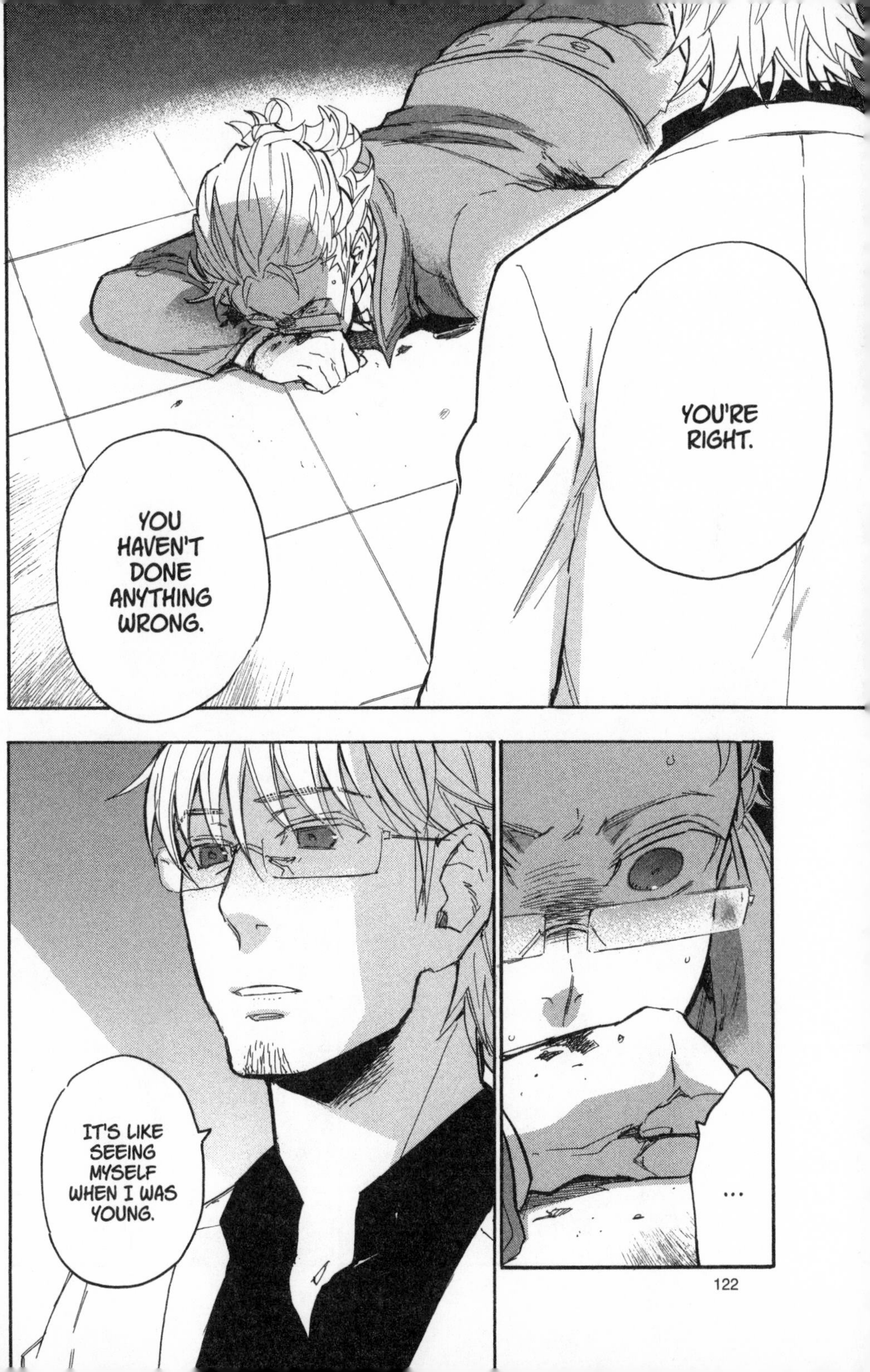
YOU'RE RIGHT.
YOU HAVEN'T DONE ANYTHING WRONG.
...
IT'S LIKE SEEING MYSELF WHEN I WAS YOUNG.

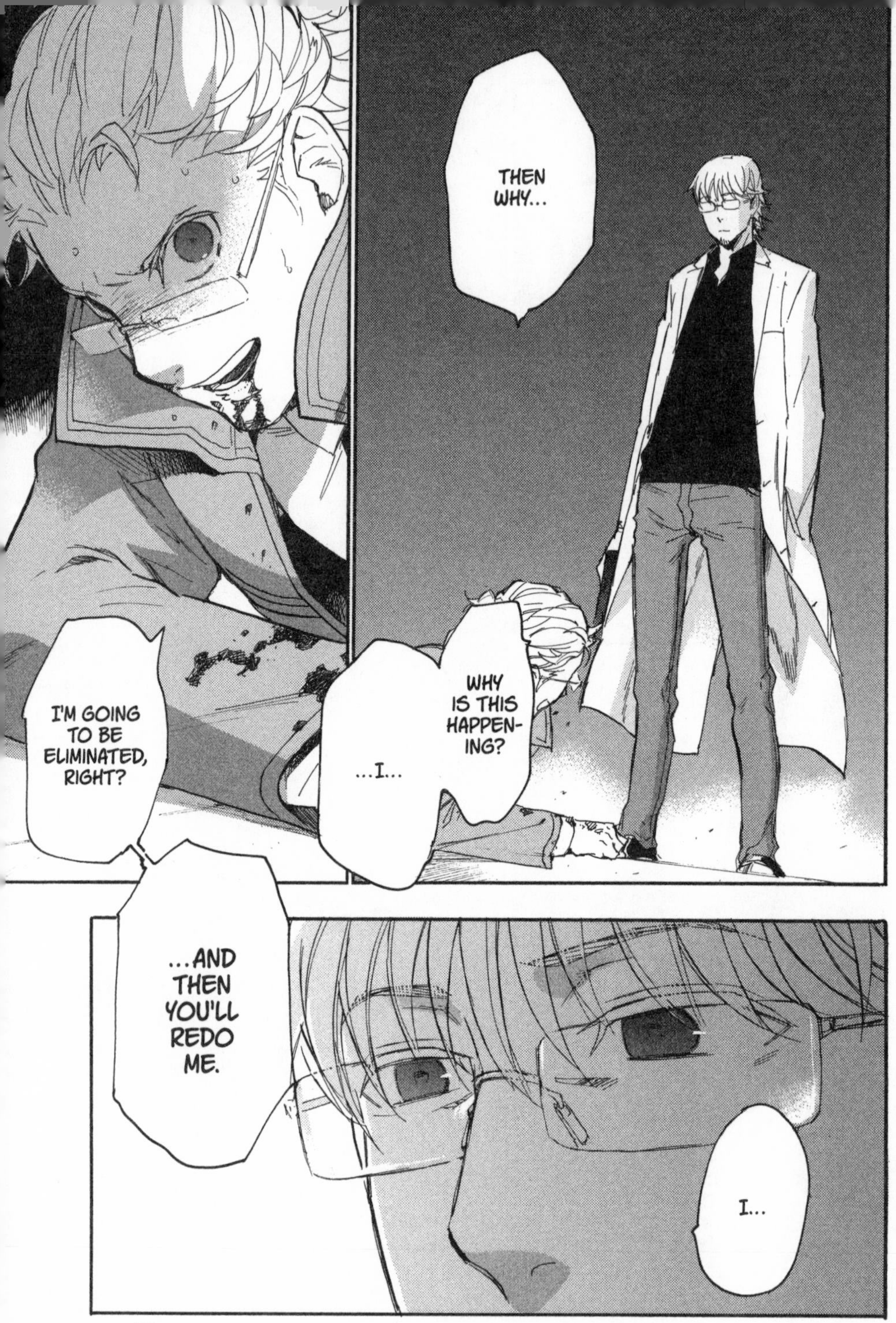
THEN WHY...
WHY IS THIS HAPPENING?
...I...
I'M GOING TO BE ELIMINATED, RIGHT?
...AND THEN YOU'LL REDO ME.
I...

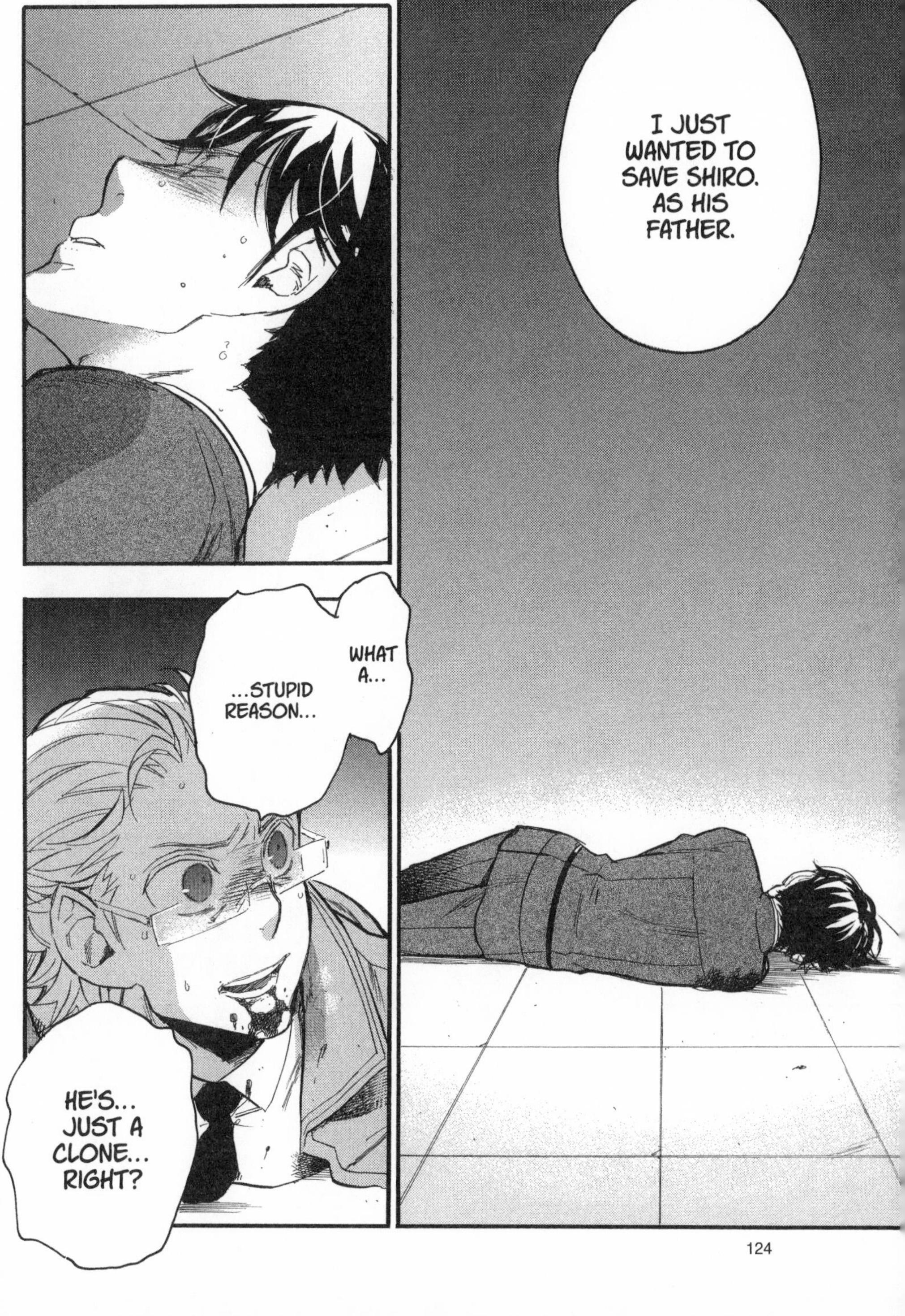
I JUST WANTED TO SAVE SHIRO. AS HIS FATHER.
WHAT A...
...STUPID REASON...
HE'S... JUST A CLONE... RIGHT?

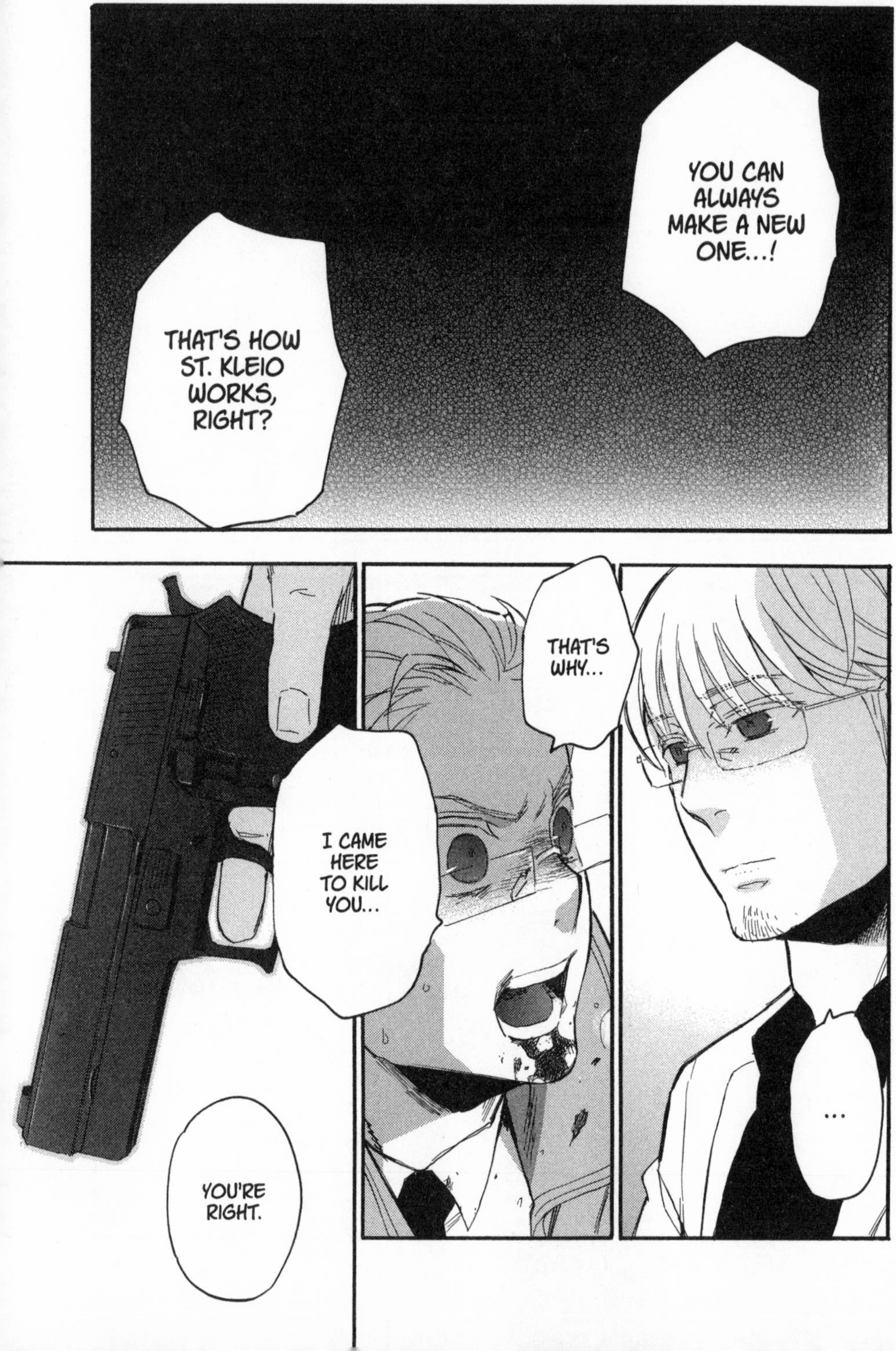
YOU CAN ALWAYS MAKE A NEW ONE...!
THAT'S HOW ST. KLEIO WORKS, RIGHT?
...
THAT'S WHY...
I CAME HERE TO KILL YOU...
YOU'RE RIGHT.

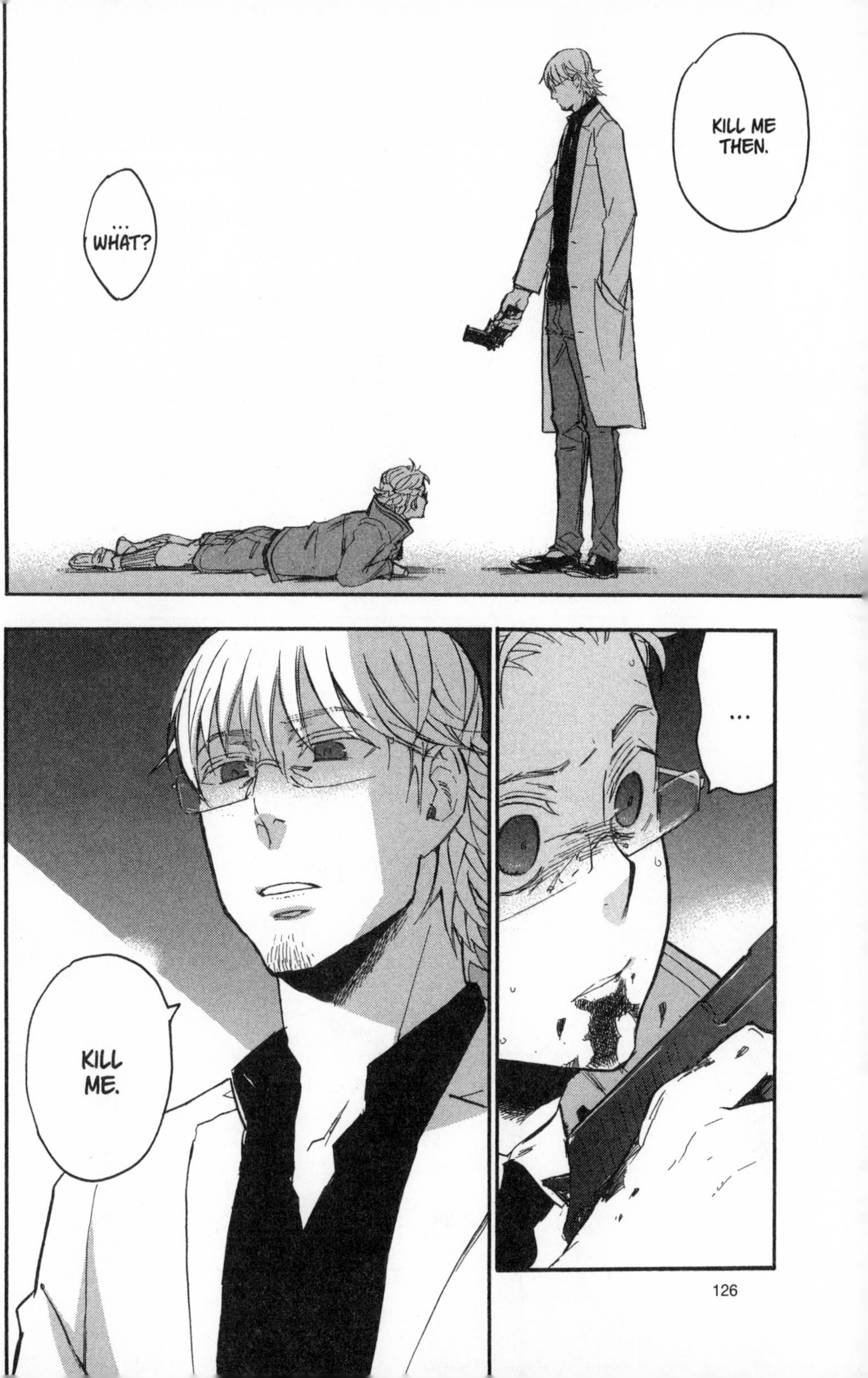
KILL ME THEN.
... WHAT?
...
KILL ME.

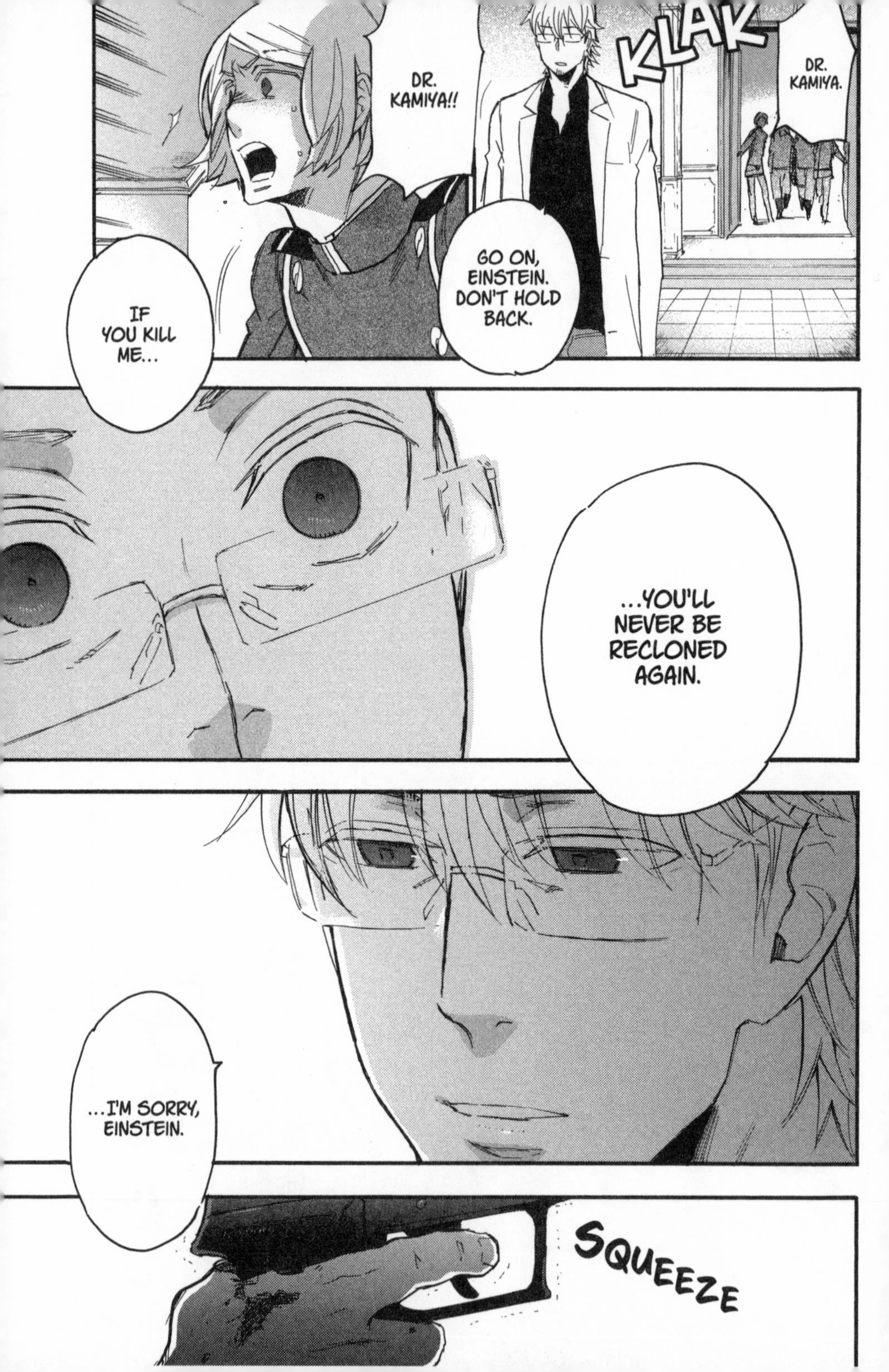
KLAK
DR. KAMIYA.
DR. KAMIYA!!
GO ON, EINSTEIN. DON'T HOLD BACK.
IF YOU KILL ME...
...YOU'LL NEVER BE RECLONED AGAIN.
...I'M SORRY, EINSTEIN.
SQUEEZE

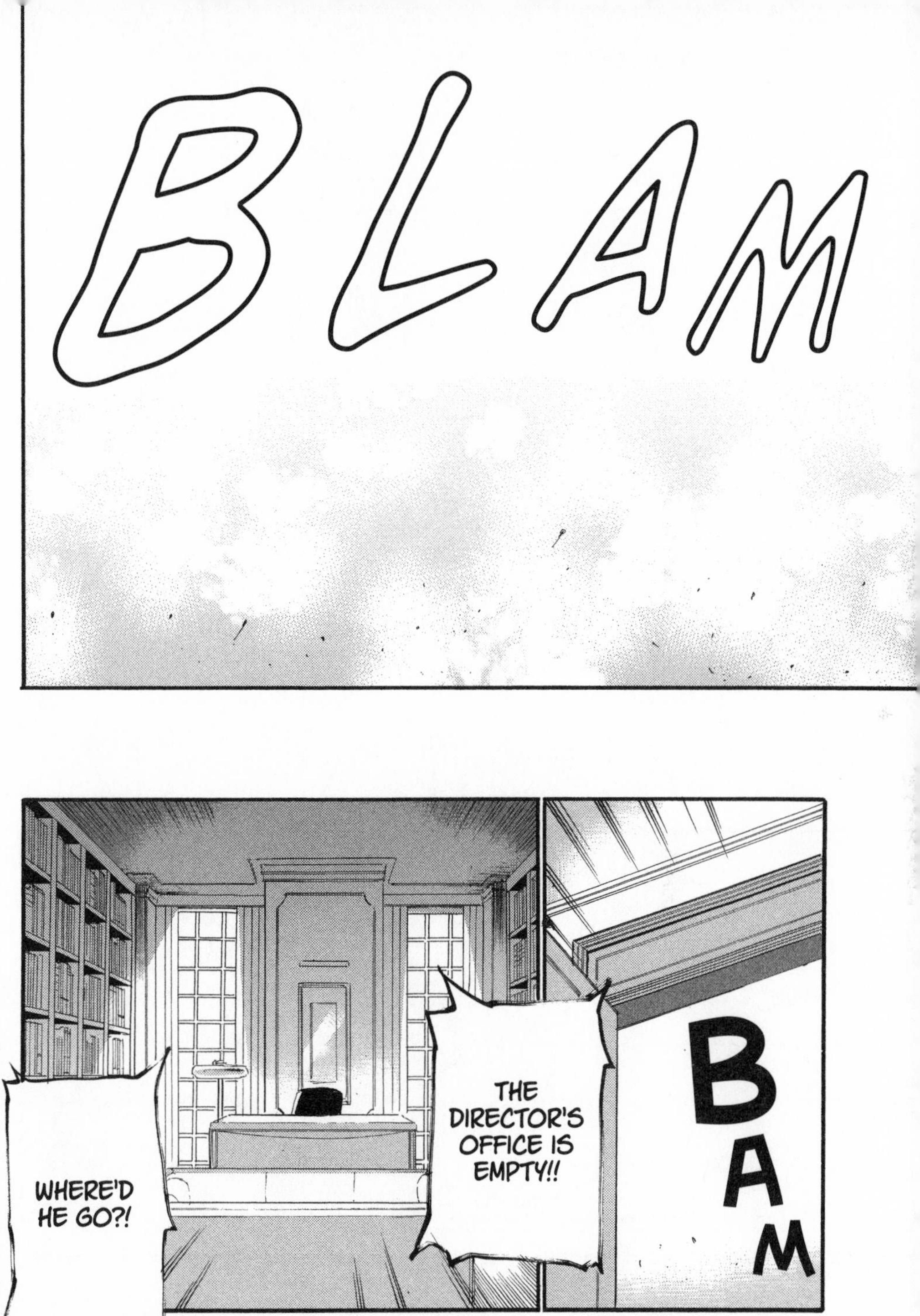
BLAM
BAM
THE DIRECTOR'S OFFICE IS EMPTY!!
WHERE'D HE GO?!

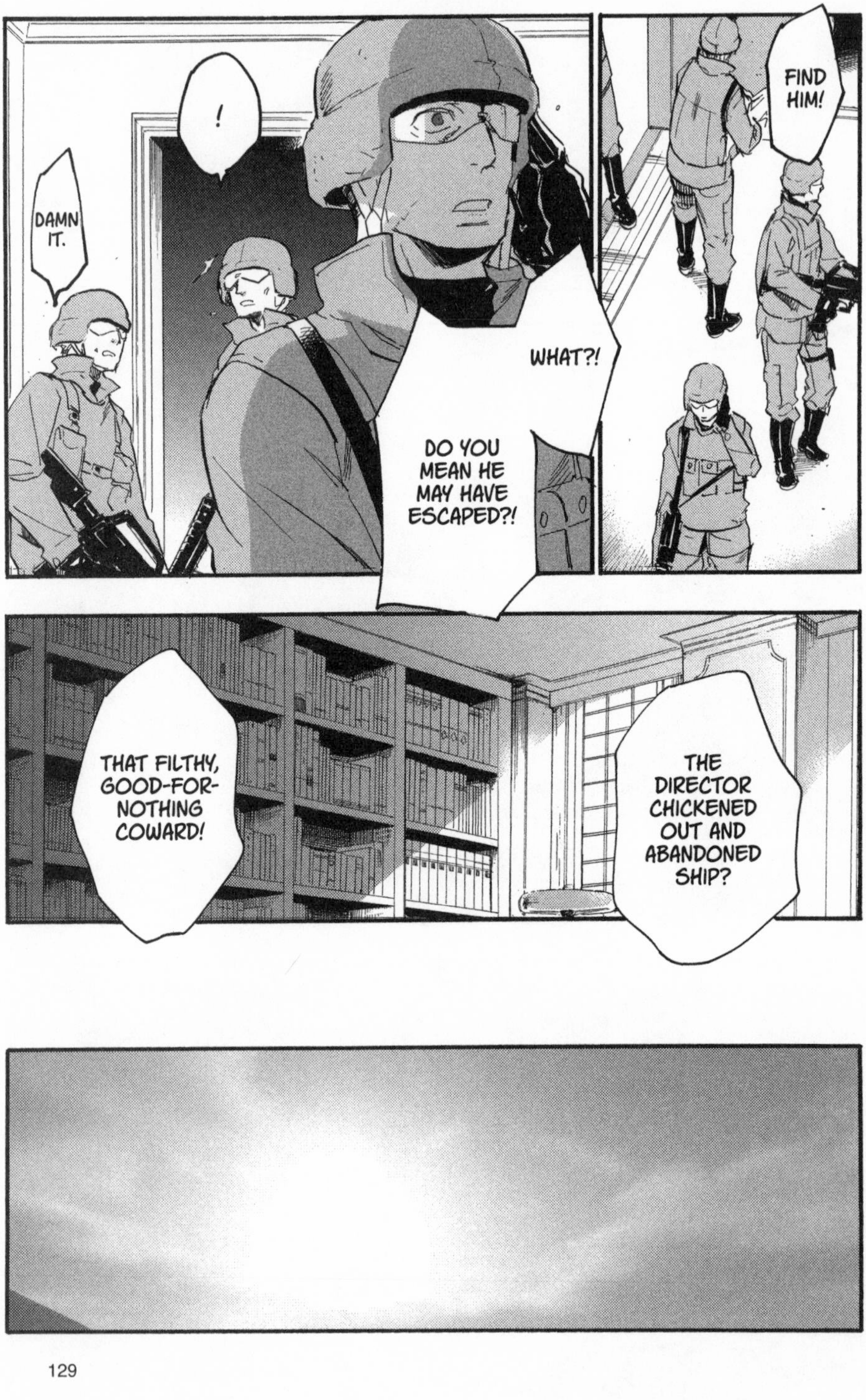
FIND HIM!
WHAT?!
DO YOU MEAN HE MAY HAVE ESCAPED?!
!
DAMN IT.
THE DIRECTOR CHICKENED OUT AND ABANDONED SHIP?
THAT FILTHY, GOOD-FOR-NOTHING COWARD!

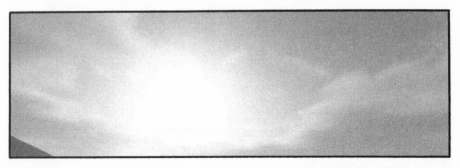

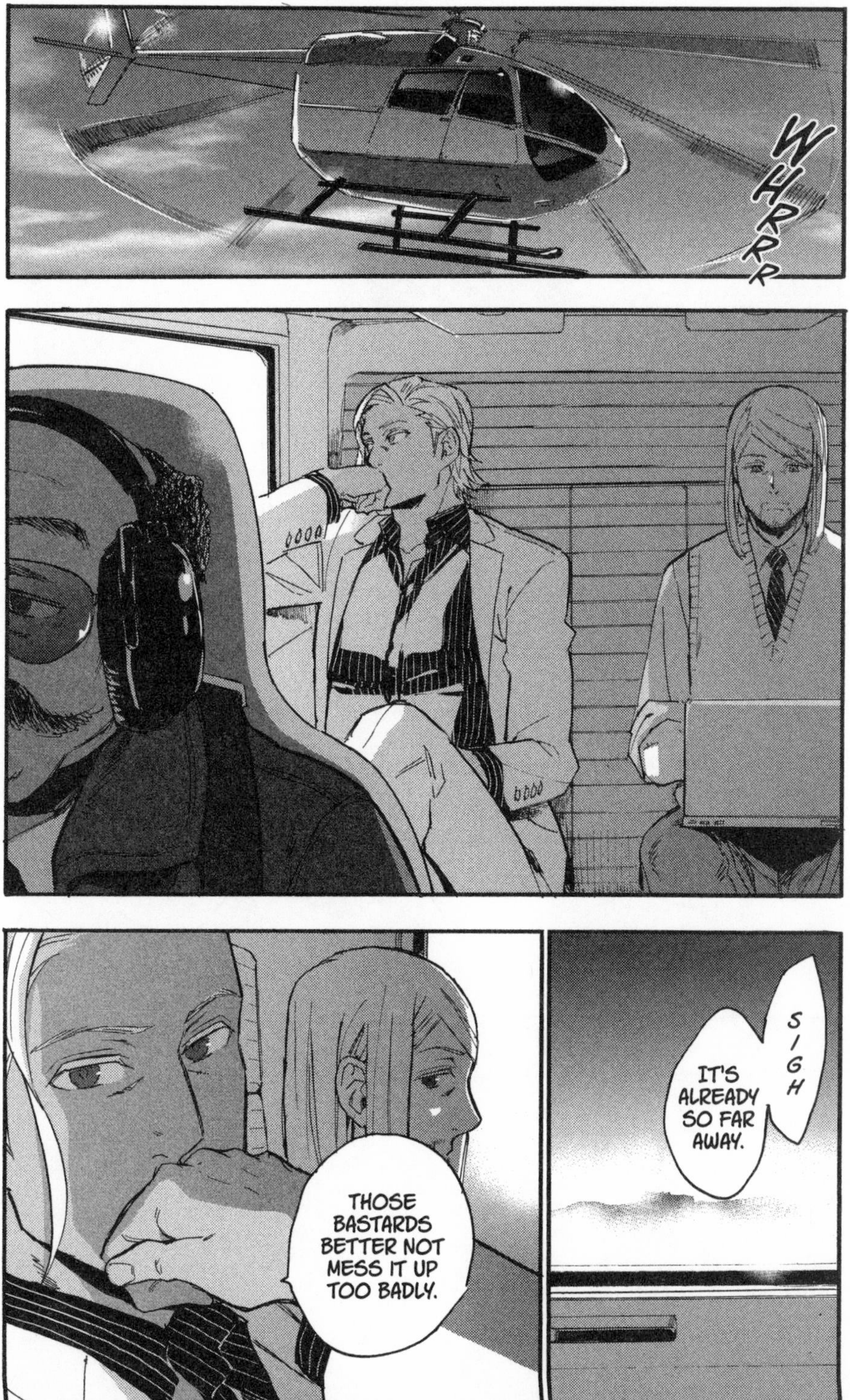
WHRRR
SIGH
IT'S ALREADY SO FAR AWAY.
THOSE BASTARDS BETTER NOT MESS IT UP TOO BADLY.

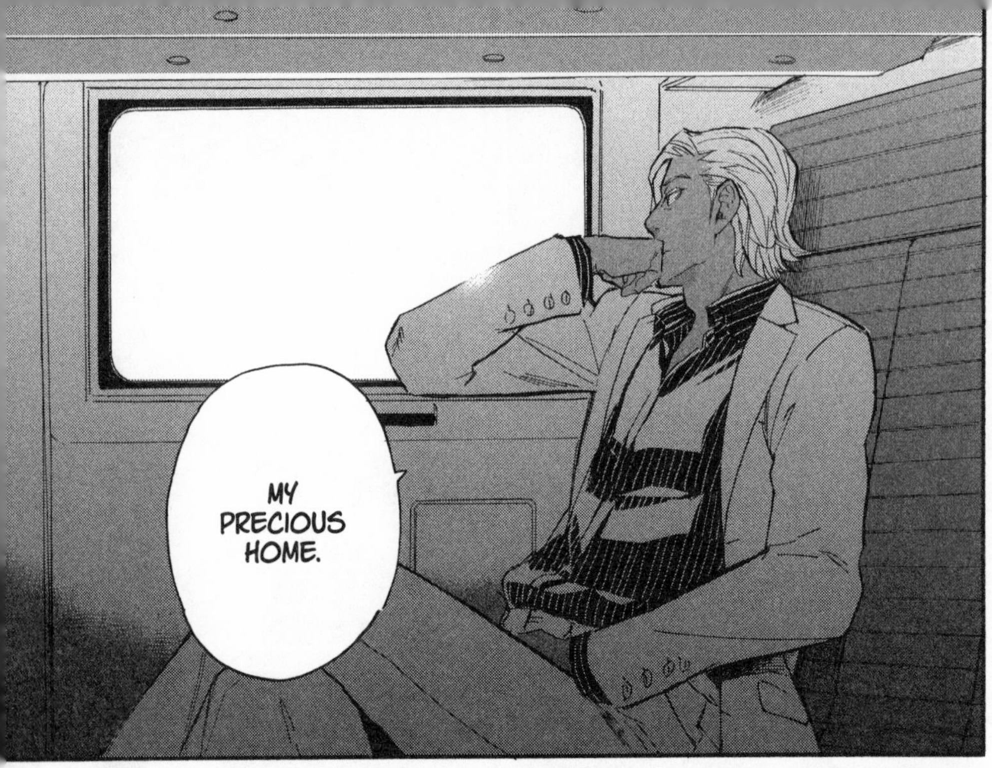
MY PRECIOUS HOME.

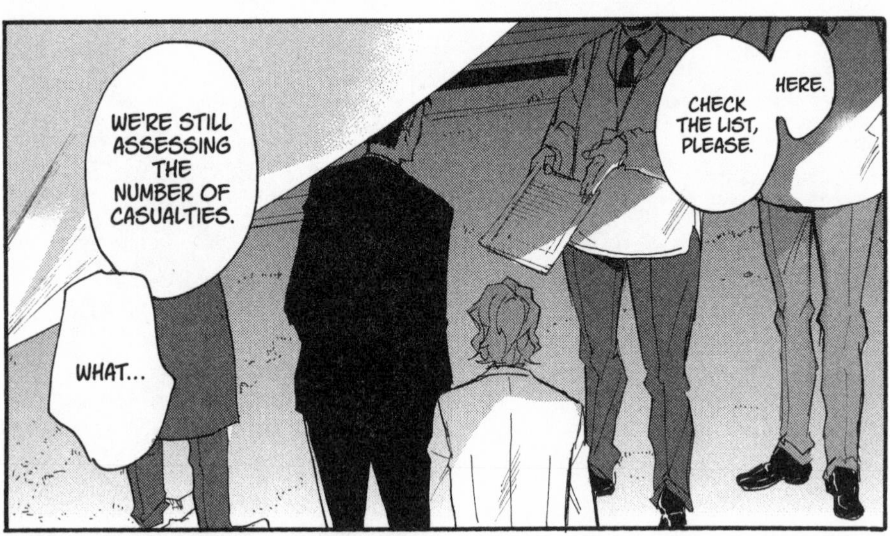
HERE.
CHECK THE LIST, PLEASE.
WE'RE STILL ASSESSING THE NUMBER OF CASUALTIES.
WHAT...

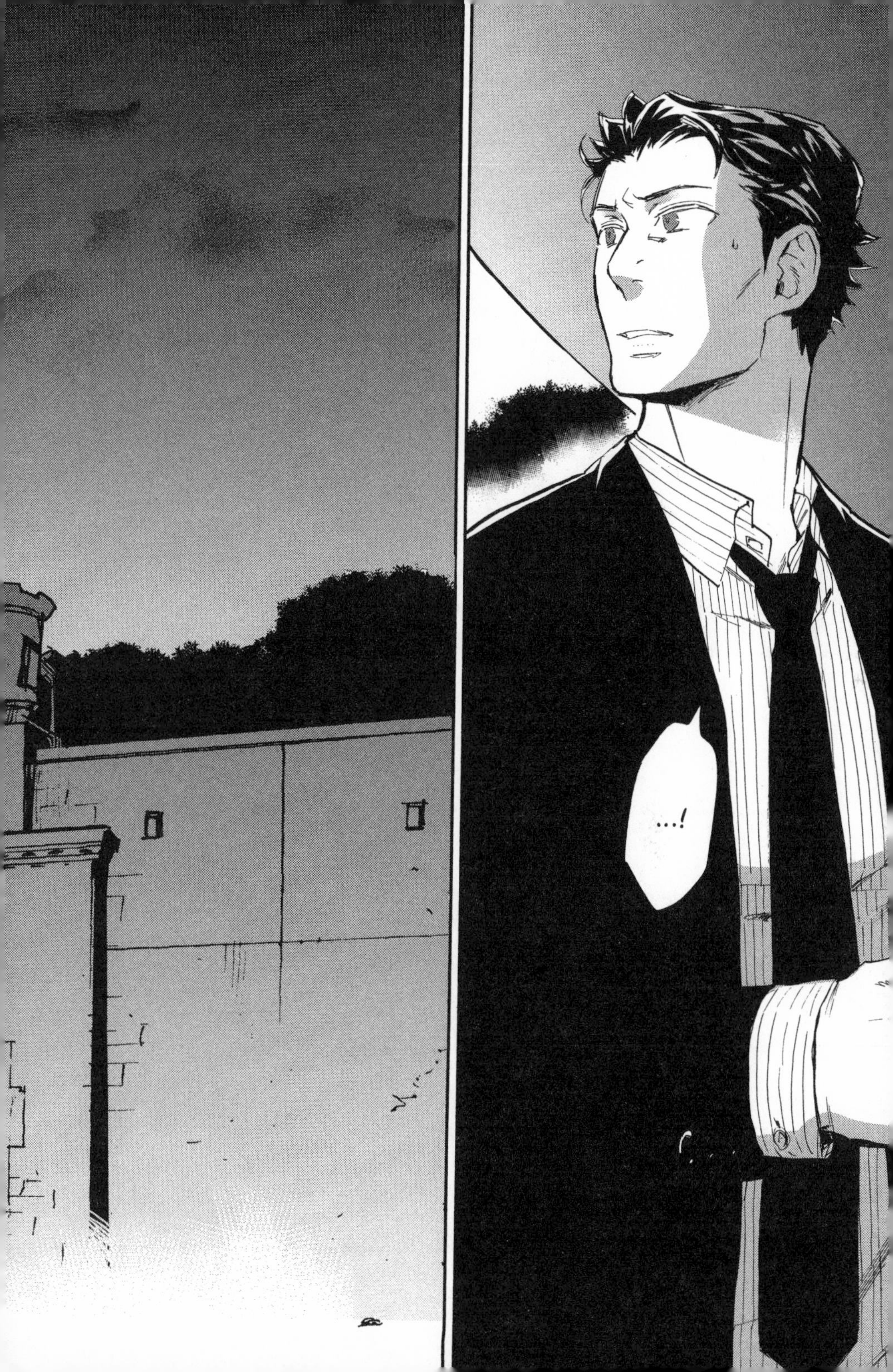
...!

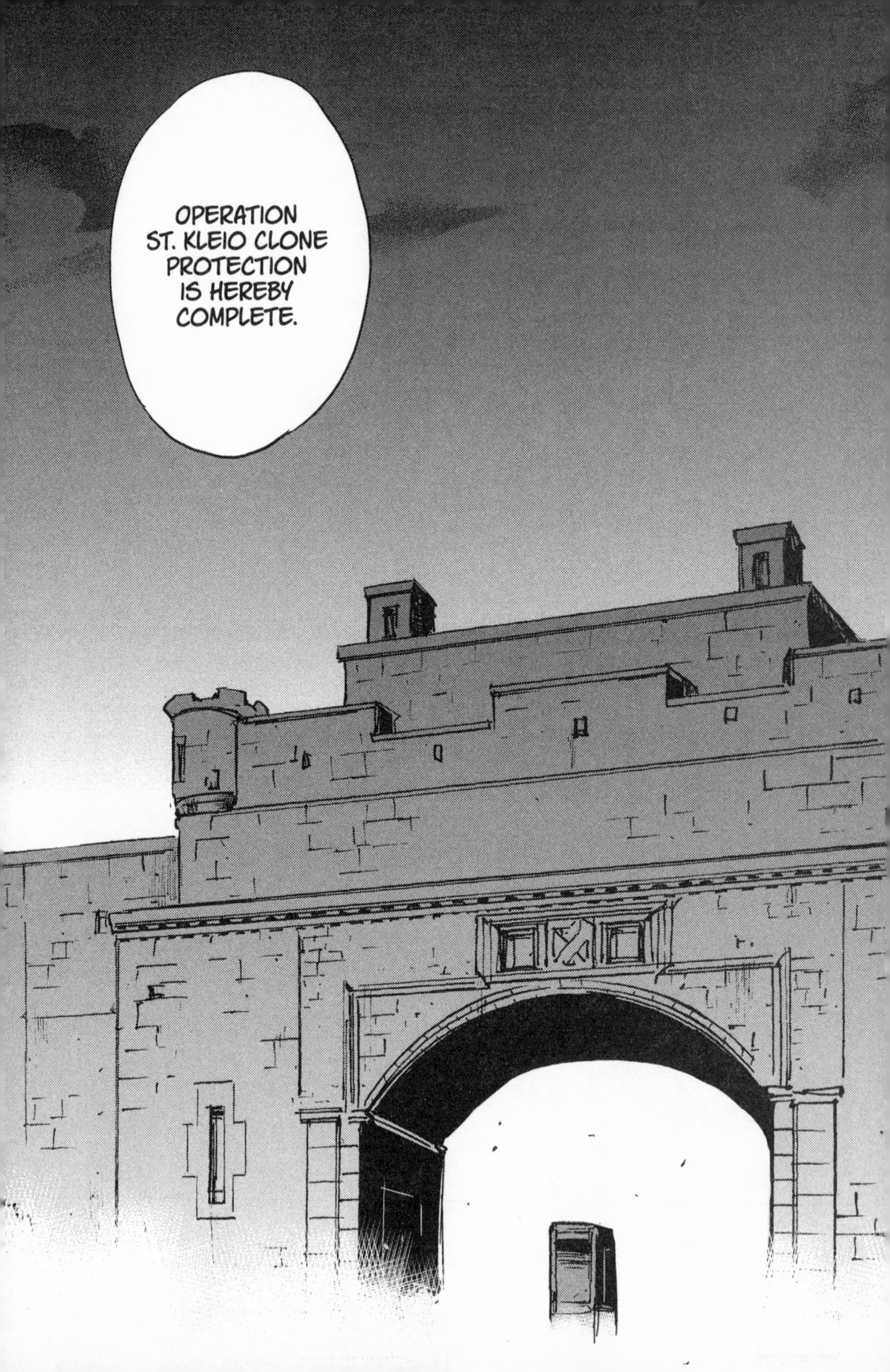
OPERATION ST. KLEIO CLONE PROTECTION IS HEREBY COMPLETE.

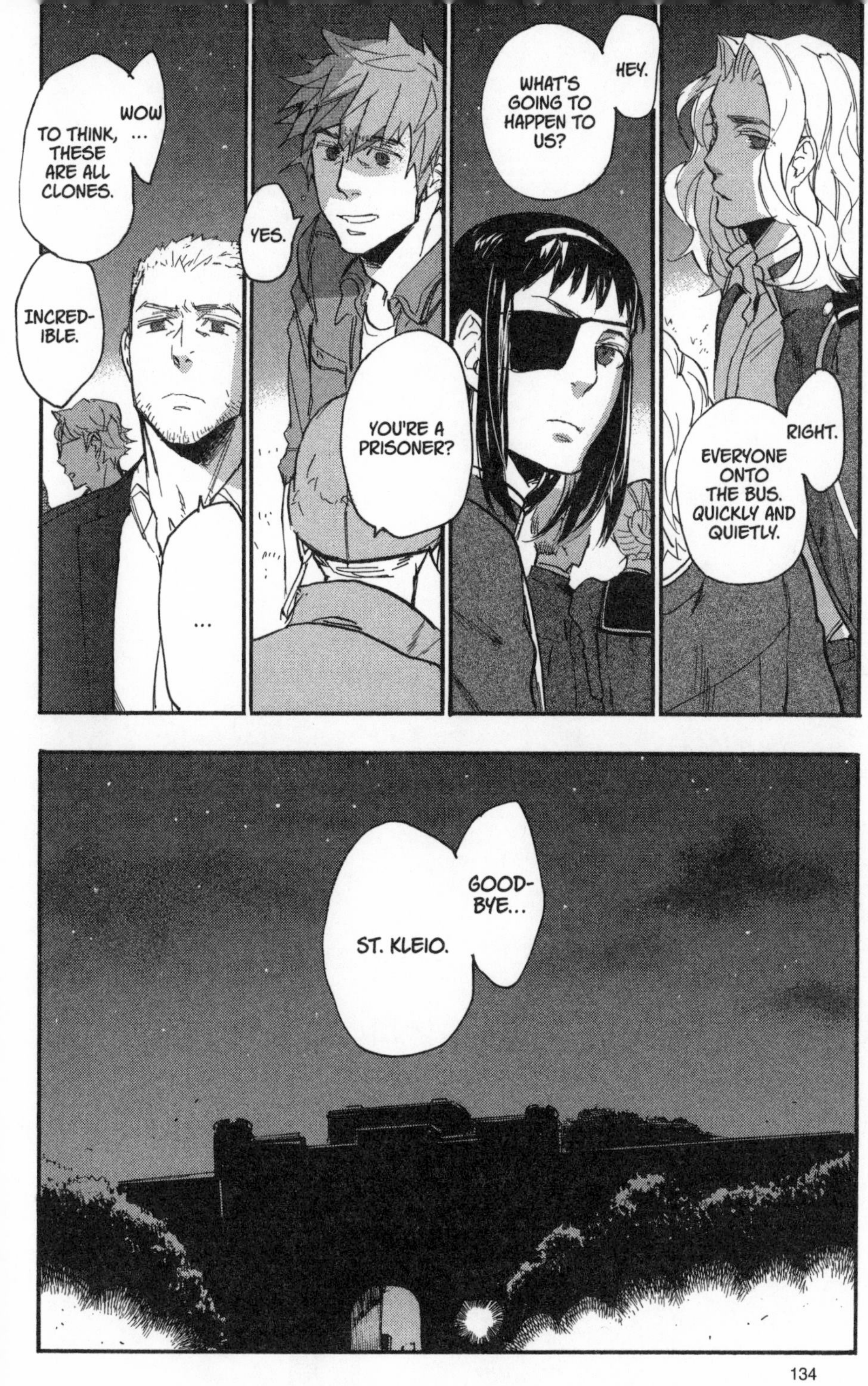
RIGHT.
EVERYONE ONTO THE BUS. QUICKLY AND QUIETLY.
HEY.
WHAT'S GOING TO HAPPEN TO US?
YOU'RE A PRISONER?
YES.
WOW...
TO THINK, THESE ARE ALL CLONES.
INCREDIBLE.
...
GOOD-BYE...
ST. KLEIO.

CHAPTER seventy-one

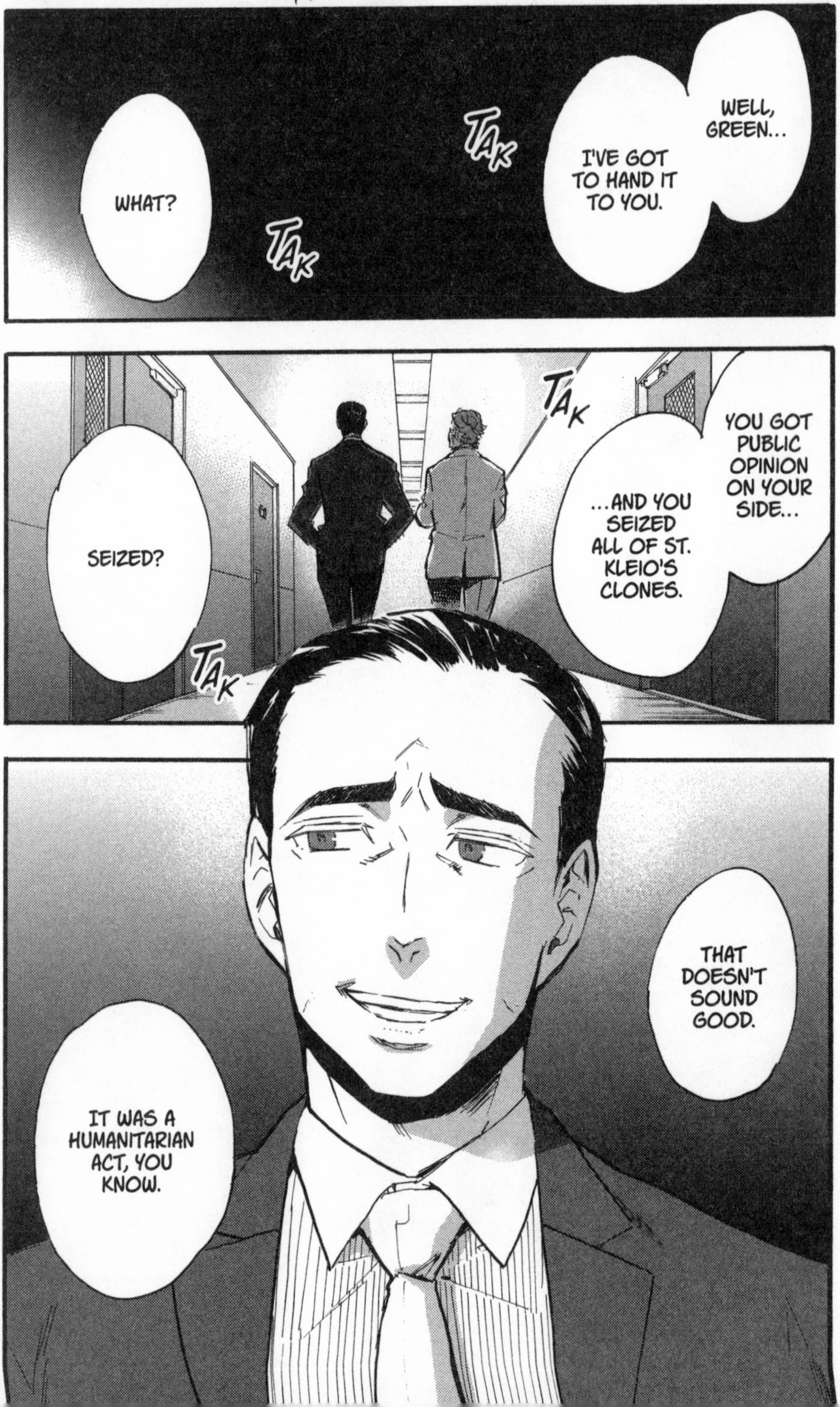
WELL, GREEN...
I'VE GOT TO HAND IT TO YOU.
TAK
TAK
WHAT?
YOU GOT PUBLIC OPINION ON YOUR SIDE...
...AND YOU SEIZED ALL OF ST. KLEIO'S CLONES.
TAK
TAK
SEIZED?
THAT DOESN'T SOUND GOOD.
IT WAS A HUMANITARIAN ACT, YOU KNOW.

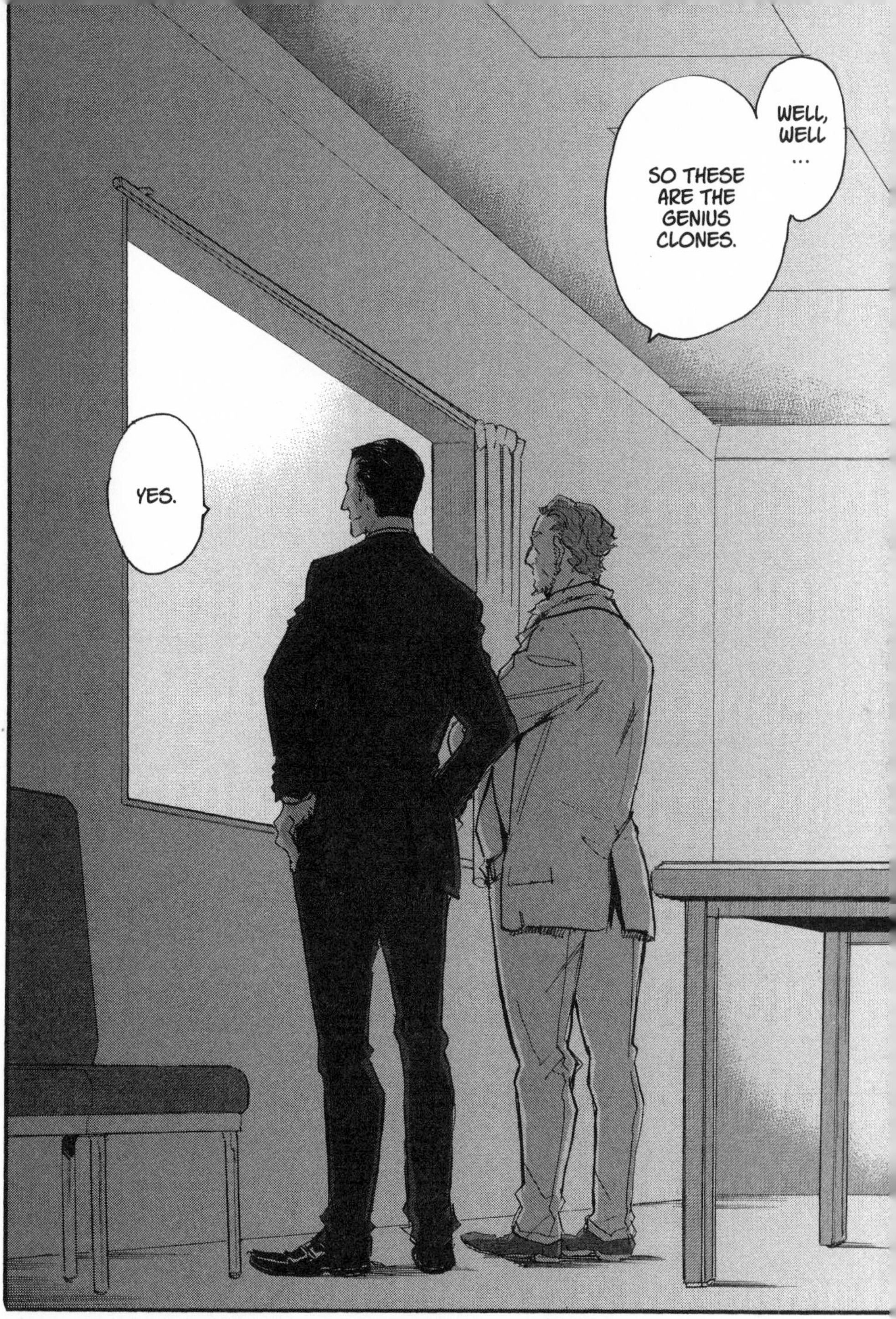
WELL, WELL ...
SO THESE ARE THE GENIUS CLONES.
YES.

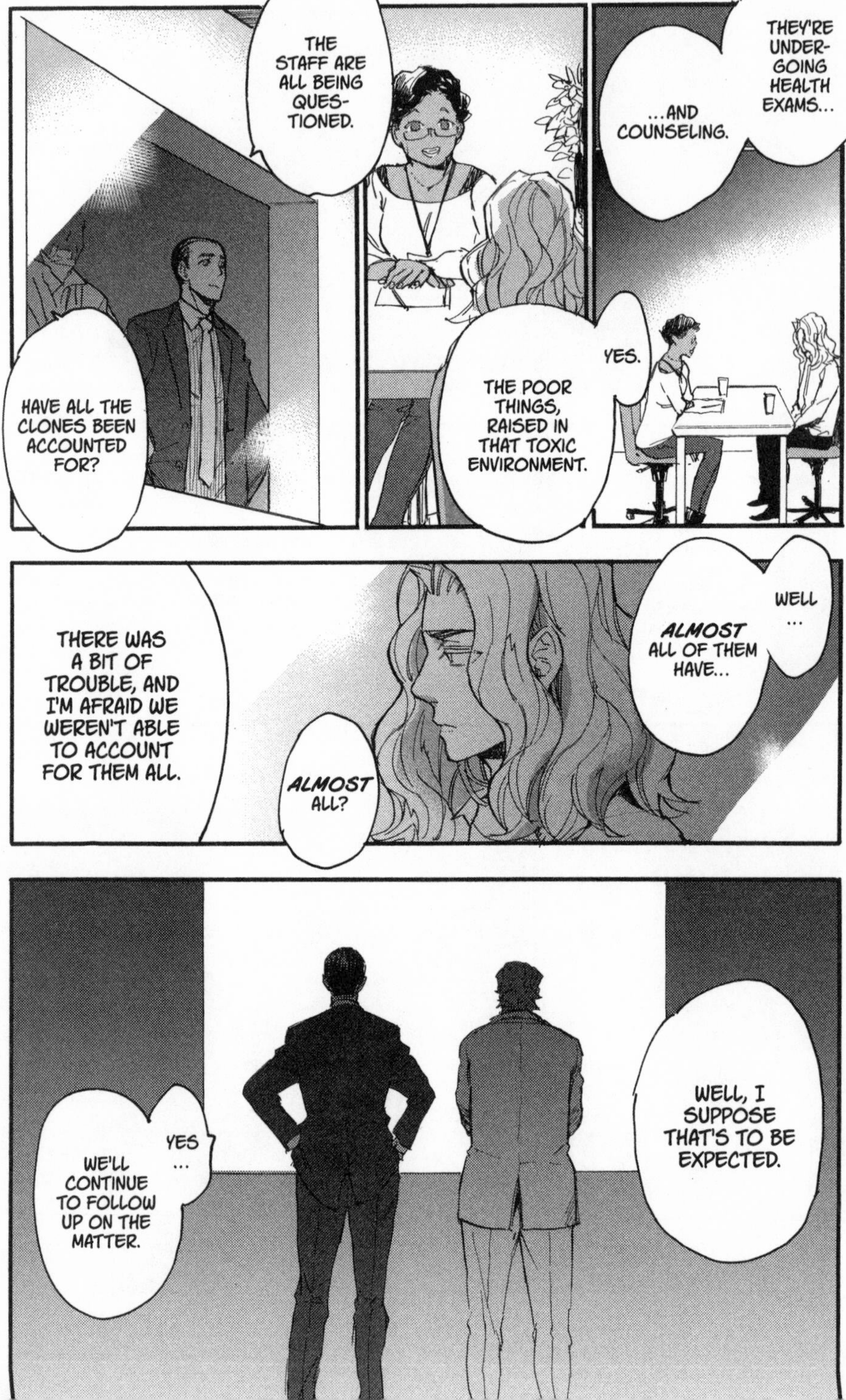
THEY'RE UNDER-GOING HEALTH EXAMS...
...AND COUNSELING.
YES.
THE POOR THINGS, RAISED IN THAT TOXIC ENVIRONMENT.
THE STAFF ARE ALL BEING QUES-TIONED.
HAVE ALL THE CLONES BEEN ACCOUNTED FOR?
WELL...
ALMOST ALL OF THEM HAVE...
ALMOST ALL?
THERE WAS A BIT OF TROUBLE, AND I'M AFRAID WE WEREN'T ABLE TO ACCOUNT FOR THEM ALL.
WELL, I SUPPOSE THAT'S TO BE EXPECTED.
YES...
WE'LL CONTINUE TO FOLLOW UP ON THE MATTER.

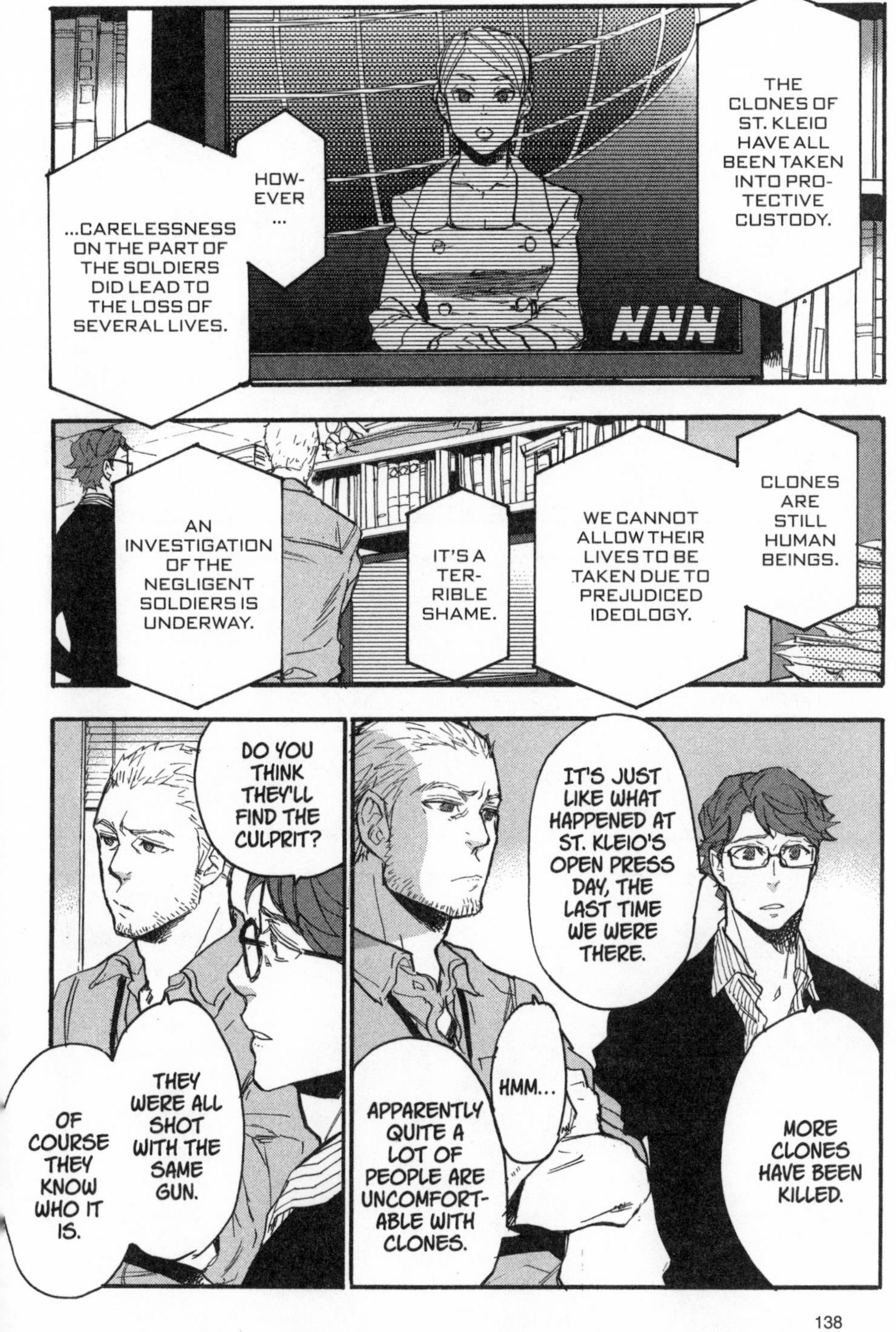
THE CLONES OF ST. KLEIO HAVE ALL BEEN TAKEN INTO PROTECTIVE CUSTODY.
HOW-EVER...
...CARELESSNESS ON THE PART OF THE SOLDIERS DID LEAD TO THE LOSS OF SEVERAL LIVES.
NNN
CLONES ARE STILL HUMAN BEINGS.
WE CANNOT ALLOW THEIR LIVES TO BE TAKEN DUE TO PREJUDICED IDEOLOGY.
IT'S A TER-RIBLE SHAME.
AN INVESTIGATION OF THE NEGLIGENT SOLDIERS IS UNDERWAY.
IT'S JUST LIKE WHAT HAPPENED AT ST. KLEIO'S OPEN PRESS DAY, THE LAST TIME WE WERE THERE.
MORE CLONES HAVE BEEN KILLED.
HMM...
APPARENTLY QUITE A LOT OF PEOPLE ARE UNCOMFORT-ABLE WITH CLONES.
DO YOU THINK THEY'LL FIND THE CULPRIT?
THEY WERE ALL SHOT WITH THE SAME GUN.
OF COURSE THEY KNOW WHO IT IS.

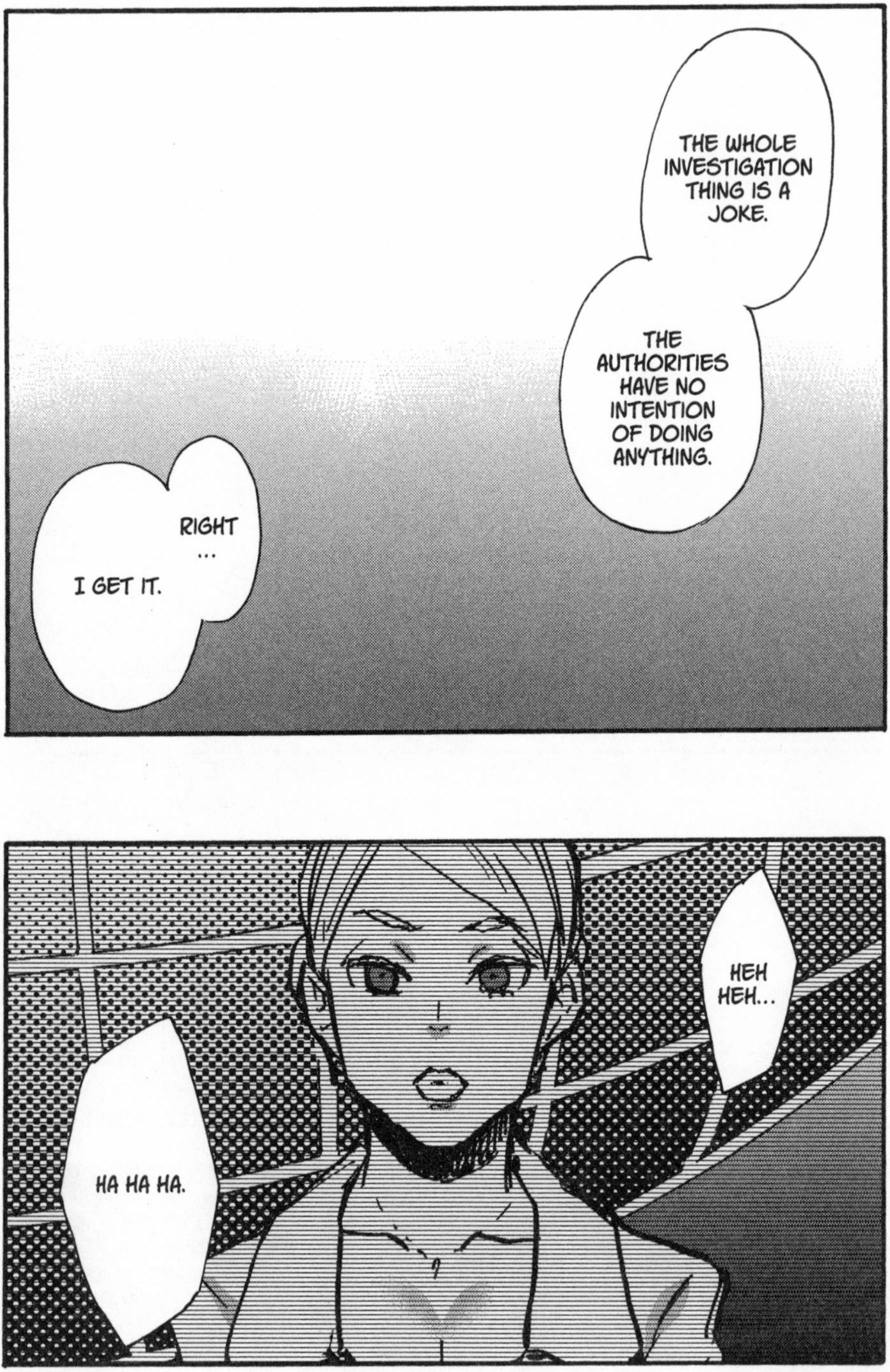
THE WHOLE INVESTIGATION THING IS A JOKE.
THE AUTHORITIES HAVE NO INTENTION OF DOING ANYTHING.
RIGHT... I GET IT.
HEH HEH...
HA HA HA.

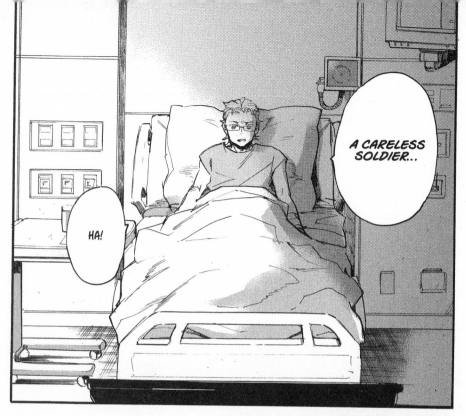

A CARELESS SOLDIER...

HA!

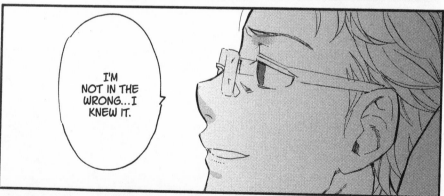

I'M NOT IN THE WRONG...I KNEW IT.

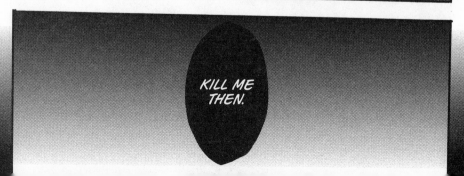

KILL ME THEN.

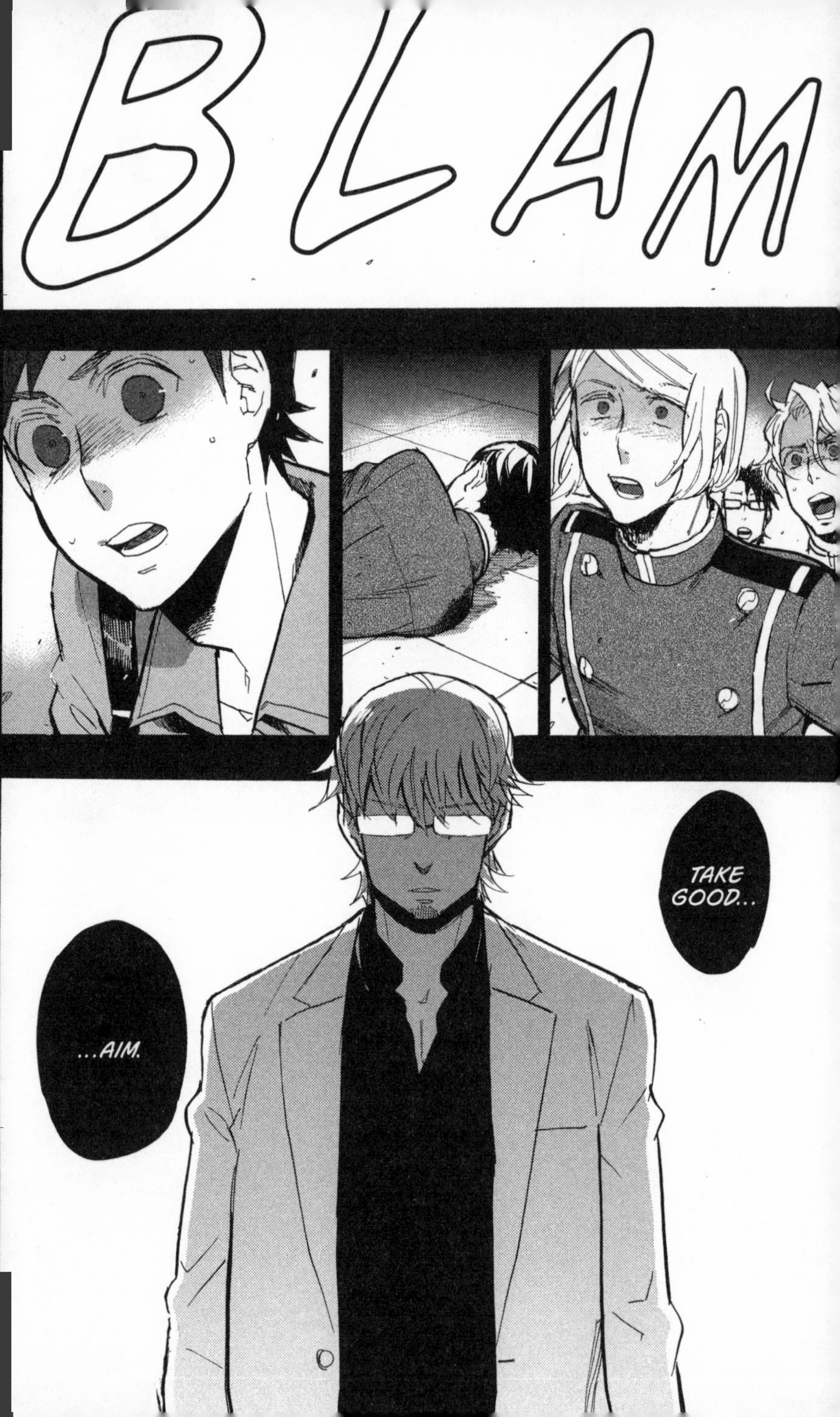
BLAM
TAKE GOOD...
...AIM.

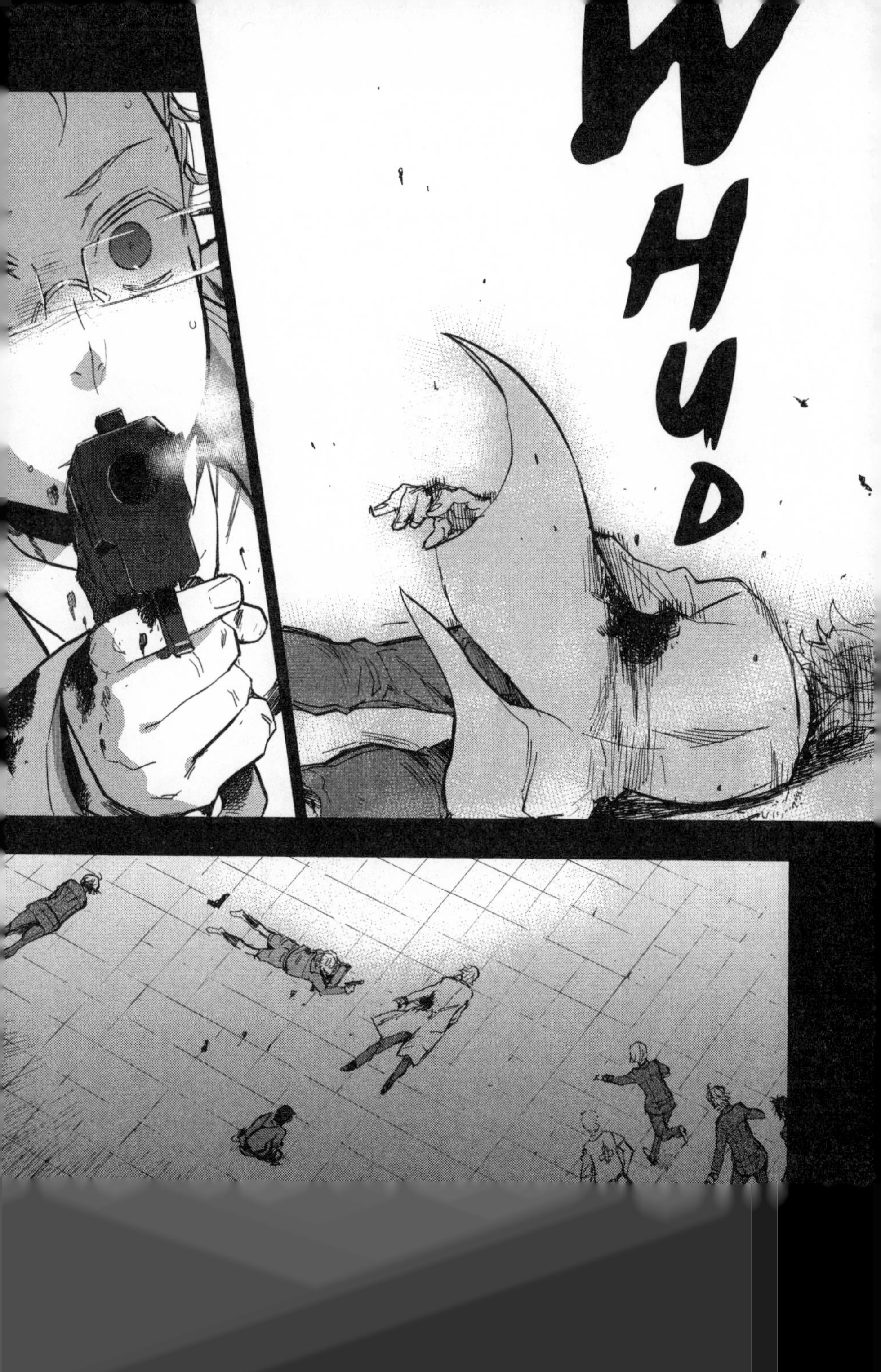
WHUD

HA HA...
THE WHOLE WORLD'S ON MY SIDE.

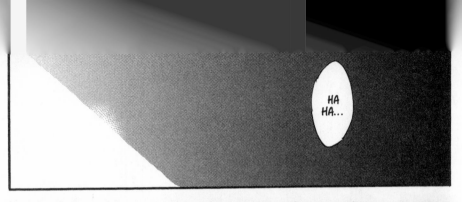

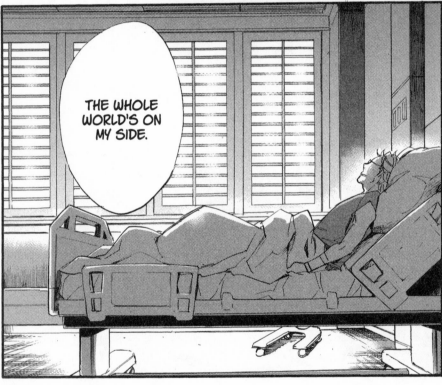

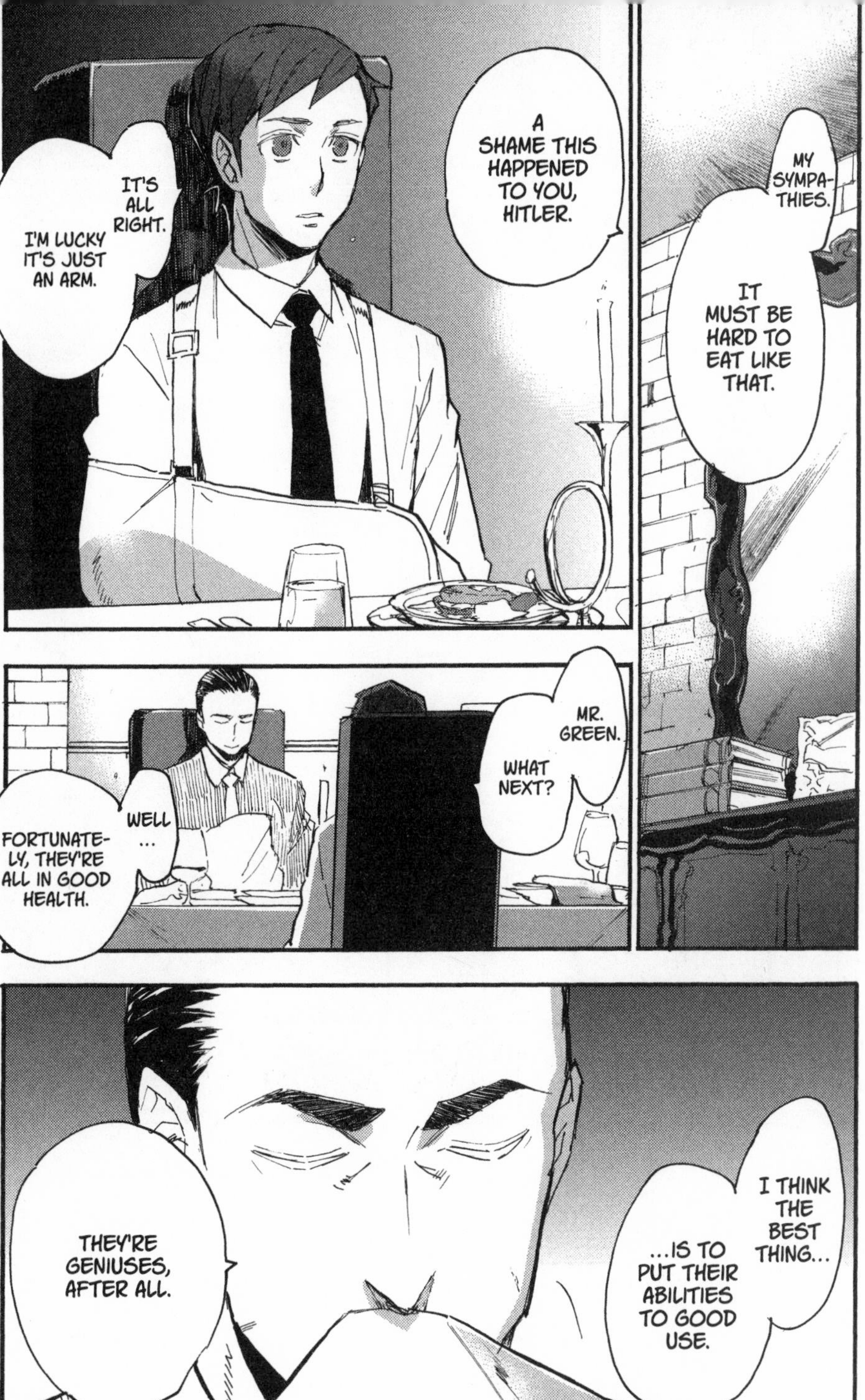
MY SYMPATHIES.
IT MUST BE HARD TO EAT LIKE THAT.
A SHAME THIS HAPPENED TO YOU, HITLER.
IT'S ALL RIGHT.
I'M LUCKY IT'S JUST AN ARM.
MR. GREEN.
WHAT NEXT?
WELL...
FORTUNATELY, THEY'RE ALL IN GOOD HEALTH.
I THINK THE BEST THING...
...IS TO PUT THEIR ABILITIES TO GOOD USE.
THEY'RE GENIUSES, AFTER ALL.

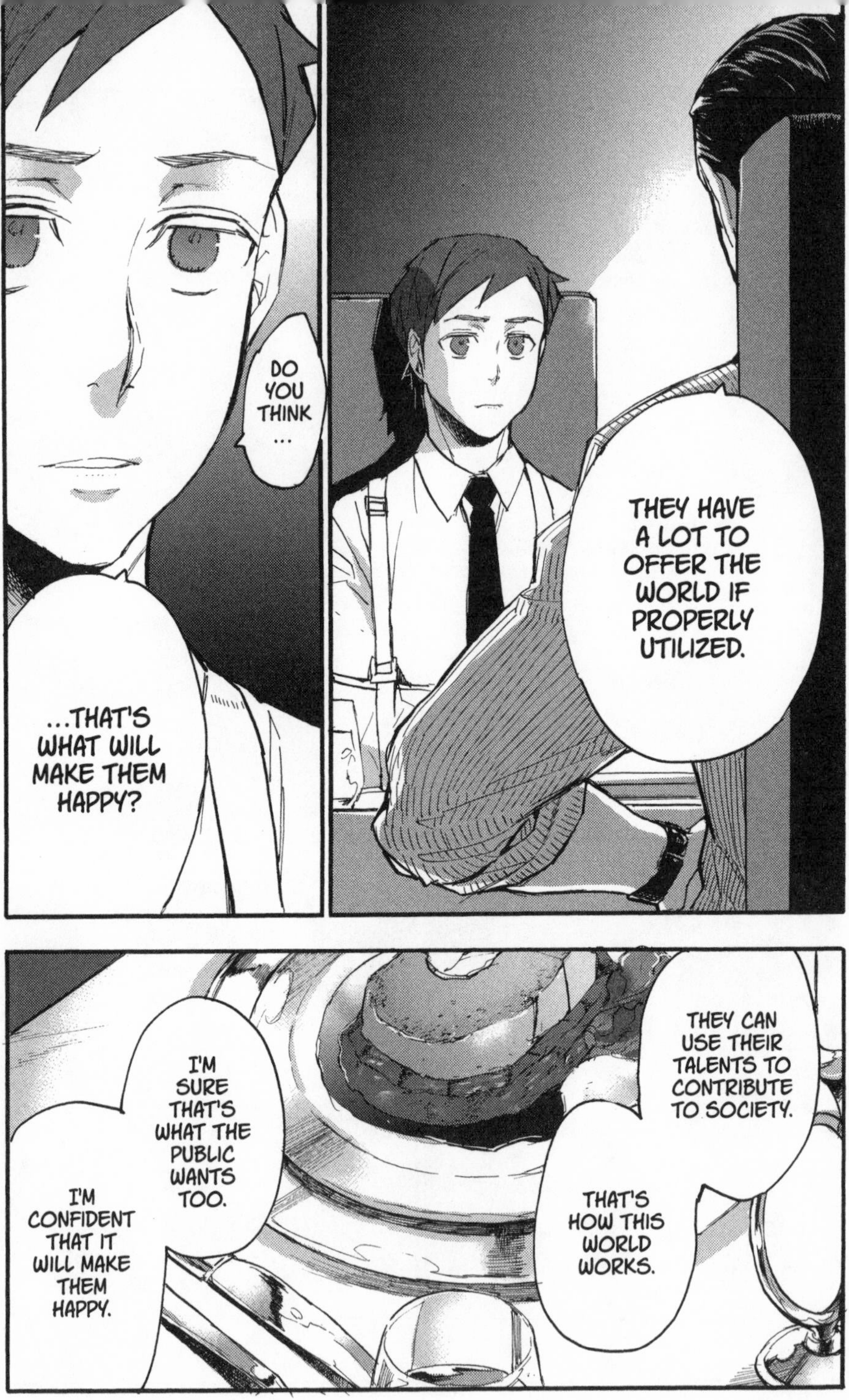
THEY HAVE A LOT TO OFFER THE WORLD IF PROPERLY UTILIZED.
DO YOU THINK ...
...THAT'S WHAT WILL MAKE THEM HAPPY?
THEY CAN USE THEIR TALENTS TO CONTRIBUTE TO SOCIETY.
THAT'S HOW THIS WORLD WORKS.
I'M SURE THAT'S WHAT THE PUBLIC WANTS TOO.
I'M CONFIDENT THAT IT WILL MAKE THEM HAPPY.

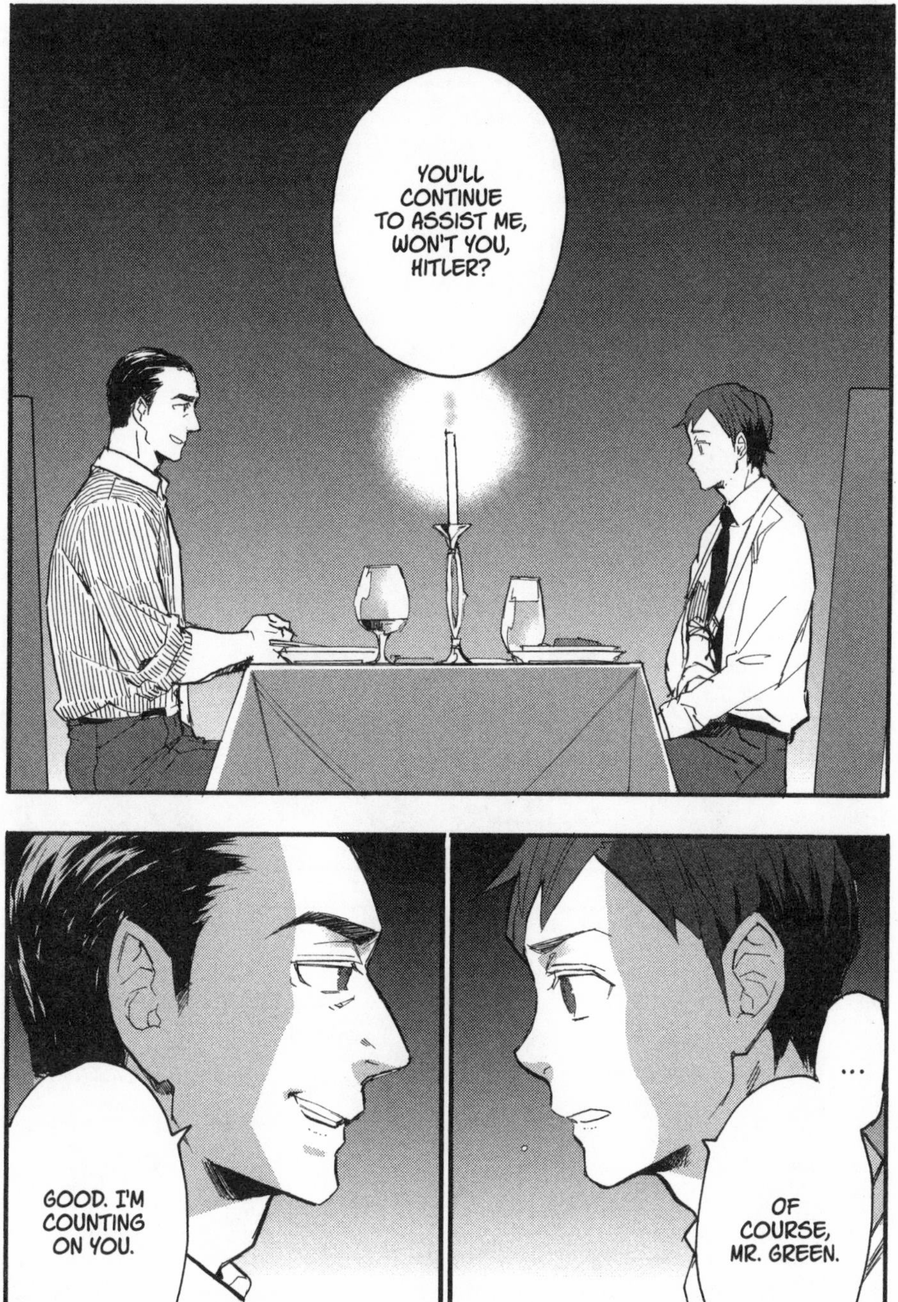
YOU'LL CONTINUE TO ASSIST ME, WON'T YOU, HITLER?
...
OF COURSE, MR. GREEN.
GOOD. I'M COUNTING ON YOU.

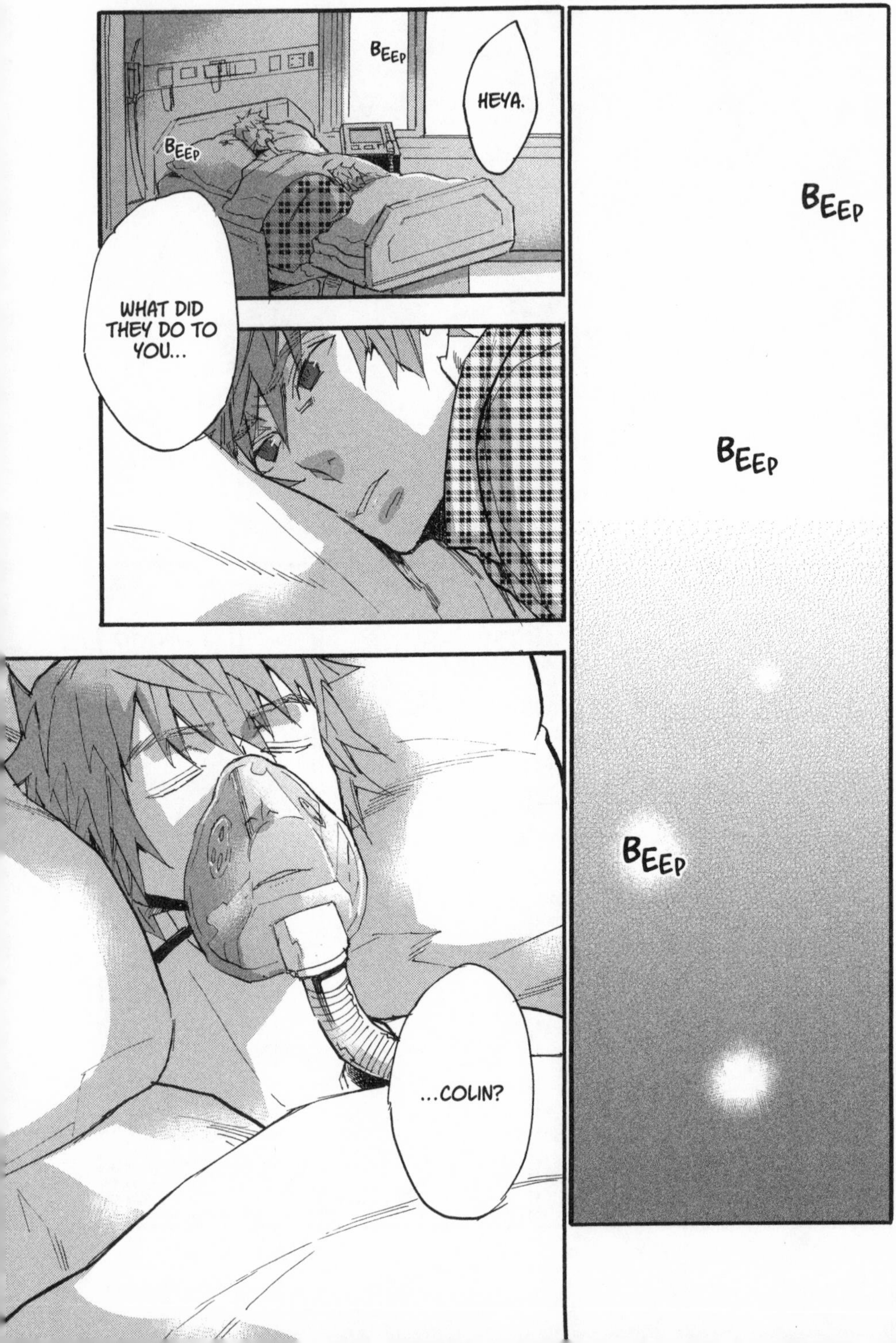
BEEP
BEEP
BEEP
BEEP
HEYA.
BEEP
WHAT DID THEY DO TO YOU...
...COLIN?

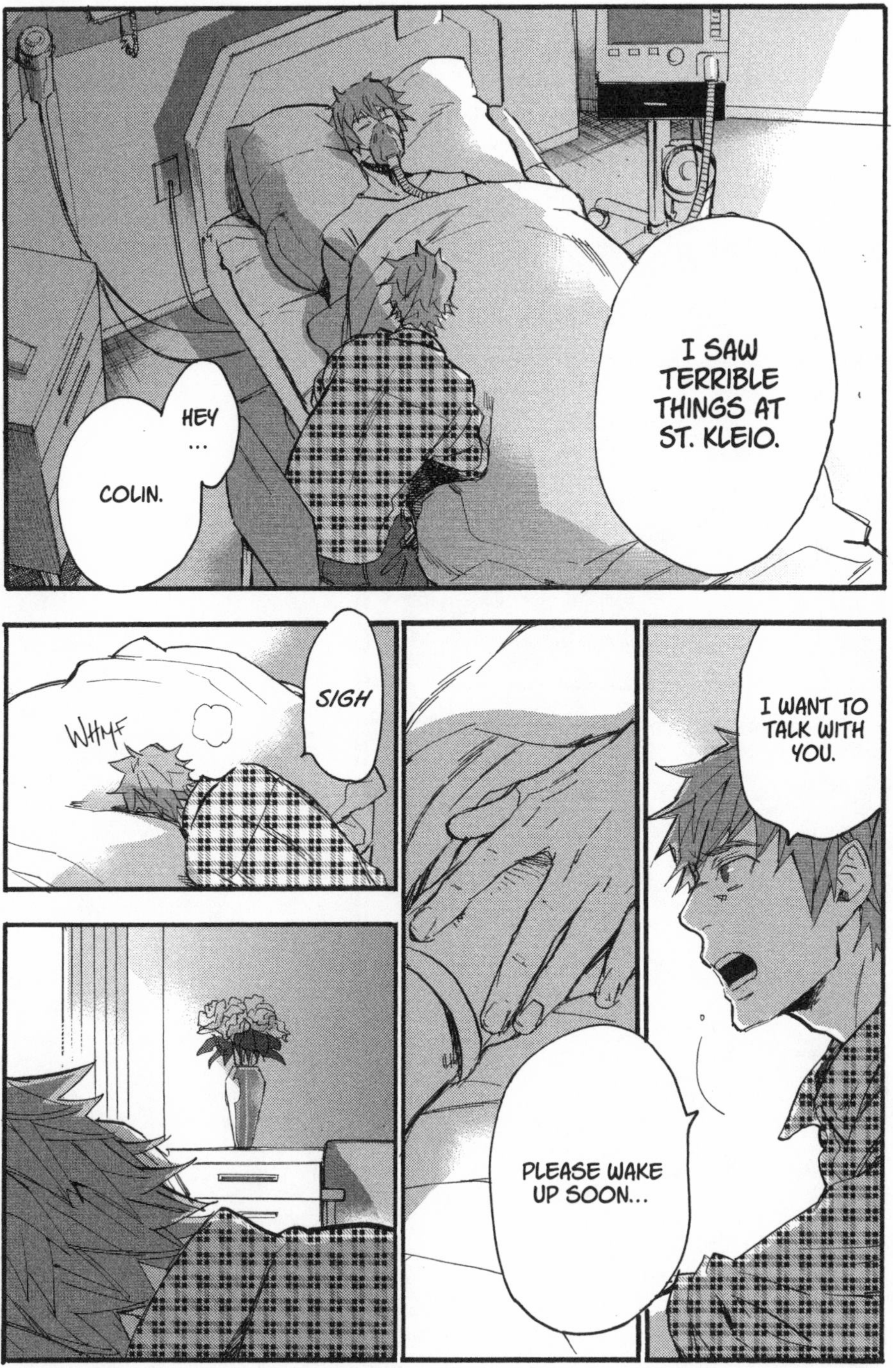
I SAW TERRIBLE THINGS AT ST. KLEIO.
HEY ...
COLIN.
I WANT TO TALK WITH YOU.
PLEASE WAKE UP SOON...
SIGH
WHMF

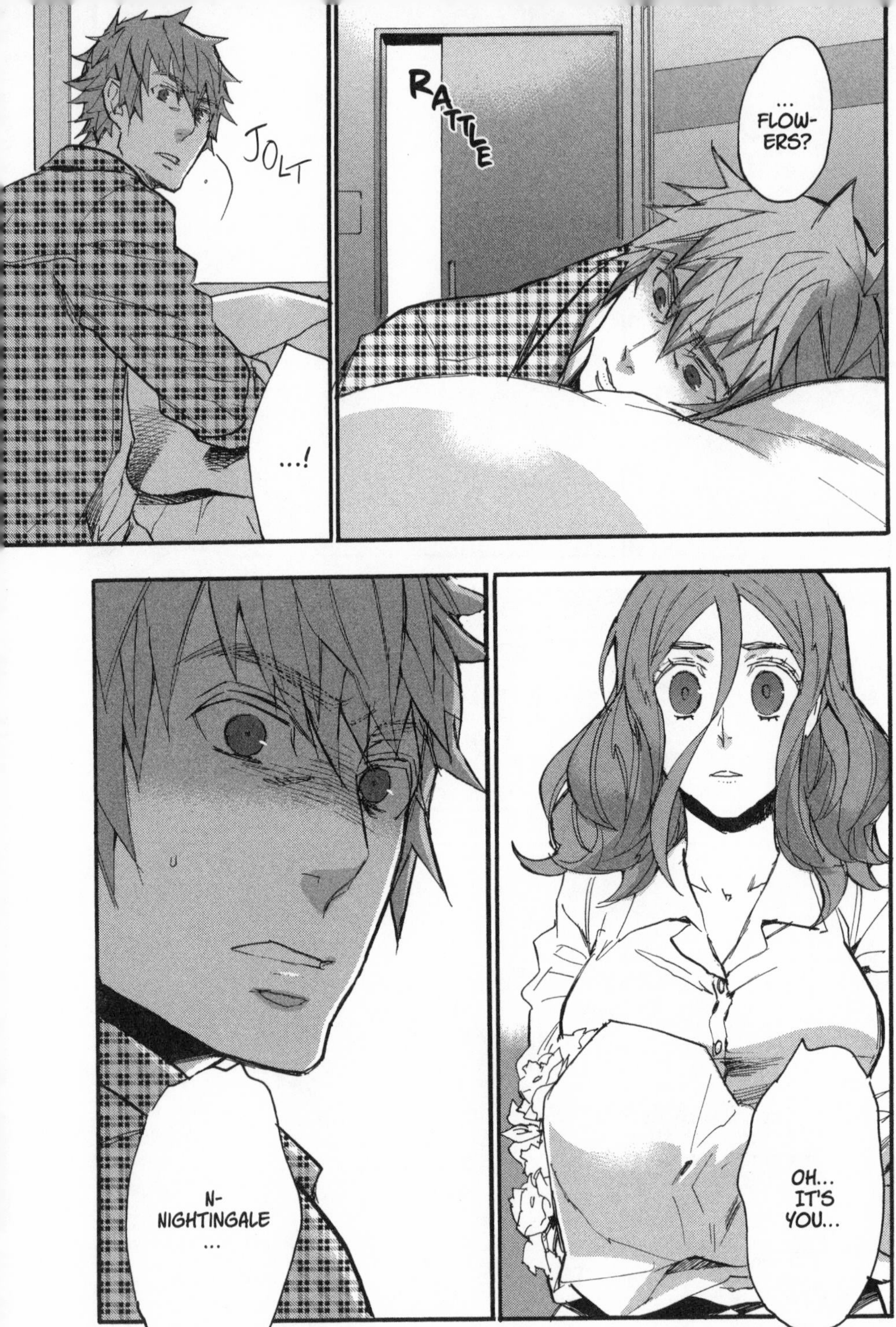
RATTLE
... FLOW-ERS?
JOLT
...!
OH... IT'S YOU...
N-NIGHTINGALE ...

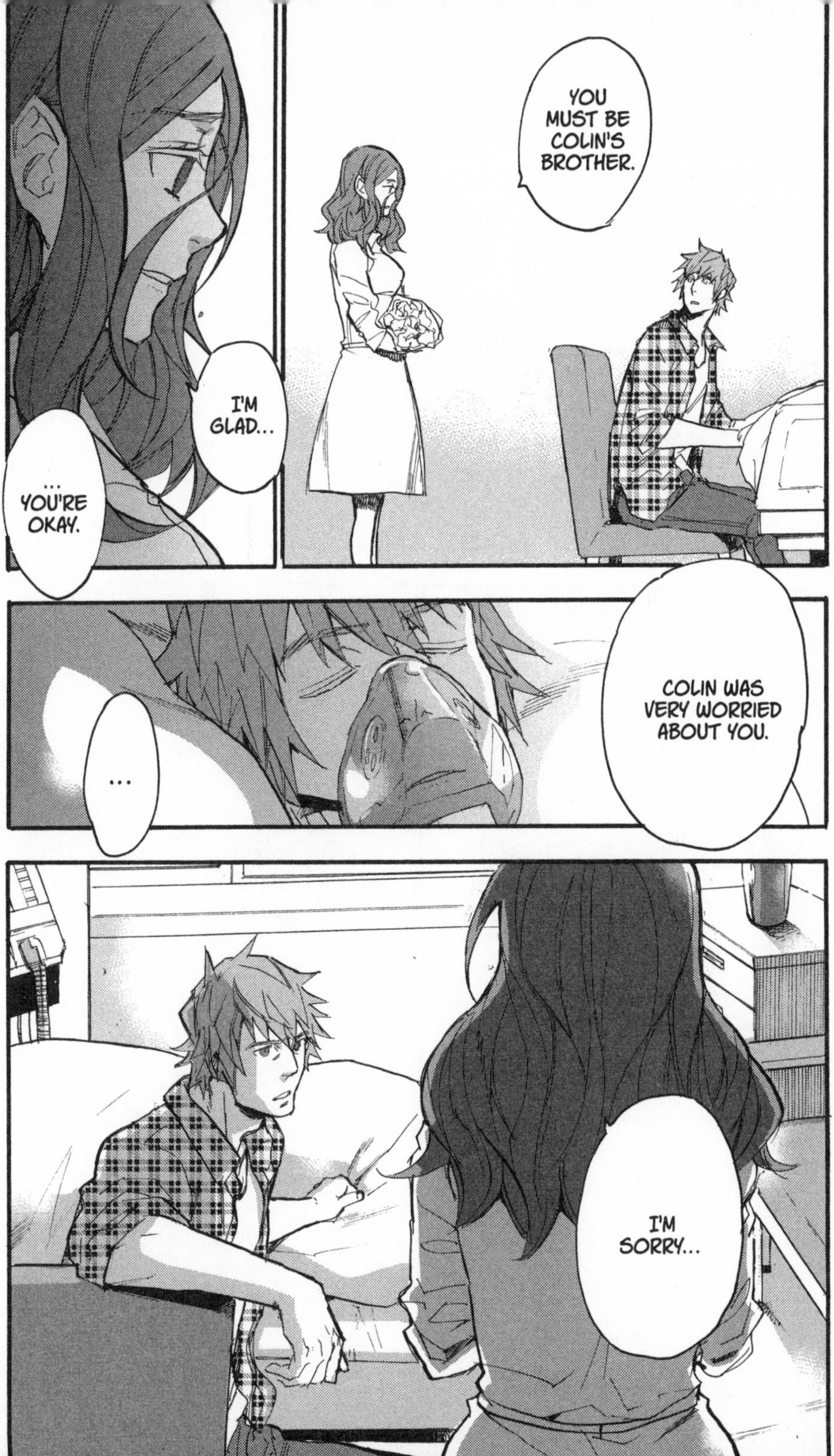
YOU MUST BE COLIN'S BROTHER.
I'M GLAD...
...YOU'RE OKAY.
COLIN WAS VERY WORRIED ABOUT YOU.
...
I'M SORRY...

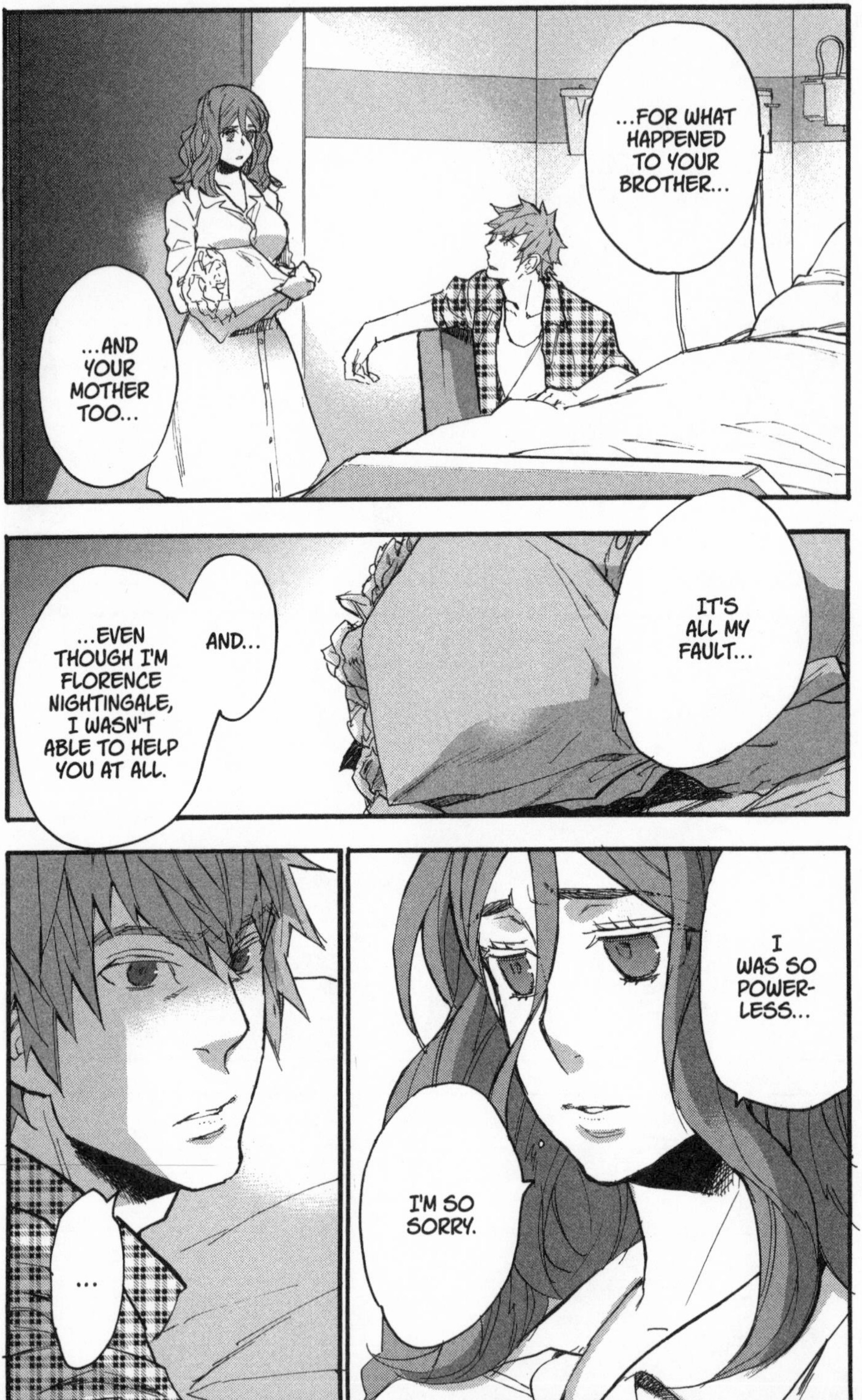
...FOR WHAT HAPPENED TO YOUR BROTHER...
...AND YOUR MOTHER TOO...
IT'S ALL MY FAULT...
AND...
...EVEN THOUGH I'M FLORENCE NIGHTINGALE, I WASN'T ABLE TO HELP YOU AT ALL.
I WAS SO POWER-LESS...
I'M SO SORRY.
...

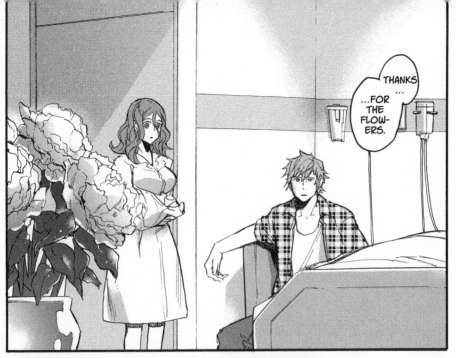

THANKS ...

...FOR THE FLOWERS.

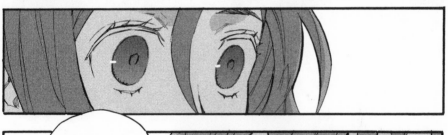

WE DON'T HAVE ANYONE TO DO STUFF LIKE THAT FOR US.

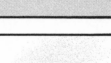

BEEP

BEEP

BEEP

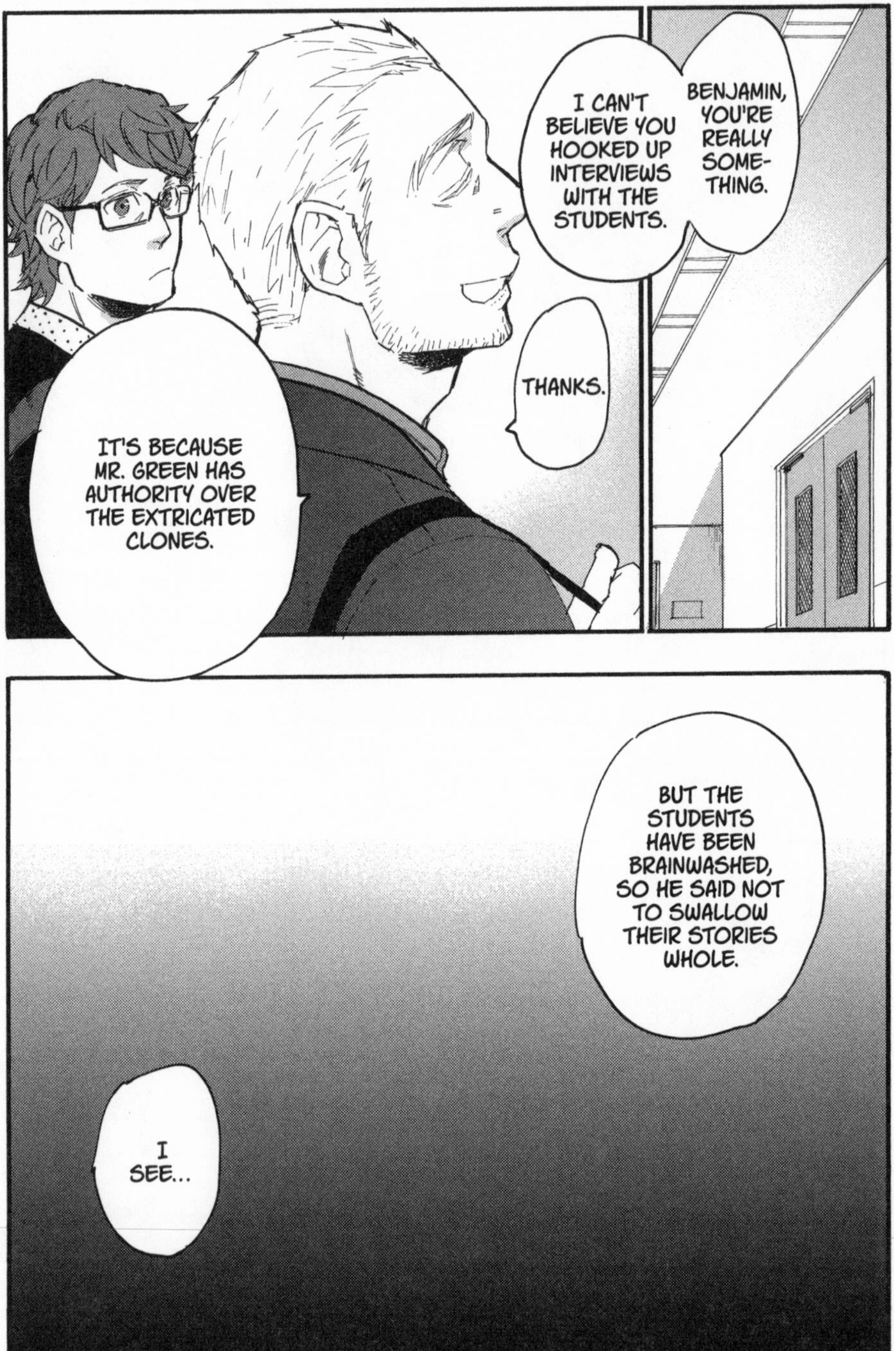
BENJAMIN, YOU'RE REALLY SOME-THING.
I CAN'T BELIEVE YOU HOOKED UP INTERVIEWS WITH THE STUDENTS.
THANKS.
IT'S BECAUSE MR. GREEN HAS AUTHORITY OVER THE EXTRICATED CLONES.
BUT THE STUDENTS HAVE BEEN BRAINWASHED, SO HE SAID NOT TO SWALLOW THEIR STORIES WHOLE.
I SEE...

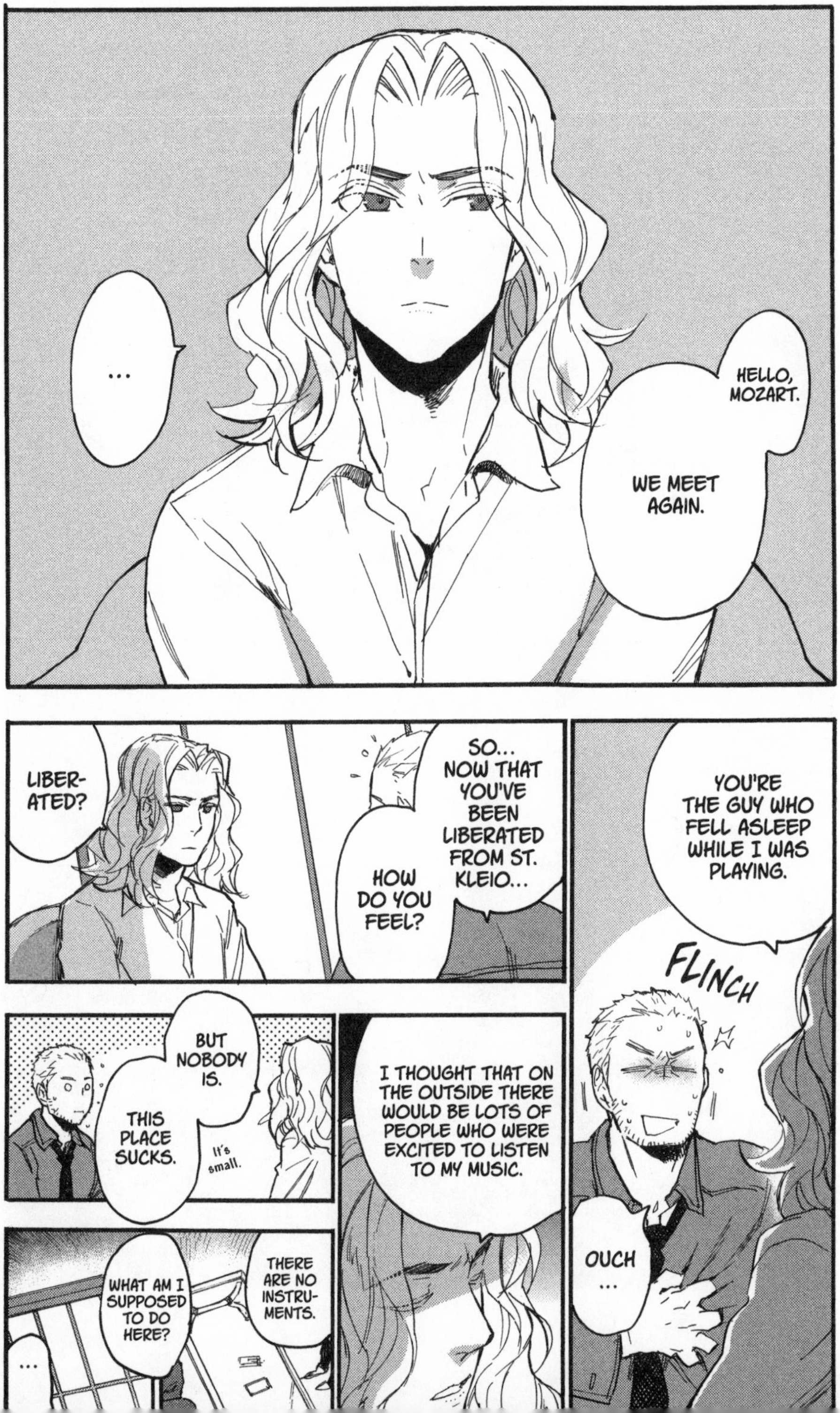
HELLO, MOZART.
WE MEET AGAIN.
...
YOU'RE THE GUY WHO FELL ASLEEP WHILE I WAS PLAYING.
FLINCH
OUCH ...
SO... NOW THAT YOU'VE BEEN LIBERATED FROM ST. KLEIO...
HOW DO YOU FEEL?
LIBER-ATED?
I THOUGHT THAT ON THE OUTSIDE THERE WOULD BE LOTS OF PEOPLE WHO WERE EXCITED TO LISTEN TO MY MUSIC.
BUT NOBODY IS.
THIS PLACE SUCKS.
It's small.
THERE ARE NO INSTRU-MENTS.
WHAT AM I SUPPOSED TO DO HERE?
...

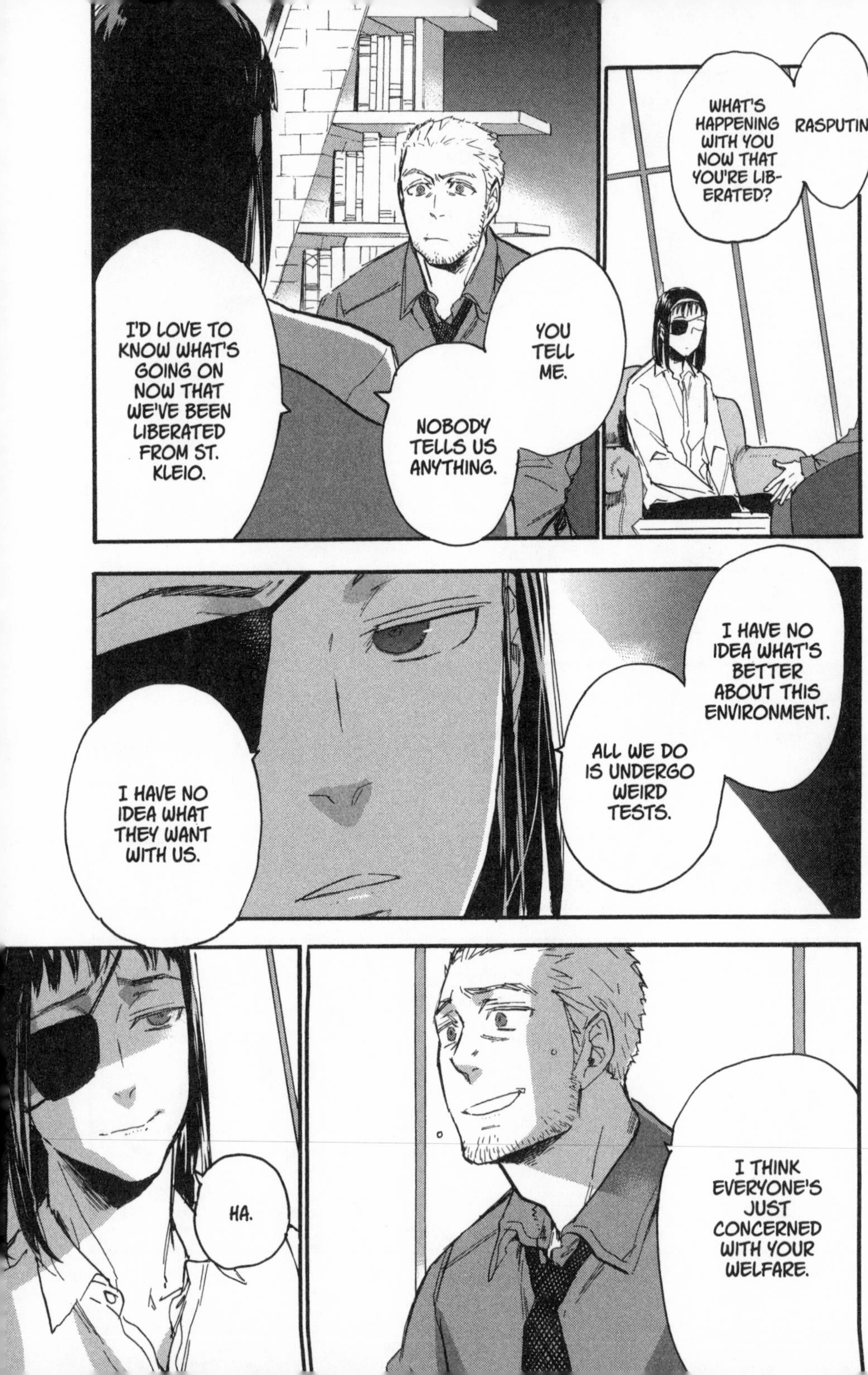
RASPUTIN.
WHAT'S HAPPENING WITH YOU NOW THAT YOU'RE LIB-ERATED?
YOU TELL ME.
NOBODY TELLS US ANYTHING.
I'D LOVE TO KNOW WHAT'S GOING ON NOW THAT WE'VE BEEN LIBERATED FROM ST. KLEIO.
I HAVE NO IDEA WHAT'S BETTER ABOUT THIS ENVIRONMENT.
ALL WE DO IS UNDERGO WEIRD TESTS.
I HAVE NO IDEA WHAT THEY WANT WITH US.
I THINK EVERYONE'S JUST CONCERNED WITH YOUR WELFARE.
HA.

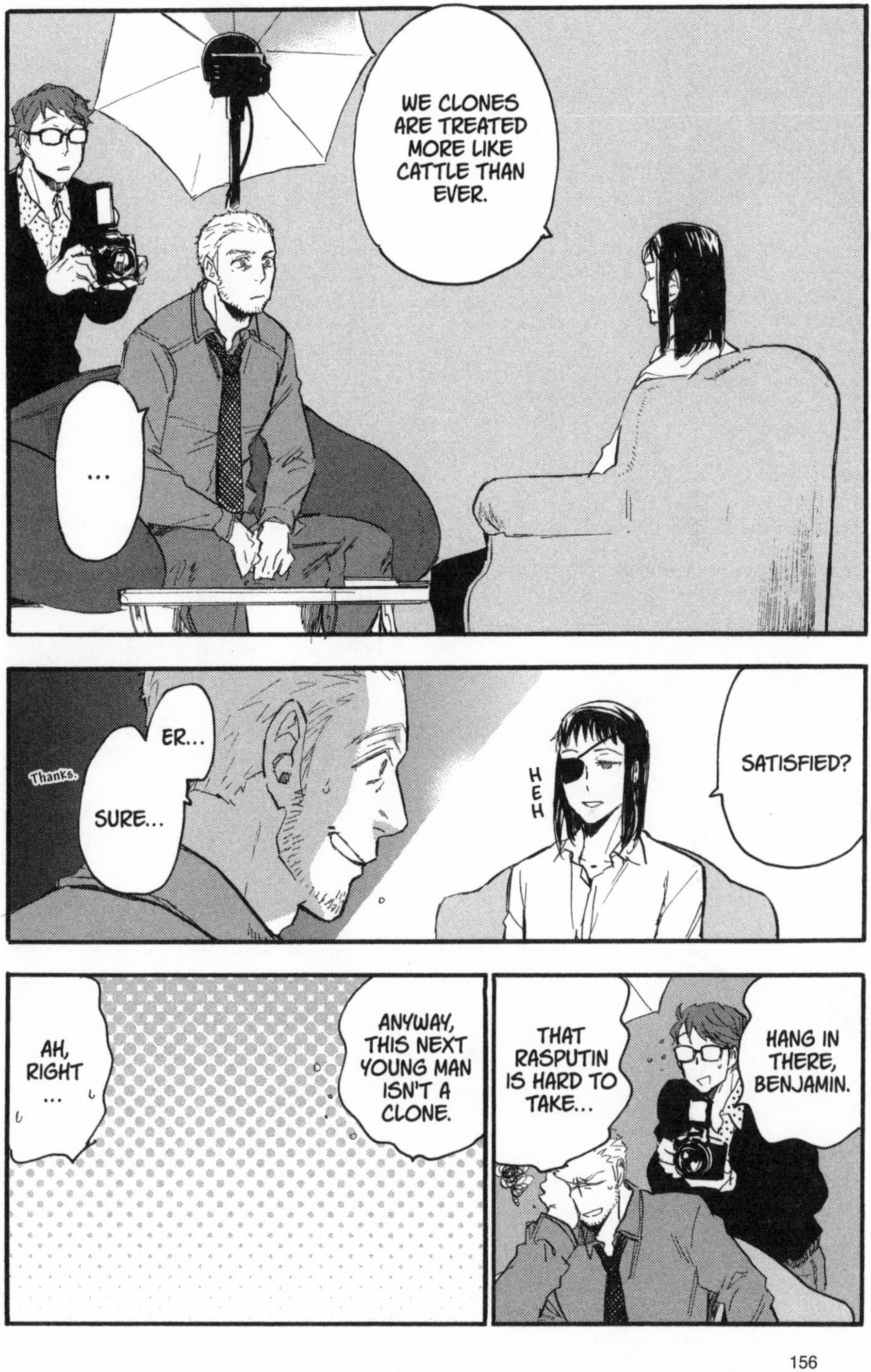
WE CLONES ARE TREATED MORE LIKE CATTLE THAN EVER.
...
SATISFIED?
HEH
ER...
SURE...
Thanks.
HANG IN THERE, BENJAMIN.
THAT RASPUTIN IS HARD TO TAKE...
ANYWAY, THIS NEXT YOUNG MAN ISN'T A CLONE.
AH, RIGHT ...

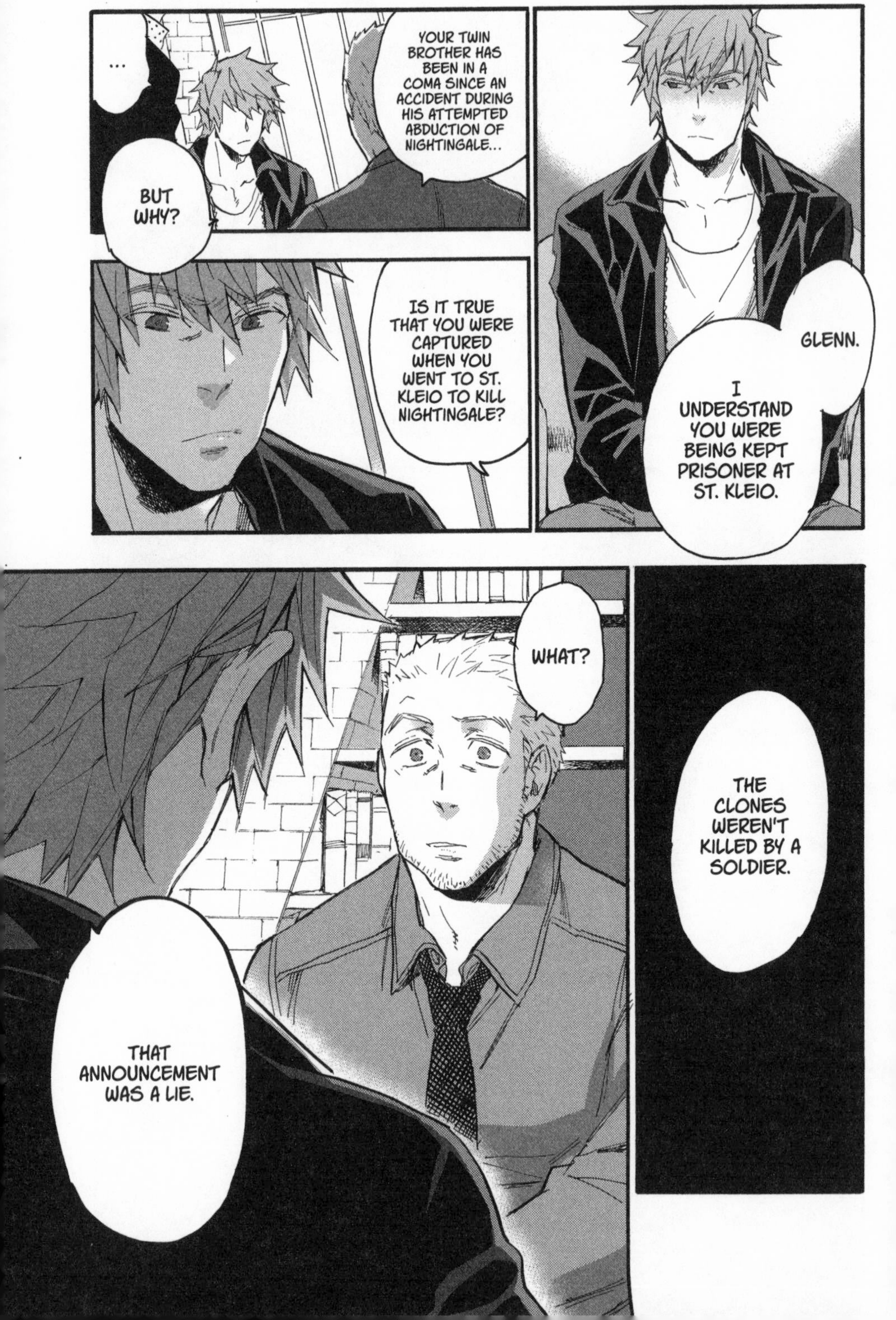
GLENN.
I UNDERSTAND YOU WERE BEING KEPT PRISONER AT ST. KLEIO.
YOUR TWIN BROTHER HAS BEEN IN A COMA SINCE AN ACCIDENT DURING HIS ATTEMPTED ABDUCTION OF NIGHTINGALE...
...
BUT WHY?
IS IT TRUE THAT YOU WERE CAPTURED WHEN YOU WENT TO ST. KLEIO TO KILL NIGHTINGALE?
THE CLONES WEREN'T KILLED BY A SOLDIER.
WHAT?
THAT ANNOUNCEMENT WAS A LIE.

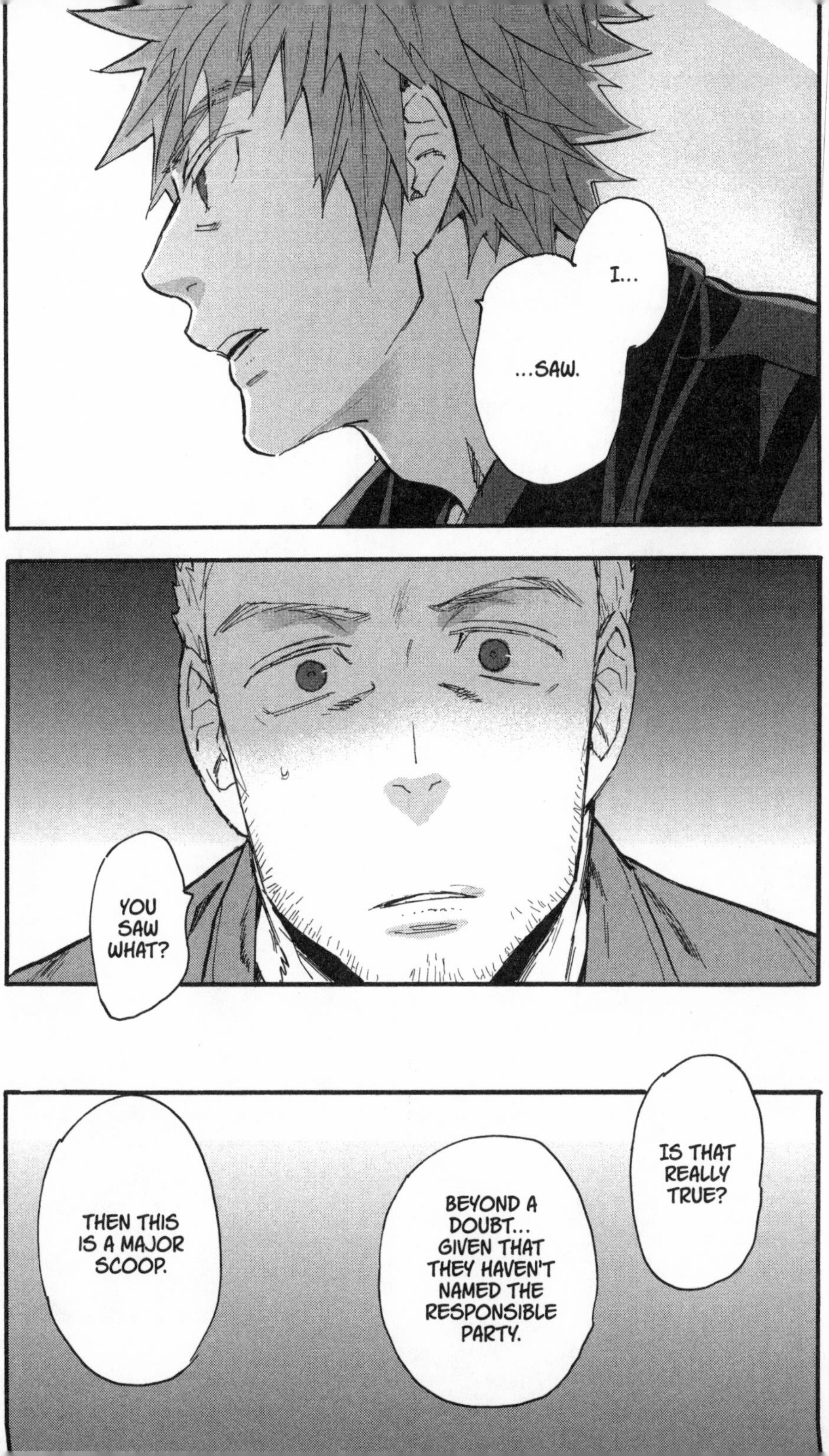
I...
...SAW.
YOU SAW WHAT?
IS THAT REALLY TRUE?
BEYOND A DOUBT... GIVEN THAT THEY HAVEN'T NAMED THE RESPONSIBLE PARTY.
THEN THIS IS A MAJOR SCOOP.

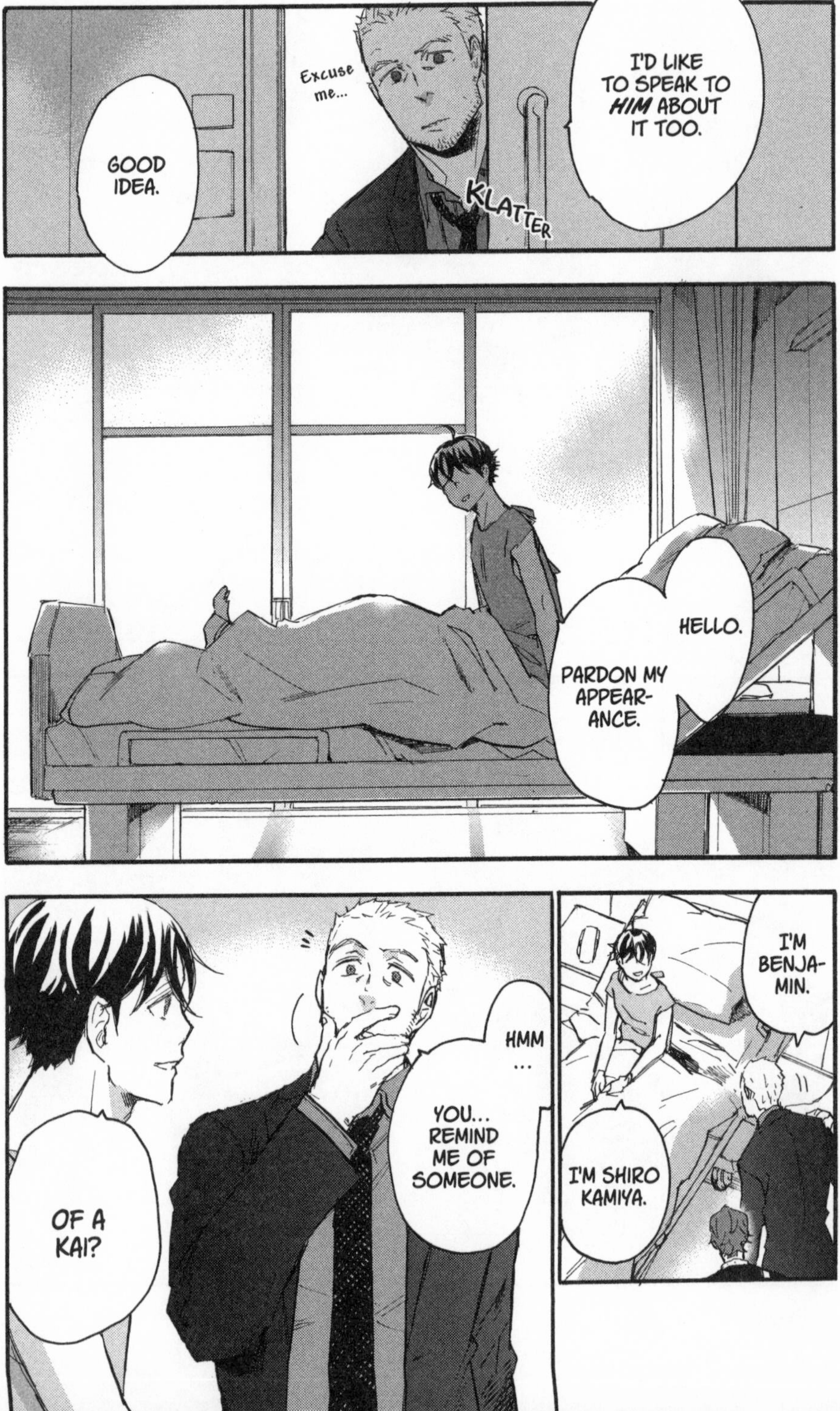
I'D LIKE TO SPEAK TO *HIM* ABOUT IT TOO.
Excuse me...
KLATTER
GOOD IDEA.
HELLO.
PARDON MY APPEAR-ANCE.
I'M BENJA-MIN.
I'M SHIRO KAMIYA.
HMM ...
YOU... REMIND ME OF SOMEONE.
OF A KAI?

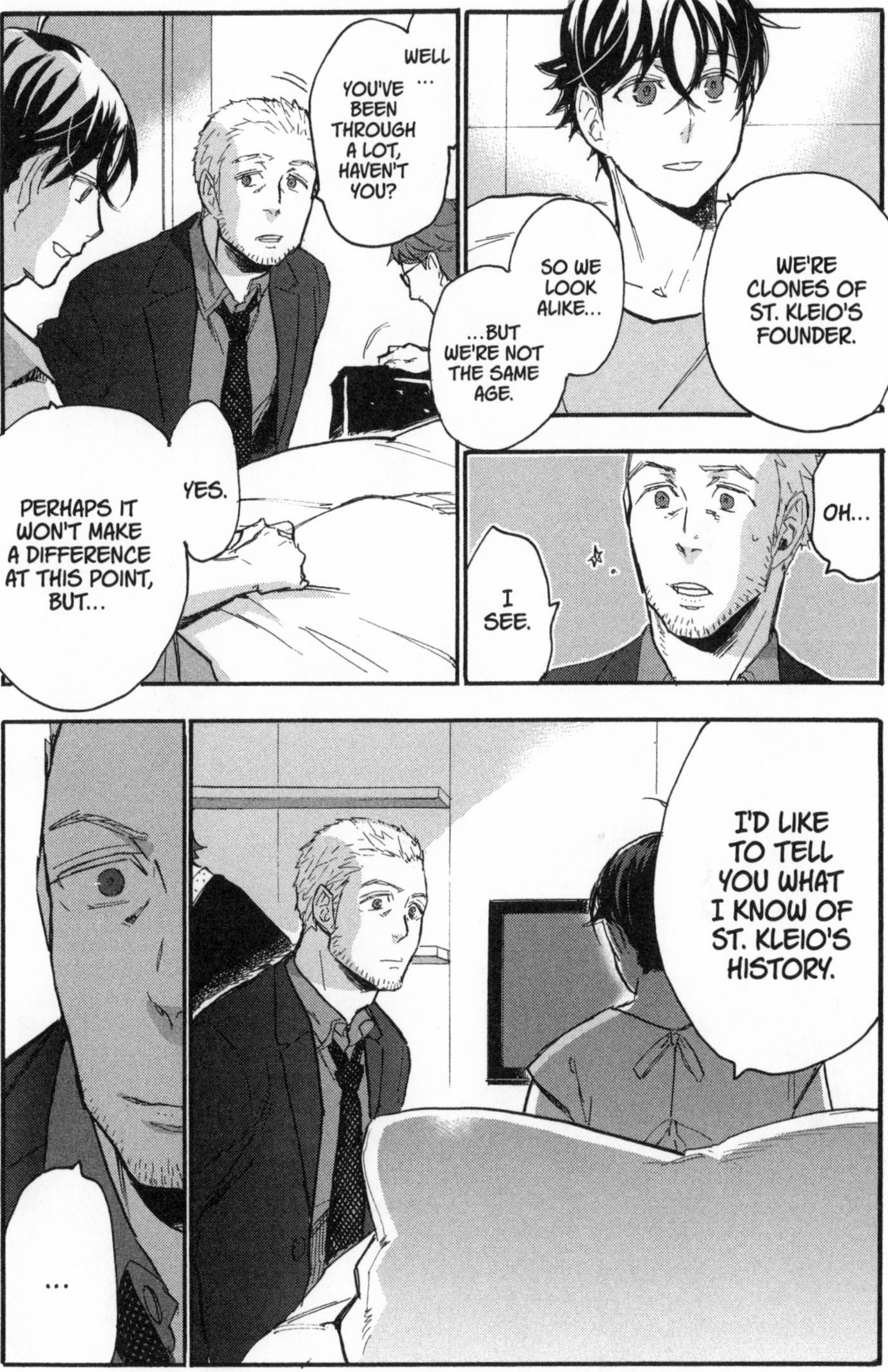
WE'RE CLONES OF ST. KLEIO'S FOUNDER.
SO WE LOOK ALIKE...
...BUT WE'RE NOT THE SAME AGE.
WELL ... YOU'VE BEEN THROUGH A LOT, HAVEN'T YOU?
OH... I SEE.
YES.
PERHAPS IT WON'T MAKE A DIFFERENCE AT THIS POINT, BUT...
I'D LIKE TO TELL YOU WHAT I KNOW OF ST. KLEIO'S HISTORY.
...

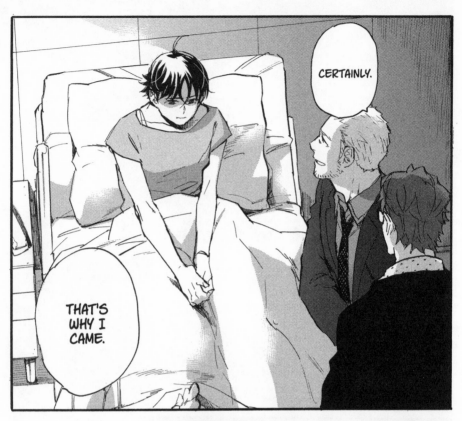

CERTAINLY.

THAT'S WHY I CAME.

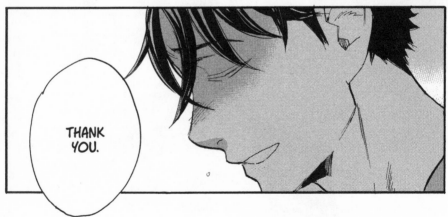

THANK YOU.

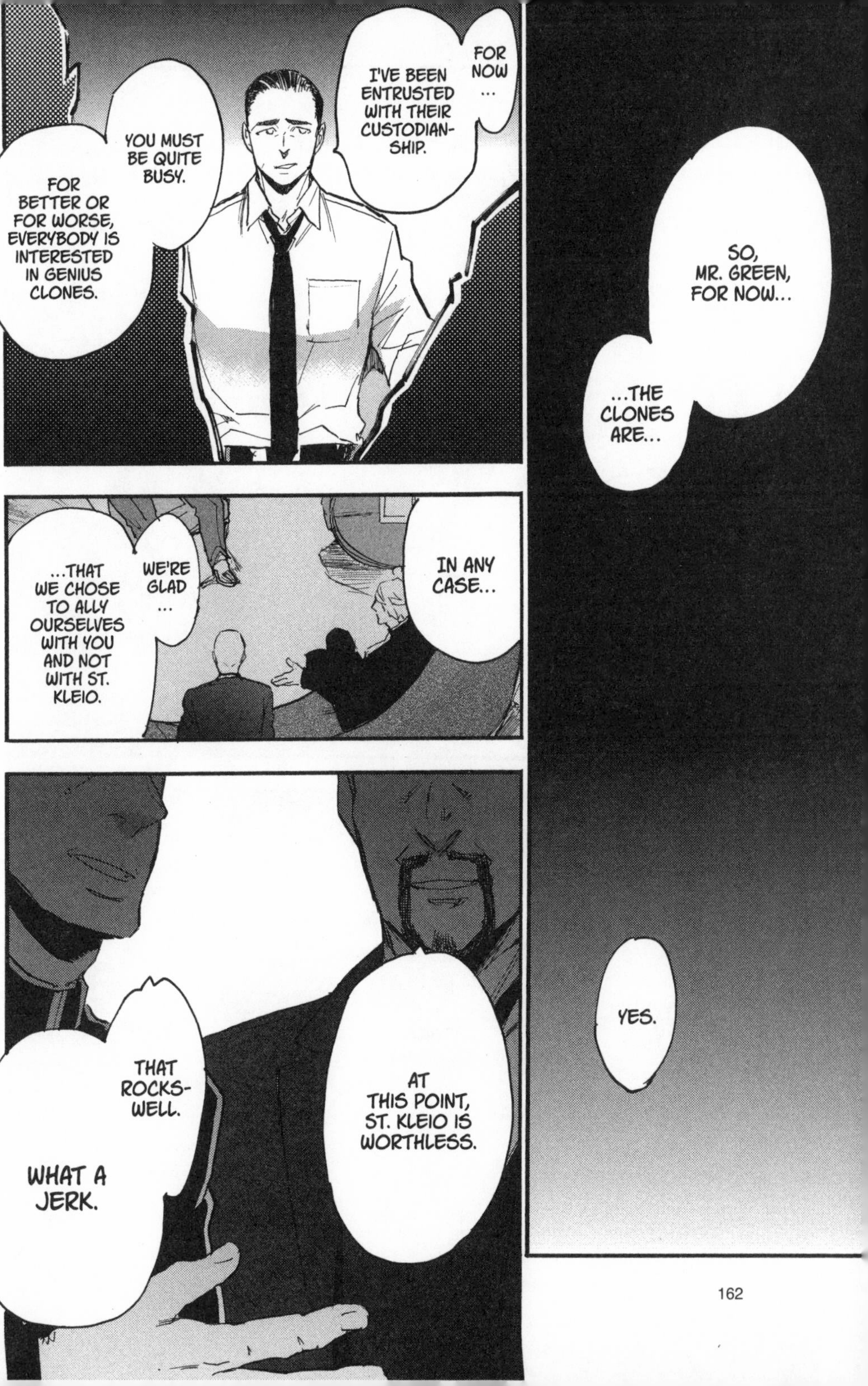
SO, MR. GREEN, FOR NOW...
...THE CLONES ARE...
YES.
FOR NOW...
I'VE BEEN ENTRUSTED WITH THEIR CUSTODIAN-SHIP.
YOU MUST BE QUITE BUSY.
FOR BETTER OR FOR WORSE, EVERYBODY IS INTERESTED IN GENIUS CLONES.
IN ANY CASE...
WE'RE GLAD...
...THAT WE CHOSE TO ALLY OURSELVES WITH YOU AND NOT WITH ST. KLEIO.
AT THIS POINT, ST. KLEIO IS WORTHLESS.
THAT ROCKS-WELL.
WHAT A JERK.

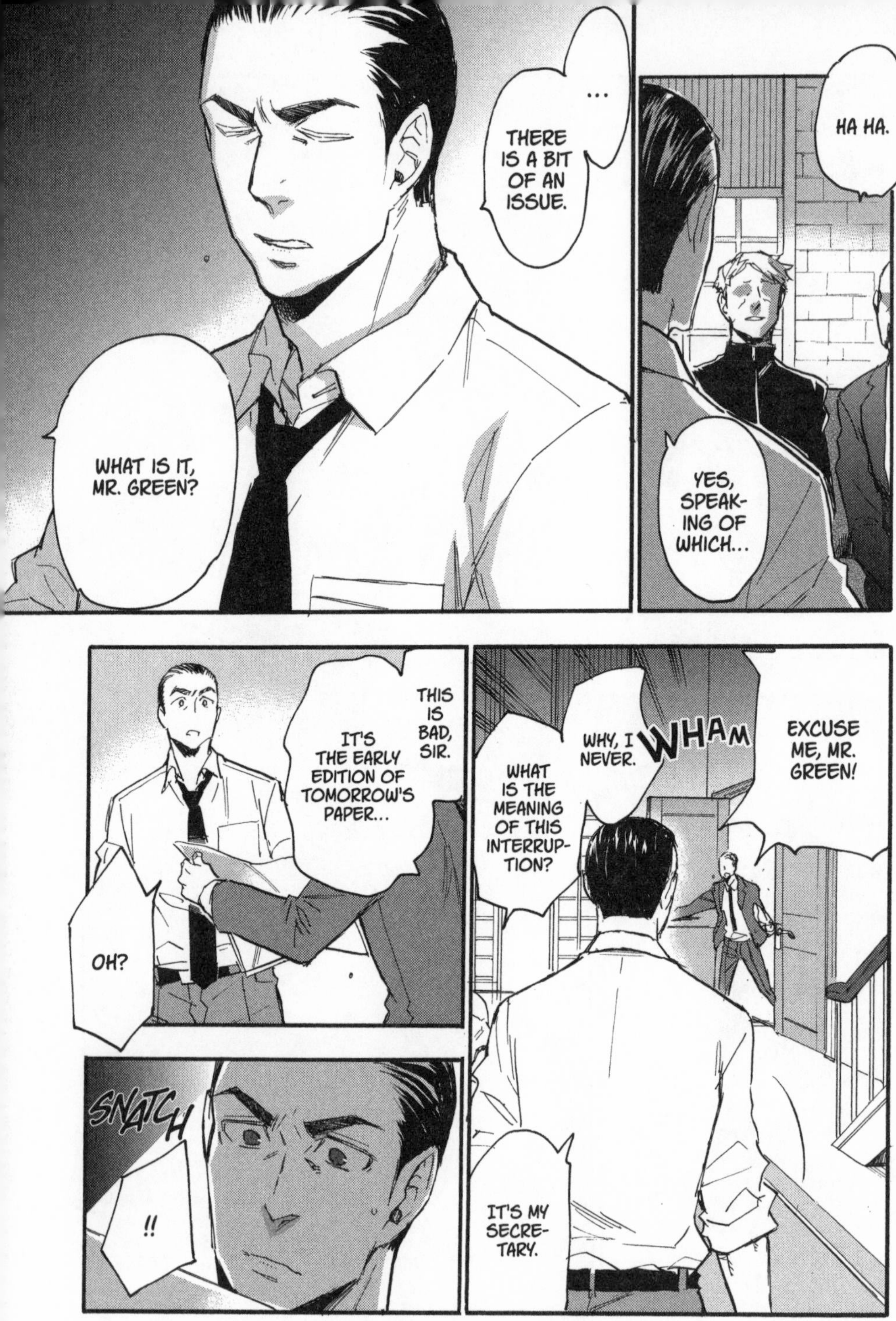
HA HA.
YES, SPEAKING OF WHICH...
...
THERE IS A BIT OF AN ISSUE.
WHAT IS IT, MR. GREEN?
EXCUSE ME, MR. GREEN!
WHAM
WHY, I NEVER.
WHAT IS THE MEANING OF THIS INTERRUPTION?
IT'S MY SECRETARY.
THIS IS BAD, SIR.
IT'S THE EARLY EDITION OF TOMORROW'S PAPER...
OH?
SNATCH
!!

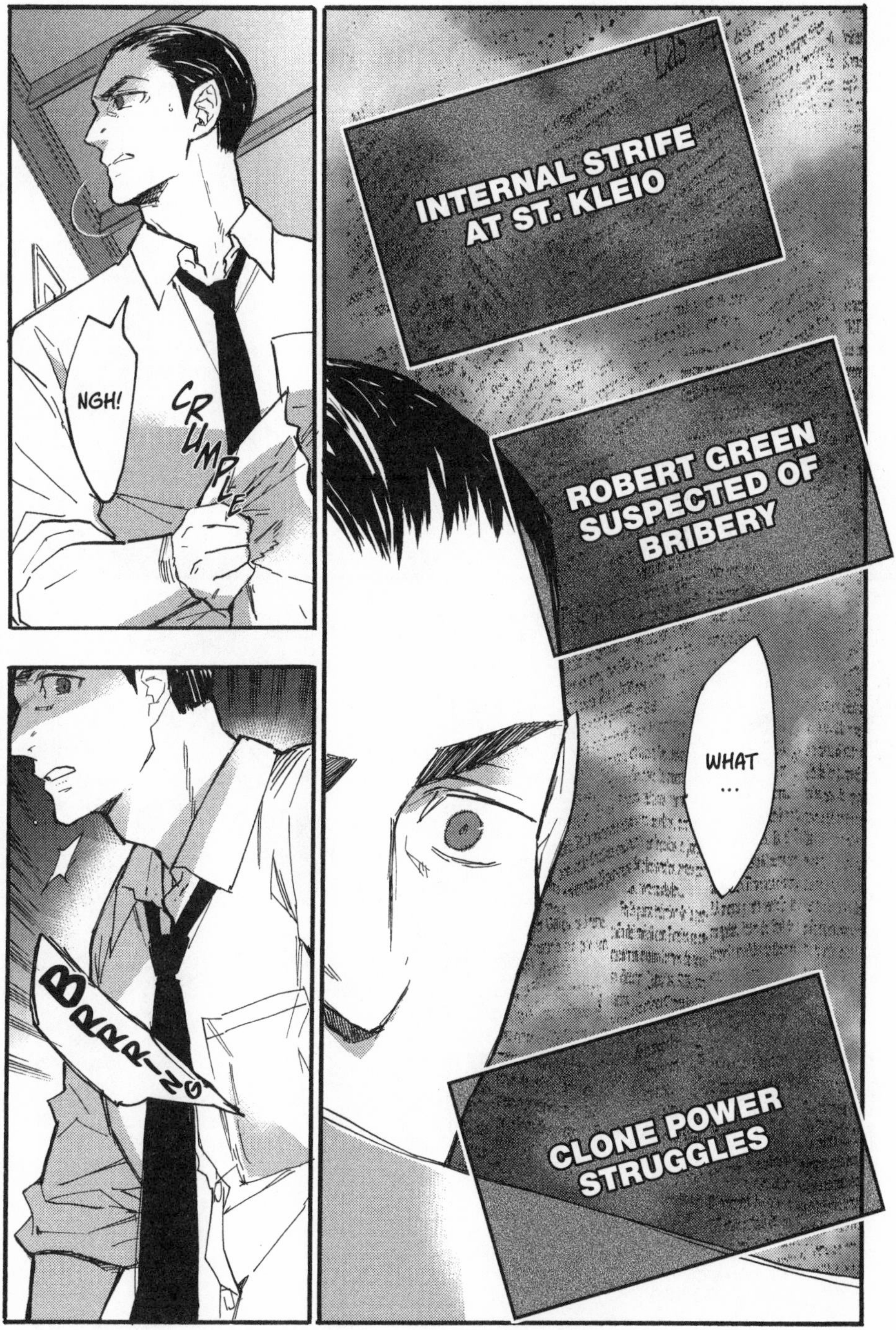
INTERNAL STRIFE AT ST. KLEIO
ROBERT GREEN SUSPECTED OF BRIBERY
WHAT...
CLONE POWER STRUGGLES
NGH!
CRUMPLE
BRRRR-NG

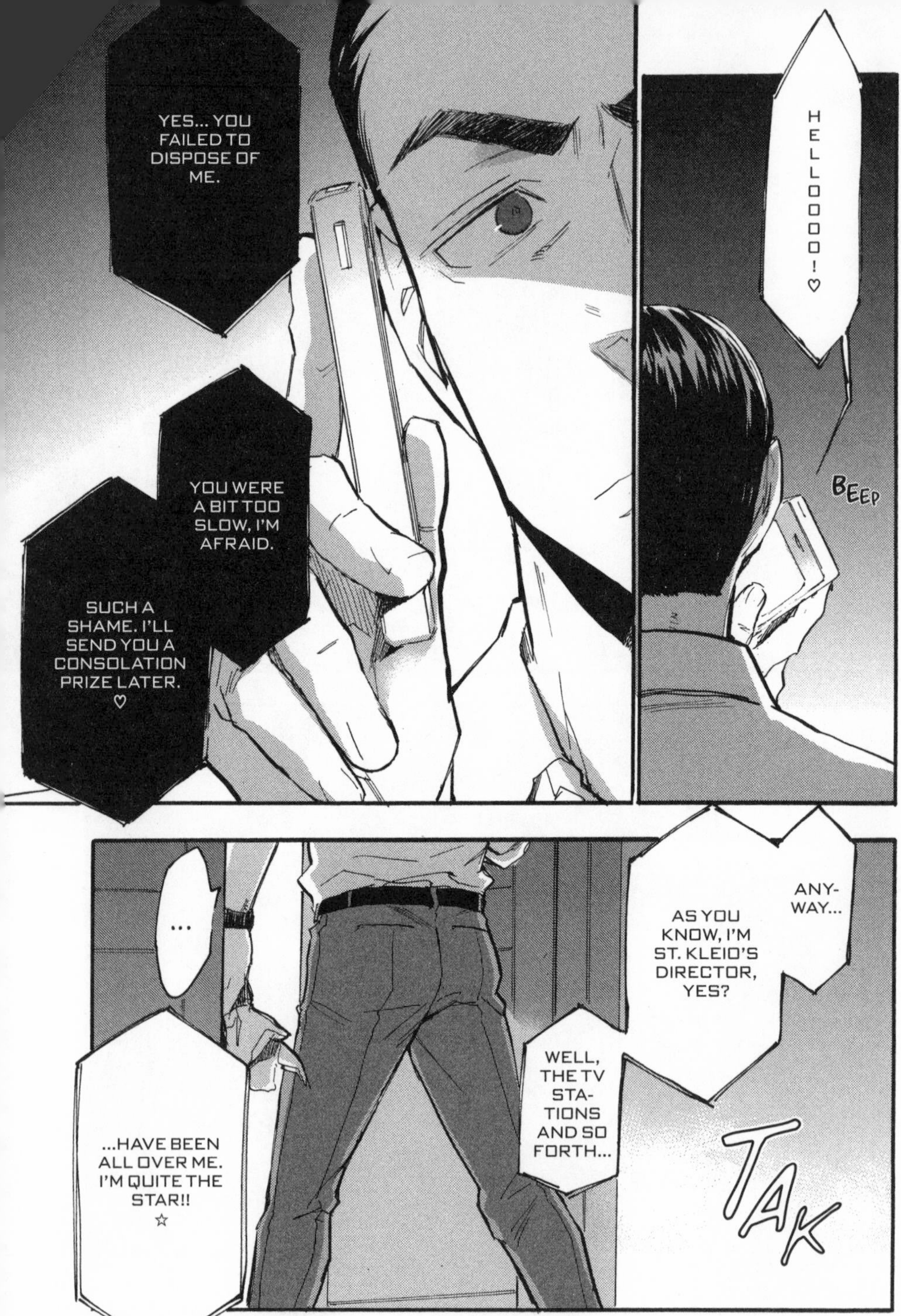
HELLOOOOO!♡
BEEP
YES... YOU FAILED TO DISPOSE OF ME.
YOU WERE A BIT TOO SLOW, I'M AFRAID.
SUCH A SHAME. I'LL SEND YOU A CONSOLATION PRIZE LATER. ♡
ANY-WAY...
AS YOU KNOW, I'M ST. KLEIO'S DIRECTOR, YES?
WELL, THE TV STA-TIONS AND SO FORTH...
TAK
...
...HAVE BEEN ALL OVER ME. I'M QUITE THE STAR!! ☆

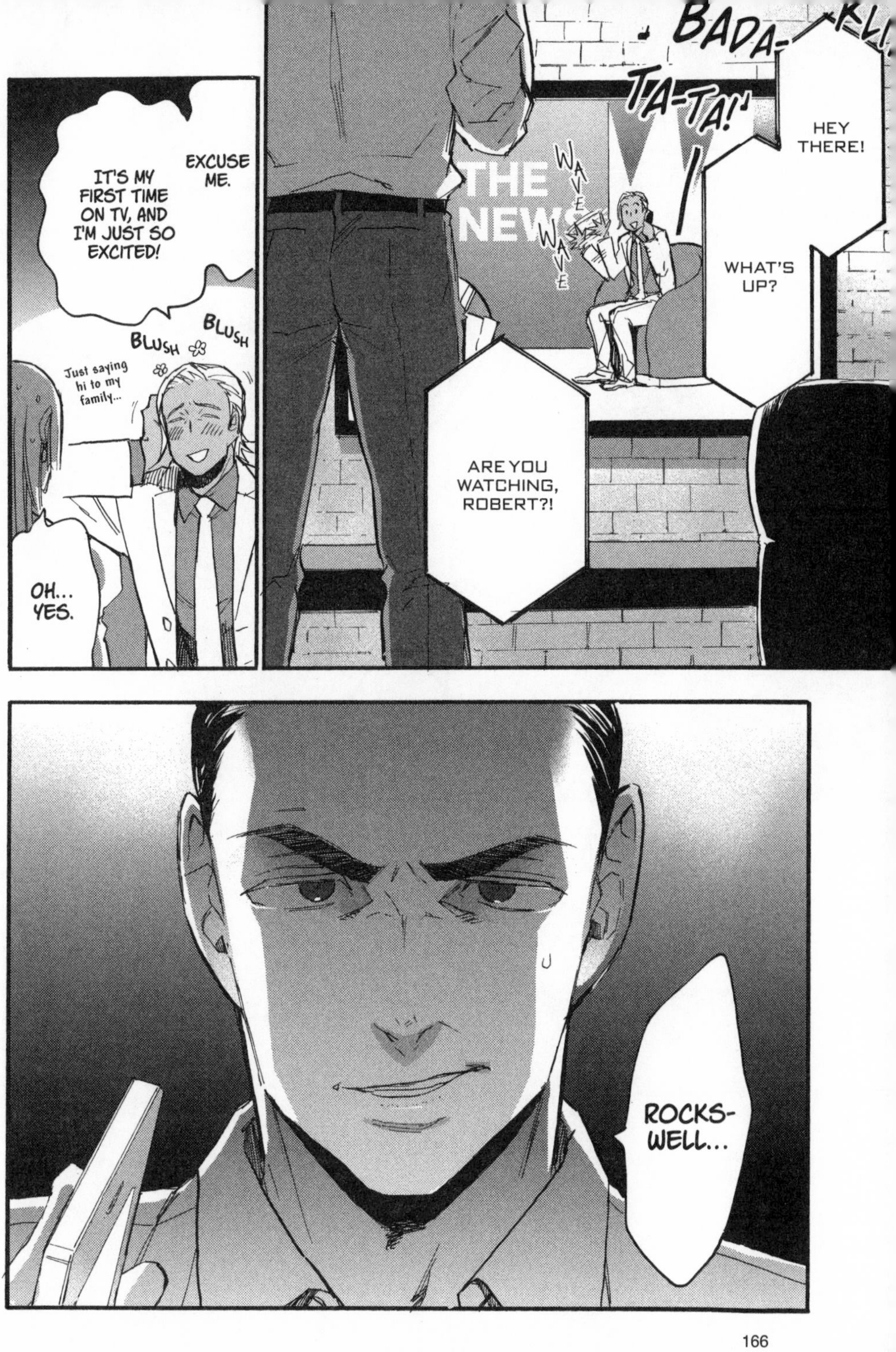
KLI
BADA-TA-TA!
HEY THERE!
WHAT'S UP?
WAVE WAVE
ARE YOU WATCHING, ROBERT?!
EXCUSE ME.
IT'S MY FIRST TIME ON TV, AND I'M JUST SO EXCITED!
BLUSH BLUSH
Just saying hi to my family...
OH... YES.
ROCKS-WELL...

FINAL CHAPTER

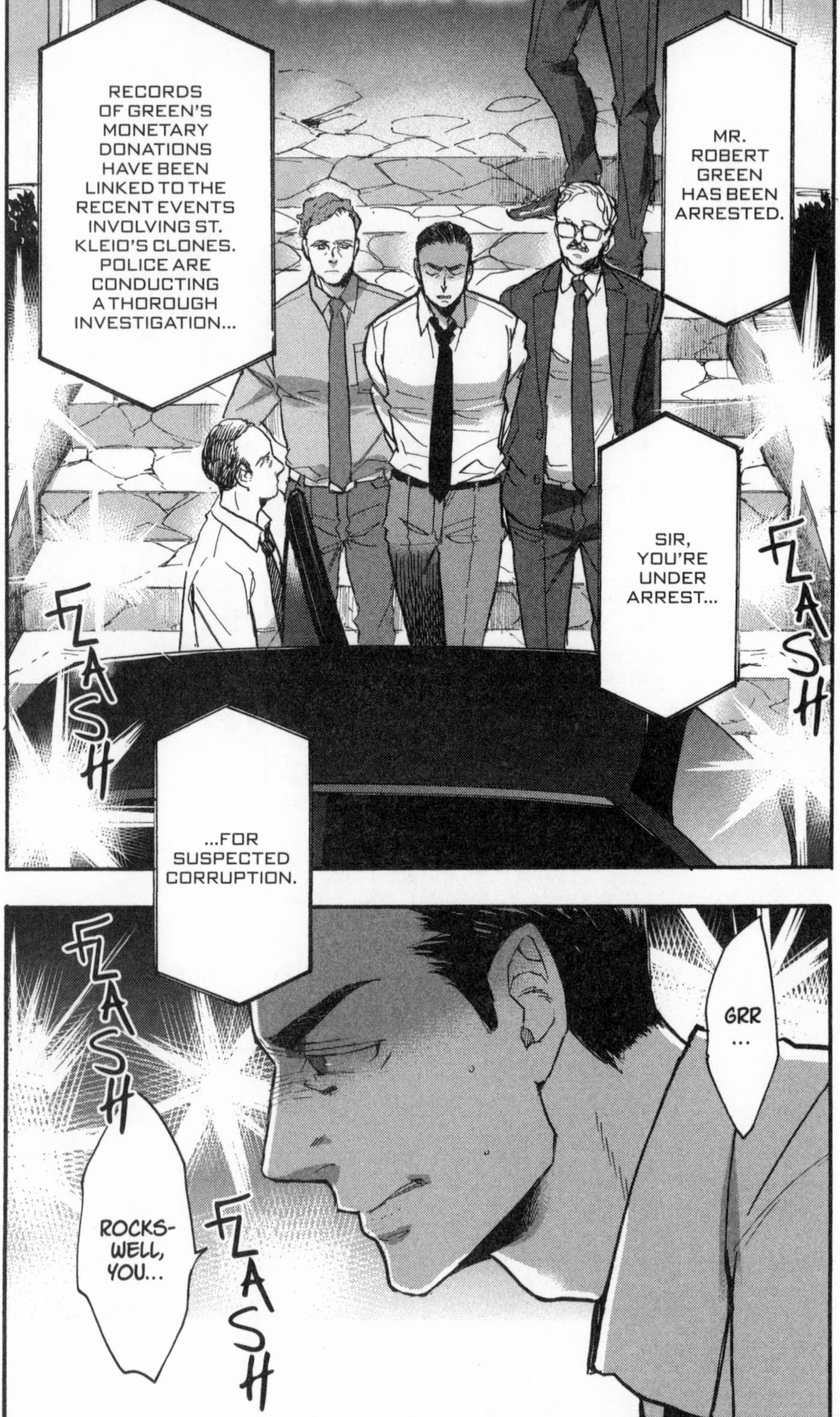
MR. ROBERT GREEN HAS BEEN ARRESTED.
RECORDS OF GREEN'S MONETARY DONATIONS HAVE BEEN LINKED TO THE RECENT EVENTS INVOLVING ST. KLEIO'S CLONES. POLICE ARE CONDUCTING A THOROUGH INVESTIGATION...
FLASH
SIR, YOU'RE UNDER ARREST...
FLASH
...FOR SUSPECTED CORRUPTION.
GRR...
FLASH
FLASH
ROCKS-WELL, YOU...

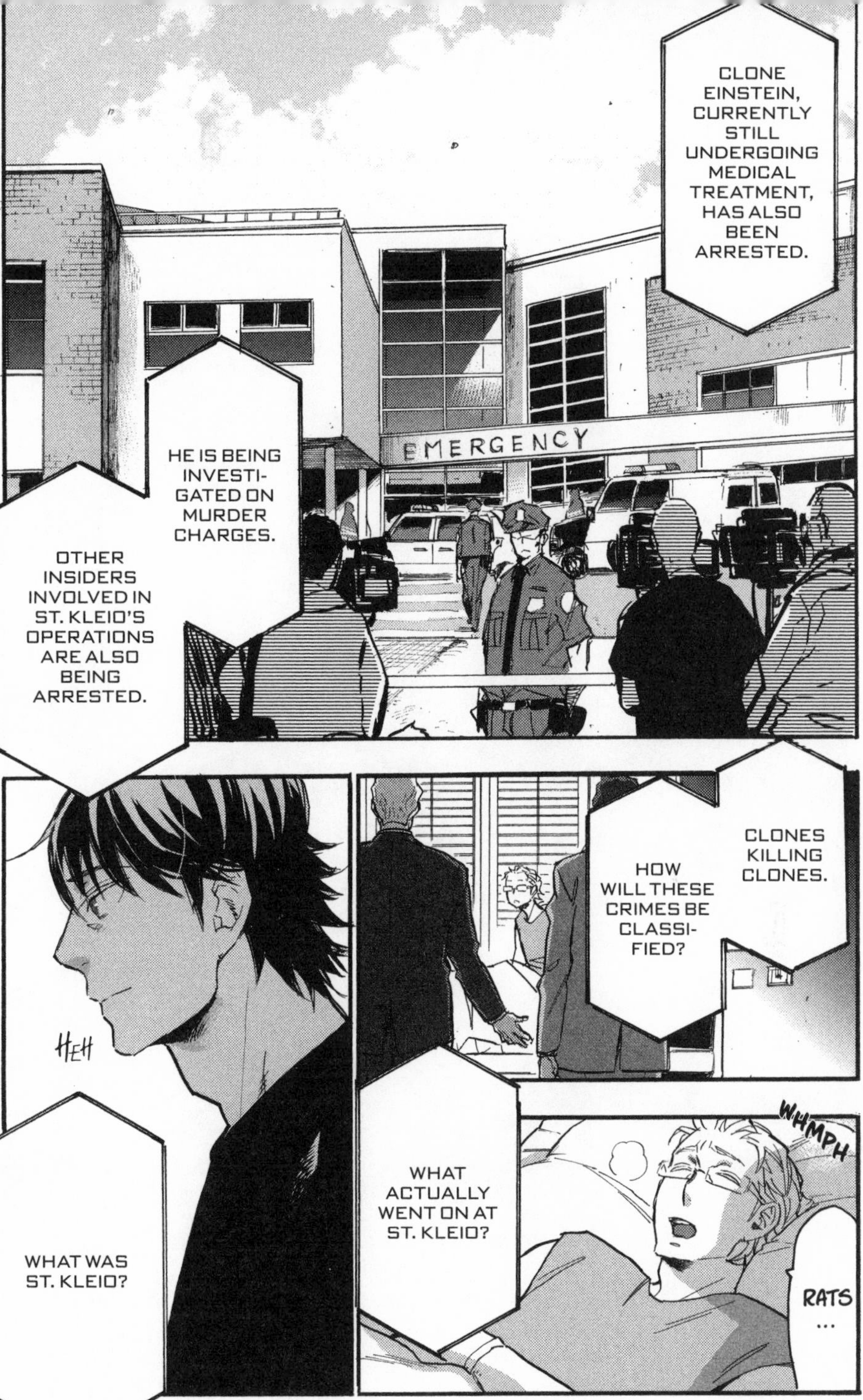

CLONE EINSTEIN, CURRENTLY STILL UNDERGOING MEDICAL TREATMENT, HAS ALSO BEEN ARRESTED.
EMERGENCY
HE IS BEING INVESTI-GATED ON MURDER CHARGES.
OTHER INSIDERS INVOLVED IN ST. KLEIO'S OPERATIONS ARE ALSO BEING ARRESTED.
CLONES KILLING CLONES.
HOW WILL THESE CRIMES BE CLASSI-FIED?
WHMPH
RATS...
WHAT ACTUALLY WENT ON AT ST. KLEIO?
HEH
WHAT WAS ST. KLEIO?

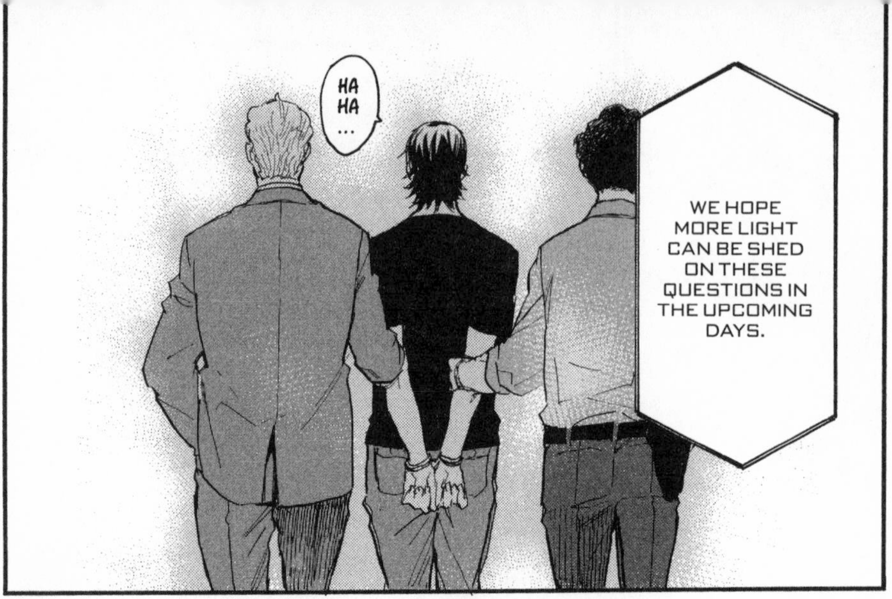
WE HOPE MORE LIGHT CAN BE SHED ON THESE QUESTIONS IN THE UPCOMING DAYS.
HA HA ...

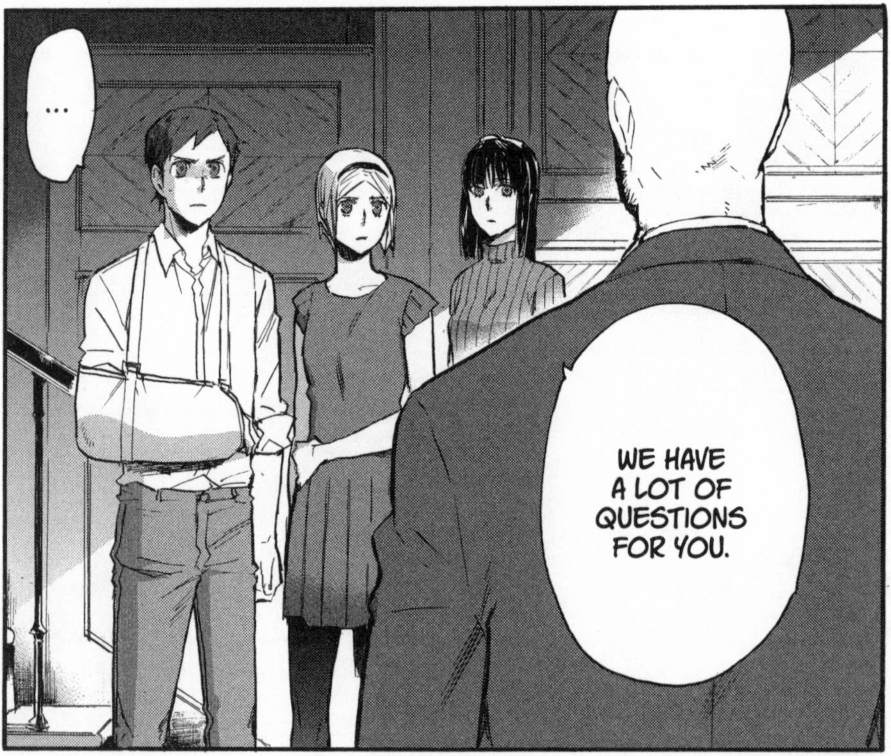
WE HAVE A LOT OF QUESTIONS FOR YOU.
...

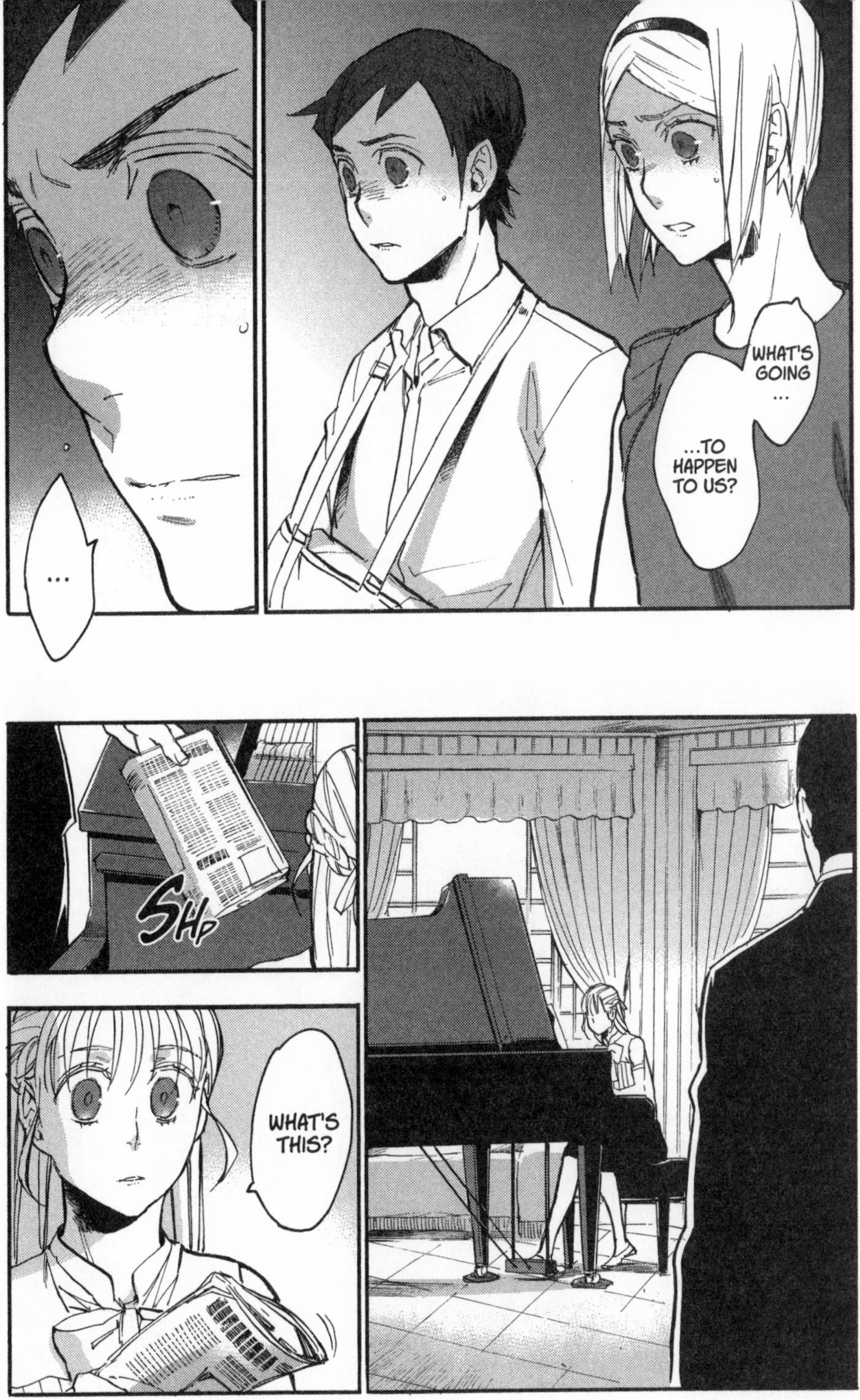
WHAT'S GOING ...
...TO HAPPEN TO US?
...
SHP
WHAT'S THIS?

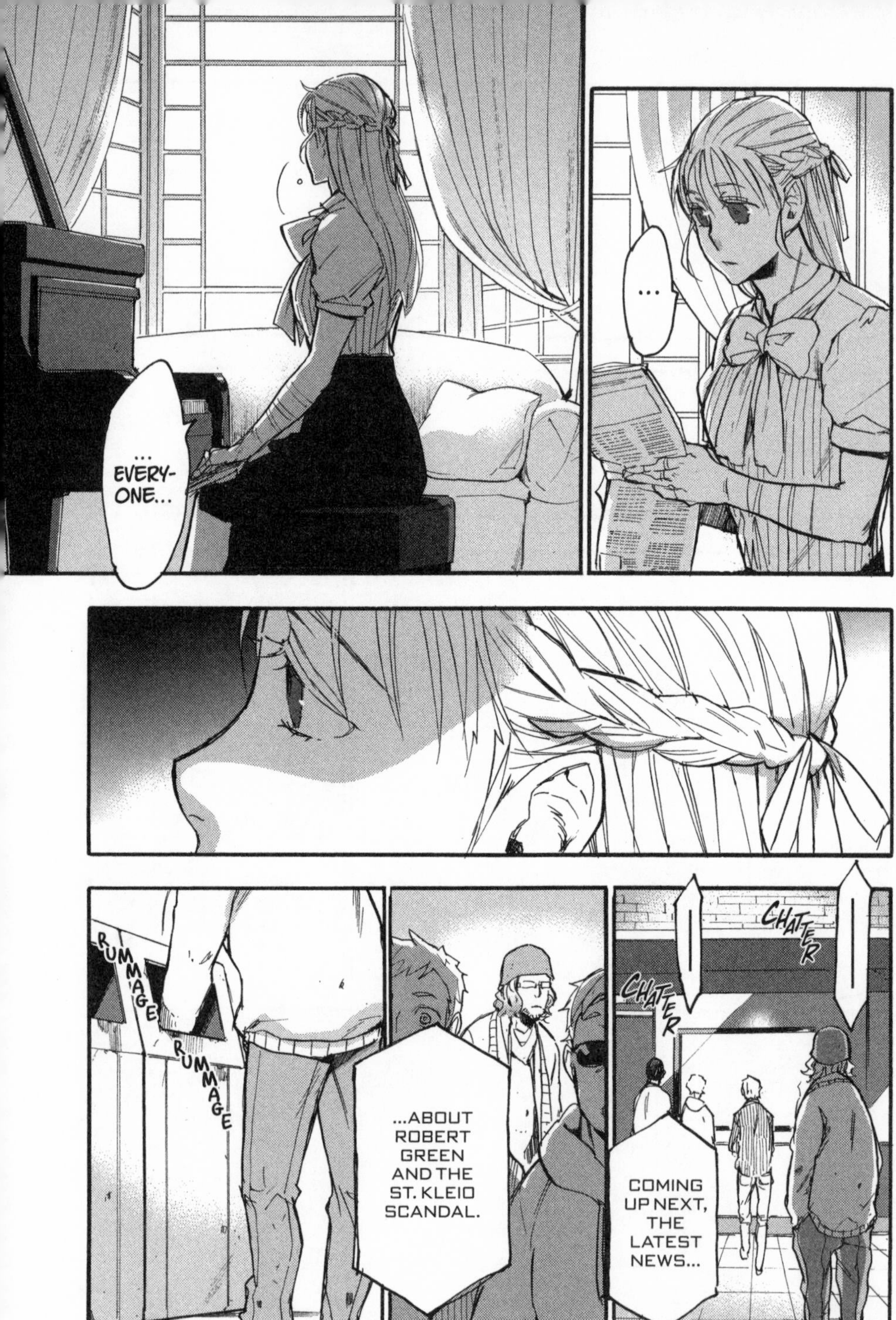
...
... EVERY-ONE...
!
!
CHATTER
CHATTER
COMING UP NEXT, THE LATEST NEWS...
...ABOUT ROBERT GREEN AND THE ST. KLEIO SCANDAL.
RUMMAGE
RUMMAGE

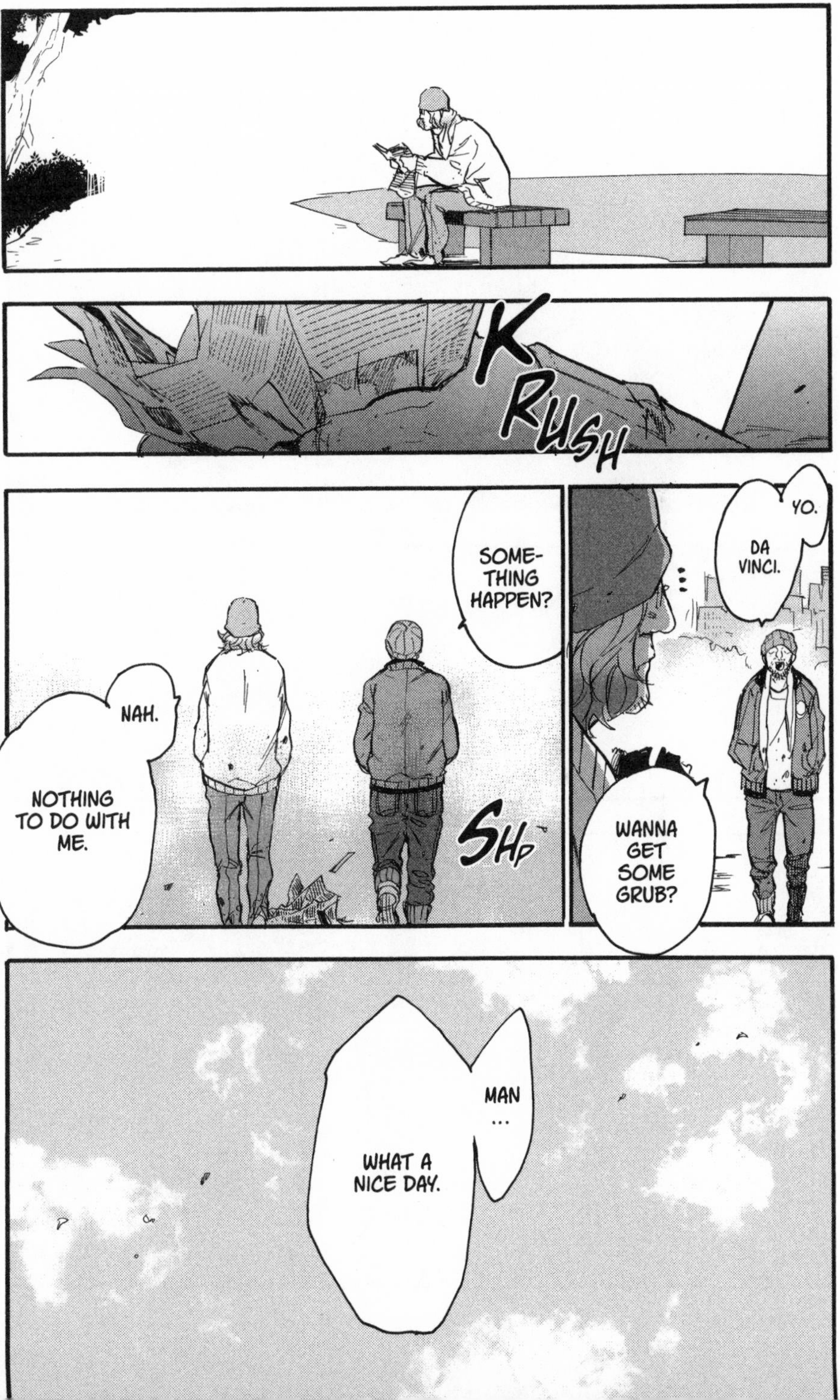
KRUSH
YO.
DA VINCI.
...
WANNA GET SOME GRUB?
SOMETHING HAPPEN?
NAH.
NOTHING TO DO WITH ME.
SHP
MAN...
WHAT A NICE DAY.

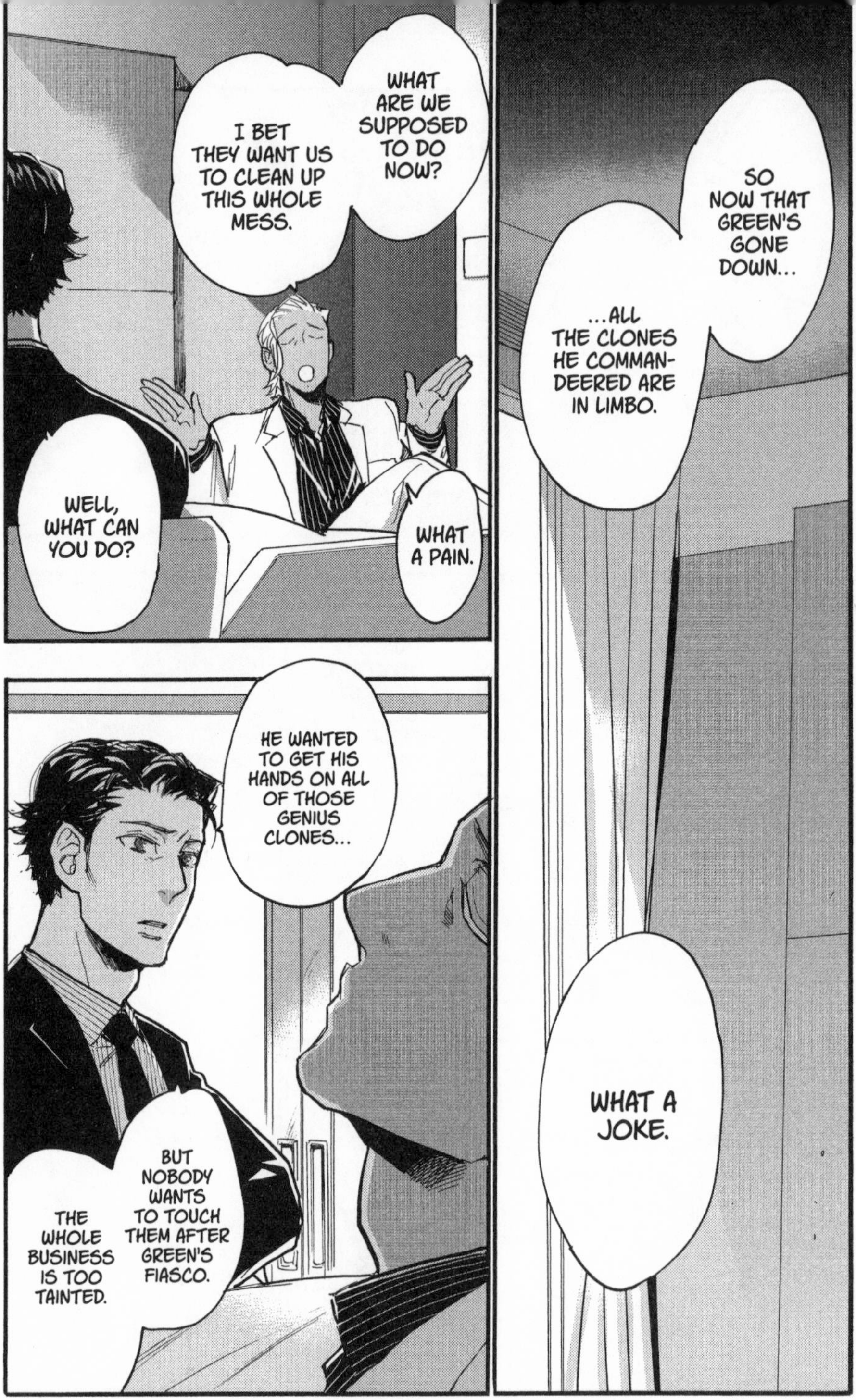
SO NOW THAT GREEN'S GONE DOWN...
...ALL THE CLONES HE COMMANDEERED ARE IN LIMBO.
WHAT A JOKE.
WHAT ARE WE SUPPOSED TO DO NOW?
I BET THEY WANT US TO CLEAN UP THIS WHOLE MESS.
WHAT A PAIN.
WELL, WHAT CAN YOU DO?
HE WANTED TO GET HIS HANDS ON ALL OF THOSE GENIUS CLONES...
BUT NOBODY WANTS TO TOUCH THEM AFTER GREEN'S FIASCO.
THE WHOLE BUSINESS IS TOO TAINTED.

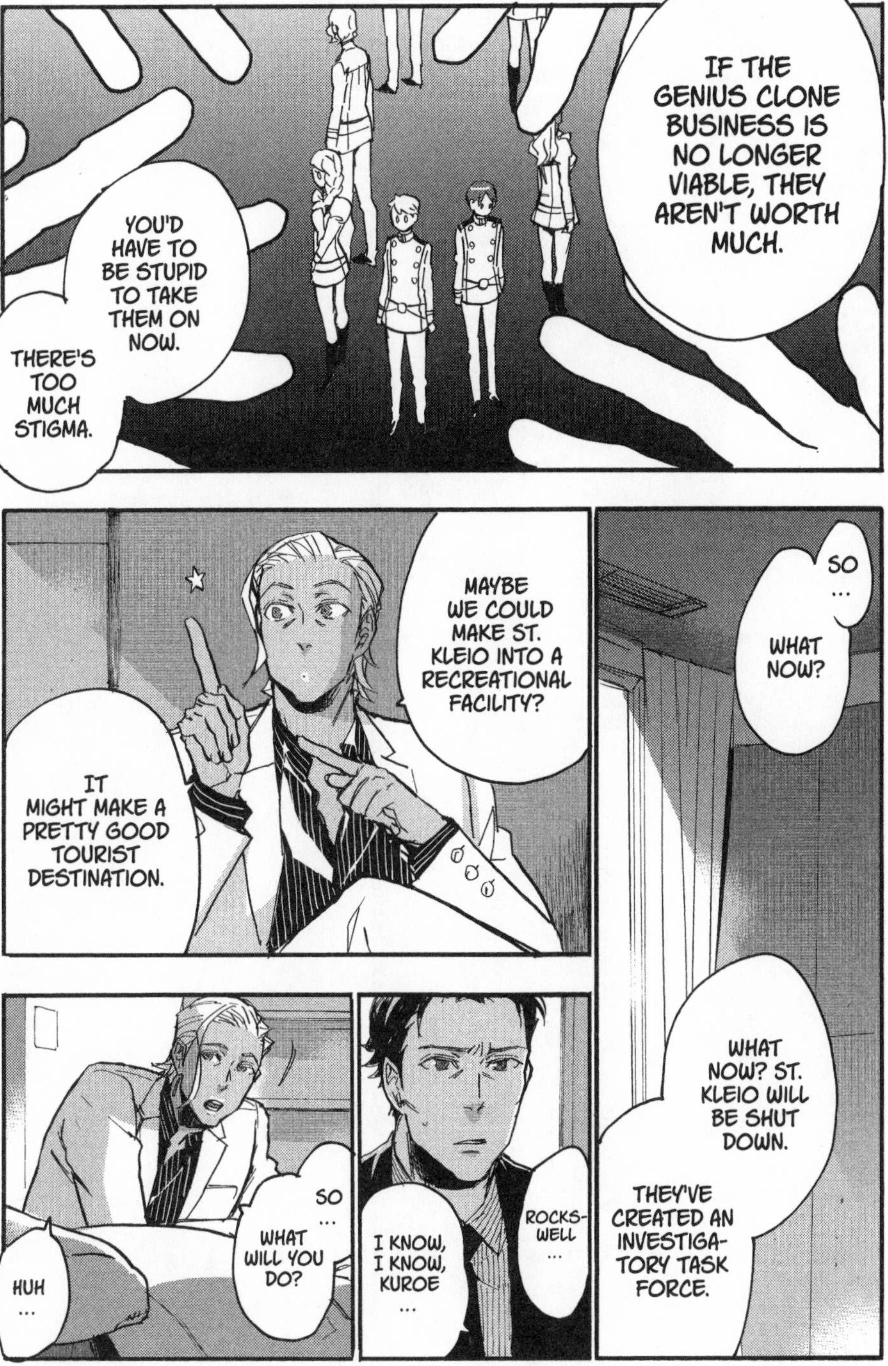

IF THE GENIUS CLONE BUSINESS IS NO LONGER VIABLE, THEY AREN'T WORTH MUCH.
YOU'D HAVE TO BE STUPID TO TAKE THEM ON NOW.
THERE'S TOO MUCH STIGMA.
SO ... WHAT NOW?
MAYBE WE COULD MAKE ST. KLEIO INTO A RECREATIONAL FACILITY?
IT MIGHT MAKE A PRETTY GOOD TOURIST DESTINATION.
WHAT NOW? ST. KLEIO WILL BE SHUT DOWN.
THEY'VE CREATED AN INVESTIGATORY TASK FORCE.
ROCKSWELL ...
I KNOW, I KNOW, KUROE ...
SO ... WHAT WILL YOU DO?
HUH ...

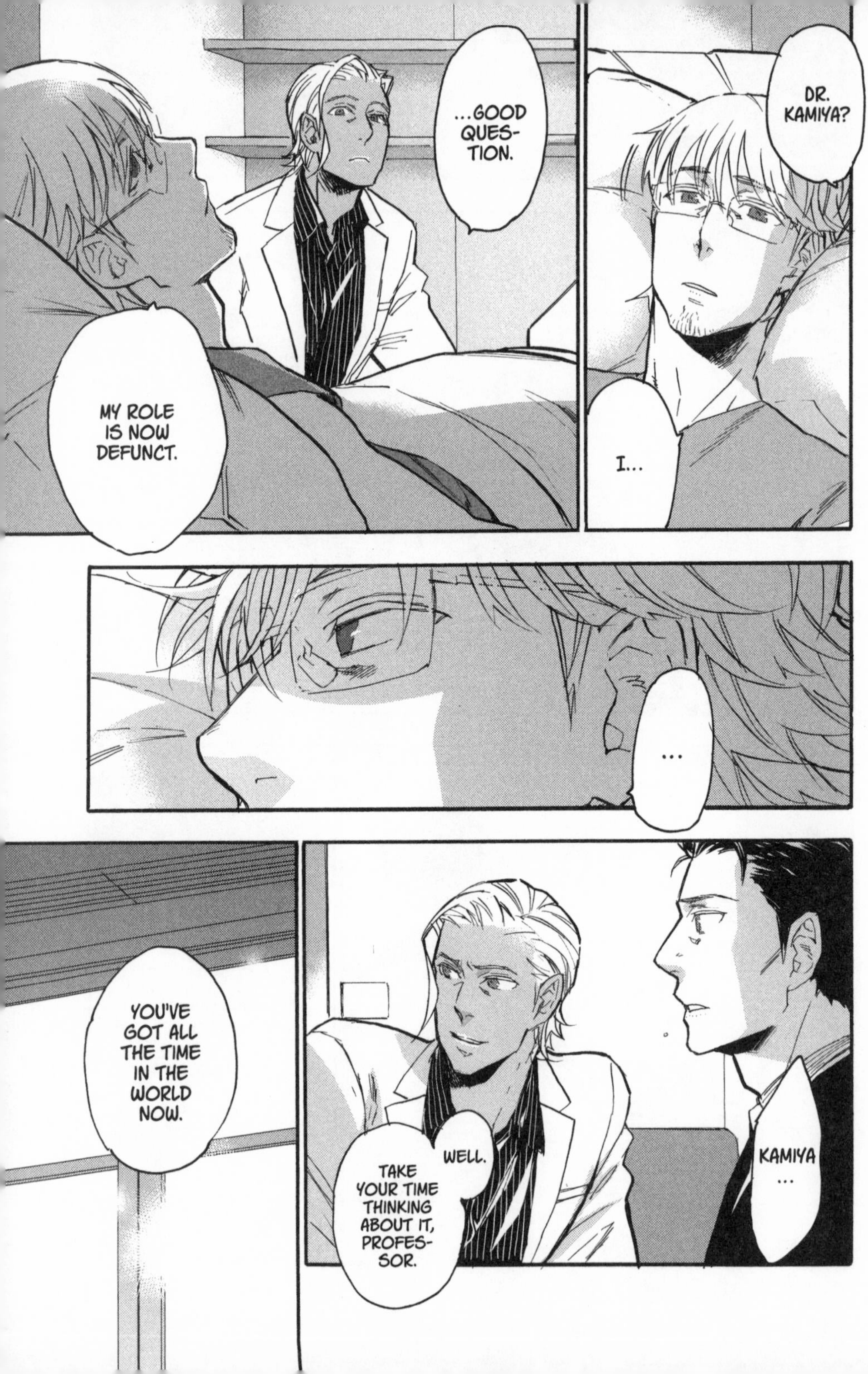
DR. KAMIYA?
I...
...GOOD QUESTION.
MY ROLE IS NOW DEFUNCT.
...
KAMIYA...
WELL.
TAKE YOUR TIME THINKING ABOUT IT, PROFESSOR.
YOU'VE GOT ALL THE TIME IN THE WORLD NOW.

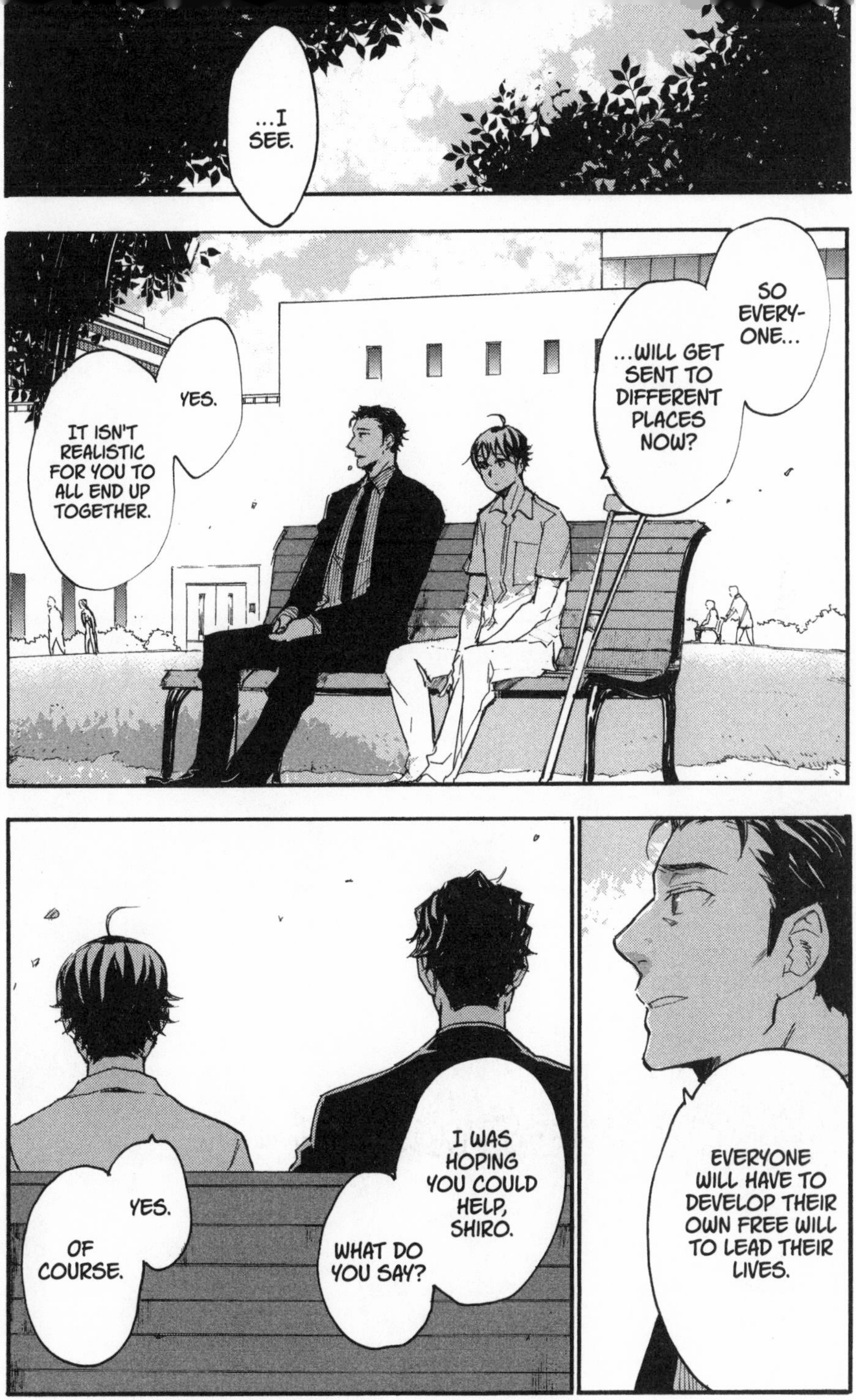
...I SEE.
SO EVERY-ONE...
...WILL GET SENT TO DIFFERENT PLACES NOW?
YES.
IT ISN'T REALISTIC FOR YOU TO ALL END UP TOGETHER.
EVERYONE WILL HAVE TO DEVELOP THEIR OWN FREE WILL TO LEAD THEIR LIVES.
I WAS HOPING YOU COULD HELP, SHIRO.
WHAT DO YOU SAY?
YES.
OF COURSE.

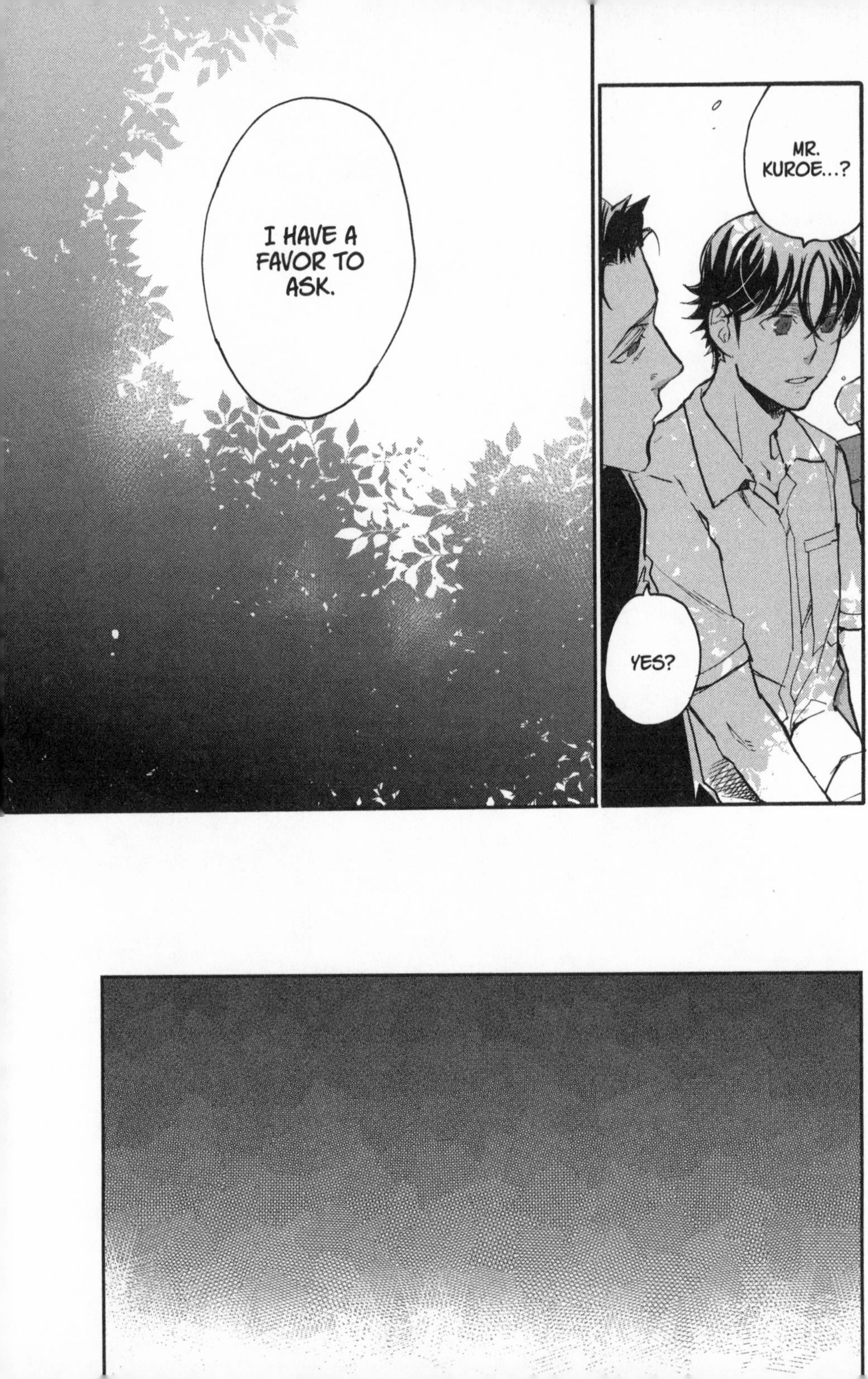
MR. KUROE...?
YES?
I HAVE A FAVOR TO ASK.

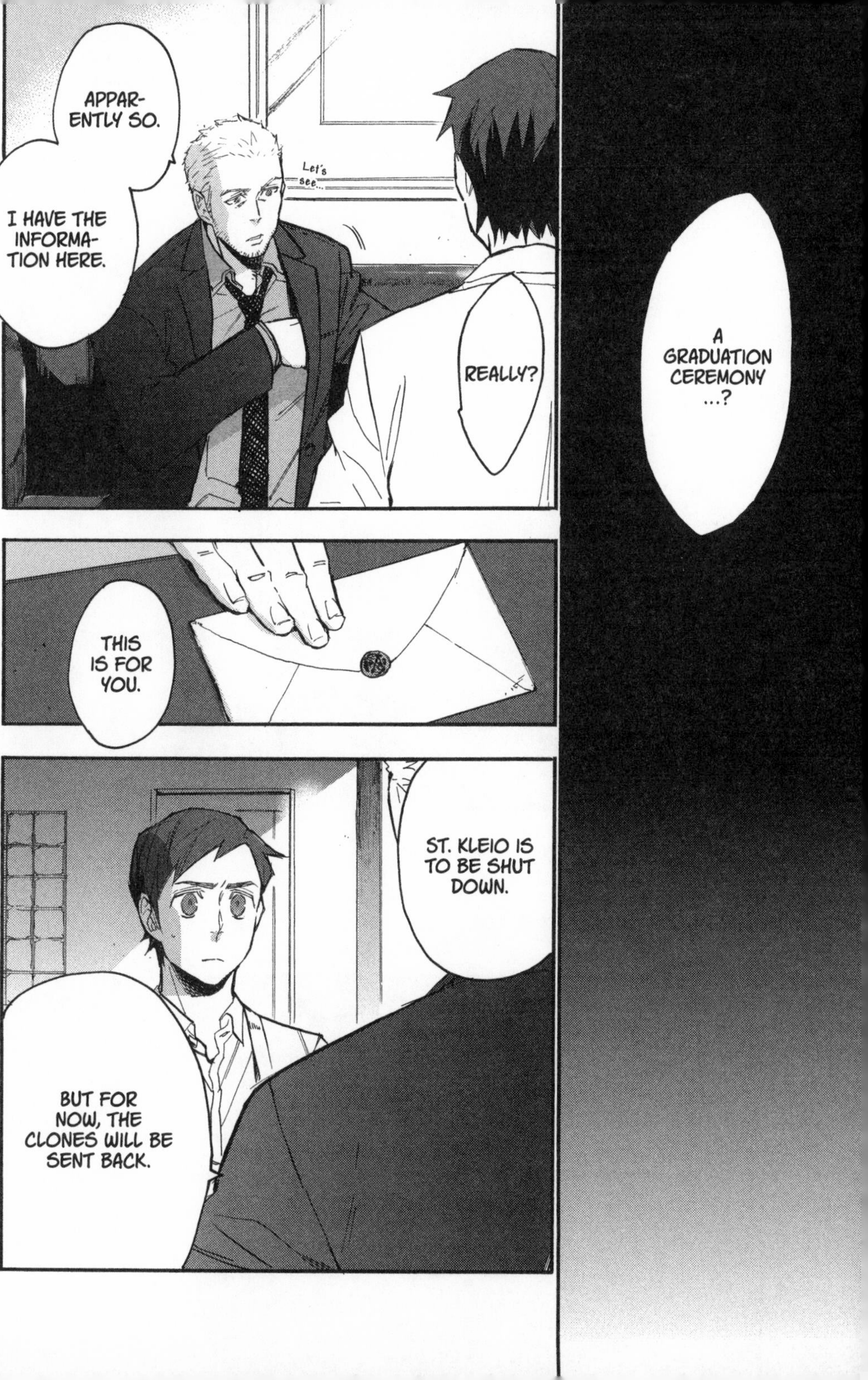
A GRADUATION CEREMONY ...?
REALLY?
APPARENTLY SO.
Let's see...
I HAVE THE INFORMATION HERE.
THIS IS FOR YOU.
ST. KLEIO IS TO BE SHUT DOWN.
BUT FOR NOW, THE CLONES WILL BE SENT BACK.

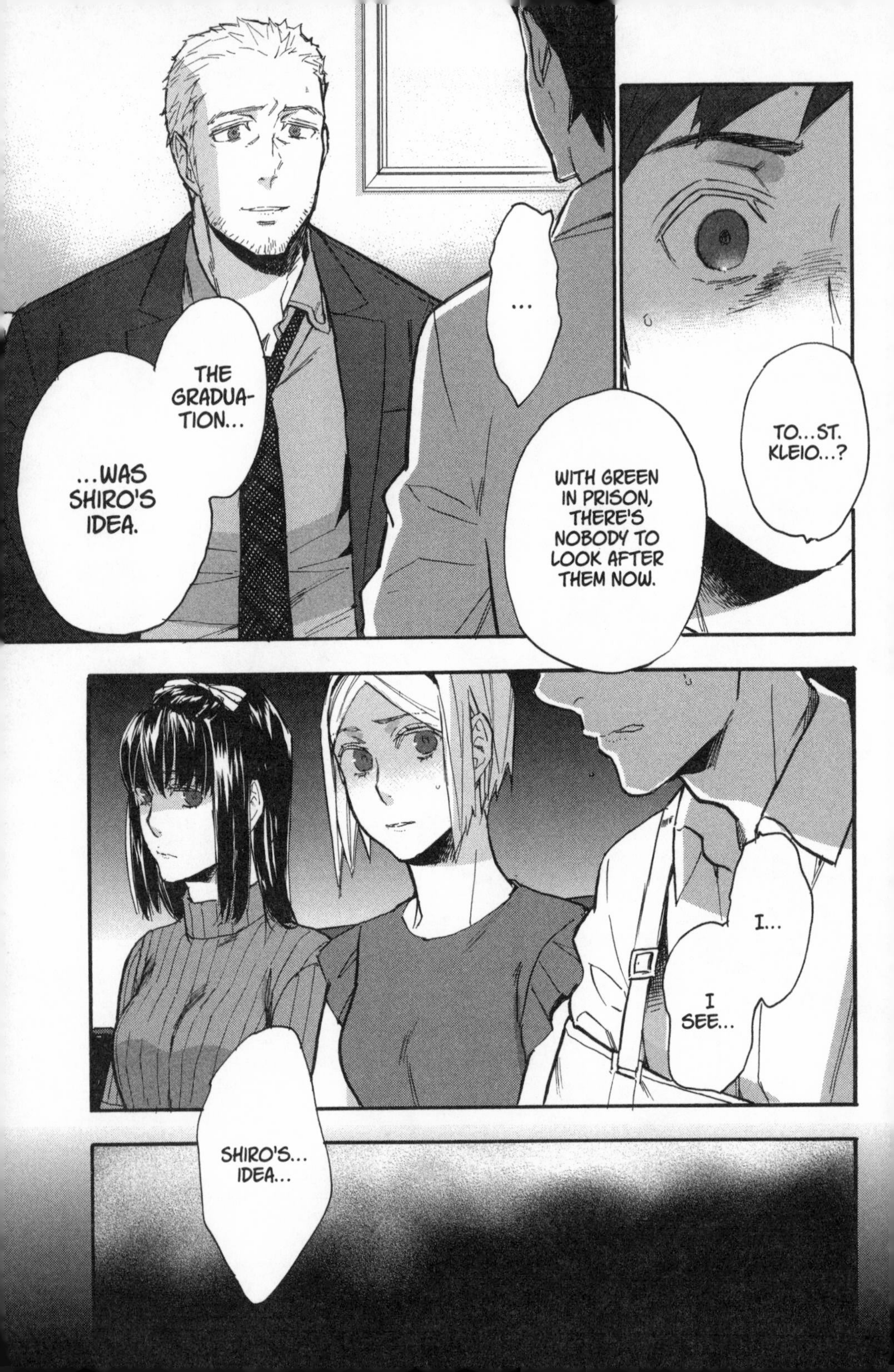
TO...ST. KLEIO...?
WITH GREEN IN PRISON, THERE'S NOBODY TO LOOK AFTER THEM NOW.
...
THE GRADUATION...
...WAS SHIRO'S IDEA.
I...
I SEE...
SHIRO'S... IDEA...

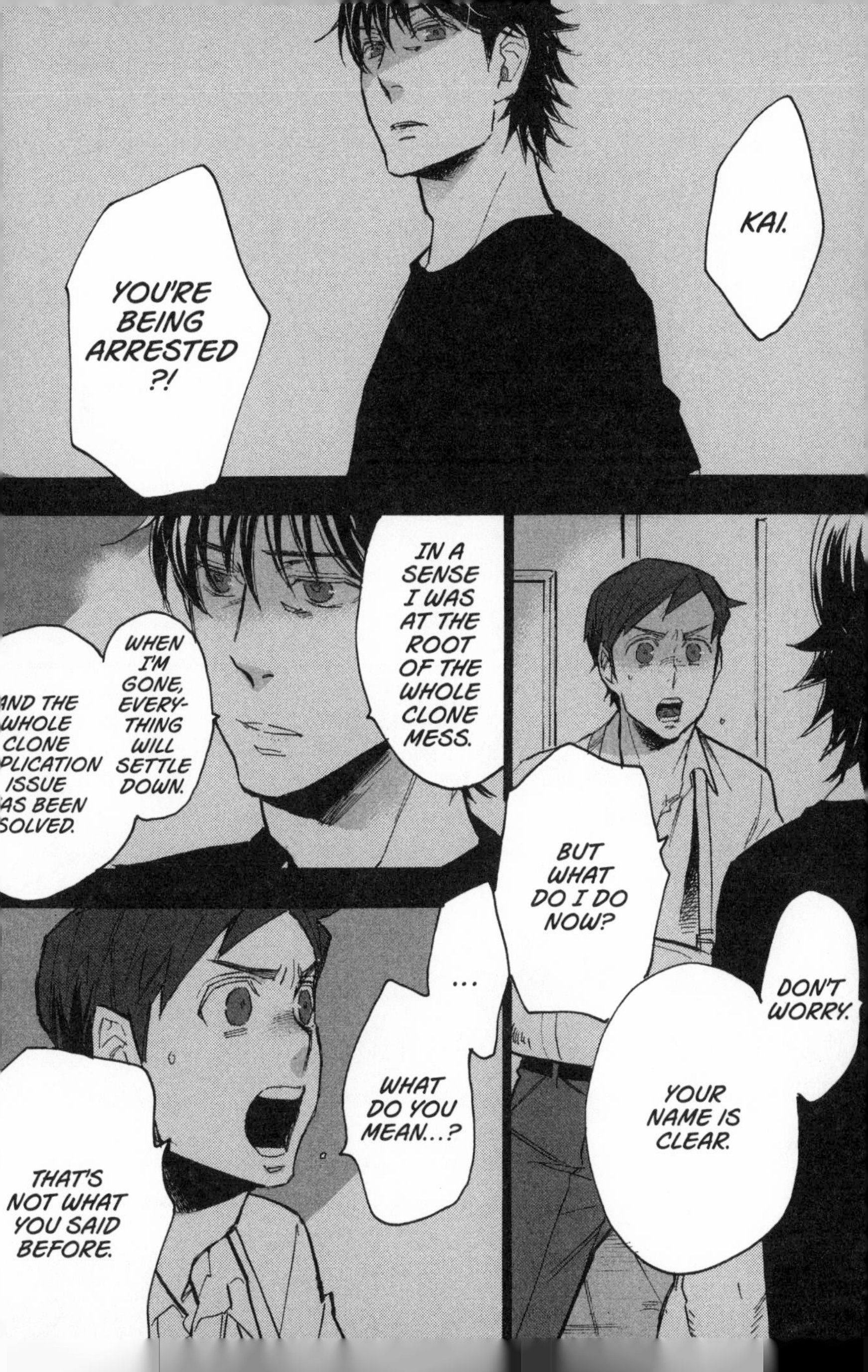
KAI.
YOU'RE BEING ARRESTED ?!
BUT WHAT DO I DO NOW?
DON'T WORRY.
YOUR NAME IS CLEAR.
IN A SENSE I WAS AT THE ROOT OF THE WHOLE CLONE MESS.
WHEN I'M GONE, EVERYTHING WILL SETTLE DOWN.
AND THE WHOLE CLONE PLICATION ISSUE AS BEEN SOLVED.
...
WHAT DO YOU MEAN...?
THAT'S NOT WHAT YOU SAID BEFORE.

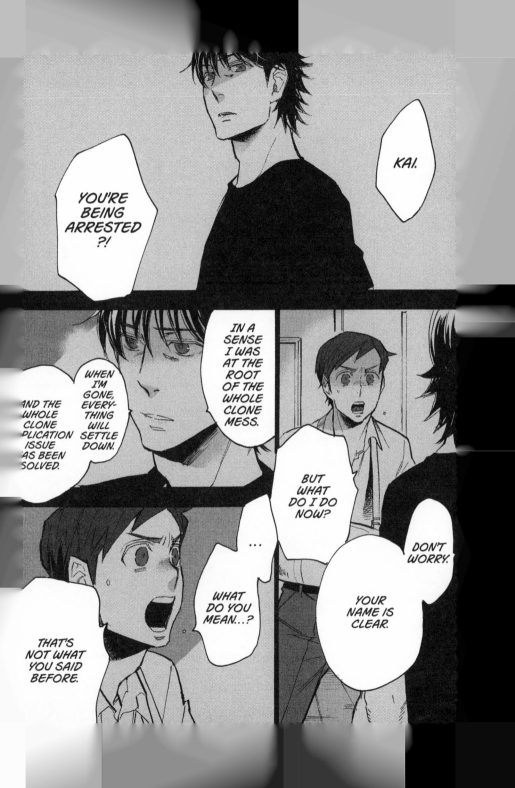

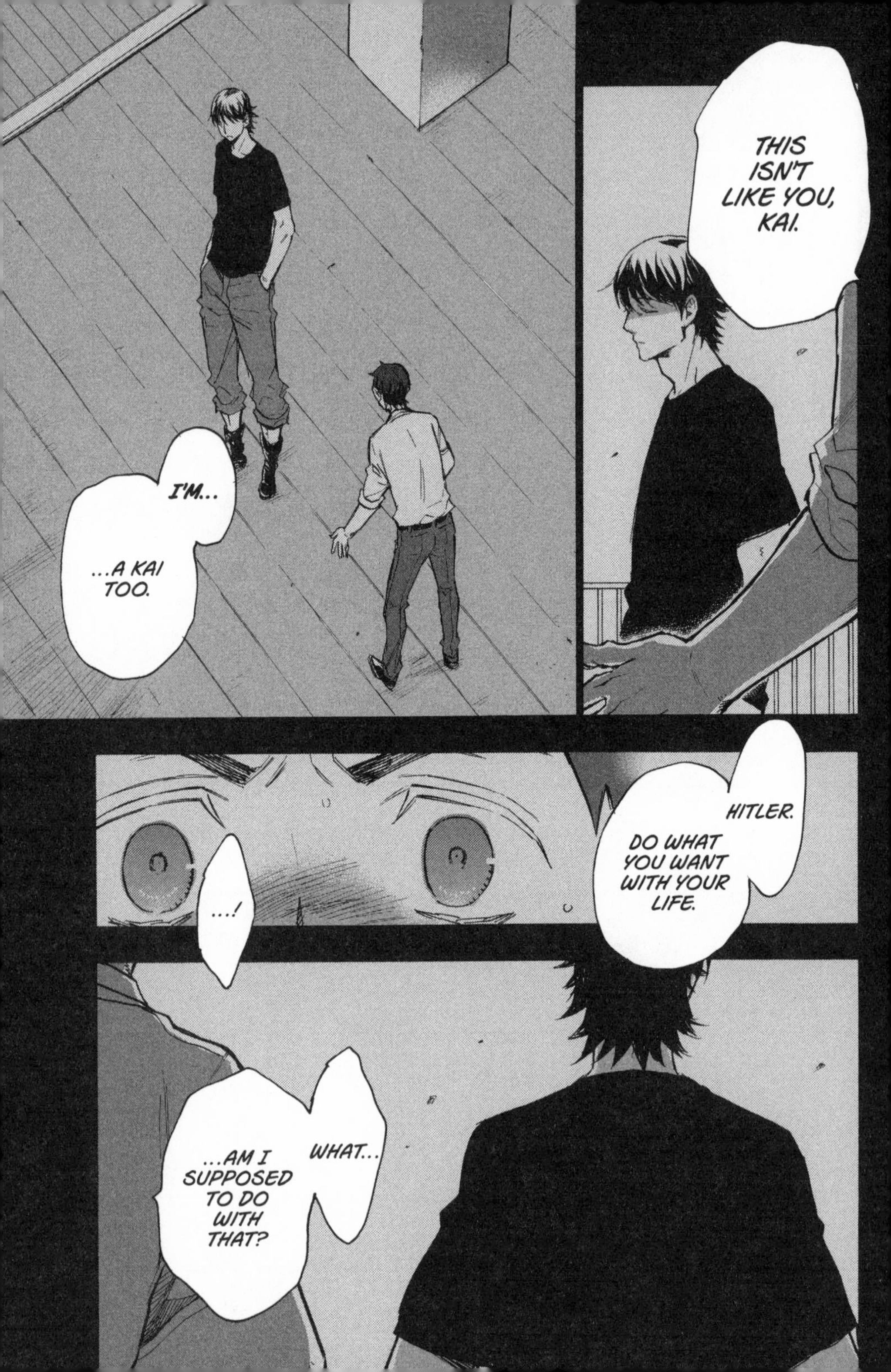
THIS ISN'T LIKE YOU, KAI.
I'M...
...A KAI TOO.
HITLER.
DO WHAT YOU WANT WITH YOUR LIFE.
...!
WHAT...
...AM I SUPPOSED TO DO WITH THAT?

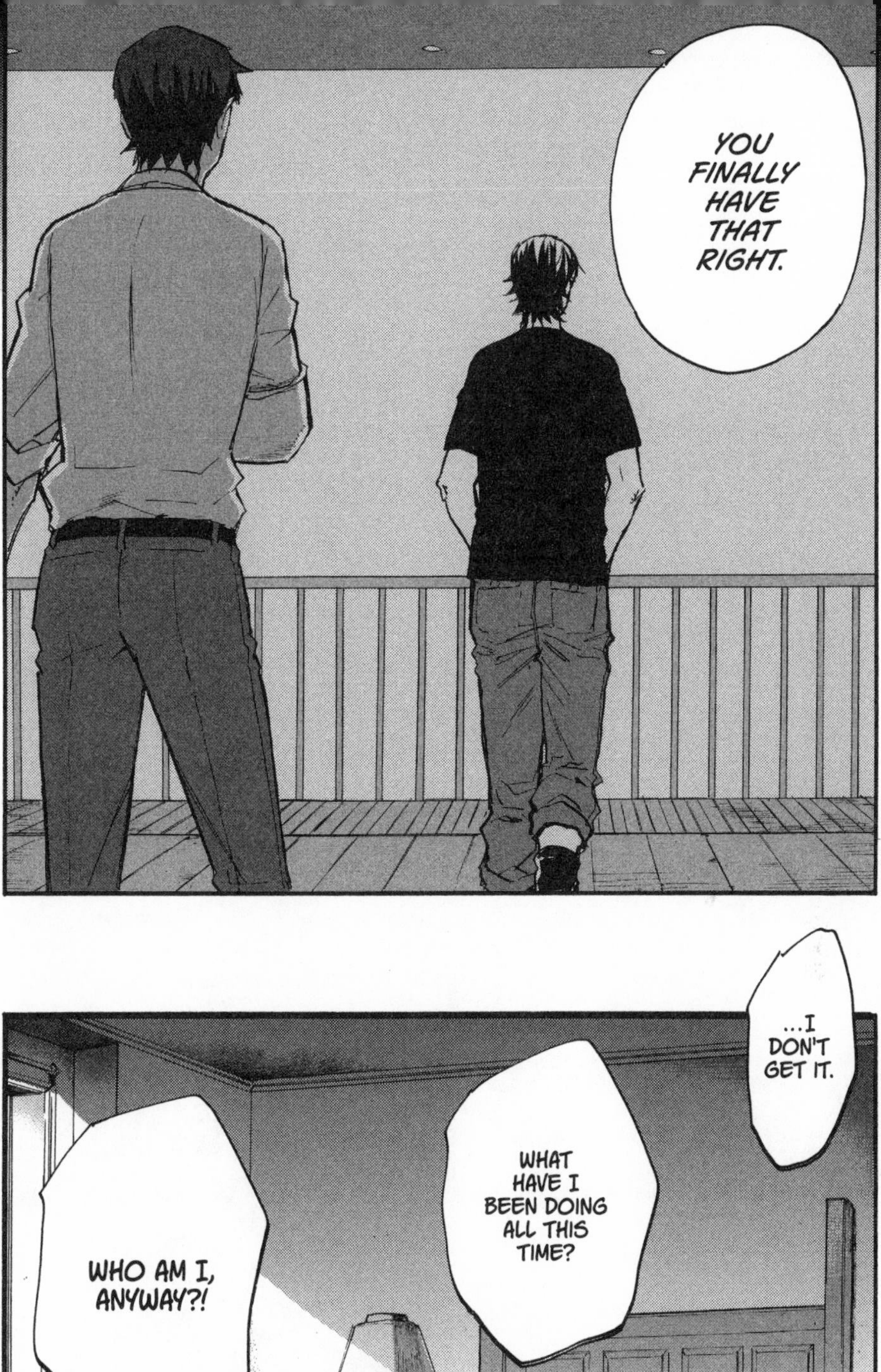
YOU FINALLY HAVE THAT RIGHT.
...I DON'T GET IT.
WHAT HAVE I BEEN DOING ALL THIS TIME?
WHO AM I, ANYWAY?!

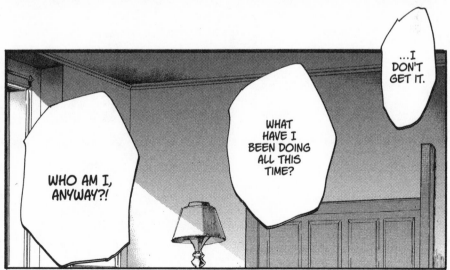

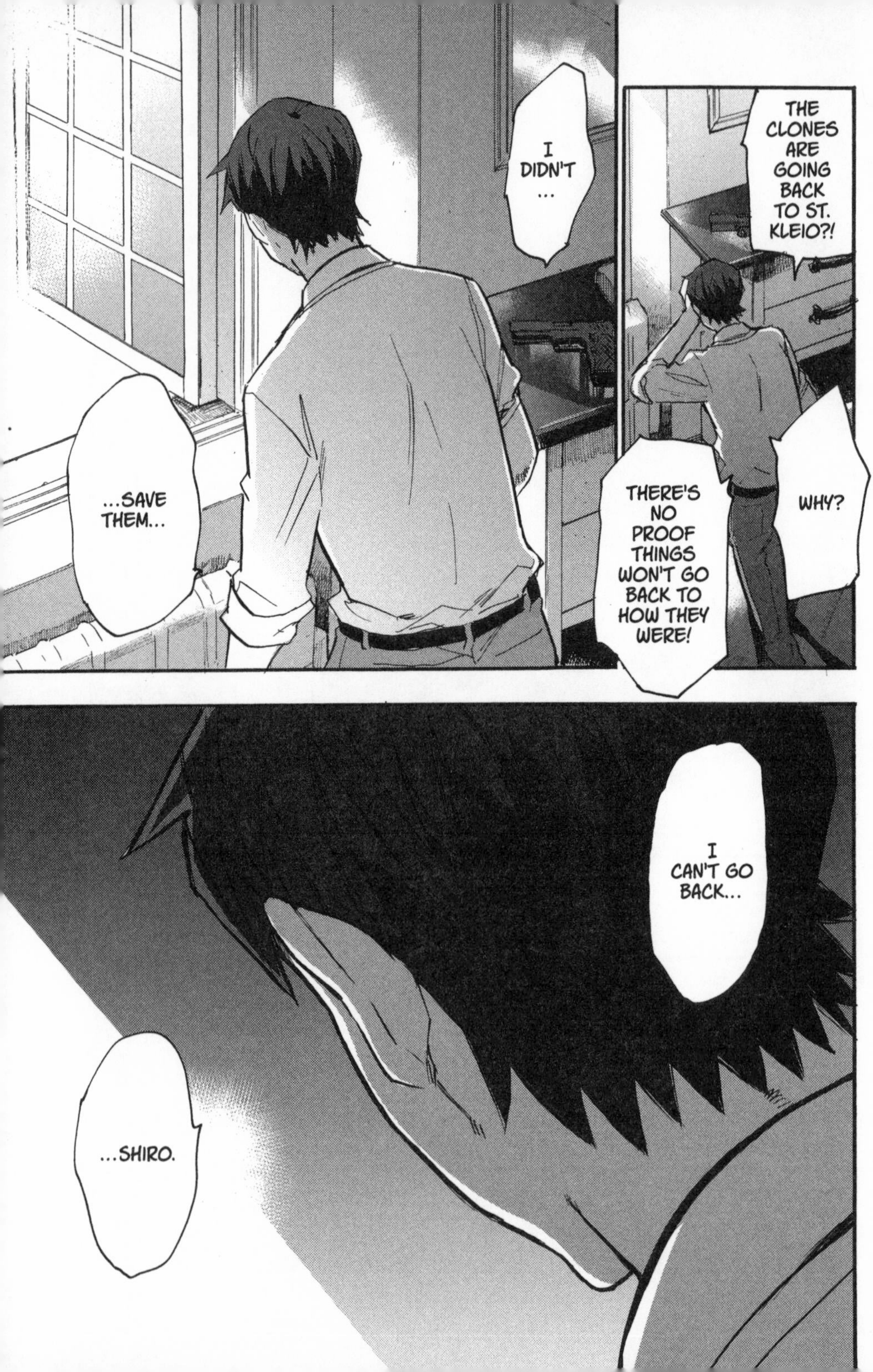
THE CLONES ARE GOING BACK TO ST. KLEIO?!
WHY?
THERE'S NO PROOF THINGS WON'T GO BACK TO HOW THEY WERE!
I DIDN'T ...
...SAVE THEM...
I CAN'T GO BACK...
...SHIRO.

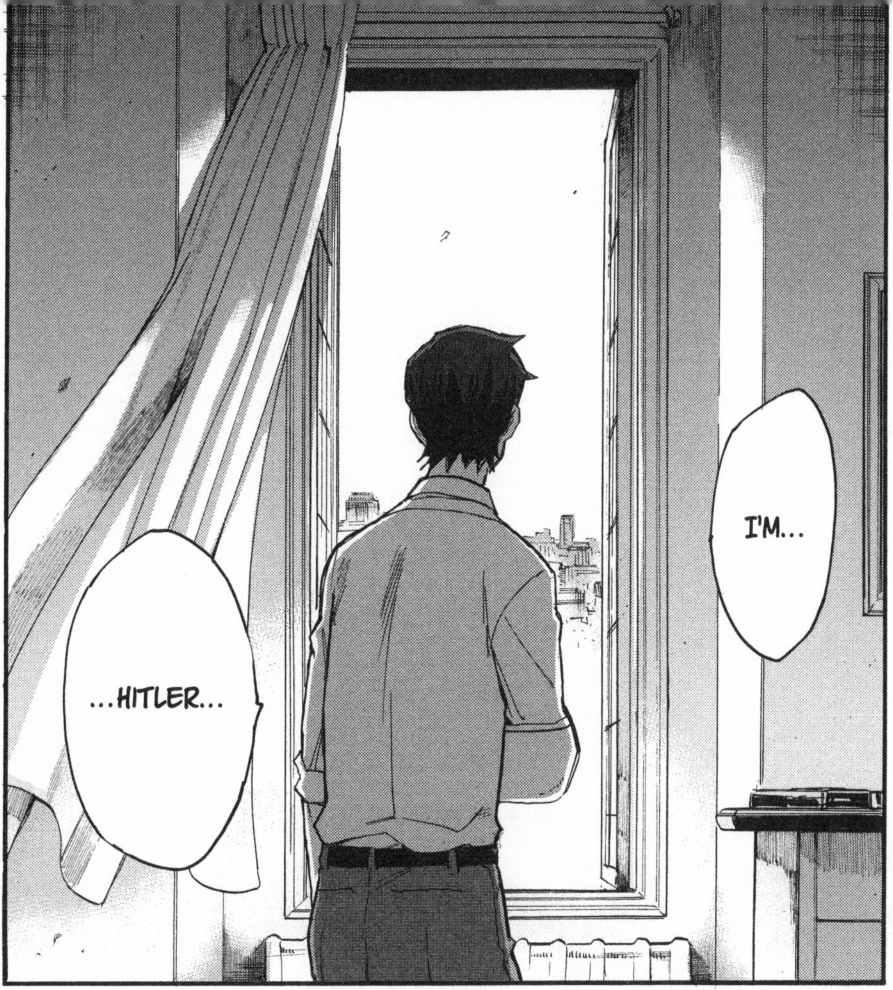
I'M...
...HITLER...

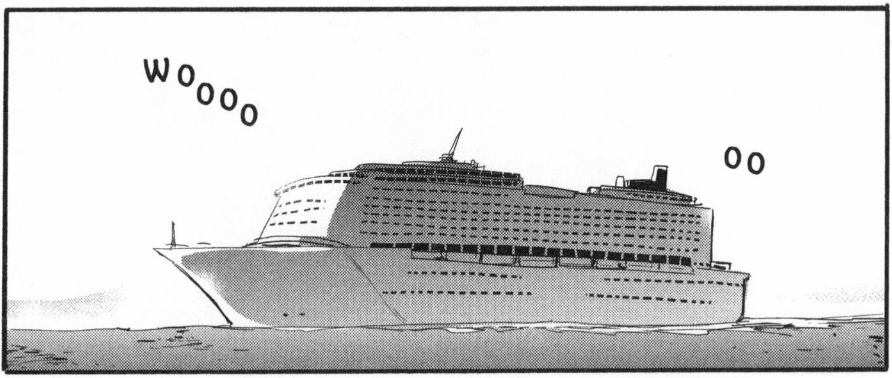
WOOOO
OO

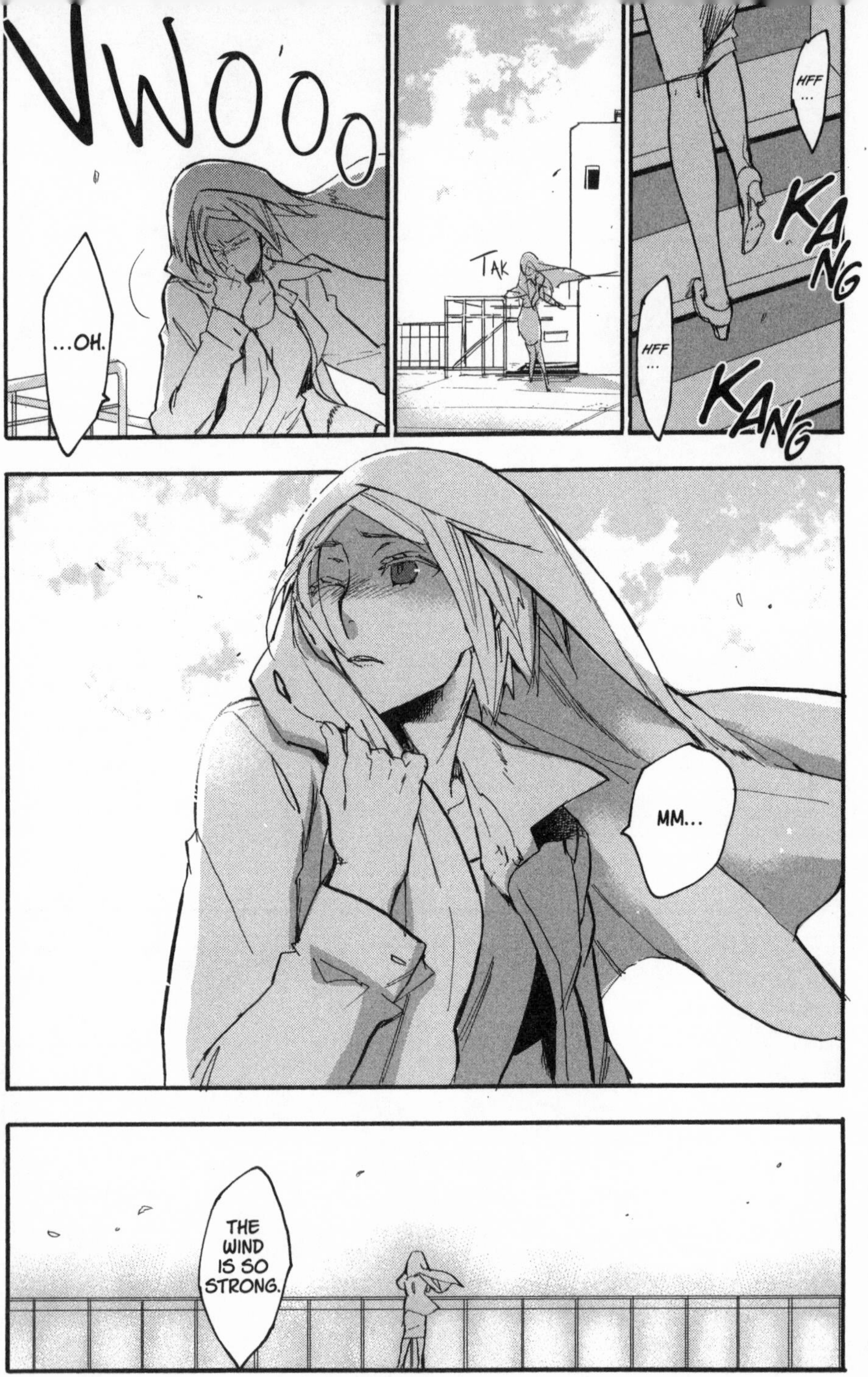
HFF...
KANG
HFF...
KANG
TAK
NWOOO
...OH.
MM...
THE WIND IS SO STRONG.

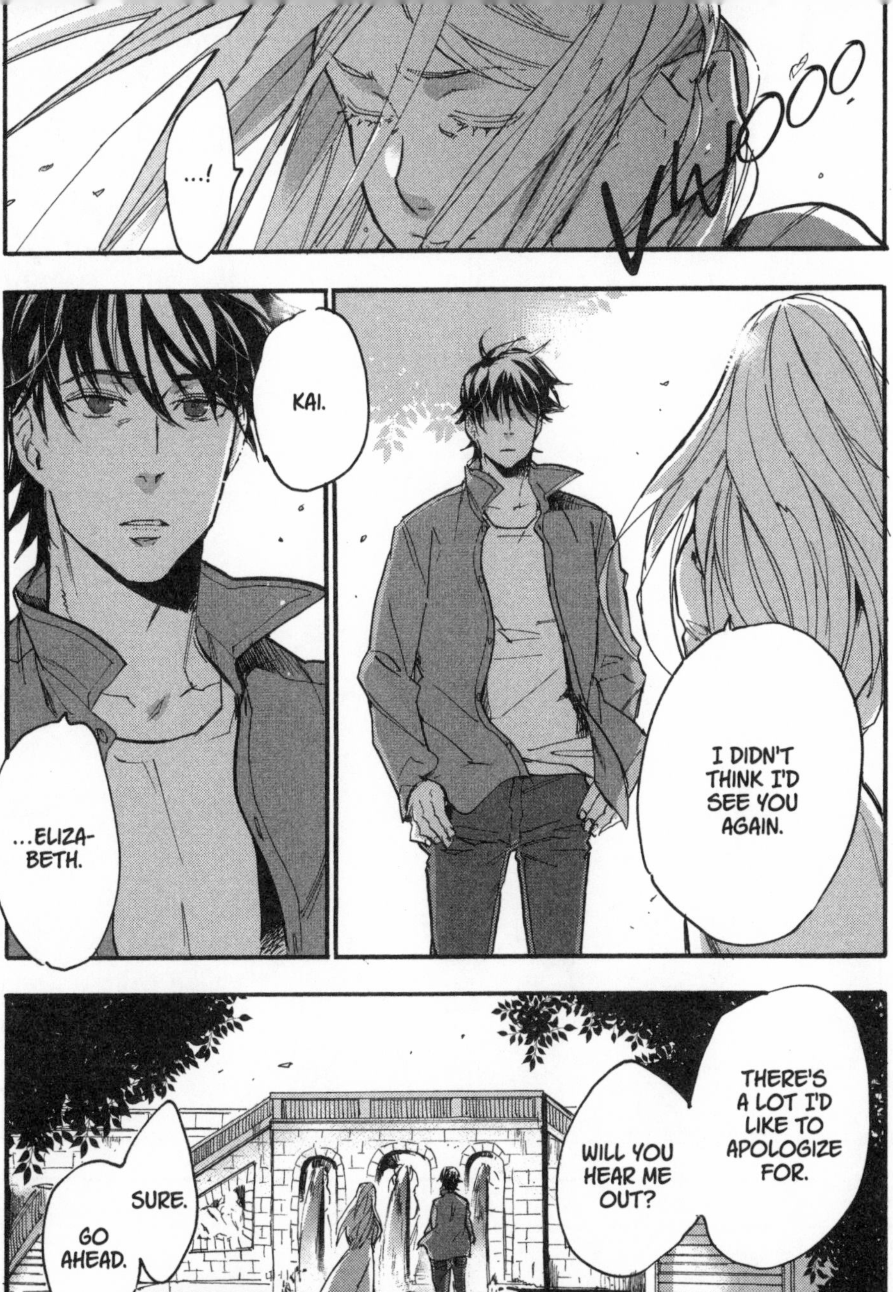
VWOOO
...!
I DIDN'T THINK I'D SEE YOU AGAIN.
KAI.
...ELIZA-BETH.
THERE'S A LOT I'D LIKE TO APOLOGIZE FOR.
WILL YOU HEAR ME OUT?
SURE.
GO AHEAD.

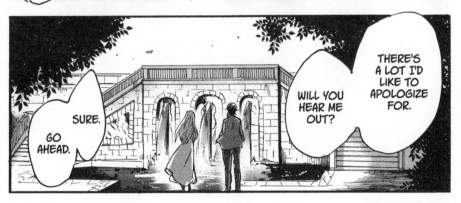

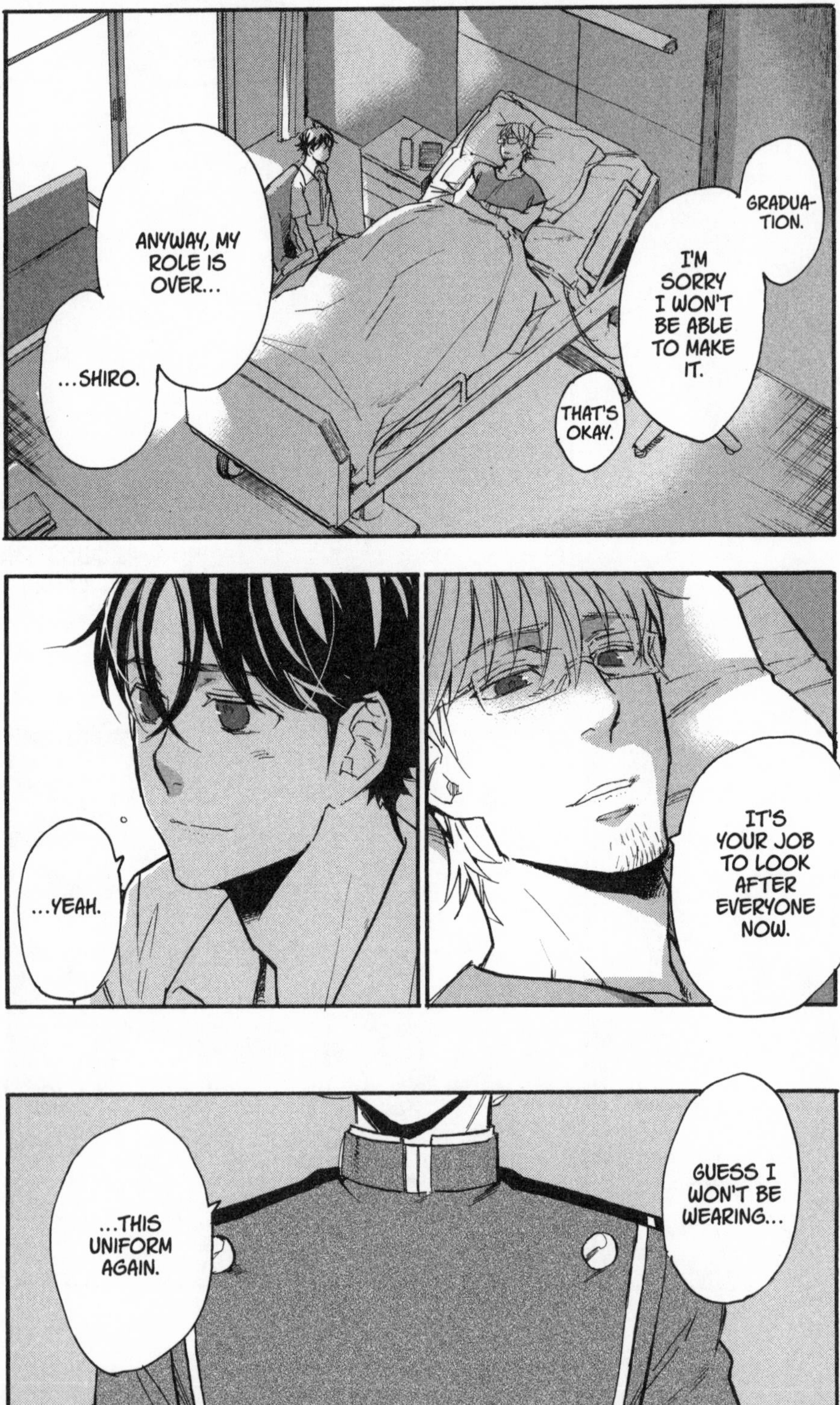
GRADUATION.
I'M SORRY I WON'T BE ABLE TO MAKE IT.
THAT'S OKAY.
ANYWAY, MY ROLE IS OVER...
...SHIRO.
IT'S YOUR JOB TO LOOK AFTER EVERYONE NOW.
...YEAH.
GUESS I WON'T BE WEARING...
...THIS UNIFORM AGAIN.

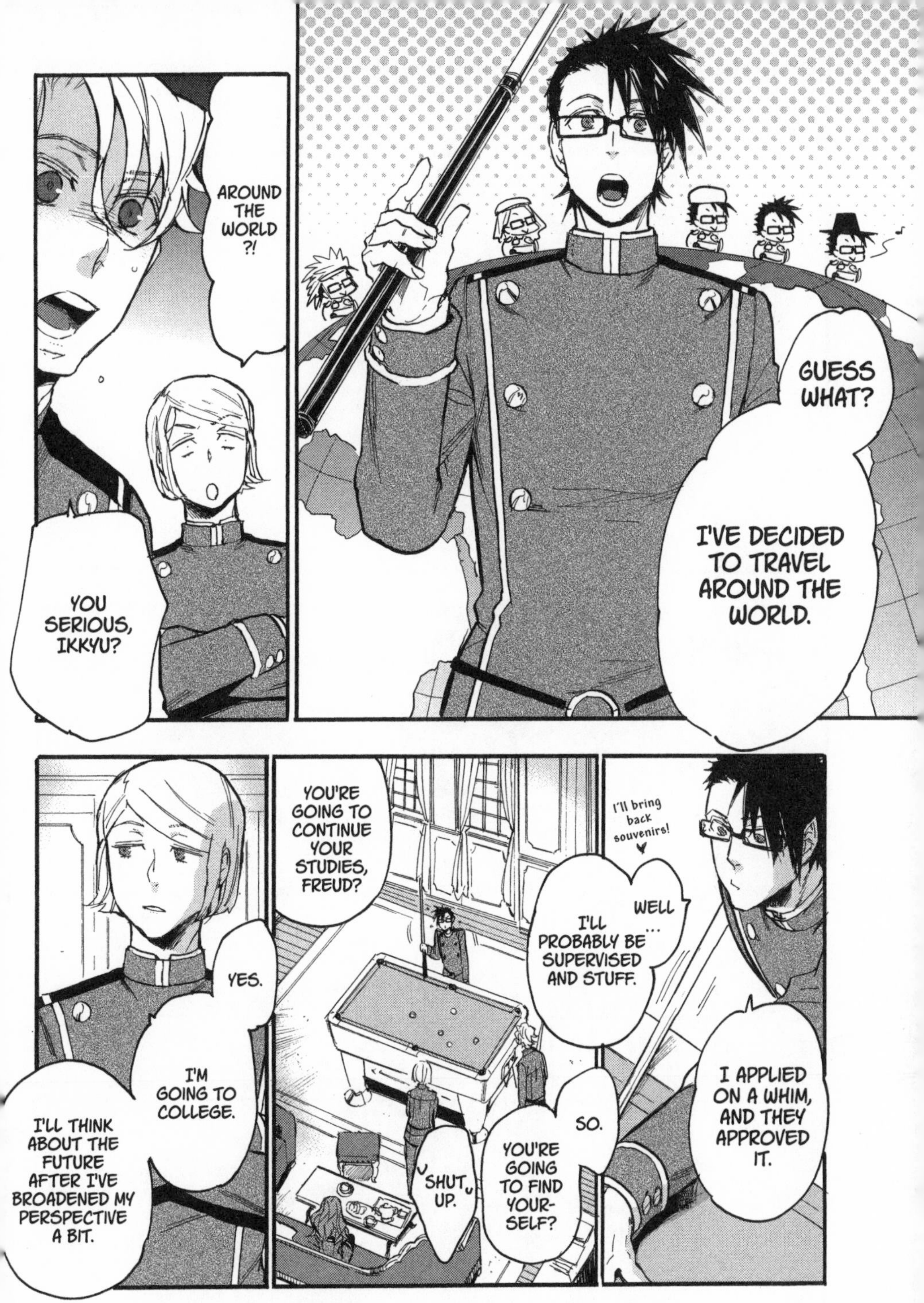
GUESS WHAT?
I'VE DECIDED TO TRAVEL AROUND THE WORLD.
AROUND THE WORLD ?!
YOU SERIOUS, IKKYU?
I'll bring back souvenirs!
I APPLIED ON A WHIM, AND THEY APPROVED IT.
WELL... I'LL PROBABLY BE SUPERVISED AND STUFF.
SO.
YOU'RE GOING TO FIND YOUR-SELF?
SHUT UP.
YOU'RE GOING TO CONTINUE YOUR STUDIES, FREUD?
YES.
I'M GOING TO COLLEGE.
I'LL THINK ABOUT THE FUTURE AFTER I'VE BROADENED MY PERSPECTIVE A BIT.

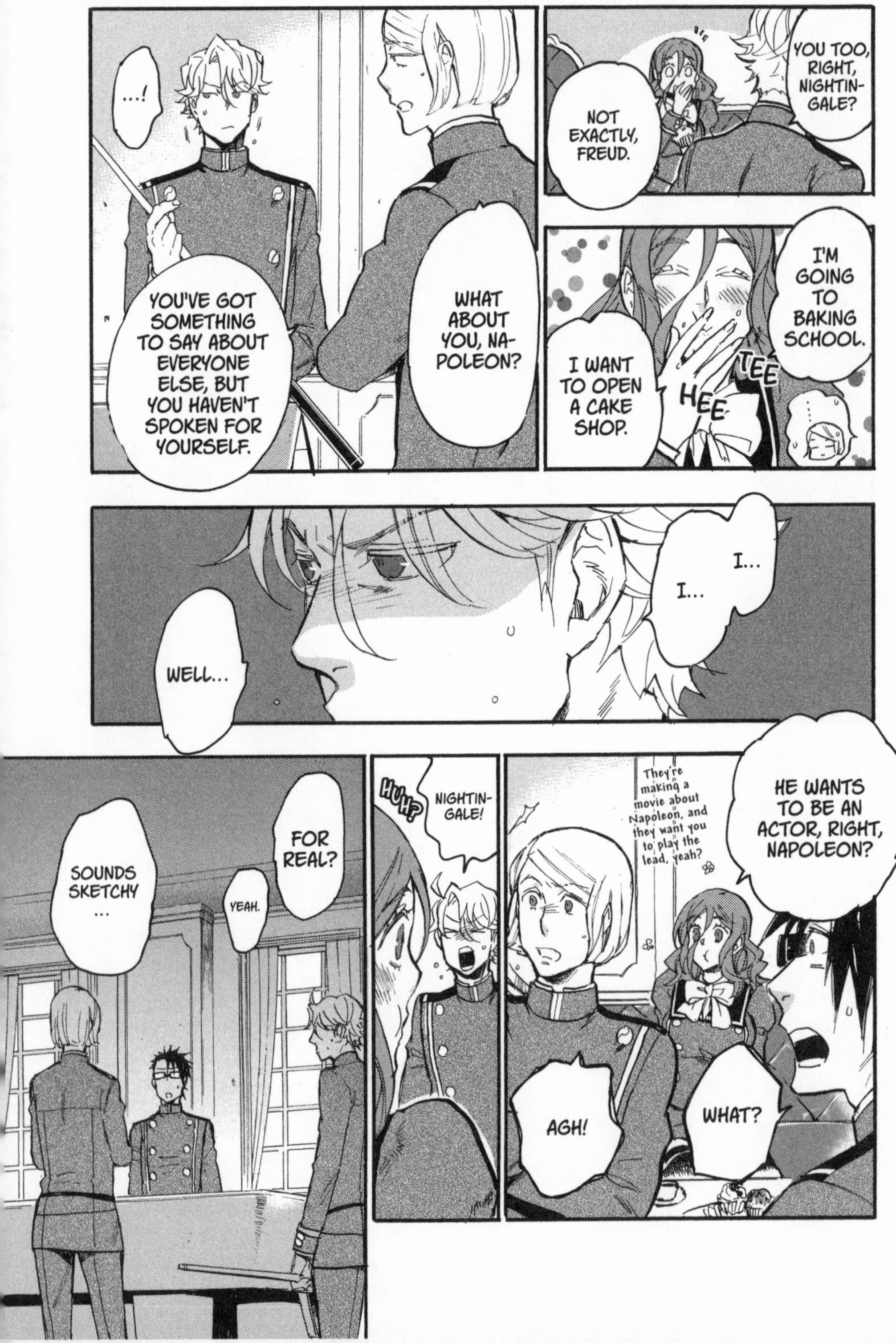
YOU TOO, RIGHT, NIGHTIN-GALE?
NOT EXACTLY, FREUD.
I'M GOING TO BAKING SCHOOL.
TEE HEE
I WANT TO OPEN A CAKE SHOP.
...
...!
WHAT ABOUT YOU, NA-POLEON?
YOU'VE GOT SOMETHING TO SAY ABOUT EVERYONE ELSE, BUT YOU HAVEN'T SPOKEN FOR YOURSELF.
I...
I...
WELL...
HE WANTS TO BE AN ACTOR, RIGHT, NAPOLEON?
They're making a movie about Napoleon, and they want you to play the lead, yeah?
WHAT?
NIGHTIN-GALE!
HUH?
AGH!
FOR REAL?
YEAH.
SOUNDS SKETCHY...

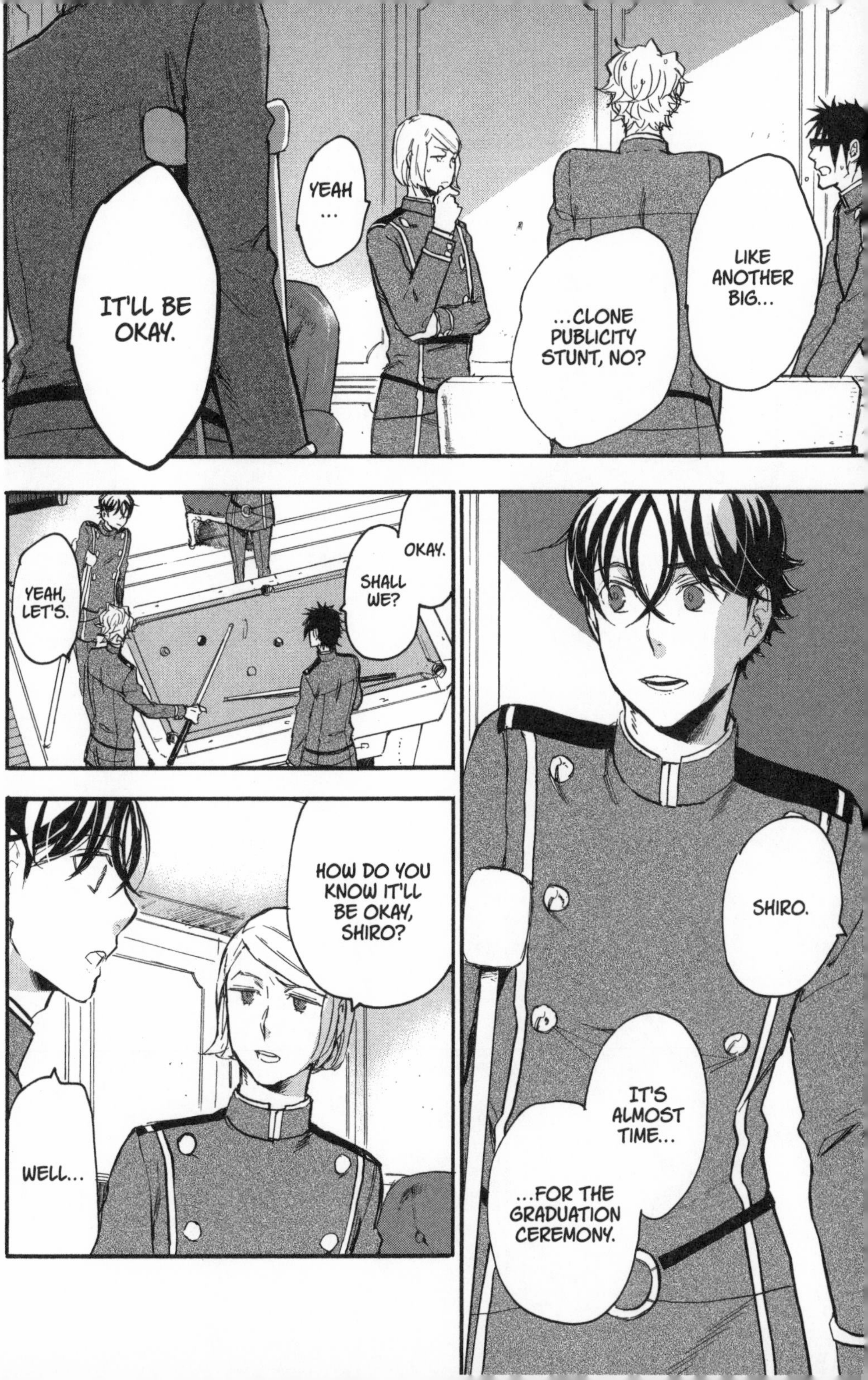
LIKE ANOTHER BIG...
...CLONE PUBLICITY STUNT, NO?
YEAH...
IT'LL BE OKAY.
SHIRO.
IT'S ALMOST TIME...
...FOR THE GRADUATION CEREMONY.
OKAY. SHALL WE?
YEAH, LET'S.
HOW DO YOU KNOW IT'LL BE OKAY, SHIRO?
WELL...

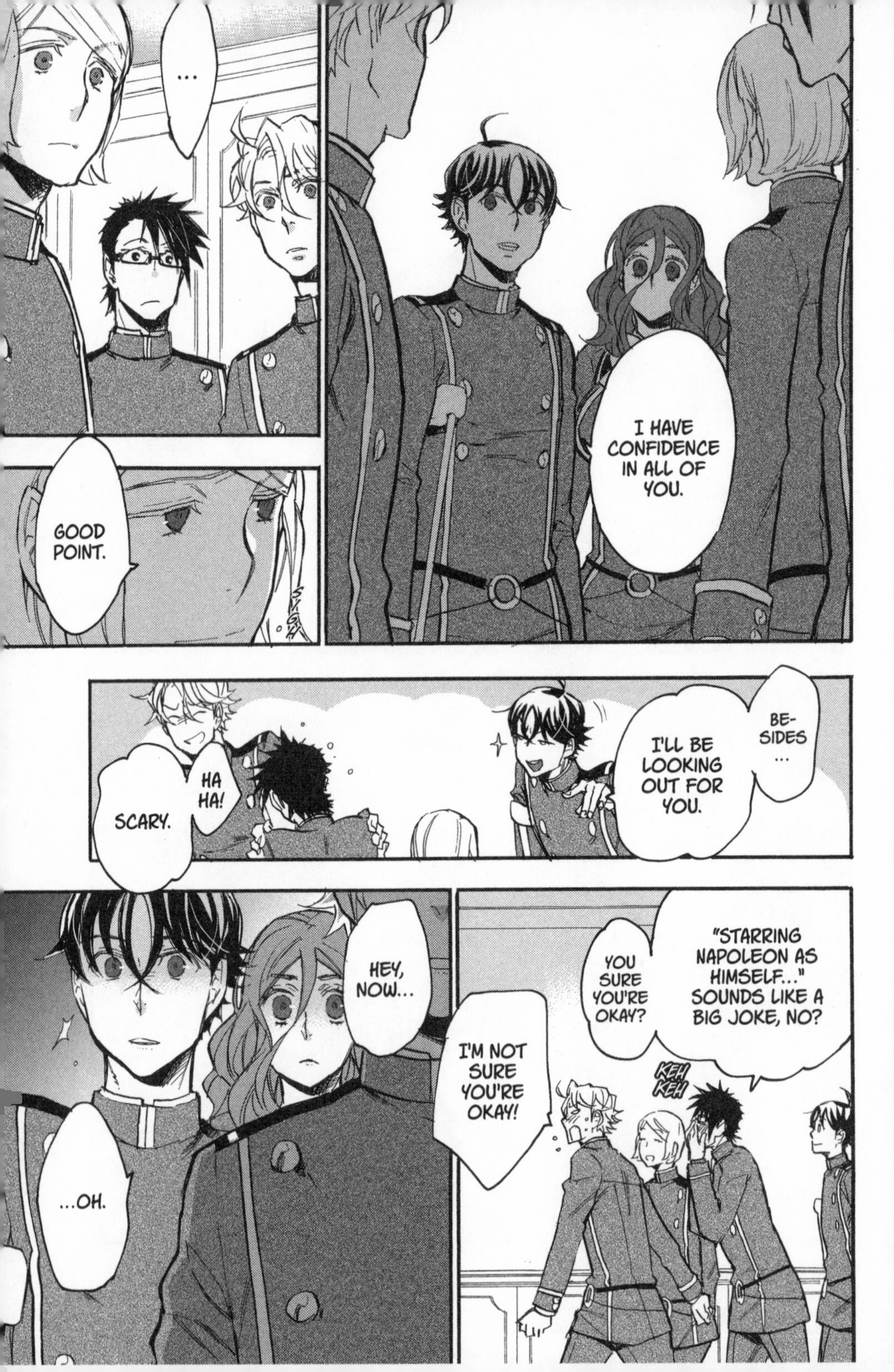
I HAVE CONFIDENCE IN ALL OF YOU.
...
GOOD POINT.
SIGH
BE-SIDES...
I'LL BE LOOKING OUT FOR YOU.
HA HA!
SCARY.
"STARRING NAPOLEON AS HIMSELF..." SOUNDS LIKE A BIG JOKE, NO?
KEH KEH
YOU SURE YOU'RE OKAY?
I'M NOT SURE YOU'RE OKAY!
HEY, NOW...
...OH.

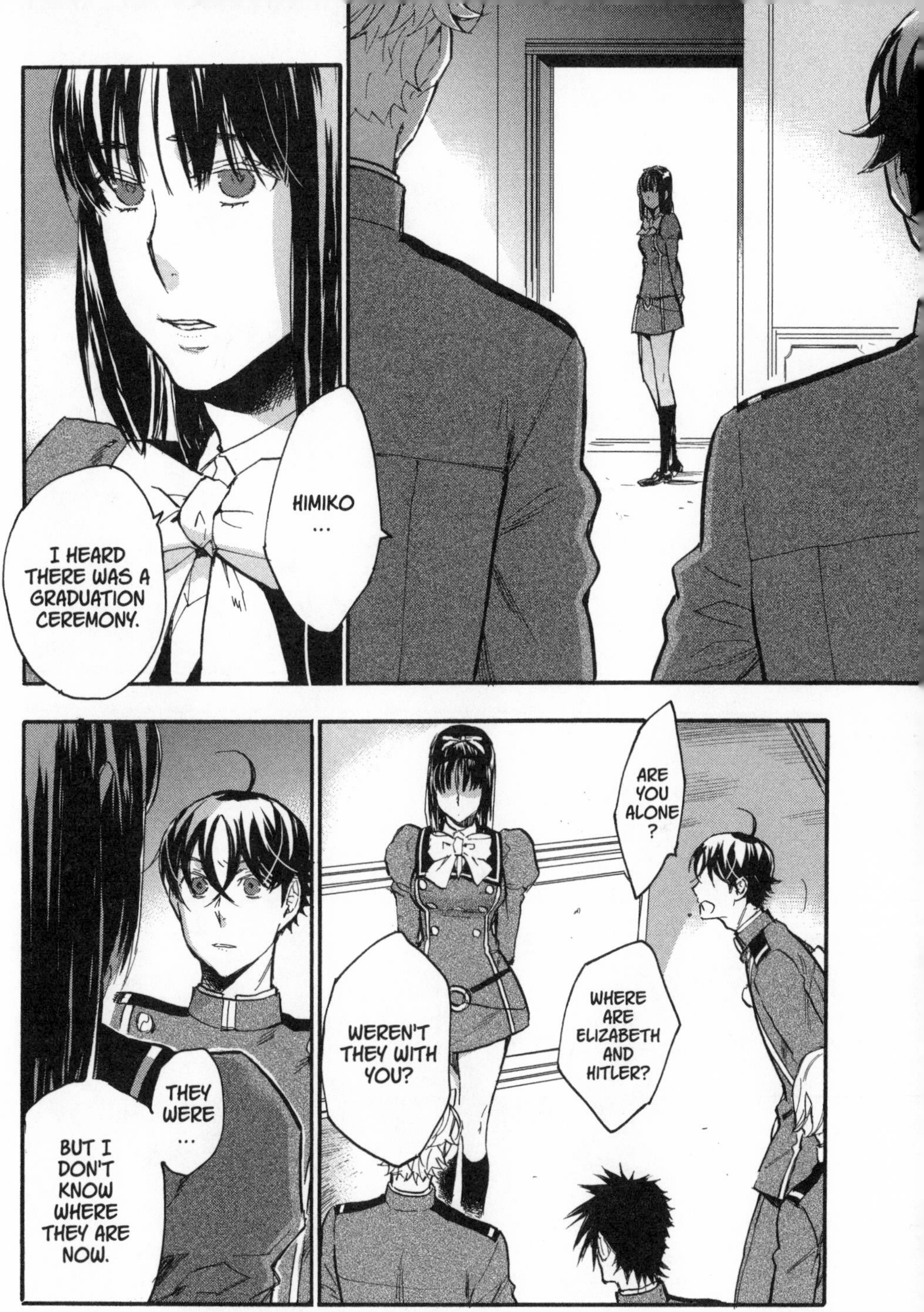
HIMIKO...
I HEARD THERE WAS A GRADUATION CEREMONY.
ARE YOU ALONE?
WHERE ARE ELIZABETH AND HITLER?
WEREN'T THEY WITH YOU?
THEY WERE...
BUT I DON'T KNOW WHERE THEY ARE NOW.

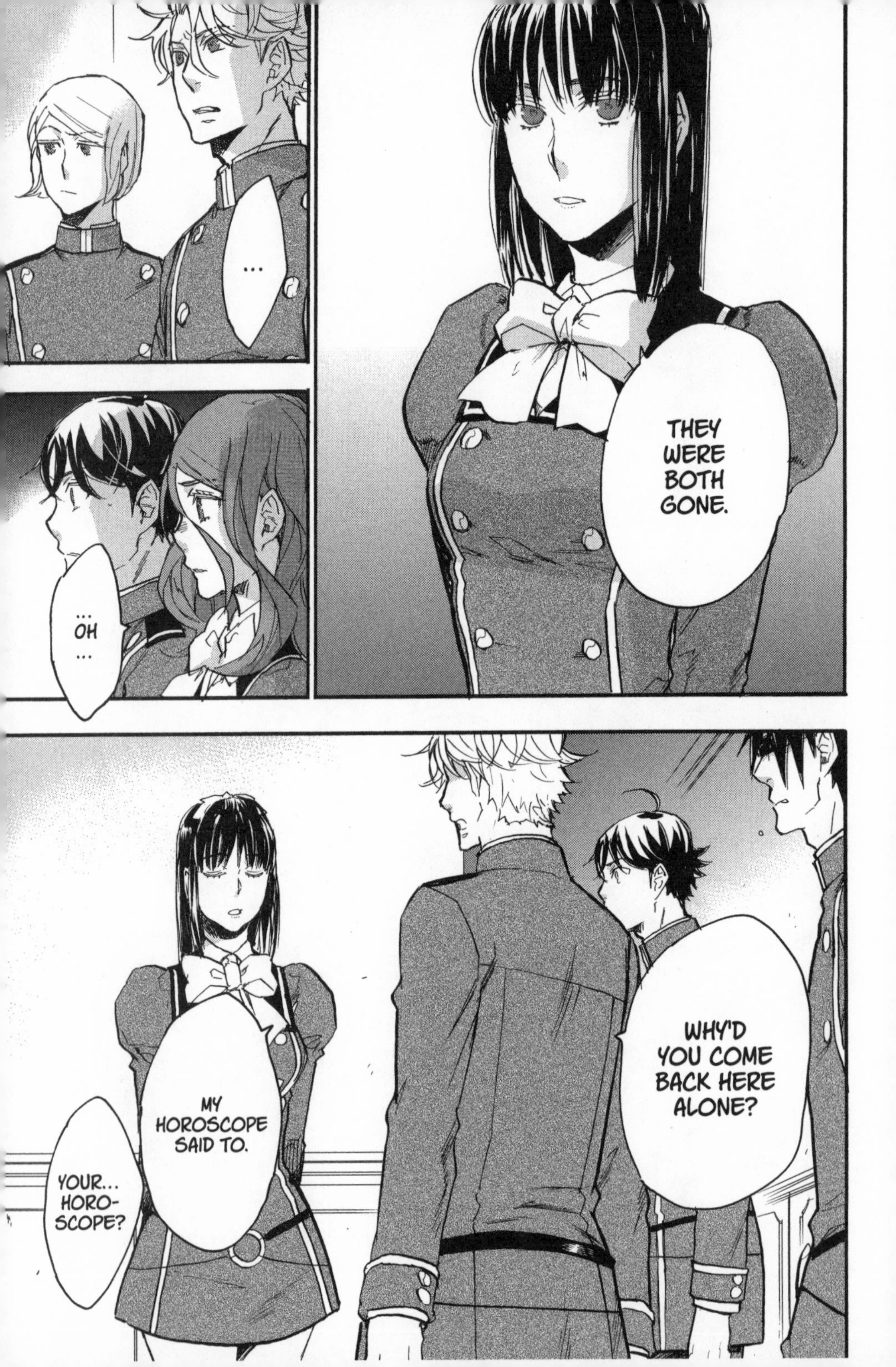
THEY WERE BOTH GONE.
...
... OH ...
WHY'D YOU COME BACK HERE ALONE?
MY HOROSCOPE SAID TO.
YOUR... HORO-SCOPE?

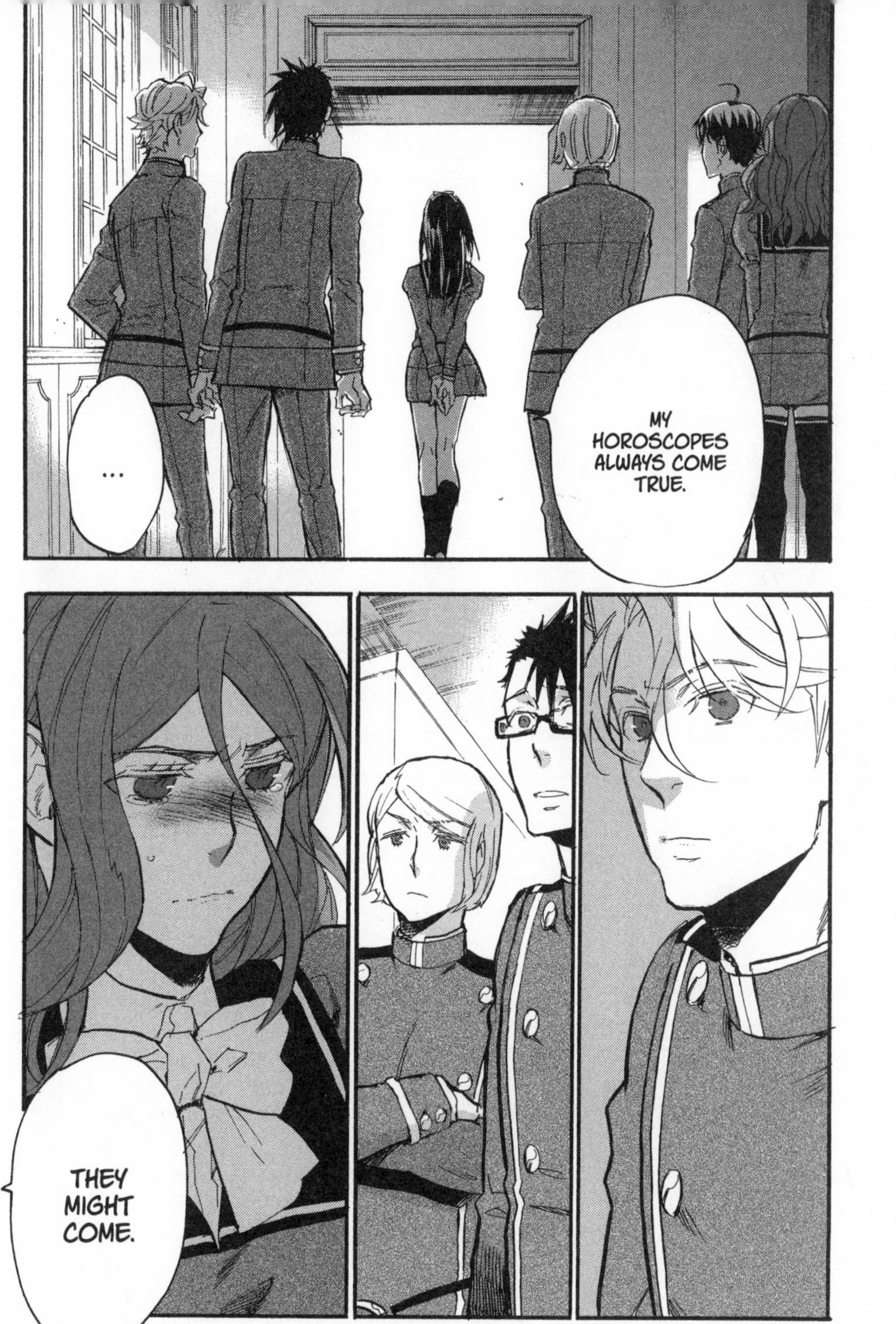
MY HOROSCOPES ALWAYS COME TRUE.
...
THEY MIGHT COME.

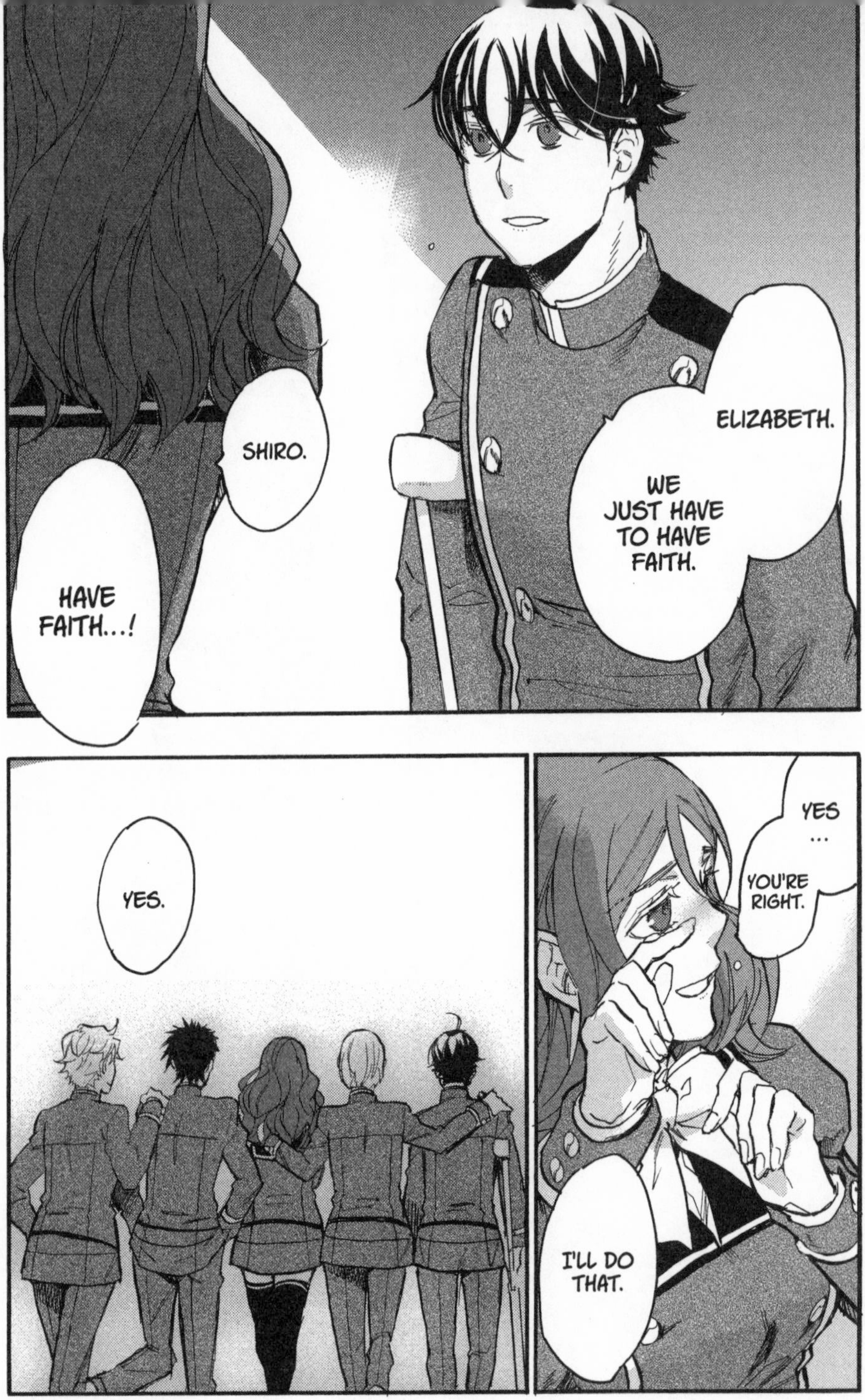
ELIZABETH.
WE JUST HAVE TO HAVE FAITH.
SHIRO.
HAVE FAITH...!
YES... YOU'RE RIGHT.
I'LL DO THAT.
YES.

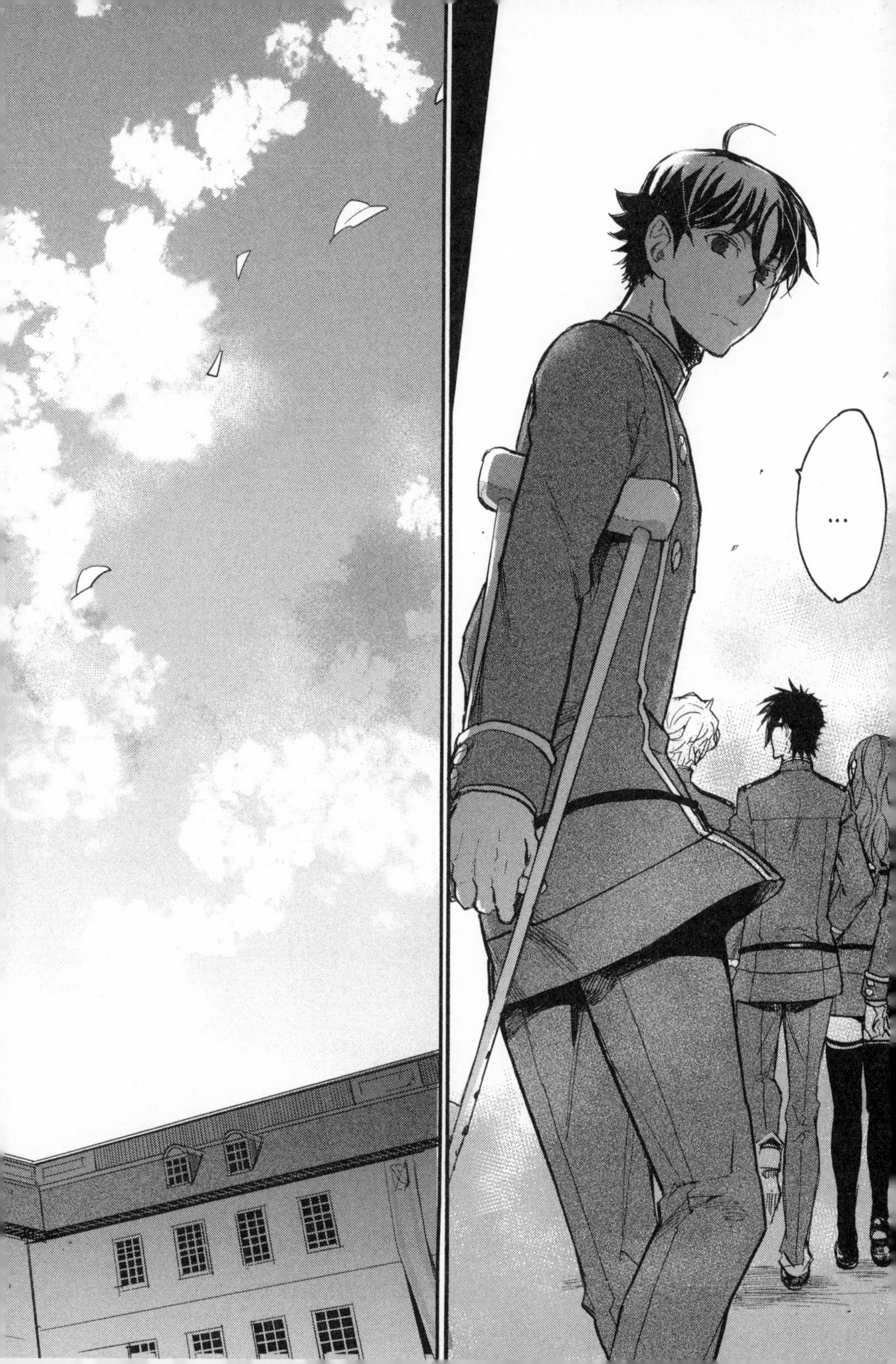
...

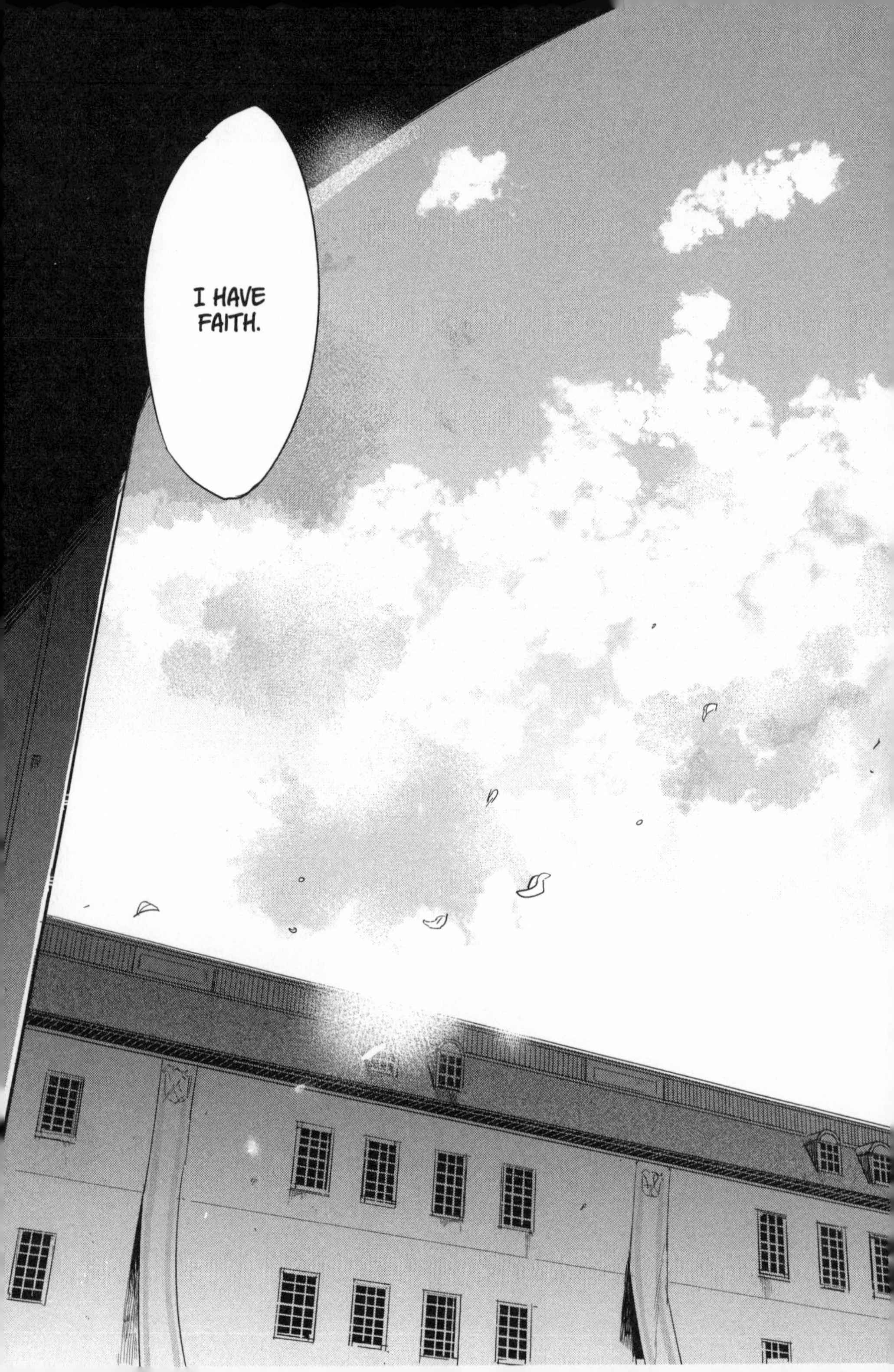
I HAVE FAITH.

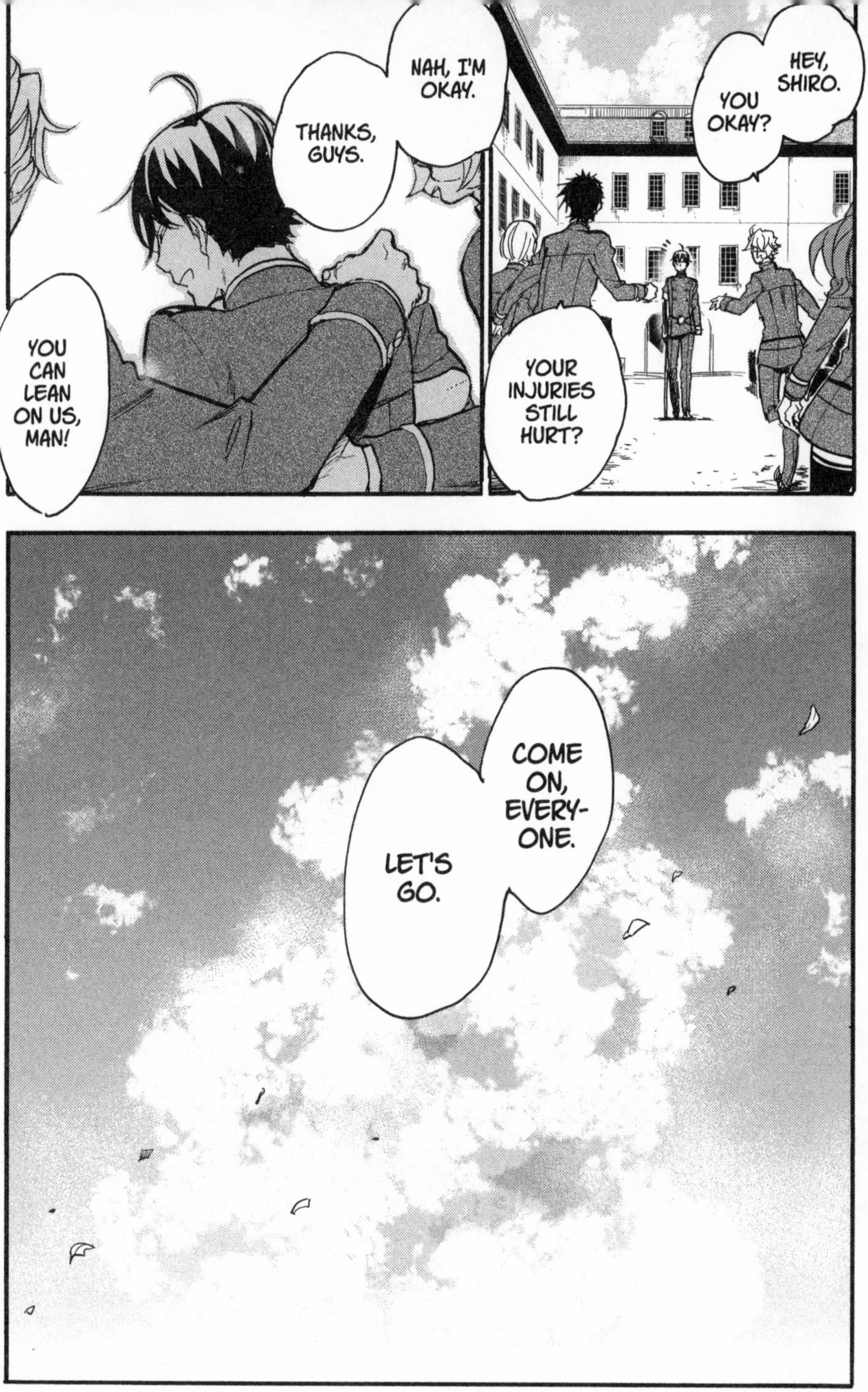
HEY, SHIRO.
YOU OKAY?
YOUR INJURIES STILL HURT?
NAH, I'M OKAY.
THANKS, GUYS.
YOU CAN LEAN ON US, MAN!
COME ON, EVERY-ONE.
LET'S GO.

afterschool charisma

end

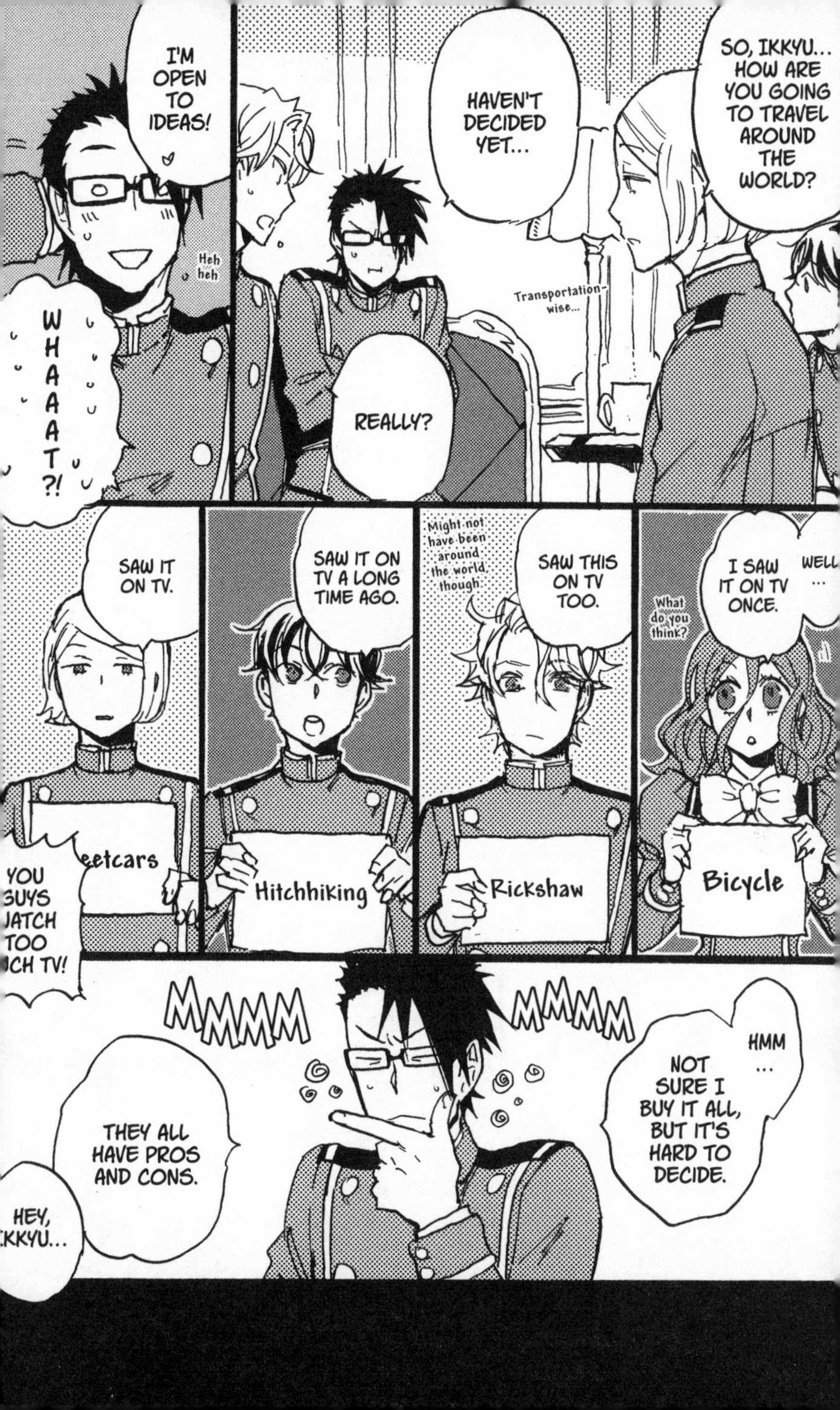
SO, IKKYU... HOW ARE YOU GOING TO TRAVEL AROUND THE WORLD?
Transportation-wise...
HAVEN'T DECIDED YET...
REALLY?
I'M OPEN TO IDEAS!
Heh heh
WHAAAAT?!
WELL...
I SAW IT ON TV ONCE.
What do you think?
Bicycle
Might not have been around the world, though.
SAW THIS ON TV TOO.
Rickshaw
SAW IT ON TV A LONG TIME AGO.
Hitchhiking
SAW IT ON TV.
eetcars
YOU GUYS ATCH TOO CH TV!
MMMM
MMMM
HMM...
NOT SURE I BUY IT ALL, BUT IT'S HARD TO DECIDE.
THEY ALL HAVE PROS AND CONS.
HEY, KKYU...

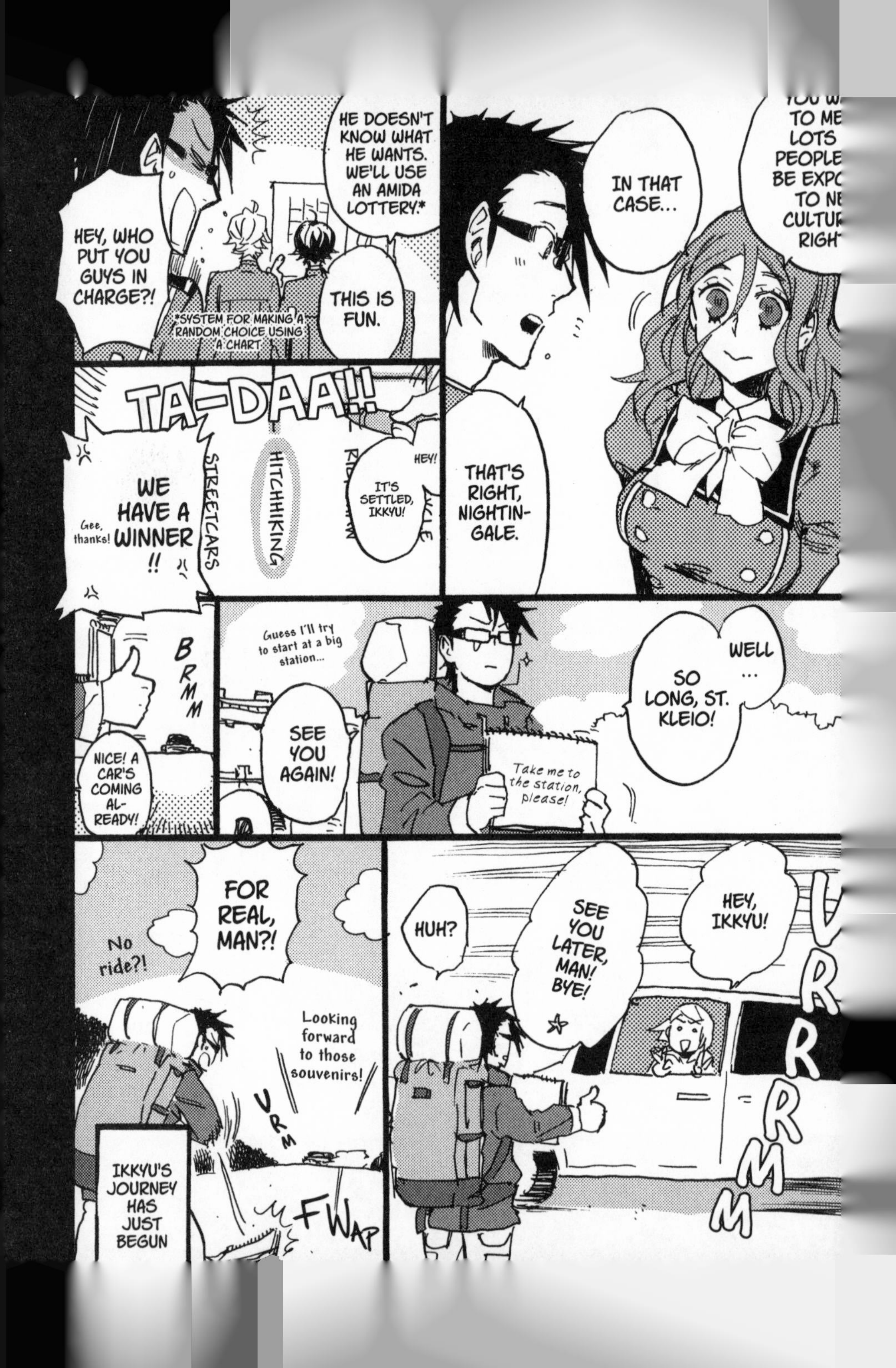
YOU W... TO ME LOTS PEOPLE BE EXPO TO NE CULTUR RIGHT
IN THAT CASE...
THAT'S RIGHT, NIGHTINGALE.
HE DOESN'T KNOW WHAT HE WANTS. WE'LL USE AN AMIDA LOTTERY.*
HEY, WHO PUT YOU GUYS IN CHARGE?!
THIS IS FUN.
*SYSTEM FOR MAKING A RANDOM CHOICE USING A CHART
TA-DAA!!
HEY!
IT'S SETTLED, IKKYU!
HITCHHIKING
STREETCARS
WE HAVE A WINNER!!
Gee, thanks!
WELL...
SO LONG, ST. KLEIO!
SEE YOU AGAIN!
Take me to the station, please!
Guess I'll try to start at a big station...
BRMM
NICE! A CAR'S COMING AL-READY!
URRRMM
HEY, IKKYU!
SEE YOU LATER, MAN! BYE!
HUH?
FOR REAL, MAN?!
No ride?!
Looking forward to those souvenirs!
URM
FWAP
IKKYU'S JOURNEY HAS JUST BEGUN

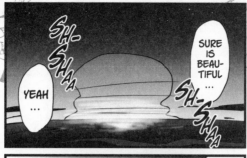

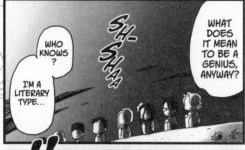

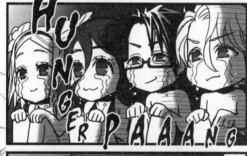

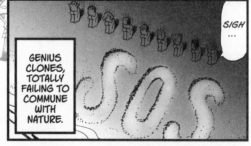

THE BATTLE OF THE GENIUS CLONES IS OVER.

SURE IS BEAUTIFUL…
SH-SHAA
SH-SHAA
YEAH…
WHAT DOES IT MEAN TO BE A GENIUS, ANYWAY?
SH-SHAA
WHO KNOWS?
I'M A LITERARY TYPE…
HUNGER PAAANG
SIGH…
GENIUS CLONES, TOTALLY FAILING TO COMMUNE WITH NATURE.
SOS

EVERYONE GOT HURT, EVERYONE CRIED.

WITH THE MAIN STORY OVER, SURELY EVERYONE HAS A COPY BY NOW… BUT JUST IN CASE…

...OR SOMETHING LIKE THAT.

For future reference...
OKAY...LOOKING BACK ON *AFTERSCHOOL CHARISMA*, WHAT THINGS COULD WE DO BETTER NEXT TIME?
OPPORTUNITIES FOR IMPROVEMENT
IF YOU HAVE ANY IDEAS, PLEASE SHARE.
CHATTER
YAPPA
CHATTER
YAPPA
I DO! I DO!
BOOBS.
POOP. WIENERS.
HUGE ORGANS.
YES...
THERE WAS A LOT OF CRUDE, CHILDISH HUMOR.
I DON'T LIKE TO ADMIT IT, BUT IT REALLY WAS A SHAME.
ME, ME!
SHOOP
YES, SHIRO.
THE FACT THAT IT'S CALLED "AFTERSCHOOL," BUT WE'RE ACTUALLY *IN* SCHOOL?
!!!!

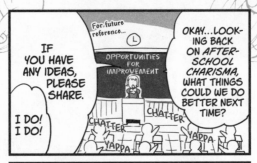

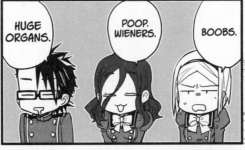

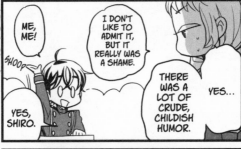

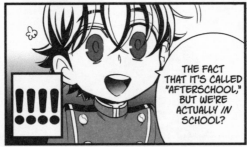

THERE'S ALWAYS ROOM FOR IMPROVEMENT.

BABY *AFTERSCHOOL CHARISMA* HOT

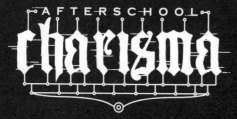

AFTERSCHOOL CHARISMA
VOLUME 12
VIZ SIGNATURE EDITION

STORY & ART BY KUMIKO SUEKANE

HOKAGO NO CHARISMA Vol. 12
by Kumiko SUEKANE
© 2009 Kumiko SUEKANE
All rights reserved.
Original Japanese edition published by SHOGAKUKAN.
English translation rights in the United States of America and Canada
arranged with SHOGAKUKAN.

Original Japanese cover design by Mitsuru KOBAYASHI (GENI A LÒIDE)

TRANSLATION –o– CAMELLIA NIEH
TOUCH-UP ART & LETTERING –o– ERIKA TERRIQUEZ
DESIGN –o– FAWN LAU
EDITOR –o– MEGAN BATES

Printed in the U.S.A.

Published by VIZ Media, LLC
P.O. Box 77010
San Francisco, CA 94107

10 9 8 7 6 5 4 3 2 1
First printing, December 2016

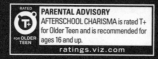

PARENTAL ADVISORY
AFTERSCHOOL CHARISMA is rated T+
for Older Teen and is recommended for
ages 16 and up.
ratings.viz.com

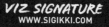

www.viz.com

VIZ SIGNATURE
WWW.SIGIKKI.COM

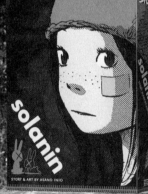

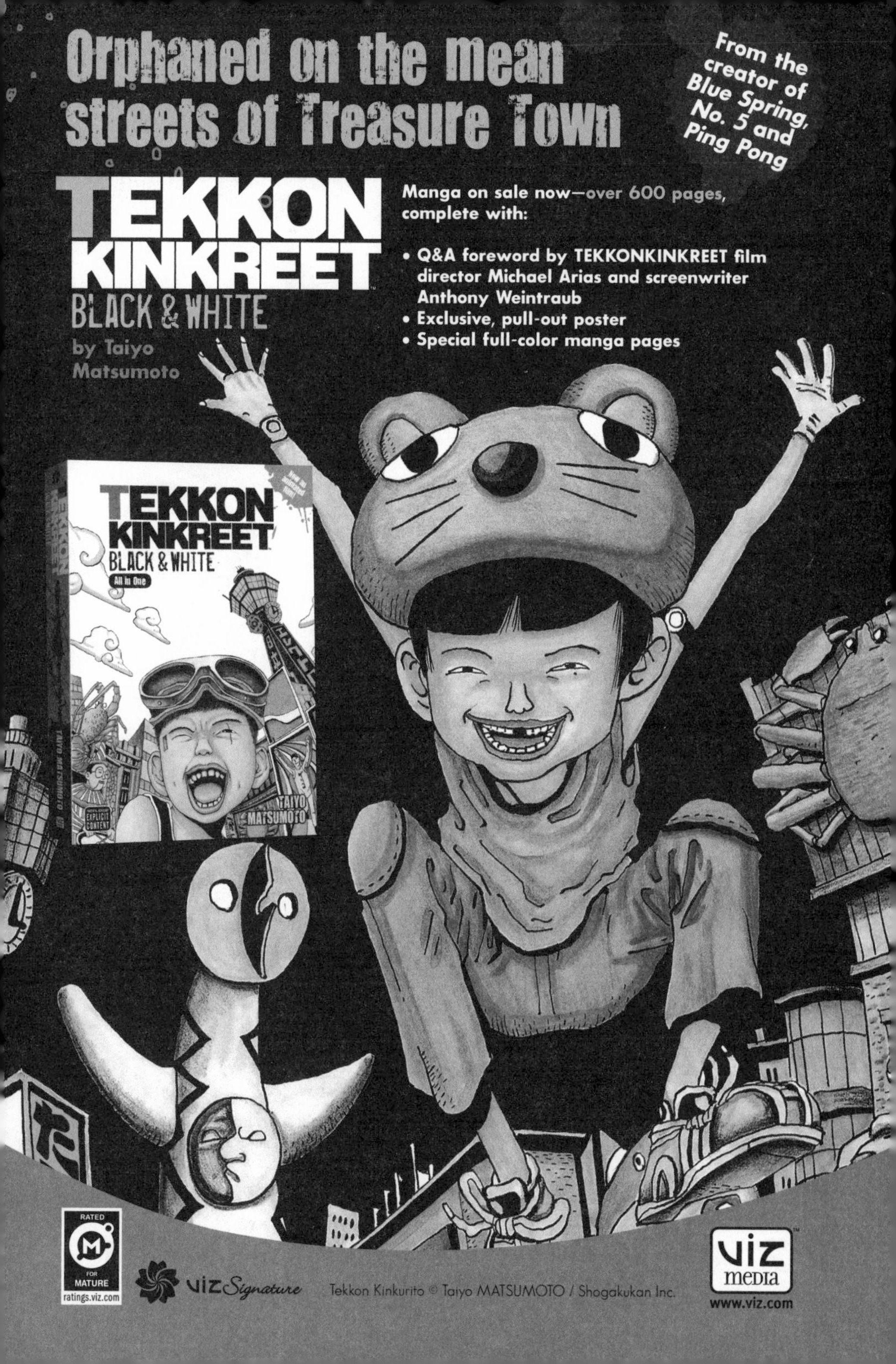
Orphaned on the mean streets of Treasure Town
From the creator of Blue Spring, No. 5 and Ping Pong
TEKKON KINKREET BLACK & WHITE
by Taiyo Matsumoto
Manga on sale now—over 600 pages, complete with:
• Q&A foreword by TEKKONKINKREET film director Michael Arias and screenwriter Anthony Weintraub
• Exclusive, pull-out poster
• Special full-color manga pages
TEKKON KINKREET BLACK & WHITE
All In One
TAIYO MATSUMOTO
EXPLICIT CONTENT
RATED M FOR MATURE
ratings.viz.com
VIZ Signature
Tekkon Kinkurito © Taiyo MATSUMOTO / Shogakukan Inc.
VIZ media
www.viz.com

UZUMAKI

Story and Art by **JUNJI ITO**

SPIRALS... THIS TOWN IS CONTAMINATED WITH SPIRALS...

Kurouzu-cho, a small fogbound town on the coast of Japan, is cursed. According to Shuichi Saito, the withdrawn boyfriend of teenager Kirie Goshima, their town is haunted not by a person or being but by a pattern: uzumaki, the spiral, the hypnotic secret shape of the world. It manifests itself in everything from seashells and whirlpools in water to the spiral marks on people's bodies, the insane obsessions of Shuichi's father and the voice from the cochlea in our inner ear. As the madness spreads, the inhabitants of Kurouzu-cho are pulled ever deeper into a whirlpool from which there is no return!

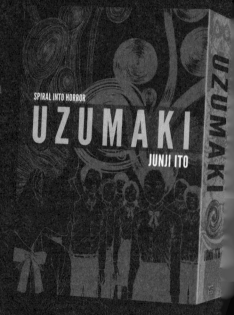

A masterpiece of horror manga, now available in a **DELUXE HARDCOVER EDITION!**

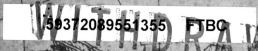

I'll tell you a story
about the sea.

It's a story that
no one knows yet.

The story of th
that only I can t

Children of the Sea

BY DAISUKE IGARASHI

Children of the Sea
Children of the Sea
DAISUKE IGARASHI
1
DAISUKE IGARASHI

Uncover the mysterious tale
with *Children of the Sea*—
BUY THE MANGA TODAY!

Read a FREE preview
at www.sigikki.com

On sale at **store.viz.com**
Also available at your local bookstore and comic store.

UNKNOWN OCEAN

VIZ SIGNATURE

RATED T+ FOR OLDER TEEN ratings.viz.com

VIZ media
www.viz.com

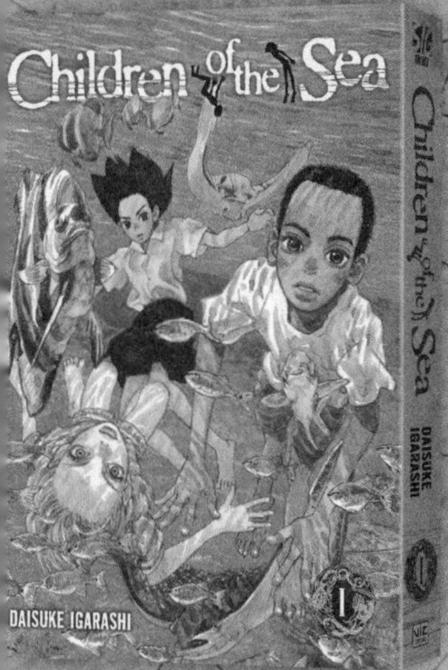